Afro-American Poetry and Drama, 1760-1975

Afro-American Poetry and Drama, 1760-1975

A GUIDE TO INFORMATION SOURCES

*Volume 17 in the American Literature, English
Literature, and World Literatures in English
Information Guide Series*

Afro-American Poetry, 1760-1975

William P. French

Michel J. Fabre

Amritjit Singh

Afro-American Drama, 1850-1975

Geneviève E. Fabre

Gale Research Company
Book Tower, Detroit, Michigan 48226

Library of Congress Cataloging in Publication Data
Main entry under title:

Afro-American poetry and drama, 1760-1975.

(American literature, English literature, and world
literatures in English ; v. 17) (Gale information guide
library)
    Includes indexes.
    CONTENTS: French, W. P., Fabre, M. J., Singh, A.
Afro-American poetry, 1760-1975.—Fabre, G.E. Afro-
American drama, 1850-1975.
    1. American literature—Afro-American authors—
Bibliography. 2. American poetry—Afro-American
authors—Bibliography. 3. American drama—Afro-
American authors—Bibliography. I. French, William P.
Afro-American poetry, 1760-1975. 1979. II. Fabre,
Geneviève. Afro-American drama, 1850-1975. 1979.
Z1229.N39F73 [PS153.N5] 016.810'9'896073 74-11518
ISBN 0-8103-1208-5

VITAE

William P. French is manager of the University Place Book Shop in New York City, specializing in Afro-American literature. With Frank Deodene he compiled two checklists: BLACK AMERICAN FICTION SINCE 1952 (1970), and BLACK AMERICAN POETRY SINCE 1944 (1971).

Michel J. Fabre is professor of American and Afro-American Studies and director of the Center for the Study of Afro-American and Third World Literatures in English at the Sorbonne Nouvelle. He has taught at the Universities of London, Nanterre, Vincennes, Paris III, and at Harvard University, Wellesley College, University of Iowa, and Yale University. He is the author of LES NOIRS AMÉRICAINS (Paris, 1970), HARLEM, VILLE NOIRE (Paris, 1971), and THE UNFINISHED QUEST OF RICHARD WRIGHT (New York, 1973).

Amritjit Singh teaches graduate students in English at the University of Hyderabad, India. He has taught at the University of Delhi, New York University, the City University of New York, and Osmania University. He is the author of THE NOVELS OF THE HARLEM RENAISSANCE and his scholarly articles have appeared in several journals in both India and the United States. Academic honors awarded him include a Ford Foundation Ethnic Studies Fellowship.

Geneviève E. Fabre is associate professor of American Studies at the University of Paris VII. She has taught at the University of Wisconsin, Madison, and Tufts University. She is the author of FRANCIS SCOTT FITZGERALD (Paris, 1969), EN MARGE: LES MINORITÉS AUX ETATS-UNIS (Paris, 1970), bilingual editions of STEPHEN CRANE, JOYCE CAROL OATES (Paris, 1971, 1974), and THE RESTLESS JOURNEY OF JAMES AGEE (New York, 1976).

CONTENTS

Contents

GENERAL PREFACE

The poetry and drama divisions of this reference guide generally follow the same arrangements and approaches, as the table of contents demonstrates, although there are some differences in emphasis. For example, the introduction to the drama is historical as well as methodological; the listing of anthologies of poetry is very important and particularly comprehensive. Readers should note the separate introductory remarks that precede the divisions for poetry and drama.

The Series Editors would like here to acknowledge the assistance of Bill French who contributed an expertise and an amount of time that went far beyond his own particular work with the primary and secondary resources for the study of Afro-American poetry in the twentieth century.

The listings in the Individual Authors sections, for both poetry and drama, endeavour to be comprehensive for published authors (unpublished plays by published dramatists are also surveyed). These listings are, thus, checklists, which should be useful to reference librarians, students, and researchers.

Theodore Grieder
Duane DeVries

AFRO-AMERICAN POETRY, 1760-1975

POETRY: INTRODUCTION

In the poetry section of this bibliography the compilers have tried to include all books and pamphlets of poetry by black authors born in the United States. Some foreign-born authors who have lived and published here have been included, with a notation of their birthplace. Sheet music, broadsides (except for the eighteenth-century works of Jupiter Hammon and Phillis Wheatley), and leaflets of fewer than five pages have been omitted.

While general background material on black history has not been included, critical and historical studies on black poetry are listed in part 1, preceded by an extensive list of bibliographies and reference works which may be consulted for additional background and peripheral studies. Some additional bibliographies are also listed in the drama section. Part 1 concludes with a list of anthologies devoted exclusively or substantially to Afro-American poetry, arranged in alphabetical order by editor, or, when no editor is named, by title, with brief notes indicating the range of content. Although the primary focus of the present bibliography is on "literary" as distinguished from "folk" or "oral" poetry, a list of collections of folk songs, blues, and spirituals is appended to the anthologies listing.

Part 2, Individual Authors, is divided into three sections: 1760-1900; 1901-45; and 1946-75. When, as frequently happens, a poet's career spans two of these periods, all his works are listed together in the period in which the bulk of his work was published; thus all of Langston Hughes's poetry, including those books published after 1945, are listed together in the 1901-45 section, with a cross-reference in the later section. A volume containing poems by two or three authors is listed under the author whose name appears first on the title page. Volumes by four or more authors are considered anthologies.

Each author's primary works (i.e., books of poetry) are listed chronologically by date of first publication. See subject index (p. 465) for page reference to authors whose works are listed in this bibliography. Titles are given in full, although in general such subtitles as "Poems" or "A Book of Verse" are omitted as redundant; other more descriptive subtitles such as "Love Poems" or "Poems of Race Inspiration" are included. Introductions, prefaces, and forewords, and their authors are noted (all as "Introd."), except those by the author of the book.

3

The pagination given is the last printed page number; preliminary pagination, if any, has been omitted. When a book's pages are not numbered we have, if possible, counted the pages and indicated the number in parentheses. In the 1946-75 section (but not elsewhere), those volumes which originally appeared only in paper covers are so indicated by "Paper" at the end of the entry. Bibliographic details of some volumes have eluded us; thus some entries are incomplete. Birth and death dates have been particularly difficult to establish for many authors, but have been included whenever possible.

Biographical and critical studies on individual authors are listed in alphabetical order following the primary works. About twenty general critical works are referred to in abbreviated form; a list of these abbreviations follows this preface. Abbreviated references to these critical works appear at the beginning of the Biography and Criticism section under each poet.

ABBREVIATIONS USED IN THE POETRY DIVISION

See Critical Studies, below, for full listings of these titles and reference works. These basic titles are cited many times in the sections on individual authors.

See also the Abbreviations Used in the Drama Division, p. 265.

Bigsby BAW2	Bigsby, C.W.E., ed. THE BLACK AMERICAN WRITER, vol. 2.
Brawley NG	Brawley, Benjamin G. THE NEGRO GENIUS
Brown NPD	Brown, Sterling A. NEGRO POETRY AND DRAMA
Chapman IPB	Chapman, Dorothy. INDEX TO BLACK POETRY
Davis FDT	Davis, Arthur P. FROM THE DARK TOWER
Gayle BA	Gayle, Addison, Jr., ed. THE BLACK AESTHETIC
Gayle BE	Gayle, Addison, Jr., ed. BLACK EXPRESSION
Gibson MBP	Gibson, Donald B., ed. MODERN BLACK POETS
Jackson BPA	Jackson, Blyden, and Louis B. Rubin, Jr. BLACK POETRY IN AMERICA
Jahn NAL	Jahn, Janheinz, NEO-AFRICAN LITERATURE
Lee DV	Lee, Don L. DYNAMITE VOICES 1971
Loggins NA	Loggins, Vernon. THE NEGRO AUTHOR
Mays NG	Mays, Benjamin E. THE NEGRO'S GOD AS REFLECTED IN HIS LITERATURE
O'Brien IBW	O'Brien, John. INTERVIEWS WITH BLACK WRITERS
'Redding TMPB	Redding, Saunders. TO MAKE A POET BLACK
Rollins FANP	Rollins, Charlemae. FAMOUS AMERICAN NEGRO POETS
Sherman IP	Sherman, Joan R. INVISIBLE POETS
Wagner BPUS	Wagner, Jean. BLACK POETS OF THE UNITED STATES

Whitlow BAL   Whitlow, Roger.   BLACK AMERICAN LITERATURE

Williams TAS   Williams, Kenny J.   THEY ALSO SPOKE

Young BW30s   Young, James O.   BLACK WRITERS OF THE THIRTIES

Part 1
POETRY: GENERAL STUDIES

1. BIBLIOGRAPHIES AND REFERENCE WORKS

Bailey, Leaonead Pack. BROADSIDE AUTHORS AND ARTISTS: AN ILLUS-TRATED BIOGRAPHICAL DIRECTORY. Detroit: Broadside, 1974. 125 p.

> Contains much useful bibliographical and biographical information on authors published by Broadside Press; according to Dudley Randall's preface, "of a total of 184 entries for authors, 166, or 90 percent, are not listed in CONTEMPORARY AUTHORS."

Bell, Barbara. BLACK BIOGRAPHICAL SOURCES: AN ANNOTATED BIB-LIOGRAPHY. New Haven, Conn.: Yale University Library, 1970.

Bergman, Peter M., et al. THE CHRONOLOGICAL HISTORY OF THE NE-GRO IN AMERICA. New York: Harper & Row, 1969. 698 p.

> The index, pages 625-98, includes over 20,000 entries.

Brasch, Ila Wales, and Walter Milton Brasch. A COMPREHENSIVE AN-NOTATED BIBLIOGRAPHY OF AMERICAN BLACK ENGLISH. Baton Rouge: Louisiana State University Press, 1974. 289 p.

Brignano, Russell C. BLACK AMERICANS IN AUTOBIOGRAPHY: AN AN-NOTATED BIBLIOGRAPHY OF AUTOBIOGRAPHIES AND AUTOBIOGRAPHICAL BOOKS WRITTEN SINCE THE CIVIL WAR. Durham, N.C.: Duke University Press, 1974. 127 p.

> Lists and annotates 291 autobiographies and 126 autobiographical books; also lists reprints of 43 pre-1865 works. An accurate and detailed work; very thoroughly indexed.

Brown, Warren Henry. CHECKLIST OF NEGRO NEWSPAPERS IN THE UNITED STATES (1827-1946). Jefferson City, Mo.: School of Journalism, Lincoln University, 1946. 37 p.

Lists 467 black newspapers, with some locations given.

Bullock, Penelope L. THE NEGRO PERIODICAL PRESS IN THE UNITED STATES, 1839-1909. Ann Arbor, Mich.: University Microfilms, 1972.

Chapman, Abraham. THE NEGRO IN AMERICAN LITERATURE, AND A BIBLIOGRAPHY OF LITERATURE BY AND ABOUT NEGRO AMERICANS. Wisconsin Council of Teachers of English, Special Publication No. 15. Oshkosh: Wisconsin Council of Teachers of English, Wisconsin State University, 1966. 135 p.

Chapman, Dorothy H. INDEX TO BLACK POETRY. Boston: G.K. Hall, 1974. 541 p.

> According to the preface, "this work attempts to provide the first index devoted solely to black poetry. Ninety-four books and pamphlets by individual poets are indexed as well as thirty-three anthologies." Among the volumes indexed is VERSES (London: Swarthmore Press, 1922), by William C. Braithwaite, a white Englishman who seems to have been included only because his first and last names are the same as those of William Stanley Braithwaite, the Afro-American poet. Among the more obvious omissions are Langston Hughes's SELECTED POEMS, J.W. Johnson's ST. PETER RELATES AN INCIDENT, Kerlin's anthology NEGRO POETS AND THEIR POEMS, Toomer's CANE, and the books of D.W. Davis, G.M. Horton, Albery Whitman, and most of the minor nineteenth-century poets. Contains indexes by title and first line, author (about 600 Afro-American poets are listed), and, more sketchily, subject. The volumes included in this index are indicated in the present bibliography by the note "In Chapman IBP" at the end of the entry.

THE CHICAGO AFRO-AMERICAN UNION ANALYTIC CATALOG: AN INDEX TO MATERIALS ON THE AFRO-AMERICAN IN THE PRINCIPAL LIBRARIES OF CHICAGO. 5 vols. Boston: G.K. Hall, 1972.

Cole, Johnetta. "Black Women in America: An Annotated Bibliography." BLACK SCHOLAR, 3 (Dec. 1971), 42-53.

Deodene, Frank, and William P. French. BLACK AMERICAN POETRY SINCE 1944: A PRELIMINARY CHECKLIST. Chatham, N.J.: Chatham Bookseller, 1971. 41 p.

> A supplement to Dorothy Porter's NORTH AMERICAN NEGRO POETS. . . 1760-1944; about 530 volumes are listed.

Dorsey, Leonia Lamier. "Negro Poetry since 1916: A Selective Bibliography." Thesis, School of Library Service, Columbia University, 1935.

DuBois, W.E.B., Guy B. Johnson, et al. ENCYCLOPEDIA OF THE NEGRO: PREPARATORY VOLUME WITH REFERENCE LISTS AND REPORTS. New York: Phelps-Stokes Fund, 1945. 207 p. Rev. and enl., 1946. 215 p.

Fisk University. DICTIONARY CATALOG OF THE NEGRO COLLECTION OF THE FISK UNIVERSITY LIBRARY. 6 vols. Boston: G.K. Hall, 1974.

Fuller, Juanita B. AN ANNOTATED BIBLIOGRAPHY OF BIOGRAPHIES AND AUTOBIOGRAPHIES OF NEGROES, 1839-1961. Rochester, N.Y.: University of Rochester Press, for the Association of College Research Libraries, 1964. (ACRL Microcard).

Hampton Institute. A CLASSIFIED CATALOG OF THE NEGRO COLLECTION IN THE COLLIS P. HUNTINGTON LIBRARY OF HAMPTON INSTITUTE. Comp. Mentor A. Howe and Roscoe E. Lewis. Hampton, Va.: Hampton Institute, 1940. 255 p.

Handy, W.C. NEGRO AUTHORS AND COMPOSERS OF THE UNITED STATES. New York: Handy Brothers Music Co., [1936?]. 24 p.

Howard University. DICTIONARY CATALOG OF THE ARTHUR B. SPINGARN COLLECTION OF NEGRO AUTHORS. 2 vols. Boston: G.K. Hall, 1972.

_____. DICTIONARY CATALOG OF THE JESSE E. MOORLAND COLLECTION OF NEGRO LIFE AND HISTORY. 9 vols. Boston: G.K. Hall, 1970. 1st supp., 3 vols., 1976.

INDEX TO PERIODICAL ARTICLES BY AND ABOUT NEGROES. March 1950- .

Published quarterly in the fifties by Central State College Library, Wilberforce, Ohio, under the title INDEX TO SELECTED PERIODI-CALS. A decennial cumulation for the years 1950-59 was published in 1961 by G.K. Hall, Boston; the same firm has published annual cumulations since, with the volume for 1960 appearing in 1962.

Jackson, Miles M., Mary W. Cleaves, and Alma L. Gray. A BIBLIOGRAPHY OF NEGRO HISTORY AND CULTURE FOR YOUNG READERS. Pittsburgh: Univ. of Pittsburgh Press for Atlanta Univ., 1969. 134 p.

Jahn, Janheinz. A BIBLIOGRAPHY OF NEO-AFRICAN LITERATURE FROM AFRICA, AMERICA AND THE CARIBBEAN. New York: Praeger, 1965. 359 p.

Attempts to list, with full bibliographic details, all editions, including translations, of "all creative works by Negro-Africans and Afro-Americans which have been published or performed on the stage, or which are ready for publication or performance." No attempt is made to include appearances in periodicals, except for a few plays. The section on North America lists about 1,400 titles, including over 500 volumes of poetry. An extensive, detailed, generally accurate, and very useful work, often overlooked by students of Afro-American literature.

Kessler, S.H. "American Negro Literature: A Bibliographical Guide." BULLETIN OF BIBLIOGRAPHY, 21 (1955), 181-85.

Lash, John S. "The American Negro and American Literature: A Checklist of Significant Commentaries." BULLETIN OF BIBLIOGRAPHY, 19 (1946), 12-15; 19 (1947), 33-36.

A list of 572 items.

Levi, Doris J., and Nerissa L. Milton. DIRECTORY OF BLACK LITERARY MAGAZINES. Washington, D.C.: Negro Bibliographic and Research Center, 1970. 19 p.

Locke, Alain L. A DECADE OF NEGRO SELF-EXPRESSION. John F. Slater Fund, Occasional Paper 26. Charlottesville: Univ. of Virginia, 1928. 20 p.

Supplemented by Locke's annual surveys of Negro literature published in the January or February issues of OPPORTUNITY for 1929 and 1931-40, and in PHYLON in 1947-53. These annual surveys were continued in PHYLON by Blyden Jackson and John S. Lash in the fifties, and by Nick Aaron Ford and Miles M. Jackson in the sixties. Another annual survey, "Books by Negro Authors," compiled by Arthur B. Spingarn, appeared in the NAACP magazine CRISIS each year, usually in the February issue, from 1936 through 1968. A more general annotated list is Ernest Kaiser's "Recent Books," published in most issues of FREEDOMWAYS since 1962.

McPherson, James M., et al. BLACKS IN AMERICA: BIBLIOGRAPHICAL ESSAYS. New York: Doubleday, 1971. 430 p.

See the section "Black Poetry," pp. 243-53.

Matthews, Geraldine O. BLACK AMERICAN WRITERS, 1773-1949: A BIBLIOGRAPHY AND UNION LIST. Comp. Geraldine O. Matthews and the African-American Materials Project Staff, School of Library Science, North Carolina Central University, Durham. Boston: G.K. Hall, 1975. 221 p.

"Catalogs over 1600 authors of monographs" with a maximum of three titles by any one author; locations are given for about 60 percent of the entries in some sixty-five libraries in five southern states (Alabama, Georgia, North Carolina, South Carolina, and Tennessee).

Miller, Elizabeth E. THE NEGRO IN AMERICA: A BIBLIOGRAPHY. Cambridge, Mass.: Harvard Univ. Press, 1966. 190 p.

"Lists over 3,500 books, documents, articles, and pamphlets written, with the exception of certain classic older works and essential background studies, since 1954." A new edition, revised by Mary L. Fisher, was published in 1970 (351 p.).

Myers, Carol. "A Selected Bibliography of Recent Afro-American Writers." CLA JOURNAL, (1972), 377-82.

Prepared as a supplement to Darwin Turner's AFRO-AMERICAN WRITERS (see below).

Myrdal, Gunnar, Richard Sterner, and Arnold Rose. AN AMERICAN DILEMMA: THE NEGRO PROBLEM AND MODERN DEMOCRACY. 2 vols. New York: Harper, 1944.

Bibliography, pp. 1144-80.

New York Public Library. DICTIONARY CATALOG OF THE SCHOMBURG COLLECTION OF NEGRO LITERATURE AND HISTORY. 9 vols. Boston: G.K. Hall, 1962. 1st supp., 2 vols., 1968; 2nd supp., 4 vols., 1974.

Olsson, Martin. A SELECTED BIBLIOGRAPHY OF BLACK LITERATURE: THE HARLEM RENAISSANCE. American Arts Pamphlet 2. Exeter, England: American Arts Documentation Centre, Univ. of Exeter, 1973. 24 p.

Page, James A. SELECTED BLACK AMERICAN AUTHORS: AN ILLUSTRATED BIO-BIBLIOGRAPHY. Boston: G.K. Hall, 1977. 398 p.

Porter, Dorothy B. "Early American Negro Writers: A Bibliographical Study." PAPERS OF THE BIBLIOGRAPHICAL SOCIETY OF AMERICA, 39 (1945), 192-270.

_____. THE NEGRO IN THE UNITED STATES: A SELECTED BIBLIOGRAPHY. Washington , D.C.: Library of Congress, 1970. 313 p.

_____. NORTH AMERICAN NEGRO POETS: A BIBLIOGRAPHICAL CHECKLIST OF THEIR WRITINGS, 1760-1944. Hattiesburg, Miss.: Book Farm, 1945. 90 p. Rpt. New York: Burt Franklin, 1963. 90 p.

_____. A WORKING BIBLIOGRAPHY ON THE NEGRO IN THE UNITED STATES. Ann Arbor, Mich.: University Microfilms, 1968. 128 p.

Pride, Armistead S. THE BLACK PRESS: A BIBLIOGRAPHY. Madison, Wis.: Association for Education in Journalism, 1968. 37 p.

_____. "A Register and History of Negro Newspapers in the United States, 1827-1950." Ph.D. dissertation, Northwestern University, 1950. 426 p.

Querry, Ronald, and Robert E. Fleming. "A Working Bibliography of Black Periodicals." STUDIES IN BLACK LITERATURE, 3 (Summer 1972), 31-36.

Rush, Theressa Gunnels, Carol Fairbanks Myers, and Esther Spring Arata. BLACK AMERICAN WRITERS PAST AND PRESENT: A BIOGRAPHICAL AND BIBLIOGRAPHICAL DICTIONARY. 2 vols. Metuchen, N.J.: Scarecrow Press, 1975. 865 p.

> Although marred by an unusually large number of errors and omis-
> sions, this is the most comprehensive bibliography of black Ameri-
> can writers to date, with extensive lists of secondary material
> (biographical and critical references, periodical appearances, re-
> views, etc.) for many authors.

Ryan, Pat M. BLACK WRITING IN THE U.S.A.: A BIBLIOGRAPHIC GUIDE. Brockport, N.Y.: Drake Memorial Library, 1969. 48 p.

Salk, Erwin A. A LAYMAN'S GUIDE TO NEGRO HISTORY. Enl. ed. New York: McGraw-Hill, 1967. 196 p.

> "Part Two: Bibliographies," pp. 81-196.

Schatz, Walter, ed. DIRECTORY OF AFRO-AMERICAN RESOURCES. New York: Bowker, 1970. 485 p.

> "Lists 2,108 institutions and 5,365 collections of resource materi-
> als," mostly manuscripts, arranged geographically and thoroughly
> indexed. Also includes a list of some 275 bibliographies.

Schomburg, Arthur A. A BIBLIOGRAPHICAL CHECKLIST OF AMERICAN NE-GRO POETRY. Bibliographica Americana, vol. 2. New York: Charles F. Heartman, 1916. 57 p.

Sherman, Joan R. INVISIBLE POETS. See under Critical Studies, below.

Shockley, Ann Allen, and Sue P. Chandler. LIVING BLACK AMERICAN AUTHORS: A BIOGRAPHICAL DIRECTORY. New York: Bowker, 1973. 220 p.

Texas Southern University. HEARTMAN NEGRO COLLECTION; CATALOGUE. Houston: Texas Southern Univ. Library, [1965?]. 325 p.

Turner, Darwin T. AFRO-AMERICAN WRITERS. Goldentree Bibliographies in Language and Literature. New York: Appleton-Century-Crofts, 1970. 117 p.

A useful selective listing of primary and secondary material. Also see Carol Myers' supplement to this work, above.

Walters, Mary Dawson. AFRO-AMERICANA: A COMPREHENSIVE BIBLIOG-RAPHY OF RESOURCE MATERIALS IN THE OHIO STATE UNIVERSITY LIBRARIES BY OR ABOUT BLACK AMERICANS. Columbus: Office of Educational Services, Ohio State Univ. Libraries, 1969. 220 p.

Welsch, Erwin K. THE NEGRO IN THE UNITED STATES: A RESEARCH GUIDE. Bloomington: Indiana Univ. Press, 1965. 142 p.

Whitlow, Roger. BLACK AMERICAN LITERATURE. See under Critical Studies, below.

Wolseley, Roland E. THE BLACK PRESS, U.S.A. Ames: Iowa State Univ. Press, 1971. Rev. printing, 1972. 362 p.

Work, Monroe N. A BIBLIOGRAPHY OF THE NEGRO IN AFRICA AND AMERICA. New York: H.W. Wilson Co., 1928. 698 p. Rpts. New York: Argosy-Antiquarian, 1965; New York: Octagon, 1966.

_____. NEGRO YEAR BOOK: AN ANNUAL ENCYCLOPEDIA OF THE NEGRO.

The subtitle varies; later "A Review of Events Affecting Negro Life." Monroe Work edited the first nine editions of this handbook, for the years 1912, 1913, 1914-15, 1916-17, 1918-19, 1921-22, 1925-26, 1931-32, and 1937-38. The tenth and eleventh editions, for the years 1941-46 and 1952, were edited by Jessie P. Guzman.

Yellin, Jean Fagan. "An Index of Literary Materials in THE CRISIS, 1910-1934: Articles, Belles Lettres, and Book Reviews." CLA JOURNAL, 14 (1971), 452-65; 15 (1971), 197-234.

2. CRITICAL STUDIES

THE AMERICAN NEGRO WRITER AND HIS ROOTS. Selected Papers from the First Conference of Negro Writers, March 1959. New York: American Society of African Culture, 1960. 70 p.

Contributors include Samuel Allen, Arna Bontemps, Langston Hughes, and Saunders Redding.

Anderson, Jervis. "Black Writing: The Other Side." DISSENT, 15 (1968), 233-42.

Aubert, Alvin. "Black American Poetry: Its Language and the Folk Tradition." In MODERN BLACK LITERATURE. Ed. S. Okechukwu Mezu. Buffalo, New York: Black Academy Press, 1971, pp. 71-80.

Baker, Houston A., Jr. "Balancing the Perspective: A Look at the Early Black American Literary Artistry." NEGRO AMERICAN LITERATURE FORUM, 6 (1972), 65-70.

_____. LONG BLACK SONG: ESSAYS IN BLACK AMERICAN LITERATURE AND CULTURE. Charlottesville: Univ. of Virginia Press, 1972. 156 p.

_____. SINGERS OF DAYBREAK: STUDIES IN BLACK AMERICAN LITERA-TURE. Washington, D.C.: Howard Univ. Press, 1974. 109 p.

Barksdale, Richard K. "Humanistic Protest in Recent Black Poetry." In Gibson MBP, pp. 157-64.

_____. "Trends in Contemporary Poetry." PHYLON, 19 (1958), 408-16.

_____. "Urban Crisis and the Black Poetic Avant-Garde." NEGRO AMERI-CAN LITERATURE FORUM, 3 (1969), 40-44.

Bell, Bernard W. "Contemporary Afro-American Poetry as Folk Art." BLACK WORLD, 22 (Mar. 1973), 16-26, 74-87.

_____. THE FOLK ROOTS OF CONTEMPORARY AFRO-AMERICAN POETRY. Detroit: Broadside, 1974. 80 p.

_____. "New Black Poetry, a Double Edged Sword." CLA JOURNAL, 15 (1971), 37-43.

Bennett, M.W. "Negro Poets." NEGRO HISTORY BULLETIN, 9 (1946), 171-72, 191.

Bigsby, C.W.E., ed. THE BLACK AMERICAN WRITER. 2 vols. Deland, Fla.: Everett, Edwards, 1969. Rpt. Baltimore: Penguin Books, 1971.

Volume 2, POETRY AND DRAMA, is referred to in the present bibliography as Bigsby BAW2.

Birnbaum, Henry. "The Poetry of Protest." POETRY, 94 (1959), 408-13.

"Black Writers Views on Literary Lions and Values." NEGRO DIGEST, 17 (Jan. 1968), 10-48, 81-89.

A symposium including statements by S.W. Allen, Gwendolyn Brooks, Margaret Danner, James Emanuel, Mari Evans, Sarah W. Fabio, K. Kgositsile, Etheridge Knight, Don L. Lee, Larry Neal, Dudley Randall, Conrad K. Rivers, Carolyn Rodgers, Alice Walker, and Margaret Walker.

Bland, Edward. "Racial Bias and Negro Poetry." POETRY, 63 (1944), 328-33.

Bone, Robert. "American Negro Poets: A French View." TRI-QUARTERLY, 4 (1965), 185-95.

_____. DOWN HOME: A HISTORY OF AFRO-AMERICAN SHORT FICTION FROM ITS BEGINNING TO THE END OF THE HARLEM RENAISSANCE. New York: Putnam, 1975. 328 p.

_____. THE NEGRO NOVEL IN AMERICA. Rev. ed. New Haven, Conn.: Yale University Press, 1965. 289 p.

Bontemps, Arna. "American Negro Poetry." CRISIS, 70 (1963), 509.

_____. "The Negro Contribution to American Letters." In THE AMERICAN NEGRO REFERENCE BOOK. Ed. John P. Davis. Englewood Cliffs, N.J.: Prentice-Hall, 1966, pp. 850-78.

_____. "Negro Poets, Then and Now." PHYLON, 11 (1950), 355-60. Also in Gayle BE, pp. 82-89.

_____. "The New Black Renaissance." NEGRO DIGEST, 11 (Nov. 1961), 52-58.

_____, ed. THE HARLEM RENAISSANCE REMEMBERED. New York: Dodd, Mead, 1972. 310 p.

Braithwaite, William Stanley. "The Negro in Literature." CRISIS, 22 (1924), 204-10.

_____. "Some Contemporary Poets of the Negro Race." CRISIS, 17 (1919), 275-80.

Brawley, Benjamin G. THE NEGRO GENIUS: A NEW APPRAISAL OF THE ACHIEVEMENTS OF THE AMERICAN NEGRO IN LITERATURE AND THE FINE ARTS. New York: Dodd, Mead, 1937. 366 p. Rpt. New York: Biblo & Tannen, 1966.

This is a revised and enlarged version of Brawley's earlier THE NEGRO IN LITERATURE AND ART IN THE UNITED STATES (New York: Duffield, 1918, 1921, 1930). "Uncritical and often tendentious . . . Brawley's critical judgments cannot be accepted without great wariness" (Wagner BPUS).

Breman, Paul. "Poetry into the Sixties." In Bigsby BAW2, pp. 99-109.

Bronz, Stephen H. ROOTS OF NEGRO RACIAL CONSCIOUSNESS: THE 1920'S: THREE HARLEM RENAISSANCE AUTHORS. New York: Libra Publishers, 1964. 101 p.

The three authors are James Weldon Johnson, Countee Cullen, and Claude McKay.

Brooks, Gwendolyn, et al. A CAPSULE COURSE IN BLACK POETRY WRITING. Detroit: Broadside, 1975. 64 p.

Contains chapters by Brooks, Keorapetse Kgositsile, Haki R. Madhubuti (Don L. Lee), and Dudley Randall.

Brooks, Russell. "The Motif of Dynamic Change in New Black Poetry." CLA JOURNAL, 15 (1971), 1-6.

Brown, Lloyd L. "Which Way for the Negro Writer." MASSES & MAINSTREAM, 4 (Mar. 1951), 53-63; (Apr. 1951), 50-59.

Brown, Lloyd W., ed. THE BLACK WRITER IN AFRICA AND THE AMERICAS. Los Angeles: Hennessey & Ingalls, 1973. 229 p.

Brown, Sterling A. "A Century of Negro Portraiture in American Literature." MASSACHUSETTS REVIEW, 7 (1966), 73-96.

_____. "Contemporary Negro Poetry, 1914-1936." In AN ANTHOLOGY OF AMERICAN NEGRO LITERATURE. Ed. Sylvestre C. Watkins. New York: Modern Library, 1944, pp. 243-61.

_____. "The Negro Author and His Publisher." NEGRO QUARTERLY, 1 (1945), 7-20.

_____. NEGRO POETRY AND DRAMA. Washington, D.C.: Associates in Negro Folk Education, 1937. 142 p. Rpt. New York: Atheneum, 1969.

No index. Referred to in the present bibliography as Brown NPD.

_____. "The New Negro in Literature (1925-1955)." In THE NEW NEGRO

THIRTY YEARS AFTERWARD. Ed. Rayford W. Logan, et al. Washington, D.C.: Howard Univ. Press, 1955, pp. 57-72.

_____. OUTLINE FOR THE STUDY OF THE POETRY OF AMERICAN NE-GROES, PREPARED TO BE USED WITH THE BOOK OF AMERICAN NEGRO POETRY. New York: Harcourt, Brace, 1931. 52 p.

> This work was prepared to be used with James Weldon Johnson's BOOK OF AMERICAN NEGRO POETRY, cited under Anthologies, below.

Budd, Louis J. "The Not So Tender Trap: Some Dilemmas of Black American Poets." INDIAN JOURNAL OF AMERICAN STUDIES, 3 (June 1973), 47-57.

Burke, Virginia M. "Black Literature for Whom?" NEGRO AMERICAN LIT-ERATURE FORUM, 9 (Spring 1975), 25-27.

Butcher, Margaret Just. THE NEGRO IN AMERICAN CULTURE. New York: Knopf, 1956. 294 p. 2nd ed., enl., 1972. 313 p.

> Based on materials left by Alain Locke. Chapter 5: "Negro Folk Poetry and Folk Thought," pp. 98-116; Chapter 6: "Formal Ne-gro Poetry," pp. 117-41.

Cartey, Wilfred. BLACK IMAGES. New York: Teachers College Press, 1970. 186 p.

> A study of modern Caribbean black poetry, with some mention of North American poets.

_____. "Four Shadows of Harlem." NEGRO DIGEST, 18 (Aug. 1969), 22-25, 83-92.

> The shadows are Garcia Lorca, Senghor, McKay, and Hughes.

Chamberlin, John. "The Negro as Writer." BOOKMAN, 70 (1930), 603-11.

Chapman, Abraham. "Black Poetry Today." ARTS IN SOCIETY, 5 (1968), 401-8.

Clark, Edward. "Studying and Teaching Afro-American Literature." CLA JOURNAL, 16 (1972), 96-105.

Clark, Margaret. "Overtones in Negro Poetry." INTERRACIAL REVIEW, 9 (July 1936), 106.

_____. "The Voice of a Race." INTERRACIAL REVIEW, 9 (Apr. 1936), 58.

Clarke, John Henrik. "The Origin and Growth of Afro-American Literature." JOURNAL OF HUMAN RELATIONS, 16 (1968), 368-84.

Clay, Eugene. "The Negro in Recent American Literature." In AMERICAN WRITERS' CONGRESS. Ed. Henry Hart. New York: International Publishers, 1935, pp. 145-53.

Collier, Eugenia W. "Heritage from Harlem." BLACK WORLD, 20 (Nov. 1970), 52-59.

———. "I Do Not Marvel, Countee Cullen." CLA JOURNAL, 11 (1967), 73-87. Also in Gibson MBP, pp. 69-83.

Culp, D.W., ed. TWENTIETH CENTURY NEGRO LITERATURE . . . BY ONE HUNDRED OF AMERICA'S GREATEST NEGROES. Naperville, Ill.: J.W. Nichols, 1902. 472 p.

See especially "The Negro as a Writer," pp. 270-86.

Davis, Arthur P. FROM THE DARK TOWER: AFRO-AMERICAN WRITERS 1900 TO 1960. Washington, D.C.: Howard Univ. Press, 1974. 306 p.

Contains chapters on Arna Bontemps, Gwendolyn Brooks, Sterling Brown, Countee Cullen, Frank M. Davis, Langston Hughes, Robert Hayden, James Weldon Johnson, Claude McKay, Melvin Tolson, Jean Toomer, Margaret Walker, and a dozen novelists of the period, illustrated with photographs of each. Bibliography, pp. 230-89. Referred to in the present bibliography as Davis FDT.

———. "The New Poetry of Black Hate." CLA JOURNAL, 14 (1970), 382-91. Also in Gibson MBP, pp. 147-56.

Daykin, Walter L. "Race Consciousness in Negro Poetry." SOCIOLOGY AND SOCIAL RESEARCH, 20 (Sept.-Oct. 1936), 45-53.

Echeruo, M.J.C. "American Negro Poetry." PHYLON, 24 (1963), 62-68.

Ellison, Martha. "Velvet Voices Feed on Bitter Fruit: A Study of American Negro Poetry." POET AND CRITIC, 4 (Winter 1967-68), 39-49.

Ely, Effie Smith. "American Negro Poetry." CHRISTIAN CENTURY, 40 (1923), 366-67.

Emanuel, James A. "America before 1950: Black Writers' Views." NEGRO DIGEST, 18 (Aug. 1969), 26-34, 67-69.

_____. "Blackness Can: A Quest for Aesthetics." In Gayle BA, pp. 192-223.

_____. "The Future of Negro Poetry." In Gayle BE, pp. 100-109.

_____. "The Invisible Men of American Literature." BOOKS ABROAD, 37 (1963), 391-94.

_____. "Renaissance Sonneteers." BLACK WORLD, 24 (Sept. 1975), 32-45.

Fabio, Sarah Webster. "Tripping with Black Writing." In Gayle BA, pp. 182-91.

_____. "Who Speaks Negro? What Is Black?" NEGRO DIGEST, 17, (Sept.-Oct. 1968), 33-37. Also in Gayle BE, pp. 115-19.

Fowler, Carolyn. "A Contemporary American Genre: Pamphlet/Manifesto Poetry." BLACK WORLD, 23 (June 1974), 4-19.

Fuller, Hoyt W. "Identity, Reality and Responsibility: Elusive Poles in the World of Black Literature." JOURNAL OF NEGRO HISTORY, 57 (1972), 83-98.

_____. "The New Black Literature: Protest or Affirmation." In Gayle BA, pp. 346-69.

_____. "Role of the Negro Writer in an Era of Struggle." NEGRO DIGEST, 13 (June 1964), 62-66.

_____. "Towards a Black Aesthetic." In Gayle BA, pp. 3-12. Also in Gayle BE, pp. 263-70.

Furay, Michael. "Africa in Negro American Poetry to 1929." AFRICAN LITERATURE TODAY, 2 (1968), 32-41.

Garrett, DeLois. "Dream Motif in Contemporary Negro Poetry." ENGLISH JOURNAL, 59 (1970), 767-70.

Garrett, Naomi M. "Racial Motifs in Contemporary American and French Negro Poetry." WEST VIRGINIA UNIV. PHILOLOGICAL PAPERS, 14 (1963), 80-101.

Gayle, Addison, Jr. "Cultural Strangulation: Black Literature and the White

Aesthetic." NEGRO DIGEST, 18 (Sept. 1969), 32-39. Also in Gayle BA, pp. 39-46.

_____. "The Harlem Renaissance: Towards a Black Aesthetic." MIDCONTINENT AMERICAN STUDIES JOURNAL, 11 (Fall 1970), 78-87.

_____. THE WAY OF THE NEW WORLD: THE BLACK NOVEL IN AMERICA. New York: Doubleday, 1975. 339 p.

_____, ed. THE BLACK AESTHETIC. New York: Doubleday, 1971. 432 p.

Referred to in the present bibliography as Gayle BA.

_____, ed. BLACK EXPRESSION: ESSAYS BY AND ABOUT BLACK AMERICANS IN THE CREATIVE ARTS. New York: Weybright & Talley, 1969. 394 p.

Referred to in the present bibliography as Gayle BE.

Gerald, Carolyn Fowler. "The Black Writer and his Role." NEGRO DIGEST, 18 (Jan. 1969), 42-48.

Gibson, Donald B., ed. MODERN BLACK POETS: A COLLECTION OF CRITICAL ESSAYS. Englewood Cliffs, N.J.: Prentice Hall, 1973, 181 p.

Twelve essays on poetry, from the Harlem Renaissance into the 1960s. Referred to in the present bibliography as Gibson MBP.

Gilman, Richard. THE CONFUSION OF REALMS. New York: Random House, 1970.

"White Standards and Black Writing," pp. 3-12; "Black Writing and White Criticism," pp. 13-21.

Glicksberg, Charles I. "The Alienation of Negro Literature." PHYLON, 11 (1950), 49-58.

_____. "Negro Poets and the American Tradition." ANTIOCH REVIEW, 6 (Summer 1946), 243-53.

Green, Elizabeth Lay. THE NEGRO IN CONTEMPORARY AMERICAN LITERATURE: AN OUTLINE FOR INDIVIDUAL AND GROUP STUDY. Chapel Hill: University of North Carolina Press, 1928. 92 p. Rpt. College Park, Md.: McGrath, 1968.

Part 1: "Poetry," pp. 7-21.

Haslam, Gerald W. "Two Traditions in Afro-American Literature." RESEARCH STUDIES (Washington State Univ.), 37 (Sept. 1969), 183-93.

Heath, Phoebe Ann. "Negro Poetry as an Historical Record." VASSAR JOURNAL OF UNDERGRADUATE STUDIES, 3 (May 1928), 34-52.

Henderson, Stephen E. "Saturation: Progress Report on a Theory of Black Poetry." BLACK WORLD, 24 (June 1975), 4-17.

_____. "'Survival Motion': A Study of the Black Writer and the Black Revolution in America." In THE MILITANT BLACK WRITER IN AFRICA AND THE UNITED STATES. Ed. by Mercer Cook and Stephen E. Henderson. Madison: Univ. of Wisconsin Press, 1969, pp. 63-129.

_____, ed. UNDERSTANDING THE NEW BLACK POETRY. See under Anthologies, below.

Hill, Herbert. "The Negro Writer and the Creative Imagination." ARTS IN SOCIETY, 5 (1968), 244-55.

_____. "New Directions of the Negro Writer." CRISIS, 70 (1963), 205-10.

_____, ed. ANGER, AND BEYOND: THE NEGRO WRITER IN THE UNITED STATES. New York: Harper, 1966. 227 p.

Horne, Frank S. "Black Verse." OPPORTUNITY, 2 (1924), 330-32.

Huggins, Nathan Irvin. HARLEM RENAISSANCE. New York: Oxford Univ. Press, 1971. 343 p.

Hughes, Langston. "How to Be a Bad Writer (in Ten Easy Lessons)." HARLEM QUARTERLY, 1 (Spring 1950), 13-14. Also in THE LANGSTON HUGHES READER. New York: George Braziller, 1958, pp. 491-92.

_____. "The Negro Artist and the Racial Mountain." NATION, 122 (1926), 692-94. Also in Gayle BA, pp. 175-81.

_____. "The Twenties: Harlem and Its Negritude." AFRICAN FORUM, 1 (Spring 1966), 11-20.

Jackson, Blyden. THE WAITING YEARS: ESSAYS ON AMERICAN NEGRO LITERATURE. Baton Rouge: Louisiana State Univ. Press, 1976. 216 p.

Jackson, Blyden, and Louis D. Rubin, Jr. BLACK POETRY IN AMERICA: TWO ESSAYS IN HISTORICAL INTERPRETATION. Baton Rouge: Louisiana State Univ. Press, 1974. 119 p.

Contains Rubin's "The Search for a Language, 1746-1923," pp. 1-
35; and Jackson's "From One 'New Negro' to Another, 1923-1972,"
pp. 37-98. Referred to in the present bibliography as Jackson BPA.

Jahn, Janheinz. A HISTORY OF NEO-AFRICAN LITERATURE: WRITING IN
TWO CONTINENTS. Trans. Oliver Coburn and Ursula Lehrburger. London:
Faber & Faber, 1968. 301 p. Reprinted as NEO-AFRICAN LITERATURE: A
HISTORY OF BLACK WRITING. New York: Grove Press, 1969.

Originally published in German as GESCHICHTE DER NEOAFRI-
KANISCHEN LITERATUR: EINE EINFUHRUNG. (Dusseldorf:
Eugen Diederichs Verlag, 1966), 285 p. The English translation
is slightly revised and enlarged. Referred to in the present bibliography as Jahn NAL.

Johnson, Ben. "Protest in American Negro Writing." MANKIND (New Delhi),
14 (Apr.-May 1970), 47-56.

Johnson, Charles S. "The Negro Renaissance and Its Significance." In THE
NEW NEGRO THIRTY YEARS AFTERWARD. Ed. Rayford W. Logan. Washington, D.C.: Howard Univ. Press, 1955, pp. 80-88.

Johnson, Guy B. "Recent Literature on the Negro." JOURNAL OF SOCIAL
FORCES, 12 (1925), 315.

Johnson, James Weldon. "The Dilemma of the Negro Author." AMERICAN
MERCURY, 15 (1928), 477-81.

_____. "Negro Authors and White Publishers." CRISIS, 36 (1929), 313-17.

_____. "Race Prejudice and the Negro Artist." HARPER'S, 157 (1928), 769-
76.

Kaiser, Ernest. "The Literature of Negro Revolt." FREEDOMWAYS, 3 (1963),
36-48.

Kent, George E. BLACKNESS AND THE ADVENTURE OF WESTERN CULTURE.
Chicago: Third World, 1972. 210 p.

Kgositsile, Keorapetse W. "Paths to the Future." NEGRO DIGEST, 17 (Sept.-
Oct. 1968), 37-48. Also in Gayle BA, pp. 248-60.

Kilgore, James C. "Toward the Dark Tower." BLACK WORLD, 19 (June
1970), 14-17.

Killens, John O. "Another Time When Black Was Beautiful." BLACK WORLD, 20 (Nov. 1970), 20-36.

On the Harlem Renaissance.

_____. "The Writer and Black Liberation." In IN BLACK AMERICA. Ed. Patricia W. Romero. Washington, D.C.: United Publishing Corp., 1969, pp. 256-71.

Kinneman, John A. "The Negro Renaissance." NEGRO HISTORY BULLETIN, 25 (1962), 200, 197-99.

Lash, John S. "Race Consciousness of the American Negro Author: Toward a Reexamination of an Orthodox Critical Concept." SOCIAL FORCES, 28 (1959-60), 24-34.

_____. "The Study of Negro Literary Expression." NEGRO HISTORY BUL-LETIN, 9 (1946), 207-11.

Lee, Don L. "Black Art/The Politics of Black Poetry." In FROM PLAN TO PLANET. Detroit: Broadside, 1973, pp. 105-13.

_____. "Black Poetry: Which Direction." NEGRO DIGEST, 17 (Sept.-Oct. 1968), 27-32.

_____. "Directions for Black Writers." BLACK SCHOLAR, 1 (Dec. 1969), 53-57.

_____. "Dynamite Voices: Black Poets of the 1970's." In AFRICAN CON-GRESS. Ed. Imamu Amiri Baraka (LeRoi Jones). New York: Morrow, 1972, pp. 200-211.

_____. DYNAMITE VOICES 1: BLACK POETS OF THE 1960'S. Detroit: Broadside, 1971. 92 p.

No index. Referred to in the present bibliography as Lee DV.

_____. "Toward a Definition: Black Poetry of the Sixties (after LeRoi Jones)." In Gayle BA, pp. 235-47.

Levin, Harry. "Literature and Cultural Identity." COMPARATIVE LITERA-TURE STUDIES, 10 (June 1973), 139-56.

Liebman, Arthur. "Patterns and Themes in Afro-American Literature." EN-GLISH RECORD, 20 (Feb. 1970), 2-12.

Locke, Alain. "The Message of the Negro Poets." CAROLINA MAGAZINE, 58 (May 1928), 5-15.

_____. "The Negro Poets of the United States." In ANTHOLOGY OF MAGAZINE VERSE FOR 1926. Ed. William S. Braithwaite. Boston: B.J. Brimmer, 1926, pp. 143-51.

_____. "The Negro's Contribution to American Art and Literature." ANNALS OF THE AMERICAN ACADEMY OF POLITICAL AND SOCIAL SCIENCE, 140 (Nov. 1928), 234-47.

_____. "Propaganda or Poetry." RACE, 1 (Summer 1936), 70-76, 87.

_____. LE ROLE DU NEGRE DANS LA CULTURE DES AMERIQUES. Port-au-Prince, Haiti: Imprimerie de l'Etat, 1943. 141 p.

Logan, Rayford W., Eugene C. Holmes, and G. Franklin Edwards, eds. THE NEW NEGRO THIRTY YEARS AFTERWARD. Washington, D.C.: Howard Univ. Press, 1955. 96 p.

Loggins, Vernon. THE NEGRO AUTHOR: HIS DEVELOPMENT IN AMERICA TO 1900. New York: Columbia Univ. Press, 1931. 480 p. Rpt. Port Washington, N.Y.: Kennikat Press, 1964.

Referred to in the present bibliography as Loggins NA.

Major, Clarence. THE DARK AND FEELING: BLACK AMERICAN WRITERS AND THEIR WORK. New York: Third Press, 1974. 153 p.

Mays, Benjamin E. THE NEGRO'S GOD AS REFLECTED IN HIS LITERATURE. Boston: Chapman & Grimes, 1938. 269 p. Rpt. New York: Atheneum, 1968.

Referred to in the present bibliography as Mays NG.

Miller, Ruth, ed. BACKGROUNDS TO BLACKAMERICAN LITERATURE. Scranton, Pa.: Chandler Publishing Co., 1971. 285 p.

Moore, W.H.A. "The New Negro Literary Movement." AFRICAN METHODIST EPISCOPAL CHURCH REVIEW, 21 (1904), 49-54.

Morpurgo, J.E. "American Negro Poetry." FORTNIGHTLY, 168 (July 1947), 16-24.

Morton, Lena Beatrice. NEGRO POETRY IN AMERICA. Boston: Stratford, 1925. 71 p.

Mphahlele, Ezekiel. "The Function of Literature at the Present Time: The Ethnic Imperative." TRANSITION (Accra), No. 45 (1974), pp. 47-53. Also in DENVER QUARTERLY, 9 (Winter 1975), 16-45.

———. "Voices in the Whirlwind: Poetry and Conflict in the Black World." In VOICES IN THE WHIRLWIND AND OTHER ESSAYS. New York: Hill & Wang, 1972, pp. 1-120.

   On Afro-American poets of the 1960s.

Neal, Larry. "The Black Arts Movement." In Bigsby BAW2, pp. 187-202.

———. "Some Reflections on the Black Aesthetic." In Gayle BA, pp. 13-16.

O'Brien, John. INTERVIEWS WITH BLACK WRITERS. New York: Liveright, 1973. 274 p.

   Among the seventeen writers interviewed are Arna Bontemps, Owen Dodson, Michael Harper, Robert Hayden, Clarence Major, Ishmael Reed, Alice Walker, and Al Young. Referred to in the present bibliography as O'Brien IBW.

Park, Robert E. "Negro Race Consciousness as Reflected in Race Literature." AMERICAN REVIEW, 1 (1923), 505-17.

Perkins, Eugene. "The Changing Status of Black Writers." BLACK WORLD, 19 (June 1970), 18-23, 95-98.

Perry, Margaret. SILENCE TO THE DRUMS: A SURVEY OF THE LITERATURE OF THE HARLEM RENAISSANCE. Westport, Conn.: Greenwood Press, 1976. 194 p.

Piquion, Rene. MANUEL DE NEGRITUDE. Port-au-Prince, Haiti: Editions Henri Deschamps, [1961?]. 335 p.

   "Negritude Americaine ou 'Renaissance Noire,'" pp. 97-111; "La Poesie des Blues," pp. 235-56.

Pool, Rosey. "The Discovery of American Negro Poetry." FREEDOMWAYS, 3 (1963), 46-51.

Portelli, Alesandro. "Cultura Poetica Afro-Americana." STUDI AMERICANE (Rome), 14 (1968), 401-29.

Ramsaran, J.A. "The 'Twice-Born' Artists' Silent Revolution." BLACK WORLD, 20 (May 1971), 58-68.

Randall, Dudley. "The Black Aesthetic in the Thirties, Forties, and Fifties." In Gayle BA, pp. 224-34. Also in Gibson MBP, pp. 34-42.

_____. "Black Poetry." In Gayle BE, pp. 109-14.

_____. BROADSIDE MEMORIES: POETS I HAVE KNOWN. Detroit: Broadside, 1975. 64 p.

Considers Brooks, Giovanni, Knight, Lorde, Madhubuti (Lee), and Sanchez.

_____. "The Poets of Broadside Press: A Personal Chronicle." BLACK ACADEMY REVIEW, 1 (Spring 1970), 40-47. Also in BROADSIDE MEMORIES (cited above), pp. 23-33.

_____. "Ubi Sunt and Hic Sum." NEGRO DIGEST, 14 (Sept. 1965), 73-76.

_____. "White Poet, Black Critic." NEGRO DIGEST, 14 (Feb. 1965), 46-48.

Record, C. Wilson. "The Negro as Creative Artist." CRISIS, 72 (1965), 153-58.

Reddick, La Bertha. "The Element of Protest in the Poetry of the Negro." Ph.D. dissertation, Fisk Univ., Nashville, Tennessee, 1940. 111 p.

Redding, J. Saunders. "American Negro Literature." AMERICAN SCHOLAR, 18 (1949), 137-48.

_____. "The Black Arts Movement in Negro Poetry." AMERICAN SCHOLAR, 42 (1973), 330-35.

_____. "The Negro Writer--Shadow and Substance." PHYLON, 11 (1950), 371-77.

_____. "Negro Writing in America." NEW LEADER, 42 (16 May 1960), 8-10.

_____. "The Problem of the Negro Writer." MASSACHUSETTS REVIEW, 6 (1964), 57-70.

_____. TO MAKE A POET BLACK. Chapel Hill: Univ. of North Carolina Press, 1939. 142 p. Rpt. College Park, Md.: McGrath, 1968.

Referred to in the present bibliography as Redding TMPB.

Redmond, Eugene B. "The Black American Epic: Its Roots, Its Writers." BLACK SCHOLAR, 2 (Jan. 1971), 15-22.

———. DRUMVOICES: THE MISSION OF AFRO-AMERICAN POETRY: A CRITICAL HISTORY. New York: Doubleday, 1976. 464 p.

> An extremely useful and comprehensive survey from Lucy Terry through the mid-1970s, with a valuable bibliographical index which includes a listing of records and tapes. Published after the present bibliography had been largely completed, DRUMVOICES is not referred to below under the individual authors with whom it deals; it should however not be overlooked, particularly for poets of the most recent period.

———. "How Many Poets Scrub the River's Bank (An Essay on Black Poetry)." CONFRONTATION, No. 2 (1971), pp. 47-53.

Reese, Carolyn. "From Jupiter Hammon to LeRoi Jones." CHANGING EDUCATION, 1 (Fall 1966), 30-34.

Rexroth, Kenneth. AMERICAN POETRY IN THE TWENTIETH CENTURY. New York: Herder & Herder, 1971. 180 p.

> Chapter 12, pp. 147-59, discusses black poets.

Rodgers, Carolyn M. "Black Poetry--Where It's At." NEGRO DIGEST, 18 (Sept. 1969), 7-16. Also in RAPPIN' AND STYLIN' OUT: COMMUNICATION IN URBAN BLACK AMERICA. Ed. Thomas Kochman. Urbana: Univ. of Illinois Press, 1972, pp. 336-45.

———. "Breakforth. In Deed." BLACK WORLD, 19 (Sept. 1970), 13-22.

———. "The Literature of Black." BLACK WORLD, 19 (June 1970), 5-14.

———. "Uh Nat'chal Thang--The Whole Truth--Us." BLACK WORLD, 20 (Sept. 1971), 4-14.

Rollins, Charlemae. FAMOUS AMERICAN NEGRO POETS. New York: Dodd, Mead, 1965. 95 p.

> Brief biographical sketches, with quotations, of a dozen poets; written for young people. Referred to in the present bibliography as Rollins FANP.

Rushing, Andrea Benton. "Images of Black Women in Afro-American Poetry." BLACK WORLD, 24 (Sept. 1975), 18-30.

Sheffey, Ruthe. "Wit and Irony in Militant Black Poetry." BLACK WORLD, 22 (June 1973), 14-21.

Sherman, Joan R. INVISIBLE POETS: AFRO-AMERICANS OF THE NINETEENTH CENTURY. Urbana: Univ. of Illinois Press, 1974. 302 p.

> Detailed biographical and critical essays on twenty-six poets, with bibliographies of thirty-eight more; a thorough and accurate work, based on extensive research. Referred to in the present bibliography as Sherman IP.

Singh, Amritjit. THE NOVELS OF THE HARLEM RENAISSANCE: TWELVE BLACK WRITERS 1923-1933. University Park: Pennsylvania State Univ. Press, 1976. 175 p.

> Gives background information for the subject.

Singh, Raman K., and Peter Fellowes, eds. BLACK LITERATURE IN AMERICA: A CASEBOOK. See under Anthologies, below.

Smitherman, Geneva. "The Power of the Rap: The Black Idiom and the New Black Poetry." TWENTIETH CENTURY LITERATURE, 19 (1973), 259-74.

"The Task of the Negro Writer as Artist: A Symposium." NEGRO DIGEST, 14 (Apr. 1965), 54-83.

> Thirty-two contributors, including three whites.

Taussig, Charlotte E. "The New Negro as Revealed in his Poetry." OPPORTUNITY, 5 (1927), 108-11.

Taylor, Clyde. "Black Folk Spirit and the Shape of Black Literature." BLACK-FOLK, 1 (Spring 1970), 11-17.

Thurman, Wallace. "Negro Poets and Their Poetry." BOOKMAN, 67 (1928), 555-61. Also in Gayle BE, pp. 70-82.

Turner, Darwin T. "Afro-American Literary Critics." BLACK WORLD, 19 (July 1970), 54-67.

_____. IN A MINOR CHORD: THREE AFRO-AMERICAN WRITERS AND THEIR SEARCH FOR IDENTITY. Carbondale: Southern Illinois Univ. Press, 1971. 153 p.

> The three writers are Jean Toomer, Countee Cullen, and Zora Neale Hurston.

Tusiani, Joseph. INFLUENZA CRISTIANA NELLA POESIA NEGRO-AMERICANA. Bologna, Italy: Editrice Nigrizia, 1971. 127 p.

Valenti, Suzanne. "The Black Diaspora: Negritude in the Poetry of West Africans and Black Americans." PHYLON, 34 (1973), 390-98.

Wagner, Jean. BLACK POETS OF THE UNITED STATES FROM PAUL LAURENCE DUNBAR TO LANGSTON HUGHES. Trans. Kenneth Douglas. Urbana: Univ. of Illinois Press, 1973. 561 p.

> Originally published in French as LES POETES NEGRES DES ETATS UNIS: LE SENTIMENT RACIAL ET RELIGIEUX DANS LA POESIE DE PAUL LAURENCE DUNBAR A LANGSTON HUGHES. (Paris: Librairie Istra, 1963), 637 p. An important and thorough study; the subtitle of the original French edition is significant, particularly in light of Jahn's criticism of Wagner as a "fanatical Christian" whose "verdict is a foregone conclusion: the evil in Afro-American poetry is represented by the influences from folklore, the Blues, the preacher style, the Spiritual, in short all Africanisms--which he tracks down with the zeal of a police inspector" (Jahn NAL). Referred to in the present bibliography as Wagner BPUS.

Walker, Margaret. "New Poets." PHYLON, 11 (1950), 345-54. Also in Gayle BE, pp. 89-100.

White, Newman Ivey. "American Negro Poetry." SOUTH ATLANTIC QUARTERLY, 20 (1921), 304-22.

_____. "Racial Feeling in Negro Poetry." SOUTH ATLANTIC QUARTERLY, 21 (1922), 14-29.

White, Walter. THE NEGRO'S CONTRIBUTION TO AMERICAN CULTURE: THE SUDDEN FLOWERING OF A GENIUS LADEN ARTISTIC MOVEMENT. Little Blue Book, 1306. Girard, Kans.: Haldeman-Julius, 1928. 64 p.

Whitlow, Roger. BLACK AMERICAN LITERATURE: A CRITICAL HISTORY WITH A 1,520 TITLE BIBLIOGRAPHY OF WORKS WRITTEN BY OR ABOUT BLACK AMERICANS. Chicago: Nelson Hall, 1973. 287 p. Rpt. Totowa, N.J.: Littlefield, Adams & Co., 1974.

> Referred to in the present bibliography as Whitlow BAL.

Williams, Kenny J. THEY ALSO SPOKE: AN ESSAY ON NEGRO LITERATURE IN AMERICA, 1787-1930. Nashville, Tenn.: Townsend Press, 1970. 319 p.

> Referred to in the present bibliography as Williams TAS.

Williams, Sherley Anne. GIVE BIRTH TO BRIGHTNESS: A THEMATIC STUDY IN NEO-BLACK LITERATURE. New York: Dial Press, 1972. 252 p.

Work, Monroe N. "The Spirit of Negro Poetry." SOUTHERN WORKMAN, 37 (1908), 73-77.

Wright, Richard. "The Literature of the Negro in the United States." In WHITE MAN LISTEN. New York: Doubleday, 1957, pp. 105-50. Also in Gayle BE, pp. 198-229.

> Originally published as "Litterature Noire Americaine," TEMPS MODERNES, 4 (1948), 193-221. On poetry from Phillis Wheatley to Robert Hayden and Margaret Walker.

Young, James O. BLACK WRITERS OF THE THIRTIES. Baton Rouge: Louisiana State Univ. Press, 1973. 257 p.

> Chapter 6, "Weavers of Jagged Words," pp. 166-202, discusses the poetry of Sterling Brown, Countee Cullen, F.M. Davis, Robert Hayden, Langston Hughes, and Margaret Walker.

Young, Roland P. "Black Words/The Death of Yakub." JOURNAL OF BLACK POETRY, No. 5 (Summer 1967), pp. 26-33.

3. ANTHOLOGIES

Anthologies indexed in Chapman IBP are so indicated. JOURNAL OF BLACK POETRY is included in this section because of its importance as a voice for Afro-American poetry.

Abdul, Raoul, ed. THE MAGIC OF BLACK POETRY. New York: Dodd, Mead, 1972. 118 p.

> Selections from forty-eight poets (twenty-four of them from the United States); "compiled for young readers." In Chapman IBP.

Adams, William, Peter Conn, and Barry Slepian, eds. AFRO-AMERICAN LITERATURE: POETRY. Boston: Houghton Mifflin, 1970. 130 p.

Adoff, Arnold, ed. BLACK OUT LOUD: AN ANTHOLOGY OF MODERN POEMS BY BLACK AMERICANS. New York: Macmillan, 1970. 86 p.

> In Chapman IBP.

_____. I AM THE DARKER BROTHER: AN ANTHOLOGY OF MODERN POEMS BY NEGRO AMERICANS. New York: Macmillan, 1968. 128 p.

> In Chapman IBP.

_____. THE POETRY OF BLACK AMERICA: ANTHOLOGY OF THE 20TH CENTURY. Introd. Gwendolyn Brooks. New York: Harper and Row, 1973. 552 p.

> One hundred forty-five poets represented in chronological order, from W.E.B. DuBois (born 1868) to Julianne Perry (born 1952).

AFRO-AMERICAN FESTIVAL OF THE ARTS MAGAZINE. Introd. Yusef Iman. Newark, N.J.: Jihad, 1966. 26 p. Mimeographed.

> 2nd ed. published as ANTHOLOGY OF OUR BLACK SELVES (Newark, N.J.: Jihad, 1967), 49 p., mimeographed; 3rd ed. (1969), [51] p., offset. The 2nd and 3rd editions have the cover title AFRO-ARTS ANTHOLOGY. Poetry by David Henderson, LeRoi Jones, Sonia Sanchez, and others, also prose selections.

AFRO-ARTS ANTHOLOGY. See preceding entry.

Alhamisi, Ahmed, and Harun Kofi Wangara, eds. BLACK ARTS: AN ANTHOLOGY OF BLACK CREATIONS. Introd. Keorapetse Kgositsile. Detroit: Black Arts Publications, 1969. 158 p.

> Poetry, pp. 97-140.

Ambrose, Amanda, ed. MY NAME IS BLACK: AN ANTHOLOGY OF BLACK POETS. New York: Scholastic Book Services, 1973. 160 p.

ANTHOLOGY: BLACK WRITERS WORKSHOP. Introd. Don L. Lee. Kansas City, Mo.: Krizna Publications, 1970. 52 p.

ANTHOLOGY OF OUR BLACK SELVES. See AFRO-AMERICAN FESTIVAL OF THE ARTS MAGAZINE, above.

Baker, Houston A., Jr., ed. BLACK LITERATURE IN AMERICA. New York: McGraw-Hill, 1971. 443 p.

> Prose and poetry. In Chapman IBP.

Barksdale, Richard, and Keneth Kinnamon, eds. BLACK WRITERS OF AMERICA: A COMPREHENSIVE ANTHOLOGY. New York: Macmillan, 1972. 917 p.

> Poetry and prose. Thirty-four poets included.

Battle, Sol, ed. GHETTO '68. New York: New World Press, 1968. 95 p. Rpt. New York: Panther House, 1968.

> "Compiled from works submitted to the Workshop for Young Writers" at Manna House in East Harlem.

Bell, Bernard W., ed. MODERN AND CONTEMPORARY AFRO-AMERICAN POETRY. Boston: Allyn & Bacon, 1972. 193 p.

BLACK ON BLACK. Stanford, Calif.: Black Student Union of Stanford University, 1967. 52 p.

BLACK POETS WRITE ON! AN ANTHOLOGY OF BLACK PHILADELPHIAN POETS. Introd. Harold Franklin. Philadelphia: Black History Museum Committee, 1970. [28] p.

Twenty-six contributors, most of them students.

Bontemps, Arna, ed. AMERICAN NEGRO POETRY. New York: Hill & Wang, 1963. 197 p.

One hundred seventy-one poems by fifty-five poets covering a span of seventy years, from James Weldon Johnson to Carl Wendell Hines. An enlarged edition of 231 p., published in 1974, adds twelve younger poets. First edition in Chapman IBP.

_____. GOLDEN SLIPPERS: AN ANTHOLOGY OF NEGRO POETRY FOR YOUNG READERS. New York: Harper, 1941. 220 p.

In Chapman IBP.

Booker, Merrel Daniel, Sr., Erma Barbour Booker, et al., eds. CRY AT BIRTH. New York: McGraw-Hill, 1971. 172 p.

Poetry and prose by ninety young authors.

Boyd, Sue Abbot, ed. POEMS BY BLACKS. Vols. 1-2. Fort Smith, Ark.: South & West, 1971-72.

For volume 3, see Pinkie Gordon Lane, below, this section.

Boyer, Jill Witherspoon, ed. THE BROADSIDE ANNUAL 1973: INTRODUCING NEW BLACK POETS. Detroit: Broadside, 1973. 24 p.

Eleven contributors. See also Jill Witherspoon, below, this section.

Brawley, Benjamin G., ed. EARLY NEGRO AMERICAN WRITERS: SELECTIONS WITH BIOGRAPHICAL AND CRITICAL INTRODUCTIONS. Chapel Hill: Univ. of North Carolina Press, 1935. Rpt. New York: Dover, 1970. 305 p.

Poetry and prose.

Breman, Paul, ed. SIXES AND SEVENS: AN ANTHOLOGY OF NEW POETRY. Heritage series, 2. London: Breman, 1962. 96 p.

Thirteen then little-known poets; George R. Bell, Ray Durem, Calvin Hernton, Audre Lorde, Conrad Kent Rivers, and James W. Thompson are the best represented.

_____. YOU BETTER BELIEVE IT: BLACK VERSE IN ENGLISH FROM AFRICA, THE WEST INDIES AND THE UNITED STATES. Baltimore: Penguin Books, 1973. 552 p.

About 125 poets, of whom some 75 are from the United States, with biographical and critical commentary on each poet.

Brewer, John Mason, ed. HERALDING DAWN: AN ANTHOLOGY OF VERSE . . . WITH A HISTORICAL SUMMARY ON THE TEXAS NEGROES' VERSE-MAKING. Introd. Henry Smith. Dallas: June Thomason, Printing, 1936. 45 p.

Twenty-four poems, many in dialect, by fifteen black Texas poets, including Gwendolyn Bennett, Bernice Love Wiggins, and the editor. In Chapman IBP.

_____. PATRIOTIC MOMENTS: A SECOND BOOK OF VERSE BY THE BELLEROPHON QUILL CLUB OF THE BOOKER T. WASHINGTON HIGH SCHOOL. Dallas: n.p., 1936. 24 p.

SENIOR SENTIMENTS AND JUNIOR JOTTINGS: A FIRST BOOK OF VERSE BY THE BELLEROPHON QUILL CLUB OF THE BOOKER T. WASHINGTON HIGH SCHOOL. Dallas: n.p., 1934. 24 p.

Brooks, Gwendolyn, ed. A BROADSIDE TREASURY. Detroit: Broadside, 1971. 188 p.

About 150 poems by fifty contemporary black authors published by Broadside Press since its founding in 1965. Brooks's introduction stresses dedication to blackness and language experimentation since 1966. In Chapman IBP.

_____. JUMP BAD: A NEW CHICAGO ANTHOLOGY. Detroit: Broadside, 1971. 188 p.

Poetry and prose by Johari Amini, Don Lee, Carolyn Rodgers, and other members of a workshop conducted by Brooks.

Brown, Patricia L., Don L. Lee, and Francis Ward, eds. TO GWEN WITH LOVE: AN ANTHOLOGY DEDICATED TO GWENDOLYN BROOKS. Chicago: Johnson Publishing Co., 1971. 149 p.

Tributes from fifty-four poets, mostly members of the Kuumba Workshop in Chicago; includes two essays and a short story. In Chapman IBP.

Brown, Sterling A., Arthur P. Davis, and Ulysses Grant, eds. THE NEGRO CARAVAN: WRITINGS BY AMERICAN NEGROES. New York: Dryden Press, 1941. 1,082 p. Rpt. New York: Arno, 1969.

> "Poetry," pp. 275-410.

Browning, Alice C., and Hildred Honore, eds. NEW VOICES IN BLACK POETRY 1972. Chicago: Browning Press, 1972. [25] p.

> Described as "an annual anthology of poetry, written by members of International Black Writers' Conference. . . ."

Bruchac, Joseph, ed. THE LAST STOP: WRITING FROM COMSTOCK PRISON. Greenfield Center, N.Y.: Greenfield Review Press, 1974. 100 p.

> Poetry and prose.

Bruchac, Joseph, and William Witherup, eds. WORDS FROM THE HOUSE OF THE DEAD: AN ANTHOLOGY OF PRISON WRITINGS FROM SOLEDAD. Greenfield Center, N.Y.: Greenfield Review Press, 1971. 67 p.

> Poetry and prose. "For obvious reasons, the names of most of the contributors have been left out."

Bryson, Clarence F., and James H. Robinson, eds. DUNDO: ANTHOLOGY OF POETRY BY CLEVELAND NEGRO YOUTH. Cleveland: January Club, 1931. 76 p.

BURNING SPEAR: AN ANTHOLOGY OF AFRO-SAXON POETRY. Washington, D.C.: Jupiter Hammon Press, 1963. 60 p.

> Eight Howard University poets, including Lance Jeffers.

Byars, J.C., Jr., ed. BLACK AND WHITE: AN ANTHOLOGY OF WASHINGTON VERSE. Washington, D.C.: Crane Press, 1927. 96 p.

Calverton, V.F., ed. ANTHOLOGY OF AMERICAN NEGRO LITERATURE. New York: Modern Library, 1929. 535 p.

> Poetry and prose. Twenty-one poets included.

Cannon, Steve, ed. JAMBALAYA. Introd. Victor Hernandez Cruz. New York: Reed, Cannon and Johnson, 1975. 117 p.

> Two of the four contributors are Afro-Americans: Lorenzo Thomas and Thulain (Barbara Davis).

Chapman, Abraham, ed. BLACK VOICES: AN ANTHOLOGY OF AFRO-AMERICAN LITERATURE. New York: New American Library, 1968. 718 p.

Rpt. New York: St Martin's Press, 1970.

    Poetry, pp. 354-492. Twenty-four poets, from Dunbar to Jones.

_____. NEW BLACK VOICES: AN ANTHOLOGY OF CONTEMPORARY AFRO-AMERICAN LITERATURE. New York: New American Library, 1972. 606 p.

    Poetry, pp. 201-390. Fifty-four poets represented.

Chicago Renaissance. CHICAGO RENAISSANCE 1. Markham, Ill.: Natural Resources Unlimited, 1975. 165 p.

    Some fifty contributors, all little known.

Clark, Peter Wellington, ed. ARROWS OF GOLD: AN ANTHOLOGY OF CATHOLIC VERSE FROM "AMERICA'S FIRST CATHOLIC COLLEGE FOR COLORED YOUTH." New Orleans: Xavier Univ. Press, 1941. 85 p.

Coleman, Edward Maceo. See Armand Lanusse, below, this section.

Coombs, Orde, ed. WE SPEAK AS LIBERATORS: YOUNG BLACK POETS. New York: Dodd, Mead, 1970. 252 p.

    Fifty-seven contributors.

Cooper, Nancy, ed. FREEDOM SCHOOL POETRY. Introd. Langston Hughes. Atlanta: Student Non-Violent Coordinating Committee, 1966. 47 p.

    By some thirty "young freedom school students of Mississippi."

Cornish, Sam, and Lucian W. Dixon, eds. CHICORY: YOUNG VOICES FROM THE BLACK GHETTO. New York: Association Press, 1969. 96 p.

    "Words overheard or written in the black ghetto of Baltimore, Maryland . . . taken from the writings in CHICORY, a magazine of poetry, fiction and commentary" published in Baltimore since 1966.

Cromwell, Otelia, Lorenzo Dow Turner, and Eva B. Dykes, eds. READINGS FROM NEGRO AUTHORS FOR SCHOOLS AND COLLEGES. New York: Harcourt, Brace, 1931. 388 p.

    Mostly prose; some fifty pages of poetry.

Cullen, Countee, ed. CAROLING DUSK: AN ANTHOLOGY OF VERSE BY NEGRO POETS. New York: Harper, 1929. 237 p.

    Two hundred twenty-eight poems by thirty-seven poets from Dunbar to the Harlem Renaissance, whose minor poets are well represented. Dialect poetry is excluded as artificial. Biographical notices written by the poets themselves. In Chapman IBP.

Cunard, Nancy. NEGRO ANTHOLOGY. Made by Nancy Cunard, 1931-33. London: Published by Nancy Cunard at Wishart & Co., 1934. 854 p. Rpt. New York: Negro Universities Press, 1969. Abr. ed. Published as NEGRO: AN ANTHOLOGY. Collected and edited by Nancy Cunard; edited and abridged with an introduction by Hugh Ford. New York: Ungar, 1970. 464 p.

Poetry and prose, by black and white authors. Both editions are large quartos with many illustrations.

Cuney, Waring, Langston Hughes, and Bruce McMarion Wright, eds. LINCOLN UNIVERSITY POETS: CENTENNIAL ANTHOLOGY. Introd. Horace Mann Bond and Jay Saunders Redding. New York: Fine Editions Press, 1954. 72 p.

In Chapman IBP.

Danner, Margaret, ed. BRASS HORSES: Richmond, Va.: 1968.

Poems by students at Virginia Union University.

_____. REGROUP. Richmond, Va.: 1969.

Poems by students at Virginia Union University.

DARK MEDITATIONS: A COLLECTION OF POEMS. Introd. Eugene Perkins. Chicago: Free Black Press, 1971. 36 p.

By "a group of young black poets who were members of the South Side Community Art Center's Writers Workshop in Chicago."

Davis, Arthur P., and Michael W. Peplow, eds. THE NEW NEGRO RENAISSANCE: AN ANTHOLOGY. New York: Holt, Rinehart and Winston, 1975. 538 p.

Prose and poetry by over fifty black writers of the twenties, with biographical and critical commentary by the editors.

Davis, Arthur P., and Saunders Redding, eds. CAVALCADE: NEGRO AMERICAN WRITING FROM 1760 TO THE PRESENT. Boston: Houghton Mifflin, 1971. 905 p.

Poetry and prose. Thirty-three poets represented. In Chapman IBP.

Dee, Ruby, ed. GLOWCHILD AND OTHER POEMS. New York: Third Press, 1972. 111 p.

Most of the contributors are black students from Albert Leonard

Junior High School and New Rochelle High School, both in New Rochelle, New York.

Dreer, Herman, ed. AMERICAN LITERATURE BY NEGRO AUTHORS. New York: Macmillan, 1950. 334 p.

Poetry and prose.

Dunbar Nelson, Alice Moore, ed. THE DUNBAR SPEAKER AND ENTERTAINER, CONTAINING THE BEST PROSE AND POETIC SELECTIONS BY AND ABOUT THE NEGRO RACE, WITH PROGRAM ARRANGED FOR SPECIAL ENTERTAINMENTS. Introd. Leslie Pinckney Hill. Naperville, Ill.: J.L. Nichols and Co., 1920. 288 p.

Poetry and prose.

ECHOES FROM THE GUMBO: WRITINGS AND WORKS FROM THE WORKSHOP OF THE FREE SOUTHERN THEATRE. New Orleans: FST Press, 1968. 69 p.

Eleazer, Robert Burns, ed. SINGERS IN THE DAWN: A BRIEF SUPPLEMENT TO THE STUDY OF AMERICAN LITERATURE. Atlanta: Conference on Education and Race Relations, 1934. 23 p.

Emanuel, James A., and Theodore L. Gross, eds. DARK SYMPHONY: NEGRO LITERATURE IN AMERICA. New York: Free Press, 1968. 604 p.

Poetry and prose, with biographical and critical commentary, bibliography, and index.

Exum, Pat Crutchfield, ed. KEEPING THE FAITH: WRITINGS BY BLACK AMERICAN WOMEN. Greenwich, Conn.: Fawcett, 1975. 288 p.

Poetry and prose.

Feaster, Bob, ed. STREET VERSES 'N SOME RIGHTEOUSNESS. New York: Manna House Workshops, 1972. 100 p.

Fifteen Harlem poets.

Fox, Hugh, and Sam Cornish, eds. THE LIVING UNDERGROUND: AN ANTHOLOGY OF CONTEMPORARY AMERICAN POETRY. East Lansing, Mich.: Ghost Dance Press, 1969. 90 p.

Giovanni, Nikki, ed. NIGHT COMES SOFTLY: ANTHOLOGY OF BLACK FEMALE VOICES. Newark, N.J.: Printed by Medic Press, 1970. 97 p.

About eighty-two contributors. Reviewed by Angela Jackson in BLACK WORLD, 20 (Apr. 1971), 90-92.

Haven, Leroy, ed. CONSCIOUSNESS: A PUBLICATION OF THE CREATIVE WRITING CLASSES OF THE ACADEMY OF BLACK CULTURE, INC. Savannah, Ga.: Academy of Black Culture, 1971. 24 p.

Hayden, Robert, ed. KALEIDOSCOPE: POEMS BY AMERICAN NEGRO POETS. New York: Harcourt, 1967. 231 p.

> Forty-two poets represented; reviewed by Don L. Lee in NEGRO DIGEST, 17 (Jan. 1968), 51-52, 90-94. In Chapman IBP.

Henderson, David, ed. UMBRA ANTHOLOGY, 1967-1968. New York: Umbra, 1967. 66 p.

> Poems by Henry Dumas, Ray Durem, Calvin Hernton, Langston Hughes, Bob Kaufman, C.K. Rivers, and some twenty-five others, including a few whites.

————. UMBRA'S BLACKWORKS 1970-1971. New York: Umbra, 1970. [40] p.

> Issued as a thirty-two-page tabloid newspaper, with Hart LeRoi Bibbs's novella DIET BOOK FOR JUNKIES as a separate eight-page supplement. Contains previously unpublished poems by David Henderson, Calvin Hernton, Langston Hughes, LeRoi Jones, Bob Kaufman, Ishmael Reed, Jay Wright, and others.

Henderson, Stephen. UNDERSTANDING THE NEW BLACK POETRY: BLACK SPEECH AND BLACK MUSIC AS POETIC REFERENCES. New York: Morrow, 1973. 394 p.

> An anthology of some seventy poets, with about eighty pages of critical discussion by Henderson. Reviewed by George E. Kent in BLACK WORLD, 23 (Feb. 1974), 51, 73-77.

Hesse, Eva, and Paridam von dem Knesebeck, eds. MEINE DUNKLEN HANDE: MODERNE NEGERLYRIK IN ORIGINAL UND NACHDICHTUNG. Munich: Nymphenburger Verlagshandlung, 1953. 90 p.

> Bilingual; English and German.

Hill, Herbert, ed. SOON, ONE MORNING: NEW WRITING BY AMERICAN NEGROES 1940-1962. New York: Knopf, 1963. 617 p.

> Poetry, pp. 557-617.

Hollo, Anselm, ed. NEGRO VERSE. London: Vista, 1964. 48 p.

> Langston Hughes, Ted Joans, LeRoi Jones, A.B. Spellman, and a dozen African and Caribbean poets are represented.

Hopkins, Lee Bennett, ed. ON OUR WAY: POEMS OF PRIDE AND PURPOSE. Introd. Augusta Baker. New York: Knopf, 1974. 63 p.

> For children.

Hopkins, Tobie, ed. SOUL GOING HOME. Los Angeles: Watts Publishing Co., 1969. 66 p.

> Local writers.

Hughes, Langston, ed. NEW NEGRO POETS U.S.A. Introd. Gwendolyn Brooks. Bloomington: Indiana Univ. Press, 1964. 127 p.

> Thirty-seven postwar poets represented, with a wide variety of style and content--from intimate, lyrical, or descriptive poetry to public protest. Some of the poets had never been published before; most have since published volumes of their own. Five sections; biographical notes. In Chapman IBP.

_____. LA POESIE NEGRO-AMERICAINE. Paris: Seghers, 1966. 317 p.

> Bilingual presentation of forty-four poets; six "precursors" and the rest equally divided between pre- and post-World War II poets, with biographical notes in French.

Hughes, Langston, and Arna Bontemps, eds. THE POETRY OF THE NEGRO, 1746-1949. New York: Doubleday, 1949. 429 p. Rev. ed. THE POETRY OF THE NEGRO, 1746-1970. New York: Doubleday, 1970. 645 p.

> The revised edition includes the work of 163 poets, "covering the widest possible range and revealing the growth of the Negro problem from regional to national and world proportions." A section of "Tributary Poems by Non-Negroes" includes 52 poets. Both editions in Chapman IBP.

Iman, Yusef, ed. THE YOUNG BLACK POETS OF BROOKLYN. Brooklyn, N.Y.: East Publications [?], 1971. 22 p.

James, Cyril, ed. THE BEST OF 40 ACRES POETRY. New York: Horizon Six, 1972. 47 p. Rev. ed., 1974. 57 p.

Johnson, Alicia L., ed. BLACK ART CREATIONS, 1970. Carbondale, Ill.: Published by the editor [?], 1970.

> Poetry and prose by students.

Johnson, Charles S., ed. EBONY AND TOPAZ: A COLLECTANEA. New York: National Urban League, 1927. 164 p. Rpt. Plainview, N.Y.: Books for Libraries, 1971.

> Focuses on the more outspoken racial poetry of the Harlem Renaissance.

Johnson, James Weldon, ed. THE BOOK OF AMERICAN NEGRO POETRY. With an Essay on the Negro's Creative Genius. New York: Harcourt, Brace, 1922. 217 p. Rev. ed.,1931. 300 p.

> The revised edition contains some 300 poems by forty authors, from Dunbar to Lucy Ariel Williams. Dialect poetry is included. Johnson says that in the revised edition "the sketches of the writers included have been made critical as well as biographical." Rev. ed. in Chapman IBP.

Jones, Jymi, ed. A VISION OF BLACKNESS: BLACK POETRY WORKSHOP. Conshohocken, Pa.: Montgomery County Community College, 1970. 29 p.

Jones, LeRoi, and Larry Neal, eds. BLACK FIRE: AN ANTHOLOGY OF AFRO-AMERICAN WRITING. New York: Morrow, 1968. 670 p.

> Poetry, pages 189-452. Includes fifty-six poets. Reviewed by Stanley Crouch in JOURNAL OF BLACK POETRY, 11 (Spring 1969), 65-69, and by Don L. Lee in NEGRO DIGEST, 18 (March 1969), 78-81.

Jordan, June, ed. SOULSCRIPT: AFRO-AMERICAN POETRY. New York: Doubleday, 1970. 146 p.

> Forty-five poets, most of them young. Selected for young readers.

Jordan, June, and Terry Bush, eds. THE VOICE OF THE CHILDREN. New York: Holt, 1970. 101 p.

Joseph, Stephen M., ed. THE ME NOBODY KNOWS: CHILDREN'S VOICES FROM THE GHETTO. New York: Avon, 1969. 81 p.

JOURNAL OF BLACK POETRY. 1966- .

> Edited by Joe Goncalves (Dingane) and published in San Francisco, the JOURNAL appears quarterly "when possible." Although a journal and not a book, it is included in this list of anthologies because of its unique status as the only continuing periodical devoted almost exclusively to Afro-American poetry. Number 1 (Spring 1966) consists of fourteen mimeographed pages; number 17 (Summer 1973), a "Special West Indian Issue," is 100 quarto pages with illustrations. With number 18 (Summer 1974) the name was changed to KITABU CHA JUA (Swahili for "Book of the Sun").

> Averaging about 100 quarto pages per issue since 1968, the JOURNAL, while maintaining a strong nationalist outlook, has published most of the major poets of the period, as well as many minor figures, including some who have not appeared elsewhere. A series of guest editors assembled the following issues: Ahmed Alhamisi (No. 8, 1968); Larry Neal (No. 9, 1968); Marvin X (No. 10,

1968); Ed Spriggs (No. 11, 1969); Clarence Major (No. 12, 1969); Askia Muhammad Toure (No. 13, 1970); Don L. Lee (No. 14, 1971); and Dudley Randall (No. 15, 1971).

An interesting and perceptive (if highly partisan) inside account of some conflicting forces in black poetry of the late sixties is contained in No. 17 (1973), pp. 86-91, in the editor's review of Don L. Lee's DYNAMITE VOICES, which is denounced as "ultimately a restatement of the white aesthetic." Another similar essay is Ahmed Akinwole Alhamisi's "On Spiritualism and the Revolutionary Spirit," in No. 15 (1971).

In spite of its bulk and durability, the JOURNAL's influence has been limited by its infrequent, and often delayed, appearance (typically, No. 16, dated Summer 1972, was not published until 1973), by its limited circulation, and, no doubt, by its radical views (in his review of DYNAMITE VOICES in No. 17 the editor says, "Many of us have sheaves of requests from white publishers . . . to re-print some of our writings. . . . It should wound us that some hunky would want to re-print anything we wrote").

Kerlin, Robert E., ed. CONTEMPORARY POETRY OF THE NEGRO. Hampton, Va.: Hampton Institute Press, 1921. 23 p.

_____. NEGRO POETS AND THEIR POEMS. Washington, D.C.: Associated Publishers, 1923. 285 p. 2nd ed. 1935, 342 p. 3rd ed. 1940, 342 p. "3rd ed." (i.e. 4th ed.) 1947, 354 p.

This is as much a history of black poetry, from the slave songs and Phillis Wheatley to the Harlem Renaissance and beyond, as an anthology. Over 200 poems and excerpts from ninety-five authors (in the 1947 edition) are used to illustrate the grouping of poets under historical or thematic headings such as "Dialect Verse," "The Heart of Negro Womanhood," and "The Poetry of Protest."

A number of minor poets found in Kerlin are not represented elsewhere.

_____. THE VOICE OF THE NEGRO, 1919. New York: Dutton, 1921. Rpt. New York: Arno, 1968. 188 p.

"A compilation from the colored press of America for the four months immediately succeeding the Washington riot" of July 1919. The anthology is entirely prose, except for section X, "The Lyric Cry," pp. 183-88, which prints ten poems by Georgia Douglas Johnson, Claude McKay, Lucian B. Watkins, and others (McKay's sonnet "To the White Fiends" appears anonymously, entitled "The Negro").

King, Woodie, ed. BLACKSPIRITS: A FESTIVAL OF NEW BLACK POETS IN AMERICA. Artistic consultant Imamu Amiri Baraka. Foreword by Nikki

Giovanni. Introd. Don L. Lee. New York: Random House, 1972. 252 p.

Thirty contributors; based on a series of poetry readings held in New York in 1971. In Chapman IBP.

_____. THE FORERUNNERS: BLACK POETS IN AMERICA. Introd. Addison Gayle, Jr., and Dudley Randall. Washington, D.C.: Howard Univ. Press, 1975. 127 p.

Sixteen contributors.

Lane, Pinkie Gordon, ed. POEMS BY BLACKS. Vol. 3. Fort Smith, Ark.: South & West, [1974?]. For volumes 1-2, see Boyd, S.A., above.

Lane, Ronnie M., ed. FACE THE WHIRLWIND. Grand Rapids, Mich.: Pilot Press, 1973. 95 p.

An anthology of ten black Michigan poets: Stella Crews, Robert Hayden, Naomi Long Madgett, Herbert Woodward Martin, Dudley Randall, James Randall, Jon Randall, Richard Thomas, June D. Whaley, and Jill Witherspoon Boyer.

Lanusse, Armand, ed. LES CENELLES: CHOIX DE POESIES INDIGENES. Nouvelle Orleans: Imprime par H. Lauve et Compagnie, 1845. 215 p. Republished as CREOLE VOICES: POEMS IN FRENCH BY FREE MEN OF COLOR, FIRST PUBLISHED IN 1845. Ed. Edward Maceo Coleman. Introd. H. Carrington Lancaster. Washington, D.C.: Associated Publishers, 1945. 128 p.

Locke, Alain L., ed. FOUR NEGRO POETS. New York: Simon & Schuster, 1927. 31 p.

The four poets are McKay, Toomer, Cullen, and Hughes. In Chapman IBP.

_____. THE NEW NEGRO: AN INTERPRETATION. New York: A. & C. Boni, 1925. 446 p. Rpts. New York: Arno, 1968; New York: Atheneum, 1968 (with a new preface by Robert Hayden); New York: Johnson Reprint, 1968.

The classic Harlem Renaissance anthology. Poetry, pp. 129-50.

Lomax, Alan, and Raoul Abdul, eds. 3000 YEARS OF BLACK POETRY. New York: Dodd, Mead, 1970. 261 p.

In Chapman IBP.

Long, Richard A., and Eugenia W. Collier, eds. AFRO-AMERICAN WRITING: AN ANTHOLOGY OF PROSE AND POETRY. 2 vols. New York: New York Univ. Press, 1972.

Twenty eight poets represented.

Lowenfels, Walter, ed. IN A TIME OF REVOLUTION: POEMS FROM OUR THIRD WORLD. New York: Random House, 1969. 151 p.

"Seventy-two poets--mostly black, some white," according to the dust jacket. Actually, two-thirds of the contributors are white.

_____. POETS OF TODAY: A NEW AMERICAN ANTHOLOGY. New York: International Publishers, 1964.

Twenty black poets are included among the eighty-five contributors.

_____. THE WRITING ON THE WALL: 198 AMERICAN POEMS OF PROTEST. New York: Doubleday, 1969. 189 p.

Some seventeen black poets represented.

Mahadi, M.A., ed. THIRD WORLD POETS SPEAK THE TRUTH. New York: Third World Publications, [1970?].

Major, Clarence, ed. THE WRITERS WORKSHOP ANTHOLOGY. New York: Harlem Educational Program, 1967. 48 p.

Poems by students aged thirteen to seventeen.

_____. THE NEW BLACK POETRY. New York: International Publishers, 1969. 156 p.

Seventy-six contributors. In Chapman IBP.

Marcus, Shmuel, ed. AN ANTHOLOGY OF REVOLUTIONARY POETRY. Introd. Ralph Cheyney and Lucia Trent. New York: Active Press, 1929. 353 p.

Includes Dunbar, Cullen, Hughes, Fenton Johnson, Georgia Douglas Johnson, James Weldon Johnson, and Claude McKay, as well as many white poets.

Miller, Adam David, ed. DICES OR BLACK BONES: BLACK VOICES OF THE SEVENTIES. Boston: Houghton Mifflin, 1970. 142 p.

Miller, Ruth, ed. BLACKAMERICAN LITERATURE 1760-PRESENT. Beverly Hills, Calif.: Glencoe Press, 1971. 724 p.

Murphy, Beatrice M., ed. EBONY RHYTHM: AN ANTHOLOGY OF CONTEMPORARY NEGRO VERSE. New York: Exposition, 1948. 162 p.

One hundred contributors. In Chapman IBP.

_____. NEGRO VOICES: AN ANTHOLOGY OF CONTEMPORARY VERSE. New York: H. Harrison, 1938. 173 p.

_____. TODAY'S NEGRO VOICES: AN ANTHOLOGY BY YOUNG NEGRO POETS. New York: Messner, 1970. 141 p.

Thirty-four contributors. In Chapman IBP.

Murray, Alma, and Robert Thomas, eds. THE JOURNEY. New York: Scholastic Book Services, 1970. 192 p.

A collection of prose and poetry for use as a seventh-grade textbook in the "Scholastic Black Literature Series." The other volumes in the series, all similar anthologies edited by Murray and Thomas, and published in 1970 and 1971, are THE SCENE, THE SEARCH, THE BLACK HERO, MAJOR BLACK WRITERS, and BLACK PERSPECTIVES, for the eighth through the twelfth grades respectively.

Nicholas, A.X., ed. THE POETRY OF SOUL. New York: Bantam, 1971. 103 p.

_____. WOKE UP THIS MORNIN': POETRY OF THE BLUES. New York: Bantam, 1973. 122 p.

Norfolk Prison Brothers. WHO TOOK THE WEIGHT? BLACK VOICES FROM NORFOLK PRISON. Introd. Elma Lewis. Boston: Little, Brown, 1972. 265 p.

Poetry and prose.

NO SHIT. By Sia, Seitu, OmeAfrika, Sekayi, Ante, Karriema, Waridi, and Sundiata. New York [?]: Published by the authors [?], 1972. [52] p.

NOUVELLE SOMME DE POESIE DU MONDE NOIR. NEW SUM OF POETRY FROM THE NEGRO WORLD. Paris: Presence Africaine, 1966.

An anthology of recent black poetry written in several languages; pages 357-94 contain selections from fourteen Afro-American poets, mostly taken from Rosey Pool's BEYOND THE BLUES (see below), with a brief presentation (in French) by Leon Damas.

NOUVELLE SOMME is a special issue (No. 57 of the new series) of PRESENCE AFRICAINE: REVUE CULTURELLE DU MONDE NOIR, a journal edited by Alioune Diop and published in Paris since 1947, at first irregularly, then bimonthly, and since 1961, quarterly. The first series, published from 1947 to 1954, included sixteen numbers; the new series, beginning in 1955, had reached No. 96 by 1975. Numbers 29-60 (except No. 57) were published in separate editions with the text in French and English. Although mainly centered on Africa, PRESENCE AFRICAINE has from the beginning included Afro-American material: Gwendolyn Brooks's "Ballad of Pearl May Lee" appeared in the first number in 1947;

a collective "Hommage a Langston Hughes" appears in number 64 (1967).

O'Brien, Helen M., Lillian W. Voorhees, and Hugh M. Gloster, eds. THE BROWN THRUSH: ANTHOLOGY OF VERSE BY NEGRO STUDENTS. [Vol. 2.]. Memphis, Tenn.: Malcolm-Roberts Publishing Co., 1935. 65 p.

For volume 1 see Lillian Voorhees, below.

Patterson, Lindsay, ed. AN INTRODUCTION TO BLACK LITERATURE IN AMERICA FROM 1746 TO THE PRESENT. New York: Publishers Co., 1968. 302 p.

In Chapman IBP.

_____. A ROCK AGAINST THE WIND: BLACK LOVE POEMS. New York: Dodd, Mead, 1973. 172 p.

Perkins, Eugene, ed. BLACK EXPRESSIONS: AN ANTHOLOGY OF NEW BLACK POETS. Chicago: Conda's Printing, 1967. 66 p.

Pitcher, Oliver, ed. ATLANTA UNIVERSITY CENTER SAMPLER. Atlanta: Afro-American Studies Center, Atlanta University, [1972?]. 122 p.

POETRY OF PRISON: POEMS BY BLACK PRISONERS. Introd. Billy Hand(s) Robinson. Chicago: DuSable Museum of Afro-American History, 1972. 48 p.

Pool, Rosey, ed. BEYOND THE BLUES: NEW POEMS BY AMERICAN NEGROES. Lympne, Kent, England: Hand & Flower Press, 1962. 188 p.

Fifty-six poets; both well known, like Claude McKay, and unknown at the time, like Bruce M. Wright and Leroy O. Stone. The emphasis, as the twenty-two-page introduction shows, is on new trends, jazz, protest, and negritude. Biographical notes often quote from authors' letters to the editor. In 1962, this anthology was the most important to appear since Hughes and Bontemps' POETRY OF THE NEGRO (1949). In Chapman IBP.

_____. IK BEN DE NIEUWE NEGER. The Hague, Netherlands: Bert Bakker, 1965. 264 p.

Bilingual.

Pool, Rosey, and Paul Breman, eds. IK ZAG HOE ZWART IK WAS (I SAW HOW BLACK I WAS): VERZEN VAN NOORD-AMERIKAANSE NEGERS. The Hague, Netherlands: Bert Bakker, 1958. 203 p.

Bilingual.

Pool, Rosey, and Eric Walrond, eds. BLACK AND UNKNOWN BARDS: A SELECTION OF NEGRO POETRY. Aldington, Kent, England: Hand & Flower Press, 1958. 43 p.

Twenty contributors.

Porter, Dorothy B., ed. EARLY NEGRO WRITING, 1760-1837. Boston: Beacon Press, 1971. 658 p.

Poetry and prose.

Randall, Dudley, ed. BLACK POETRY: A SUPPLEMENT TO ANTHOLOGIES WHICH EXCLUDE BLACK POETS. Detroit: Broadside, 1969. 48 p.

Twenty-five authors, from McKay to Giovanni.

_____. THE BLACK POETS. New York: Bantam Books, 1972. 353 p.

Black American poetry from the slave songs to the present day, stressing turning away from white models and returning to ethnic roots. Large selection of folk seculars and spirituals, with little literary poetry before the twentieth century. Renaissance and post-Renaissance sections comparatively slender compared to that for the 1960s which are represented mostly by Broadside Press poets. Useful list of publishers, periodicals, records, video tapes, and films.

Randall, Dudley, and Margaret G. Burroughs, eds. FOR MALCOLM: POEMS ON THE LIFE AND THE DEATH OF MALCOLM X. Preface and eulogy by Ossie Davis. Detroit: Broadside, 1967. 127 p.

Forty-three contributors; reviewed by Conrad Kent Rivers in NEGRO DIGEST, 16 (June 1967), 68-70. In Chapman IBP.

Rawls, Isetta Crawford, ed. COME TO THINK OF IT. [Denver, 1972?].

Redmond, Eugene, ed. SIDES OF THE RIVER: A MINI-ANTHOLOGY OF BLACK WRITINGS. East St. Louis, Ill.: Published by the editor, 1969. 31 p.

Rhode, Gerald, ed. MAY WE SPEAK. Pittsburgh: Signals Press, 1968.

An anthology of local black poets, including Michael Harper.

Robinson, William H., ed. EARLY BLACK AMERICAN POETS. Dubuque, Iowa: William C. Brown Co., 1969. 275 p.

Sections devoted to orator poets, formalist poets, romantic poets, and dialect poets. There are also appendices and a bibliography devoted to poets not among the twenty-nine selected for representation. In Chapman IBP.

Rochon, Noel J., ed. NO BIG THING. New Orleans: Noret Press, 1967. 107 p.

Poetry and prose by four New Orleans authors.

Rollins, Charlemae H., ed. CHRISTMAS GIF': AN ANTHOLOGY OF CHRISTMAS POEMS, SONGS AND STORIES, WRITTEN BY AND ABOUT NE-GROES. Chicago: Follett, 1963. 119 p.

In Chapman IBP.

Sanchez, Sonia, ed. THREE HUNDRED AND SIXTY DEGREES OF BLACKNESS COMIN AT YOU: AN ANTHOLOGY OF THE SONIA SANCHEZ WRITERS WORKSHOP AT COUNTEE CULLEN LIBRARY IN HARLEM. New York: 5X Publishing Co., 1971. 190 p.

Poetry (pp. 1-86), fiction, and drama by some forty workshop members.

Schulberg, Budd, ed. FROM THE ASHES: VOICES OF WATTS. New York: New American Library, 1967. 277 p. Rpt. New York: Meridian Books, 1969.

Johnie Scott and a dozen other poets are included in this collection of writings from the Watts Writers Workshop.

The Scribes. SING, LAUGH, WEEP: A BOOK OF POEMS BY THE SCRIBES. Introd. Alta Edmund. St. Louis: Press Publishing Co., 1944. 126 p.

Senna, Carl. PARACHUTE SHOP BLUES AND OTHER WRITINGS OF NEW ORLEANS. New Orleans: Dinstuhl Printing & Publishing, [1972?]. 82 p.

Shuman, R. Baird, ed. A GALAXY OF BLACK WRITING. Durham, N.C.: Moore Publishing Co., 1970. 441 p.

Poetry, pp. 228-429. Thirty-six contributors.

_____. NINE BLACK POETS. Durham, N.C.: Moore Publishing Co., 1968. 236 p.

Charles Cooper, Kattie M. Cumbo, Julia Fields, Carole Gregory, William J. Harris, Lance Jeffers, Alicia Loy Johnson, James Arlington Jones, and Richard W. Thomas.

Simmons, Gloria M., and Helene D. Hutchinson, eds. BLACK CULTURE: READING AND WRITING BLACK. New York: Holt, Rinehart and Winston, 1972. 328 p.

Poetry and prose.

Singh, Raman K., and Peter Fellowes, eds. BLACK LITERATURE IN AMERICA: A CASEBOOK. New York: Crowell, 1970. 354 p.

Poetry and prose.

SOUL SESSION: ANTHOLOGY OF THE B.C.D. Newark, N.J.: Jihad, 1969. [36] p.

A collection of poems by fifteen young Newark writers, dedicated to Imamu Baraka. B.C.D. is the "Black Community Defence."

Spratt, Talmadge, ed. BLACK LIGHT: SELECTED WRITINGS FROM AMERICAN NEGRO LITERATURE. Kansas City: Hallmark Editions, 1973. 61 p.

Poetry and prose.

Stanford, Barbara Dodds, ed. I, TOO, SING AMERICA: BLACK VOICES IN AMERICAN LITERATURE. New York: Hayden Book Co., 1971. 308 p.

Poetry and prose.

STONES ASKING STARS: AN ANTHOLOGY OF POETRY BY STUDENTS OF DILLARD UNIVERSITY. New Orleans: Department of English, Dillard Univ., 1974. 43 p.

TEN: AN ANTHOLOGY OF DETROIT POETS. Fort Smith, Ark.: South and West, 1968. 52 p.

Five of the ten contributors are black (Gloria Davis, Oliver La Grone, Naomi Long Madgett, Dudley Randall, and Joyce Whitsitt).

Tisdale, Celes, ed. BETCHA AIN'T: POEMS FROM ATTICA. Detroit: Broadside, 1974. 62 p.

Twenty-two contributors.

Troupe, Quincy, ed. WATTS POETS: A BOOK OF NEW POETRY AND ESSAYS. Los Angeles: House of Respect, 1968. 90 p.

Poems by Elaine Browne, Stanley Crouch, Lance Jeffers, Curtis Lyle, Blossom Powe, Herbert A. Simmons, Troupe, and a dozen others.

Troupe, Quincy, and Rainer Schulte, eds. GIANT TALK: AN ANTHOLOGY OF THIRD WORLD WRITINGS. New York: Random House, 1975. 546 p.

Poetry and prose. 160 contributors, including about 50 Afro-American poets.

Turner, Darwin T., ed. BLACK AMERICAN LITERATURE: POETRY. Columbus,

Ohio: Charles E. Merrill Publishing Co., 1969. 132 p.

Twenty-three poets from Wheatley to Don L. Lee.

_____. BLACK DRAMA IN AMERICA: AN ANTHOLOGY. Greenwich, Conn.: Fawcett Publications, 1971. 630 p.

Plays by Willis Richardson, Langston Hughes, Theodore Ward, Owen Dodson, Louis Peterson, Randolph Edmunds, Ossie Davis, LeRoi Jones, and Kingsley Bass, Jr., edited with an introduction and a bibliography.

Turner, Darwin T., Jean M. Bright, and Richard Wright, eds. VOICES FROM THE BLACK EXPERIENCE: AFRICAN AND AFRO-AMERICAN LITERATURE. Lexington, Mass.: Ginn and Co., 1972. 280 p.

Poetry and prose.

Voorhees, Lillian Welch, and Robert W. O'Brien, eds. THE BROWN THRUSH: AN ANTHOLOGY OF VERSE BY NEGRO STUDENTS. Vol. 1. Bryn Athyn, Pa.: Lawson-Roberts Publishing Co., 1932. 67 p.

For volume 2 see O'Brien, R.W., above. In Chapman IBP.

Washington, William D., and Samuel Beckoff, eds. BLACK LITERATURE: AN ANTHOLOGY OF OUTSTANDING BLACK WRITERS. New York: Simon and Schuster, 1972. 316 p.

A high-school textbook, mostly prose, with thirty-two poems by nineteen authors.

Weisman, Leon, and Elfreda S. Wright, eds. BLACK POETRY FOR ALL AMERI-CANS. New York: Globe Book Co., 1971. 120 p.

Wertheim, Bill, and Irma Gonzalez, eds. TALKIN' ABOUT US: WRITINGS BY STUDENTS IN THE UPWARD BOUND PROGRAM. New York: New Century, 1970. 176 p.

Wheeler, Benjamin Franklin, ed. CULLINGS FROM ZION'S POETS. Mobile, Ala.: Published by the editor, 1907. 384 p.

"Sacred poems written by the clergy and laity" of the African Methodist Episcopal Zion Church. Includes biographical sketches of some of the contributors.

WHEN ONE OF US FALLS. Chicago: Artists United, 1970. 18 p.

Poems by Margaret Burroughs and other Chicago writers "dedicated to the living ideals of Fred Hampton and Mark Clark, murdered leaders of the Illinois Black Panther Party."

White, Newman Ivey, and Walter Clinton Jackson, eds. AN ANTHOLOGY OF VERSE BY AMERICAN NEGROES. Introd. James Hardy Dillard. Durham, N.C.: Trinity College Press, 1924. 250 p. Rpt. Durham, N.C.: Moore Publishing Co., 1968.

> From Wheatley to Cullen. In Chapman IBP.

WHITE PAPER, BLACK PAPER:. A BLACK TORNADO. Corona, N.Y.: A Colnoized [sic] Few, 1971. [40] p.

> Poems by Kiidh, Eric Rawlins, Lorraine Taylor, and Randolph Latimer, Jr.

Wilentz, Ted, and Tom Weatherly, eds. NATURAL PROCESS: AN ANTHOLOGY OF NEW BLACK POETRY. New York: Hill and Wang, 1970. 181 p.

> Seventeen young poets, of whom Conyus, Sam Cornish, William J. Harris, L.V. Mack, Lennox Raphael, Tom Weatherly, and Jay Wright were the least well known at the time. "Designed to show what has happened since the breakthrough of the 'New American poetry'. . . ." Short introduction and substantial biographical notes.

Witherspoon, Jill, ed. THE BROADSIDE ANNUAL 1972, INTRODUCING NEW BLACK POETS. Detroit: Broadside, 1972. 22 p.

> See also Boyd, J.W., above.

Wood, Clement, ed. NEGRO SONGS. Little Blue Book No. 626. Girard, Kans.: Haldeman-Julius Co., 1924. 64 p.

Wormley, Beatrice F., and Charles W. Carter, eds. AN ANTHOLOGY OF NEGRO POETRY BY NEGROES AND OTHERS. [Trenton?], N.J.: Works Progress Administration, 1937. 138 p.

> In Chapman IBP.

Yardbird Reader. 4 vols. Berkeley, Calif.: Yardbird Publishing Cooperative, 1972-75.

> Volume 1, published in 1975, was edited by Ishmael Reed; introduced by Chester Himes, Ishmael Reed, Al Young, and Cecil Brown; 184 pages. Volume 2, published in 1973, was edited and introduced by Al Young, 224 pages. Contains poetry and prose by some Umbra poets and others, including several young West Coast poets, and the "mysterious, elusive, irascible" O.O. Gabugah. Volume 3, published in 1974, is devoted to Asian-American writers. Volume 4, published in 1975 and edited by William Lawson, focuses on African and Afro-American writers.

Zu-Bolton, Ahmos II, and E. Ethelbert Miller, eds. SYNERGY: AN ANTHOL-

OGY OF WASHINGTON D.C. BLACKPOETS. Washington, D.C.: Energy
BlackSouth Press, 1975. 107 p.

Forty contributors.

Anthologies: Appendix of Folk Songs, Blues, and Spirituals

Allen, William Francis, Charles Pickard Ware, and Lucy McKim Garrison, eds.
SLAVE SONGS OF THE UNITED STATES. New York: A. Simpson & Co.,
1867. 115 p.

_____. SLAVE SONGS OF THE UNITED STATES: THE COMPLETE ORIGINAL
COLLECTION (136 SONGS) . . . WITH NEW PIANO ARRANGEMENTS AND
GUITAR CHORDS BY IRVING SCHLEIN. New York: Oak Publications, 1965.
175 p.

Blades, William C. NEGRO POEMS, MELODIES, PLANTATION PIECES, CAMP
MEETING SONGS. Boston: R.J. Badger, 1921. 168 p.

Boatner, Edward, and Willa A. Townsend, eds. SPIRITUALS TRIUMPHANT
OLD AND NEW. Nashville, Tenn.: Sunday School Publishing Board, National Baptist Convention USA, 1927. [98] p.

Burlin, Natalie Curtis. NEGRO FOLK SONGS. 4 vols. New York: Schirmer,
1918-19.

Carawan, Guy, and Carawan, Candie, eds. FREEDOM IS A CONSTANT
STRUGGLE: SONGS OF THE FREEDOM MOVEMENT. New York: Oak Publications, 1968. 224 p.

Charters, Samuel B. THE COUNTRY BLUES. New York: Rinehart, 1959.
288 p.

_____. THE POETRY OF THE BLUES. New York: Oak Publications, 1963.
111 p.

Cook, Bruce. LISTEN TO THE BLUES. New York: Scribner, 1973. 263 p.

Courlander, Harold. NEGRO FOLK MUSIC, U.S.A. New York: Columbia
Univ. Press, 1963. 324 p.

_____. NEGRO SONGS FROM ALABAMA. Music transcribed by John Benson
Brooks. 2nd ed. rev. and enl. New York: Oak Publications, 1963. 111 p.

Dett, Robert Nathaniel. RELIGIOUS FOLK-SONGS OF THE NEGRO, AS SUNG AT HAMPTON INSTITUTE. Hampton, Va.: Hampton Institute Press, 1927. 236 p.

Fenner, Thomas P., ed. "Cabin and Plantation Songs, as Sung by the Hampton Students." In HAMPTON AND ITS STUDENTS, by two of its teachers, Mrs. M.F. Armstrong and Helen W. Ludlow. With Fifty Cabin and Plantation Songs, arranged by Thomas P. Fenner. New York: Putnam, 1874, pp. 171-255. Enl. ed. published as RELIGIOUS FOLK SONGS OF THE NEGRO, AS SUNG ON THE PLANTATIONS. Arranged by the musical directors of the Hampton Normal and Agricultural Institute, from the original ed. by Thomas P. Fenner. Hampton, Va.: Institute Press, 1916. 178 p.

> The enlarged edition contains about 140 songs.

Fisher, Miles Mark. NEGRO SLAVE SONGS IN THE UNITED STATES. Ithaca, N.Y.: Cornell Univ. Press, 1953. 223 p.

Fisher, William Arms, ed. SEVENTY NEGRO SPIRITUALS. Boston: Oliver Ditson, 1926. 212 p.

Gellert, Lawrence. NEGRO SONGS OF PROTEST. New York: American Music League, 1936. 47 p.

Hallowell, Emily, ed. CALHOUN PLANTATION SONGS. Boston: C.W. Thompson and Co., 1907. 74 p.

> Contains sixty-nine songs sung by the students at the Calhoun Colored School.

Handy, William Christopher, ed. BLUES: AN ANTHOLOGY. Introd. Abbe Niles. New York: Boni, 1926. 180 p.

_____. A TREASURY OF THE BLUES. With an historical and critical text by Abbe Niles. New York: Boni, 1949. 258 p.

Jackson, George Pullen. WHITE AND NEGRO SPIRITUALS: THEIR LIFE SPAN AND KINSHIP . . . WITH 116 SONGS AS SUNG BY BOTH RACES. New York: J.J. Augustin, 1944. 349 p.

Johnson, James Weldon, and J. Rosamund Johnson, eds. THE BOOK OF AMERICAN NEGRO SPIRITUALS. New York: Viking, 1925. 187 p.

_____. THE BOOKS OF AMERICAN NEGRO SPIRITUALS. 2 vols. in 1. New York: Viking, 1940.

_____. THE SECOND BOOK OF AMERICAN NEGRO SPIRITUALS. New York: Viking, 1926. 189 p.

Keil, Charles. URBAN BLUES. Chicago: Univ. of Chicago Press, 1966. 231 p.

Kennedy, R. Emmet. MELLOWS: A CHRONICLE OF UNKNOWN SINGERS. New York: Boni, 1925. 183 p.

_____. MORE MELLOWS. New York: Dodd, Mead, 1931. 178 p.

Krehbiel, Henry Edward. AFRO-AMERICAN FOLKSONGS: A STUDY IN RACIAL AND NATIONAL MUSIC. New York: Schirmer, 1914. 176 p.

Marsh, J.B.T. THE STORY OF THE JUBILEE SINGERS. With Supplement Containing an Account of Their Six Years' Tour around the World, and Many New Songs. New ed. Cleveland: Cleveland Printing and Publishing Co., 1892. 311 p.

    With 139 songs, (words and music).

THE NEGRO SINGER'S OWN BOOK: CONTAINING EVERY NEGRO SONG THAT HAS EVER BEEN SUNG OR PRINTED. Philadelphia: Turner and Fisher, [1846?]. 448 p.

Odum, Howard W., and Guy B. Johnson. THE NEGRO AND HIS SONGS: A STUDY OF TYPICAL NEGRO SONGS IN THE SOUTH. Chapel Hill: Univ. of North Carolina Press, 1925. 306 p.

_____. NEGRO WORKADAY SONGS. Chapel Hill: Univ. of North Carolina Press, 1926. 287 p.

Oliver, Paul. BLUES FELL THIS MORNING: THE MEANING OF THE BLUES. Introd. Richard Wright. London: Horizon Press, 1960. 355 p.

_____. CONVERSATION WITH THE BLUES. New York: Horizon, 1965. 217 p.

Pike, G.D. THE JUBILEE SINGERS, AND THEIR CAMPAIGN FOR TWENTY THOUSAND DOLLARS. Boston: Lee and Shepard, 1873. 219 p.

    With sixty songs (words and music).

Sackheim, Eric. THE BLUES LINE: A COLLECTION OF BLUES LYRICS. New York: Grossman Publishers, 1969. 500 p.

Scarborough, Dorothy. ON THE TRAIL OF NEGRO FOLK SONGS. Cambridge, Mass.: Harvard Univ. Press, 1925. 289 p.

Seward, Theodore F., ed. JUBILEE SONGS: AS SUNG BY THE JUBILEE SINGERS, OF FISK UNIVERSITY (NASHVILLE, TENN.) UNDER THE AUSPICES OF THE AMERICAN MISSIONARY SOCIETY. New York: Biglow and Main, 1872. 28 p.

Talley, Thomas. NEGRO FOLK RHYMES, WISE AND OTHERWISE. New York: Macmillan, 1922. 347 p.

White, Clarence Cameron. FORTY NEGRO SPIRITUALS. Compiled and Arranged for Solo Voice with Pianoforte Accompaniment. Philadelphia: Theodore Presser, 1927. 129 p.

White, Newman Ivey. AMERICAN NEGRO FOLK SONGS. Cambridge, Mass: Harvard Univ. Press, 1928. 700 p.

Work, Frederick Jerome, ed. FOLK SONGS OF THE AMERICAN NEGRO. Introd. John W. Work. Nashville, Tenn.: Published by the author, 1907. 94 p.

Work, John Wesley. AMERICAN NEGRO SONGS: A COMPREHENSIVE COLLECTION OF 230 FOLK SONGS, RELIGIOUS AND SECULAR. New York: Howell, Soskin and Co., 1940. 259 p.

_____. FOLK SONG OF THE AMERICAN NEGRO. Nashville, Tenn.: Fisk Univ. Press, 1915. 131 p.

Part 2
POETRY: INDIVIDUAL AUTHORS

1. 1760-1900

Only two of the poets of this period, Phillis Wheatley and Paul Laurence Dunbar, received any wide recognition during their lives; neither lived to be thirty-five. Joan Sherman, in her INVISIBLE POETS (see under Critical Studies, above), has painstakingly assembled information on many lesser nineteenth-century poets; nevertheless, painful gaps in documentation are evident, even for such relatively major figures as George Moses Horton and Frances E.W. Harper.

In this section, primary works are listed first, in chronological order, followed by secondary works, in alphabetical order. Works indexed in Chapman IBP are so indicated.

BATSON, FLORA. See MILLAR, GERALD, below, this section.

BEADLE, SAMUEL ALFRED

SKETCHES FROM LIFE IN DIXIE. Chicago: Scroll Publishing and Literary Syndicate, 1899. 127 p.

> Seven prose and thirty-seven verse sketches of a beautiful country "where the rage of the vulture, the love of the turtle/now melt into sorrow, now madden to crime."

LYRICS OF THE UNDER WORLD. Introd. W.E. Mollison. Jackson, Miss.: W.A. Scott, 1912. 148 p.

BELL, JAMES MADISON (1826-1902)

A POEM. San Francisco: S.F. Sterett, 1862. 10 p.

A POEM ENTITLED THE DAY AND THE WAR, DELIVERED JANUARY 1, 1864 . . . AT THE CELEBRATION OF THE FIRST ANNIVERSARY OF PRESIDENT LINCOLN'S EMANCIPATION PROCLAMATION. San Francisco: Agnew and Deffeback, Printer, 1864. 27 p.

> Included in POETICAL WORKS (below).

AN ANNIVERSARY POEM ENTITLED THE PROGRESS OF LIBERTY, DELIVERED JANUARY 1st, 1866 . . . AT THE CELEBRATION OF THE THIRD ANNIVERSARY OF PRESIDENT LINCOLN'S PROCLAMATION. San Francisco: Agnew and Deffeback, Printer, 1866. 28 p.

> Included in POETICAL WORKS (below).

A POEM, ENTITLED THE TRIUMPH OF LIBERTY, DELIVERED APRIL 7, 1870 . . . ON THE OCCASION OF THE FIFTEENTH AMENDMENT TO THE CON-STITUTION OF THE UNITED STATES. Detroit: Tunis Steam Printing Co., 1870. 32 p.

> Included in POETICAL WORKS (below).

THE POETICAL WORKS OF JAMES MADISON BELL. With a Biography by Bishop B.W. Arnett. Lansing, Mich.: Press of Wynkoop, Hallenbeck and Crawford, 1901. 208 p. 2nd ed. 1901. 221 p. Rpt. New York: AMS Press, 1974.

> Twenty-seven poems on slavery, John Brown and related topics; the second edition adds five poems.

Biography and Criticism

Brown NPD; Mays NG; Redding TMPB; Sherman IP; Williams TAS.

BENJAMIN, ROBERT C.O.

POETIC GEMS. Charlottesville, VA.: Peck and Allan, 1883, 14 p.

> Eighteen poems, most of them on love; with two on political themes and one on the "colored" press.

BIBB, ELOISE A. [ELOISE BIBB THOMPSON] (1878-1927)

POEMS. Boston: Monthly Review Press, 1895. 107 p.

> Twenty-six poems.

Biography and Criticism

Sherman IP.

BLACKSON, LORENZO DOW (1817- ?)

THE RISE AND PROGRESS OF THE KINGDOMS OF LIGHT & DARKNESS; OR, THE REIGN OF KINGS ALPHA AND ABADON. Philadelphia: J. Nicholas, Printer, 1867. 288 p.

> An allegorical prose narrative, with an 800-line verse summary on pages 250-73.

BOYD, FRANCIS A. (1844- ?)

COLUMBIANA: OR, THE NORTH STAR, COMPLETE IN ONE VOLUME. Chicago: Steam Job and Book Printing House of B. Hand, 1870. 69 p.

CAMPBELL, ALFRED GIBBS (1826?- ?)

POEMS. Newark, N.J.: Advertiser Printing House, 1883, 120 p.

> Fifty-four poems, most of them on religion and abolitionism.

CAMPBELL, JAMES EDWIN (1867-95)

DRIFTINGS AND GLEANINGS. Charleston, W. Va.: 1887. 96 p.

> No copy located.

ECHOES FROM THE CABIN AND ELSEWHERE. Chicago: Donohue and Henneberry, Printers, 1895. 86 p.

> Divided into two sections, "Echoes from the Cabin" (sixteen dialect poems), and "Elsewhere" (twenty-eight poems in standard English), dealing with "the simplicity, the philosophy and the humor" of the antebellum Negro. Includes contents of DRIFTINGS AND GLEANINGS (above).

Biography and Criticism

Brown NPD; Redding TMPB; Sherman IP; Wagner BPUS; Williams TAS.

Woodson, Carter G. "James Edwin Campbell, a Forgotten Man of Letters." NEGRO HISTORY BULLETIN, 2 (1938), 11.

CANNON, NOAH CALWELL W. (1796?-1850)

THE ROCK OF WISDOM: AN EXPLANATION OF THE SACRED SCRIPTURES . . . TO WHICH ARE ADDED SEVERAL INTERESTING HYMNS. [New York?]: n.p., 1833. 144 p.

> Prose, with seventeen poems on pages 133-44.

Biography and Criticism

Loggins NA; Mays NG; Sherman IP.

Weyman, Alexander W. MY RECOLLECTIONS OF AFRICAN M.E. MINISTERS. Philadelphia: A.M.E. Book Rooms, 1881, pp. 7-10.

CLARK, BENJAMIN CUTLER (1825?- ?)

THE PAST, PRESENT AND FUTURE, IN PROSE AND POETRY. Toronto, Ontario: Adam, Stevenson and Co., 1867. 168 p.

> Sixty-five poems.

CLEM, CHARLES DOUGLAS. See under the section 1901-45, below.

COFFIN, FRANK BARBOUR (1870?-1951)

COFFIN'S POEMS WITH AJAX' ORDEALS. Little Rock, Ark.: Colored Advocate Printers, 1897. 248 p.

> Ninety poems.

FACTUM FACTORUM. New York: Haven Press, 1947. 190 p.

> Fifty poems and prose.

CORROTHERS, JAMES DAVID (1869-1917)

No collection of poems is available, but individual poems can be found in the following:

> CENTURY MAGAZINE, n.s. 35-45 (1888-1904);
>
> HOWARD'S AMERICAN MAGAZINE (1899-1900);
>
> COLORED AMERICAN, 3 (1901);
>
> VOICE OF THE NEGRO, 6 (Apr. 1904), 156; (June 1904), 247; 7 (Jan. 1905), 686; (Mar. 1904), 186;
>
> CRISIS, 5 (1913), 121; 6 (191-93), 39; 8 (1914), 79-80; 9 (1915), 138; 10 (1915), 304.

Biography and Criticism

Corrothers, James David. IN SPITE OF THE HANDICAP. New York: George H. Doran, 1916. 238 p.

> An autobiography.

COTTER, JOSEPH SEAMON, SR. See section for 1901-45, below.

DAVIS, DANIEL WEBSTER (1862-1913)

IDLE MOMENTS, CONTAINING EMANCIPATION AND OTHER POEMS. Introd. John H. Smythe. Baltimore, Md.: Educator of Morgan College, 1895. 81 p.

Thirty-eight poems.

'WEH DOWN SOUF, AND OTHER POEMS. Introd. John H. Smythe. Cleveland: Helman-Taylor Co., 1897. 136 p.

Some forty poems on religious and racial themes, many in dialect.

Biography and Criticism

Brown NPD; Redding TMPB; Sherman IP; Wagner BPUS.

Harrison, Lottie D. "Daniel Webster Davis." NEGRO HISTORY BULLETIN, 18 (Dec. 1954), 55-57.

Sherman, Joan R. "Daniel Webster Davis: A Black Virginia Poet in the Age of Accommodation." VIRGINIA MAGAZINE OF HISTORY AND BIOGRAPHY, 81 (1973), 457-78.

DUNBAR, ALICE RUTH MOORE. See MOORE, ALICE RUTH, below, this section.

DUNBAR, PAUL LAURENCE (1872-1906)

OAK AND IVY. Dayton, Ohio: Press of United Brethren Publishing House, 1893. 62 p.

Fifty-six poems.

MAJORS AND MINORS. Toledo, Ohio: Hadley and Hadley, Printers and Binders, 1895. 148 p. Rpt. Miami, Fla.: Mnemosyne Publishing Co., 1969.

One hundred poems. Reviewed by William Dean Howells in HARPER'S WEEKLY, 40 (27 June 1896), 630.

LYRICS OF LOWLY LIFE. Introd. William Dean Howells. New York: Dodd, Mead, 1896. 208 p. Rpt. Upper Saddle River, N.J.: Gregg Press, 1968.

Contains 103 poems, including many from MAJORS AND MINORS (above). In Chapman IBP.

LYRICS OF THE HEARTHSIDE. New York: Dodd, Mead, 1899. 227 p. Rpts. Freeport, N.Y.: Books for Libraries, 1970; New York: AMS Press, 1972.

Contains 109 poems.

POEMS OF CABIN AND FIELD. New York: Dodd, Mead, 1899. 125 p.

Eight poems, all previously published.

CANDLE-LIGHTIN' TIME. New York: Dodd, Mead, 1901. 127 p.

Nine poems, all but one taken from previous Dunbar books. In Chapman IBP.

LYRICS OF LOVE AND LAUGHTER. New York: Dodd, Mead, 1903. 180 p.

Ninety-nine poems, all but eleven taken from OAK AND IVY and MAJORS AND MINORS (both cited above).

WHEN MALINDY SINGS. New York: Dodd, Mead, 1903. 144 p.

Twenty poems, all but one previously published. In Chapman IBP.

LIL' GAL. New York: Dodd, Mead, 1904. 123 p.

Twenty-two poems, all but four previously published. In Chapman IBP.

HOWDY HONEY HOWDY. New York: Dodd, Mead, 1905. [125] p.

Twenty-one poems, all previously published.

LYRICS OF SUNSHINE AND SHADOW. New York: Dodd, Mead, 1905. 109 p. Rpts. Freeport, N.Y.: Books for Libraries, 1970; New York: AMS Press, 1972.

Seventy-eight poems.

JOGGIN' ERLONG. New York: Dodd, Mead, 1906. 119 p.

Twenty poems, all but one previously published.

CHRIS'MUS IS A'COMIN' & OTHER POEMS. New York: Dodd, Mead, 1907. 48 p.

Fourteen poems, all previously published.

THE LIFE AND WORKS OF PAUL LAURENCE DUNBAR, CONTAINING HIS COMPLETE POETICAL WORKS, HIS BEST SHORT STORIES, NUMEROUS ANEC-DOTES AND A COMPLETE BIOGRAPHY OF THE FAMOUS POET BY LIDA KECK WIGGINS. Introd. William Dean Howells. Naperville, Ill.: J.L. Nichols & Co., 1907. 430 p. Rpt. Nendeln, Liechtenstein: Kraus, 1971.

About 400 poems.

A PLANTATION PORTRAIT. New York: Dodd, Mead, 1911. 50 p.

Fourteen poems, all previously published.

THE COMPLETE POEMS OF PAUL LAURENCE DUNBAR. Introd. William Dean Howells. New York: Dodd, Mead, 1913. 239 p.

Four hundred seventeen poems, all but four previously published. In Chapman IBP.

SPEAKIN' O' CHRISTMAS, AND OTHER CHRISTMAS AND SPECIAL POEMS. New York: Dodd, Mead, 1914. 96 p.

Nineteen poems, all previously published.

LITTLE BROWN BABY: PAUL LAURENCE DUNBAR POEMS FOR YOUNG PEOPLE. Selections, with Biographical Sketch by Bertha Rodgers. New York: Dodd, Mead, 1940. 106 p.

Twenty-five poems, all previously published.

A CABIN TALE. Introd. Welvin Stroud. San Francisco: Julian Richardson Associated, 1969. [27] p.

First separate edition of a poem originally published in LYRICS OF THE HEARTHSIDE (1905), above.

THE PAUL LAURENCE DUNBAR READER: A SELECTION OF THE BEST OF PAUL LAURENCE DUNBAR'S POETRY AND PROSE. INCLUDING WRITINGS NEVER BEFORE AVAILABLE IN BOOK FORM. Ed. Jay Martin and Gossie H. Hudson. New York: Dodd, Mead, 1975. 477 p.

Contains sixty-seven poems, thirty-seven of them not in THE COM-PLETE POEMS. Also includes essays, fiction, letters, bibliog-raphy, and commentary.

NOTE: Most of Dunbar's books were repeatedly reissued with various dates by Dodd, Mead in the early years of the century, and in recent years numerous reprint houses have published them. BOOKS IN PRINT 1975 lists over fifty currently available reprints of his books; notably absent are OAK AND IVY and LYRICS OF LOVE AND LAUGHTER.

Bibliographies

Blanck, Jacob, comp. "Paul Laurence (Lawrence) Dunbar 1872-1906." In BIBLIOGRAPHY OF AMERICAN LITERATURE. New Haven, Conn.: Yale Univ. Press, 1957. pp. 498-505.

Describes all of Dunbar's first editions (with details of collation, binding, and issue points), with a briefer list of reprinted material and references; Dunbar is the only Afro-American among the 281 authors included in this standard reference work.

Burris, Andrew M. "A Bibliography of Works by Paul Laurence Dunbar, Negro Poet and Author." AMERICAN COLLECTOR, 5 (Nov. 1927), 69-73.

Metcalf, E.W., Jr. PAUL LAURENCE DUNBAR: A BIBLIOGRAPHY. Metuchen, N.J.: Scarecrow Press, 1975. 193 p.

Biography and Criticism

Brown NPD; Jackson BPA; Jahn NAL; Loggins NA; Redding TMPB; Rollins FANP; Wagner BPUS; Whitlow BAL; Williams TAS.

Achille, Louis T. "Paul Laurence Dunbar, poète nègre." REVUE ANGLO-AMERICAINE, 12 (1934), 504-20.

Allen, Walker. "Paul Dunbar, a Study in Genius." PSYCHOANALYTIC RE-VIEW, 25 (1938), 53-82.

Arnold, Edward F. "Some Personal Reminiscences of Paul Laurence Dunbar." JOURNAL OF NEGRO HISTORY, 17 (1932), 400-408.

Baker, Houston A., Jr. "Paul Laurence Dunbar: An Evaluation." BLACK WORLD, 21 (Nov. 1971), 3-37. Also in SINGERS OF DAYBREAK. Washington, D.C.: Howard Univ. Press, 1974, pp. 33-41.

_____. "Report on a Celebration: Dunbar's One-Hundredth Year." BLACK WORLD, 22 (Feb. 1973), 81-85.

Brawley, Benjamin. PAUL LAURENCE DUNBAR: POET OF HIS PEOPLE. Chapel Hill: Univ. of North Carolina Press, 1936. 159 p.

Burch, Charles F. "Dunbar's Poetry in Literary English." SOUTHERN WORK-MAN, 50 (1921), 469-73.

_____. "The Plantation Negro in Dunbar's Poetry." SOUTHERN WORKMAN, 50 (1921), 227-29.

Clark, Davis W., ed. PAUL LAURENCE DUNBAR LAUREL-DECKED. Boston: Paul Laurence Dunbar Scholarship Fund, 1909. 32 p.

Clarke, John Henrik. "Paul Laurence Dunbar." FREEDOMWAYS, 12 (1972), 316-18.

Cunningham, Virginia. PAUL LAURENCE DUNBAR AND HIS SONG. New York: Dodd, Mead, 1947. 283 p. Rpt. New York: Biblo and Tannen, 1969.

Daniel, T.W. "Paul Laurence Dunbar and the Democratic Ideal." NEGRO HISTORY BULLETIN, 6 (1943), 206-8.

Dunbar, Mrs. Paul Laurence, W.S. Scarborough, and Reverdy C. Ransom. PAUL LAURENCE DUNBAR: POET LAUREATE OF THE NEGRO RACE. Philadelphia: R.C. Ransom, 1914. 32 p.

> Three articles reprinted from A.M.E. CHURCH REVIEW, 31 (Oct. 1914), 121-42, 192-95.

Fox, Allan B. "Behind the Mask: Paul Laurence Dunbar's Poetry in Literary English." TEXAS QUARTERLY, 14 (Summer 1971), 7-19.

Gayle, Addison, Jr. OAK AND IVY: A BIOGRAPHY OF PAUL LAURENCE DUNBAR. New York: Doubleday, 1971. 175 p.

> For young readers.

Gould, Jean. THAT DUNBAR BOY: THE STORY OF AMERICA'S FAMOUS NEGRO POET. New York: Dodd, Mead, 1958. 245 p.

> For children.

Henry, Thomas M. "The First Black World Poet." POET LORE, 40 (1929), 303-12.

_____. "Old School of Negro 'Critics' Hard on Paul Laurence Dunbar." MESSENGER, 6 (1924), 310-11.

Howells, William Dean. "Paul Laurence Dunbar." NORTH AMERICAN REVIEW, 23 (1906), 185-86.

Lawson, Victor. DUNBAR CRITICALLY EXAMINED. Washington, D.C.: Associated Publishers, 1941. 151 p.

Martin, Jay, ed. A SINGER IN THE DAWN: REINTERPRETATIONS OF PAUL LAURENCE DUNBAR. Afterword by Nikki Giovanni. New York: Dodd, Mead, 1975. 255 p.

> Includes essays on Dunbar's poetry by Dickson D. Bruce, Jr., James A. Emanuel, Myron Simon, and Darwin T. Turner; poems on Dunbar by Michael S. Harper, Raymond Patterson, Lorenzo Thomas, and Margaret Walker.

Phillips, Waldo. "Paul Laurence Dunbar: A New Perspective." NEGRO HISTORY BULLETIN, 29 (1965), 7-8.

Stronks, James B. "Paul Laurence Dunbar and William Dean Howells." OHIO HISTORICAL QUARTERLY, 67 (1958), 95-108.

Turner, Darwin T. "Paul Laurence Dunbar: The Poet and the Myths." CLA JOURNAL, 18 (1974), 155-71.

_____. "Paul Laurence Dunbar: The Rejected Symbol." JOURNAL OF NE-GRO HISTORY, 52 (1967), 1-13.

Young, Pauline A. "Paul Laurence Dunbar: An Intimate Glimpse." FREEDOM-WAYS, 12 (1972), 319-29.

FORDHAM, MARY WESTON (1862?- ?)

MAGNOLIA LEAVES. Introd. Booker T. Washington. Charleston, S.C.: Walker, Evans and Cogswell Co., 1897. 104 p.

FORTEN, CHARLOTTE. See GRIMKE, CHARLOTTE L. FORTEN, below, this section.

FORTUNE, MICHAEL. "New Year's Anthem as Sung in the African Episcopal Church of St. Thomas, Jan. 1, 1808." In A THANKSGIVING SERMON, PREACHED JANUARY 1, 1808, IN ST. THOMAS'S, OR THE AFRICAN EPIS-COPAL CHURCH, PHILADELPHIA; ON ACCOUNT OF THE ABOLITION OF THE AFRICAN SLAVE TRADE, by Absalom Jones. Philadelphia: Printed for the use of the Congregation, Fry and Kammerer, Printers, 1808. 24 p.

Fortune's poem appears on pages 22-24.

FORTUNE, TIMOTHY THOMAS (1856-1928)

DREAMS OF LIFE: MISCELLANEOUS POEMS. New York: Fortune and Peterson, 1905. 192 p. Rpt. Freeport, N.Y.: Books for Libraries, 1974.

Biography and Criticism

Loggins NA; Sherman IP.

Slocum, A. Terry. "Timothy Thomas Fortune: A Negro in American Society." Dissertation, Princeton Univ., 1967.

Thornbrough, Emma Lou. T. THOMAS FORTUNE: MILITANT JOURNALIST. Chicago: Univ. of Chicago Press, 1972. 388 p.

FRANKLIN, JAMES THOMAS

MID-DAY GLEANINGS: A BOOK FOR HOME AND HOLIDAY READING. Memphis, Tenn.: Tracy Printing and Stationery Co., 1893. 144 p. Rpt. New York: AMS Press, 1974.

Forty-six poems. Also contains prose.

JESSAMINE POEMS. Memphis, Tenn.: n.p., [1900?].

No copy located.

GORDON, CHARLES BENJAMIN WILLIAM (1861- ?)

SELECT SERMONS. Vol. 1. 4th ed. Introd. Mrs. Maggie W. Gordon. Petersburg, Va.: C.B.W. Gordon and Co., 1889. 420 p.

Sermons and poetry. Apparently only one volume was published.

GRIMKE, CHARLOTTE L. FORTEN (1837-1914)

LIFE AND WRITINGS OF THE GRIMKE FAMILY. Ed. Anna Julia Cooper. 2 vols. in 1. N.p.: Published by the editor, 1951.

Volume 2, "The Life and Writings of Charlotte Forten Grimke," contains most of her fourteen published poems; Sherman IP, p. 215, lists periodical appearances for the rest.

Biography and Criticism

Loggins NA; Sherman IP.

Billington, Ray A., ed. THE JOURNAL OF CHARLOTTE L. FORTEN. New York: Dryden Press, 1953.

Brown, William Wells. THE BLACK MAN. Boston: James Redpath, 1863. pp. 190-99.

HAMMON, JUPITER (1711-1800?)

AN EVENING THOUGHT. SALVATION BY CHRIST, WITH PENETENTIAL CRIES. Composed by Jupiter Hammon, a Negro Belonging to Mr. Lloyd, of Queen's Village, on Long-Island, the 25th of December, 1760. No imprint. [1761?]. Broadside.

AN ADDRESS TO MISS PHILLIS WHEATLY, ETHIOPIAN POETESS, IN BOSTON, WHO CAME FROM AFRICA AT EIGHT YEARS OF AGE, AND SOON BECAME ACQUAINTED WITH THE GOSPEL OF JESUS CHRIST. [At end of text:] Composed by Jupiter Hammon, a Negro Man Belonging to Mr. Joseph Lloyd, of Queen's Village, on Long Island, now in Hartford. Hartford, Conn.: Published by the Author, and a Number of His Friends, 1778. Broadside.

A WINTER PIECE: BEING A SERIOUS EXHORTATION, WITH A CALL TO THE UNCONVERTED: AND A SHORT CONTEMPLATION ON THE DEATH OF JESUS CHRIST. Written by Jupiter Hammon, a Negro Man Belonging to Mr. John Lloyd of Queen's Village, on Long Island, now in Hartford. Published by the Author with the Assistance of His Friends. Hartford, Conn.: Printed for the Author, 1782. 24 p.

> Prose except for the last two pages, which contain "A Poem for Children with Thoughts on Death."

AN EVENING'S IMPROVEMENT. SHEWING, THE NECESSITY OF BEHOLDING THE LAMB OF GOD. TO WHICH IS ADDED, A DIALOGUE, ENTITLED, THE KIND MASTER AND DUTIFUL SERVANT. Written by Jupiter Hammon, A Negro Man Belonging to Mr. John Lloyd, of Queen's Village on Long-Island, now in Hartford. Hartford, Conn.: Printed for the Author, by the Assistance of His Friends, [1790?]. 28 p.

> Poetry and prose.

JUPITER HAMMON--AMERICAN NEGRO POET. SELECTIONS FROM HIS WRITINGS AND A BIBLIOGRAPHY. Ed. Oscar Wegelin. New York: Charles F. Heartman, 1915. 51 p.

> In Chapman IBP.

AMERICA'S FIRST NEGRO POET: THE COMPLETE WORKS OF JUPITER HAMMON OF LONG ISLAND. Biographical Sketch of Jupiter Hammon by Oscar Wegelin. Critical Analysis of the Works of Jupiter Hammon by Vernon Loggins. Ed. and introd. Stanley Austin Ransom, Jr. Port Washington, N.Y.: Kennikat Press, 1970. 122 p.

Biography and Criticism

Brawley NG; Loggins NA; Mays NG; Redding TMPB; Rollins FANP; Williams TAS.

Costanzo, Angelo. "Three Black Poets in Eighteenth Century America." SSC REVIEW (Shippenberg State College, Pa.), (1973), pp. 89-101.

Hammon, Jupiter. AN ADDRESS TO THE NEGROES IN THE STATE OF NEW YORK. New York: Printed by Carroll and Patterson, 1787. 20 p. Another ed. Philadelphia: Daniel Humphreys, 1787. 15 p. Later ed. New York: Samuel Wood, 1806. 22 p.

Palmer, R. Roderick. "Jupiter Hammon's Poetic Exhortations." CLA JOURNAL, 18 (1974), 22-29.

Ransom, Stanley Austin, Jr., ed. AMERICA'S FIRST NEGRO POET (1970).

See above, under Primary Works, cited by title.

Reese, Carolyn. "From Jupiter Hammon to LeRoi Jones." CHANGING EDUCATION, 1 (Fall 1966), 30-34.

Vertanes, Charles A. "Jupiter Hammon: Early Negro Poet of Long Island." NASSAU COUNTY HISTORICAL JOURNAL, 18 (Winter 1957), 4-21.

Wegelin, Oscar. JUPITER HAMMON, AMERICAN NEGRO POET (1915).

See above, under Primary Works, cited by title.

_____. "Was Phillis Wheatley America's First Negro Poet?" LITERARY COLLECTOR, August 1904, pp. 117-18.

HARPER, FRANCES ELLEN WATKINS (1824-1911)

POEMS ON MISCELLANEOUS SUBJECTS, BY FRANCES ELLEN WATKINS. 2nd ed. Introd. William Lloyd Garrison. Boston: J.B. Yerrinton and Son, Printers, 1854, 40 p. Later ed. 10th Thousand. Philadelphia: Merrihew and Thompson, Printers, 1857. 48 p. 20th ed., by Frances Ellen Watkins Harper. Philadelphia: Merrihew and Son, Printers, 1871. 56 p. Rpt. New York: AMS Press, 1974.

The edition of 1854 contains nineteen poems and three prose pieces; the edition of 1857 has four poems added; the edition of 1871 has twenty-six poems.

MOSES: A STORY OF THE NILE. 2nd ed. Philadelphia: Merrihew and Son, Printers, 1869. 2nd ed. Philadelphia: Published by the author, 1889. 52 p. Later ed. 1893. 64 p.

POEMS. Philadelphia: Merrihew and Son, Printers, 1871. 48 p. Later ed. Providence, R.I.: A. Crawford Greene and Sons, Printers, 1880. 48 p. Later ed. Philadelphia: Published by the author, 1896. 74 p. New ed. 1900. 90 p.

The edition of 1880 contains thirty-one poems; the edition of 1900 has thirty-six poems.

SKETCHES OF SOUTHERN LIFE. Philadelphia: Merrihew and Son, Printers, 1872. 24 p. Later ed. Philadelphia: Ferguson Bros. and Co., Printers, 1888. 58 p. Later ed. 1891. 58 p. Later ed. 1896. 48 p.

> The edition of 1888 contains sixteen poems; the edition of 1891 has fifteen poems; the edition of 1896 has only ten.

THE SPARROW'S FALL AND OTHER POEMS. No imprint. [1890?]. 22 p.

> Ten poems.

THE ALABAMA MARTYR AND OTHER POEMS. No imprint. [1894?]. 24 p.

> Twelve poems, of which nine are included in ATLANTA OFFER-ING (see below).

ATLANTA OFFERING. Philadelphia: Published by the author, 1895. 70 p.

> Thirty-four poems, all but nine of them from previous books.

LIGHT BEYOND THE DARKNESS. Chicago: Donohue and Henneberry, n.d. 8 p.

Biography and Criticism

Brawley NG; Loggins NA; Mays NG; Redding TMPB; Rollins FANP; Sherman IP; Williams TAS.

Daniel, Theodora Williams. "The Poems of Frances E.W. Harper, Edited with a Biographical and Critical Introduction, and Bibliography." M.A. thesis, Howard University, 1937. 256 p.

Riggins, Linda N. "The Works of Frances E.W. Harper." BLACK WORLD, 22 (Dec. 1972), 30-36.

Still, William. THE UNDERGROUND RAIL ROAD. Philadelphia: Porter and Coates, 1872, pp. 755-80.

HEARD, JOSEPHINE DELPHINE HENDERSON (1861- ?)

MORNING GLORIES. Introd. Bishop Benjamin Tucker Tanner. Philadelphia: Published by the author, 1890. 108 p. 2nd ed. Atlanta: Franklin Printing and Publishing Co., 1901. 142 p.

> The first edition contains seventy-eight poems divided into three sections headed "Musings," "The Race Problem," and "Obituaries," aimed at encouraging and inspiring "the youth of the Race to pure

and noble motives," according to the author's preface. The second
edition adds sixty-six poems.

Biography and Criticism

Heard, William Henry. FROM SLAVERY TO THE BISHOPRIC IN THE A.M.E.
CHURCH: AN AUTOBIOGRAPHY. Philadelphia: A.M.E. Book Concern,
1924. 104 p.

Majors, Monroe A. NOTED NEGRO WOMEN, THEIR TRIUMPHS AND
ACTIVITIES. Chicago: Donohue and Henneberry, 1893, pp. 261-68.

HOLLY, JOSEPH CEPHAS (1825-54)

FREEDOM'S OFFERING. Rochester, N.Y.: Chas. H. McDonnell, 1853.
39 p.

HORTON, GEORGE MOSES (1797?-1883?)

THE HOPE OF LIBERTY. CONTAINING A NUMBER OF POETICAL PIECES.
Raleigh, N.C.: Printed by J. Gales and Son, 1829. 22 p.

> Twenty-one poems on love, death, slavery, and liberty.

POEMS BY A SLAVE. 2nd ed. Philadelphia: Lewis Gunn, 1837. 23 p.

> A new edition of THE HOPE OF LIBERTY (see above), with the
> text unchanged. Also published in MEMOIR AND POEMS OF
> PHILLIS WHEATLEY . . . ALSO, POEMS BY A SLAVE. 3rd edi-
> tion. Boston: I. Knapp, 1838. 155 p.

THE POETICAL WORKS OF GEORGE M. HORTON, THE COLORED BARD OF
NORTH-CAROLINA, TO WHICH IS PREFIXED THE LIFE OF THE AUTHOR,
WRITTEN BY HIMSELF. Hillsborough, N.C.: Printed by D. Heartt, 1845.
99 p.

> Forty-four poems, with little or no mention of slavery or liberty.

NAKED GENIUS. Rev. and comp. Capt. W.W.S. Banks, 9th Michigan Cav.
Raleigh, N.C.: Wm. B. Smith and Co., Southern Field and Fireside Book
Publishing House, 1865. 160 p.

> One hundred thirty-two poems: forty-two from the POETICAL
> WORKS (see above), and ninety new pieces.

Biography and Criticism

Brawley NG; Jackson BPA; Loggins NA; Redding TMPB; Sherman IP; Williams
TAS.

Battle, Kemp P. "George Horton, the Slave Poet." NORTH CAROLINA UNIVERSITY MAGAZINE, 7 (May 1888), 229-32.

Brawley, Benjamin. "Three Negro Poets: Horton, Mrs. Harper and Whitman." JOURNAL OF NEGRO HISTORY, 2 (1917), 384-92.

Cobb, Collier. "An American Man of Letters: George Moses Horton, the Negro Poet." UNIVERSITY OF NORTH CAROLINA MAGAZINE, 27 (Oct. 1909), 3-10.

Farrison, W.E. "George Moses Horton: Poet for Freedom." CLA JOURNAL, 14 (1971), 227-41.

Hentz, Caroline Lee (Whiting). LOVELL'S FOLLY, A NOVEL. Cincinnati: Hubbard & Edmands, 1833. 333 p.

A character in this novel of New England life is based on Horton.

Jarrett, Calvin. "George Moses Horton, Slave, Illiterate Genius." NEGRO DIGEST, 13 (July 1964), 62-69.

Lakin, Mattie T. "George Moses Horton." M.A. thesis, North Carolina College, Durham, 1951.

Oldham, Edward A. "North Carolina Poets--Past and Present--George Moses Horton." NORTH CAROLINA POETRY REVIEW, 2 (Jan.-Feb. 1935).

Richmond, Merle A. BID THE VASSAL SOAR: INTERPRETIVE ESSAYS ON THE LIFE AND POETRY OF PHILLIS WHEATLEY (CA. 1753-1784) AND GEORGE MOSES HORTON (CA. 1797-1883). Washington, D.C.: Howard Univ. Press, 1974. 216 p.

Walser, Richard. THE BLACK POET: BEING THE REMARKABLE STORY . . . OF GEORGE MOSES HORTON, A NORTH CAROLINA SLAVE. New York: Philosophical Library, 1966. 120 p.

Weeks, Stephen B. "George Moses Horton: Slave Poet." SOUTHERN WORK-MAN, 43 (1914), 571-77.

JACKSON, A.J.

A VISION OF LIFE, AND OTHER POEMS. Hillsborough, Ohio: Printed at the Highland News Office, 1869. 52 p.

LAMBERT, MARY ELIZA [PERINE] TUCKER (1838- ?)

LOEW'S BRIDGE, A BROADWAY IDYL. New York: M. Doolady, 1867. 78 p.

POEMS. New York: M. Doolady, 1867. 216 p.

McCLELLAN, GEORGE MARION (1860-1934)

POEMS. Nashville, Tenn.: A.M.E. Church Sunday School Union, 1895.
145 p. Rpt. Freeport, N.Y.: Books for Libraries, 1974.
> Fifty-seven poems and prose.

SONGS OF A SOUTHERNER. Boston: Press of Rockwell and Churchill, 1896.
16 p.
> Twelve poems, all from POEMS (above).

THE PATH OF DREAMS. Louisville, Ky.: John P. Morton, 1916. 76 p.

THE PATH OF DREAMS AND GABE YOWL. Nashville, Tenn.: A.M.E. Sunday School Union, 1916. 206 p.
> THE PATH OF DREAMS--forty-three poems on love, nature, and religion--occupies the first fifty-seven pages of this volume; pages 58-206 contain a novel.

Biography and Criticism

Sherman IP.

Sherman, Joan R. "Tennessee's Black Poet: George Marion McClellan."
TENNESSEE STUDIES IN LITERATURE, 18 (1973), 147-62.

McGIRT, JAMES EPHRAIM (1874-1930)

AVENGING THE MAINE, A DRUNKEN A.B. AND OTHER POEMS. Raleigh,
N.C.: Edwards and Broughton, Printers and Binders, 1899. 86 p. 2nd ed.,
enl. 1900. 109 p. 3rd ed., rev. and enl. Philadelphia: George F. Lasher,
Printer and Binder, 1901. 119 p.
> The first edition contains forty-two poems, the second fifty-nine,
> and the third sixty-one.

SOME SIMPLE SONGS AND A FEW MORE AMBITIOUS ATTEMPTS. Philadelphia: George F. Lasher, Printer and Binder, 1901. 72 p.
> Twenty-one poems.

FOR YOUR SWEET SAKE. Philadelphia: John C. Winston Co., 1906. 79 p.
2nd ed. 1909. 77 p.

> The first edition contains forty-four poems, the second fifty-one.
> The first edition is in Chapman IBP.

Biography and Criticism

Sherman IP.

Parker, John William. "James E. McGirt: Poet of 'Hope Deferred.'" NEGRO HISTORY BULLETIN, 16 (1953), 123-27; also in NORTH CAROLINA HISTORICAL REVIEW, 31 (1954), 321-35.

_____. "James E. McGirt: Tar Heel Poet." CRISIS, 60 (May 1953), 286-89.

MENARD, JOHN WILLIS (1838-93)

LAYS IN SUMMER LANDS. With the Press Notices of His Speech and His Appearance in Congress, and a Biographical Preface by F.J. Barbadoes. Washington, D.C.: Enterprise Publishing Co., 1879. 84 p.

> Sixty-three poems on personal and public themes.

Biography and Criticism

Sherman IP.

Gibbs, Thomas V. "John Willis Menard, the First Congressman elect." A.M.E. CHURCH REVIEW, 3 (1887), 426-32.

MILLAR, GERALD

LIFE, TRAVELS AND WORKS OF MISS FLORA BATSON, DECEASED QUEEN OF SONG. By Gerald Millar the Basso, for Ten Years her Manager and Professional Associate, Interspersed with Comments from Leading Characters of the World, and Original Poems Heretofore Unpublished. N.p.: T.M.R.M. Co., Gerald Millar, [19- ?]. 92 p.

> The majority of the fifteen songs included in the volume are presumably by Gerald Millar. Flora Batson is portrayed by Millar as a soprano singer of remarkable depth and range.

MOORE, ALICE RUTH (1875-1935)

VIOLETS AND OTHER TALES. New Orleans: n.p., 1895. 176 p.

> Prose and poetry by Paul Laurence Dunbar's future wife.

NELSON, ALICE RUTH MOORE DUNBAR. See MOORE, ALICE RUTH, above.

PAYNE, DANIEL ALEXANDER (1811-93)

THE PLEASURES AND OTHER MISCELLANEOUS POEMS. Baltimore: Sherwood and Co., 1850. 43 p.

Biography and Criticism

Brawley NG; Loggins NA; Mays NG.

Coan, Josephus R. DANIEL ALEXANDER PAYNE, CHRISTIAN EDUCATOR. Philadelphia: A.M.E. Book Concern, 1935. 139 p.

Payne, Daniel Alexander. RECOLLECTIONS OF SEVENTY YEARS. Nashville, Tenn.: A.M.E. Sunday School Union, 1888. 335 p. Rpt. New York: Arno Press, 1968.

PETERS, PHILLIS. See WHEATLEY, PHILLIS, below, this section.

PLATO, ANN (1820?- ?)

ESSAYS: INCLUDING BIOGRAPHIES AND MISCELLANEOUS PIECES, IN PROSE AND POETRY. Introd. James C.W. Pennington. Hartford, Conn.: Printed for the author, 1841. 122 p.

> Twenty poems and prose.

Biography and Criticism

Loggins NA; Sherman IP.

PURVIS, T.T.

HAGAR; THE SINGING MAIDEN, WITH OTHER STORIES AND RHYMES. Philadelphia: Walton and Co., 1881. 228 p. Rpt. New York: AMS Press, 1974.

> Poetry and prose.

RAY, HENRIETTA CORDELIA (1852?-1916)

LINCOLN. WRITTEN FOR THE OCCASION OF THE UNVEILING OF THE FREEDMEN'S MONUMENT IN MEMORY OF ABRAHAM LINCOLN, APRIL 14, 1876. New York: Press of J.J. Little and Co., 1893. 11 p.

SONNETS. New York: Press of J.J. Little and Co., 1893. 29 p.

Twelve poems.

POEMS. New York: Grafton Press, 1910. 169 p.

Contains 146 poems; includes her SONNETS (cited above). Reviewed by Jessie Fauset in CRISIS, 4 (1912), 183.

Biography and Criticism

Sherman IP.

Brown, Hallie Q. HOMESPUN HEROINES AND OTHER WOMEN OF DISTINCTION. Xenia, Ohio: Aldine Publishing Co., 1926, pp. 171-75.

REASON, CHARLES LEWIS (1818-93)

According to Sherman IP, p. 220, Reason's uncollected poems are to be found in the following:

"Freedom." In THE MAN: THE HERO: THE CHRISTIAN: . . . THOMAS CLARKSON . . . TOGETHER WITH FREEDOM: A POEM, READ ON THE SAME OCCASION BY MR. CHARLES L. REASON, by Alexander Crummell. New York: Egbert, Hovey & King, 1847, pp. 39-44.

"Hope and Confidence." In AUTOGRAPHS FOR FREEDOM. Ed. Julia Griffiths. Auburn, N.Y.: Alden, Beardsley and Co., 1854, pp. 226-29.

"The Spirit Voice; or Liberty Call to the Disfranchised (State of New York)" and "Silent Thoughts." In MEN OF MARK; EMINENT, PROGRESSIVE AND RISING, by William Simmons. Cleveland: George M. Rewell and Co., 1887, pp. 1108-12.

Biography and Criticism

Loggins NA; Sherman IP.

Brown, William Wells. THE RISING SON. Boston: A.G. Brown and Co., 1874, pp. 442-44.

Mayo, Anthony R. CHARLES LEWIS REASON, PIONEER NEW YORK EDUCATOR AND LEADER OF THE MOVEMENT TO SECURE EQUAL OPPORTUNITIES FOR NEGROES IN THE NEW YORK PUBLIC SCHOOL SYSTEM: A BRIEF SKETCH OF HIS LIFE, COMMEMORATING THE FIFTIETH ANNIVERSARY OF HIS DEATH AUGUST 16TH, 1893. N.p.: [1943?]. 12 p.

Payne, Daniel Alexander. RECOLLECTIONS OF SEVENTY YEARS. Nashville,

Tenn.: A.M.E. Sunday School Union, 1888, pp. 46-48, 118, 327.

Roy, J.M. "Charles Reason: Teacher." NEGRO HISTORY BULLETIN, 16 (1953), 204-5.

RHODES, JACOB (1835?- ?)

THE NATION'S LOSS: A POEM ON THE LIFE AND DEATH OF THE HON. ABRAHAM LINCOLN, LATE PRESIDENT OF THE UNITED STATES, WHO DEPARTED THIS LIFE, IN WASHINGTON, D.C., APRIL 15, 1865. Newark, N.J.: F. Starbuck, Printer, 1866. 18 p.

Poetry and prose.

ROGERS, ELYMAS PAYSON (1815-61)

A POEM ON THE FUGITIVE SLAVE LAW. Newark, N.J.: A. Stephen Holbrook, Printer, 1856. 24 p.

THE REPEAL OF THE MISSOURI COMPROMISE CONSIDERED. Newark, N.J.: A. Stephen Holbrook, Printer, 1856. 24 p.

Biography and Criticism

Loggins NA; Sherman IP.

Wilson, Joseph M. THE PRESBYTERIAN HISTORICAL ALMANAC . . . FOR 1862, pp. 191-95.

ROWE, GEORGE CLINTON (1853-1903)

THOUGHTS IN VERSE. Charleston, S.C.: Kahrs, Stolze and Welch, Printers, 1887. 113 p.

Seventy-one poems written with the objective of "stirring up our young people to higher aspirations."

OUR HEROES: PATRIOTIC POEMS ON MEN, WOMEN AND SAYINGS OF THE NEGRO RACE. Charleston, S.C.: Walker, Evans and Cogswell Co., Printers, 1890. 68 p.

Fifteen poems.

A MEMORIAL SOUVENIR OF REV. T. WOFFORD WHITE. Charleston, S.C.: Published by the author, 1890. 9 p.

A NOBLE LIFE: MEMORIAL SOUVENIR OF REV. JOS. C. PRICE. Charleston, S.C.: Published by the author, 1894. 7 p.

REV. SALEM MITCHELL: A MEMORIAL SOUVENIR. Charleston, S.C.: Published by the author, 1903. 7 p.

Biography and Criticism

Sherman IP.

SHOEMAN, CHARLES HENRY

A DREAM AND OTHER POEMS. Ann Arbor, Mich.: George Wahr, 1899. 146 p. 2nd ed. 1900. 202 p.

> The first edition contains forty-six poems, the second contains sixty-eight.

SIDNEY, ROBERT Y.

"Anthems, Composed by R.Y. Sidney, for the National Jubilee of the Abolition of the Slave Trade, January 1st, 1909." In AN ORATION, COMMEMORATIVE OF THE ABOLITION OF THE SLAVE TRADE IN THE UNITED STATES; DELIVERED BEFORE THE WILBERFORCE PHILANTHROPIC ASSOCIATION, IN THE CITY OF NEW YORK, ON THE SECOND OF JANUARY, 1809, by Joseph Sidney. New York: J. Seymour, Printer, 1809, pp. 19-20.

> Robert Sidney's anthems are republished in EARLY NEGRO WRITING, ed. Dorothy B. Porter (Boston: Beacon Press, 1971), pages 565-67.

SIMPSON, JOSHUA McCARTER (1820?-76)

THE EMANCIPATION CAR, BEING AN ORIGINAL COMPOSITION OF ANTI-SLAVERY BALLADS, COMPOSED EXCLUSIVELY FOR THE UNDER GROUND RAIL ROAD. Zanesville, Ohio: Printed by Sullivan and Brown, 1874. 152 p.

> Fifty-six poems and five essays, mostly on slavery and its abolition.

Biography and Criticism

Sherman IP.

TANNER, BENJAMIN TUCKER (1835-1923)

STRAY THOUGHTS. No imprint. 20 p.

TEMPLE, GEORGE HANNIBAL

THE EPIC OF COLUMBUS' BELL AND OTHER POEMS. Reading, Pa.: Reading Eagle, 1900. 80 p.

TERRY, LUCY [MRS. LUCY TERRY PRINCE] (1730-1821, born in Africa)

"Bars Fight," her only known poem, is a twenty-eight-line vivid doggerel description of a 1746 Indian raid on Deerfield, Massachusetts, and of the massacre of various white citizens ("Samuel Amsden they found dead/ Not many rods off from his head."). Written contemporaneously but first published a century and a half later by George Sheldon (see below), it is the earliest known piece of Afro-American poetry. The text is available in the following anthologies: L. Hughes and A. Bontemps, THE POETRY OF THE NEGRO (1949, 1973), p. 3; L. Patterson, INTRODUCTION TO BLACK LITERATURE IN AMERICA (1968), p. 27; D. Randall, THE BLACK POETS (1972), p. 37; and W. Robinson, EARLY BLACK AMERICAN POETS (1969), p. 4.

Biography and Criticism

Constanzo, Angelo. "Three Black Poets in Eighteenth Century America." SSC REVIEW (Shippenburg State College, Pa.) (1973), pp. 89-101.

Greene, Lorenzo J. THE NEGRO IN COLONIAL NEW ENGLAND. New York: Columbia Univ. Press, 1942, pp. 242-43, 314-15.

Katz, Bernard. "A Second Version of Lucy Terry's Early Ballad." NEGRO HISTORY BULLETIN, 29 (1966), 183-84.

Sheldon, George. A HISTORY OF DEERFIELD, MASSACHUSETTS. Vol. 1. Greenfield, Mass.: Press of E.M. Hall, 1895, pp. 545-49.

_____. "Slavery in Old Deerfield." NEW ENGLAND MAGAZINE, 8 (Mar. 1893), 49-60.

Wright, Martha R. "Bijah's Luce of Guilford." NEGRO HISTORY BULLETIN, 27 (1965), 152-53, 159.

THOMPSON, AARON BELFORD (1883-1929)

MORNING SONGS. Rossmoyne, Ohio: Published by the author, 1899. 84 p.
    Forty poems.

ECHOES OF SPRING. Rossmoyne, Ohio: Published by the author, 1901. 78 p.
    Thirty-seven poems.

HARVEST OF THOUGHTS. Introd. James Whitcomb Riley. Indianapolis: Published by the author, 1907. 106 p.

Forty-five poems, including twenty-two taken from his earlier book.

THOMPSON, ELOISE BIBB. See BIBB, ELOISE, above, this section.

TURNER, HENRY McNEAL (1834-1915)

THE CONFLICT FOR CIVIL RIGHTS. Washington, D.C.: Published by the author, 1881. 14 p.

VANDYNE, WILLIAM JOHNSON

REVELS OF FANCY. Boston: A.F. Grant, 1891. 55 p.

VASHON, GEORGE BOYER (1824-78)

According to Sherman IP, p. 222, Vashon's uncollected poems are to be found in the following:

> "A Life Day." In THE SEMI-CENTENARY AND THE RETROSPECTION OF THE A.M.E. CHURCH IN THE UNITED STATES OF AMERICA, by Daniel A. Payne. Baltimore: Sherwood and Co., 1866, pp. 172-75.
>
> "Ode on the Proclamation of the Fifteenth Amendment." NEW ERA, 1 (7 Apr. 1870).
>
> "Vincent Oge." In AUTOGRAPHS FOR FREEDOM. Ed. Julia Griffiths. Auburn, N.Y.: Alden, Beardsley and Co., 1854, pp. 44-60; an extract appears in EARLY BLACK AMERICAN POETS, (1969), ed. W.H. Robinson.

Biography and Criticism

Brawley NG; Loggins NA; Sherman IP.

Brown, William Wells. THE RISING SON. Boston: A.G. Brown and Co., 1874, pp. 476-78.

WALDEN, ALFRED ISLAY (1847?-84)

WALDEN'S MISCELLANEOUS POEMS, WHICH THE AUTHOR DESIRES TO DEDICATE TO THE CAUSE OF EDUCATION AND HUMANITY. Washington, D.C.: Reed and Woodward, Printers, 1872. 50 p. 2nd ed. Washington, D.C.: Published by the author, 1873. 96 p.

Fifty-five poems.

WALDEN'S SACRED POEMS, WITH A SKETCH OF HIS LIFE. New Brunswick, N.J.: Terhune and Van Anglen's Press, 1877. 23 p.

Thirteen poems.

Biography and Criticism

Loggins NA; Sherman IP.

WATKINS, FRANCES ELLEN. See HARPER, FRANCES ELLEN WATKINS, above, this section.

WATKINS, JAMES ROBERT (1821?- ?)

POEMS, ORIGINAL AND SELECTED, BY JAMES WATKINS, A FUGITIVE SLAVE. Manchester, England: A. Heywood, Printer, [1859?]. 16 p.

Biography and Criticism

Watkins, James Robert. NARRATIVE OF THE LIFE OF JAMES WATKINS, FORMERLY A SLAVE IN MARYLAND, U.S., CONTAINING AN ACCOUNT OF HIS ESCAPE FROM SLAVERY, AND HIS SUBSEQUENT HISTORY. Manchester, England: n.p., 1859. 96 p.

_____. STRUGGLES FOR FREEDOM; OR, THE LIFE OF JAMES WATKINS. 19th ed. Manchester, England: n.p., 1860. 104 p.

WHEATLEY, PHILLIS [PHILLIS PETERS] (1753?-84, born in West Africa)

AN ELEGIAC POEM, ON THE DEATH OF THAT CELEBRATED DIVINE, AND EMINENT SERVANT OF JESUS CHRIST, THE REVEREND AND LEARNED GEORGE WHITEFIELD, CHAPLAIN TO THE RIGHT HONOURABLE THE COUNTESS OF HUNTINGDON, ETC., WHO MADE HIS EXIT FROM THE TRANSITORY STATE, TO DWELL IN THE CELESTIAL REALMS OF BLISS, ON LORD'S DAY, 30TH OF SEPTEMBER, 1770, WHEN HE WAS SEIZ'D WITH A FIT OF THE ASTHMA, AT NEWBURY-PORT, NEAR BOSTON, IN NEW ENGLAND. IN WHICH IS A CONDOLATORY ADDRESS TO HIS TRULY NOBLE BENEFACTRESS THE WORTHY AND PIOUS LADY HUNTINGDON; AND THE ORPHAN-CHILDREN IN GEORGIA, WHO, WITH MANY THOUSANDS ARE LEFT, BY THE DEATH OF THIS GREAT MAN, TO LAMENT THE LOSS OF A FATHER, FRIEND AND BENEFACTOR. By Phillis, a Servant Girl, of 17 Years of Age, belonging to Mr. J. Wheatley, of Boston; She Has Been but 9 Years in this Country from Africa. Boston: Ezekiel Russell and John Boyles, 1770. 8 p.

Also published in 1770 as a broadside with the same imprint; with no imprint, and in separate Newport, R.I., New York, Philadel-

phia, and London broadside editions, with some variations in title.
A revised version appears in POEMS ON VARIOUS SUBJECTS
(1773), as "On the Death of the Rev. Mr. George Whitefield."

TO MRS. LEONARD, ON THE DEATH OF HER HUSBAND. Boston: n.p.,
1771. Broadside.

A revised version appears in POEMS ON VARIOUS OCCASIONS
(1773), as "To a Lady on the Death of Her Husband."

TO THE REV. MR. PITKIN, ON THE DEATH OF HIS LADY. Boston: n.p.,
1772. Broadside.

A revised version appears in POEMS ON VARIOUS OCCASIONS
(1773), as "To a Clergyman on the Death of His Lady."

TO THE HON'BLE THOMAS HUBBARD, ESQ; ON THE DEATH OF MRS.
THANKFULL LEONARD. Boston: n.p., 1773. Broadside.

A revised version appears in POEMS ON SEVERAL OCCASIONS
(1773), as "To the Honourable T.H. Esq; on the Death of His
Daughter."

AN ELEGY, TO MISS MARY MOORHEAD, ON THE DEATH OF HER FATHER,
THE REV. MR. JOHN MOORHEAD. Boston: William M'Alpine, 1773. Broadside.

POEMS ON VARIOUS SUBJECTS, RELIGIOUS AND MORAL. London: Printed
for A. Bell, . . . and Sold by Messrs. Cox and Berry, . . . Boston, 1773.
124 p.

Thirty-nine poems. Later editions:

Philadelphia: Reprinted, and Sold by Joseph Crukshank, 1786.
66 p. Same, 1789.

Albany, N.Y.: Reprinted from the London Edition, by Barber and
Southwick, for Thomas Spencer, 1793. 89 p.

Walpole, N.H.: Printed for Thomas and Thomas, by David New-
hall, 1802. 86 p.

Hartford, Conn.: Printed by Oliver Steele, 1804. 92 p.

"Reprinted in New England," 1816. 120 p.

With memoirs by W.H. Jackson. Cleveland: Rewell, 1886.
149 p. Denver, Colo.: W.H. Lawrence & Co., 1887. 149 p.

Reprint of 1773 ed. Nendeln, Liechtenstein: Kraus, 1970. 124 p.

Reprint of 1786 ed. New York: AMS Press, 1974. 66 p.

Also published in THE NEGRO EQUALLED BY FEW EUROPEANS

by J. La Vallee. 2 vols. Philadelphia: William W. Woodward, 1801; and in THE INTERESTING NARRATIVE OF THE LIFE OF OLAUDAH EQUIANO, OR GUSTAVAS VASSA, THE AFRICAN, by Olaudah Equiano. Halifax, N.S.: Printed at the Office of J. Nicholoson [sic] and Co., 1813. 514 p. Rpts. Halifax: Nicholson and Co., 1814; Halifax: M. Garlick, 1819. Wheatley's poems do not appear in any of the numerous other editions of Equiano's NARRATIVE, which was first published in London in 1789.

AN ELEGY, SACRED TO THE MEMORY OF THAT GREAT DIVINE, THE REVEREND AND LEARNED DR. SAMUEL COOPER, WHO DEPARTED THIS LIFE DECEMBER 29, 1783, AETATIS 59. By Phillis Peters. Boston: Printed and Sold by E. Russell, 1784. [6] p.

LIBERTY AND PEACE, A POEM. By Phillis Peters. Boston: Printed by Warden and Russell, 1784. 4 p.

POEMS ON COMIC, SERIOUS AND MORAL SUBJECTS. 2nd ed., corrected. London: Printed for J. French, 1787. 124 p.

Apparently a reissue of the 1773 POEMS ON VARIOUS SUBJECTS, unchanged save for the title page.

A BEAUTIFUL POEM ON PROVIDENCE; WRITTEN BY A YOUNG FEMALE SLAVE. TO WHICH IS SUBJOINED A SHORT ACCOUNT OF THIS EXTRAORDINARY WRITER. Halifax, N.S.: Printed by E. Gay, 1805. 8 p.

This poem is in POEMS ON VARIOUS SUBJECTS (1773) under the title "Thoughts on the Works of Providence."

MEMOIR AND POEMS OF PHILLIS WHEATLEY, A NATIVE AFRICAN AND A SLAVE. Boston: Geo. W. Light, 1834. 103 p. 2nd ed. Boston: Light and Horton, 1835. 114 p. 3rd ed. Boston: Isaac Knapp, 1838. 155 p. Rpt. Miami, Fla.: Mnemosyne Publishing Co., 1969.

In the last forty pages of the third edition is "Poems by a Slave" (George Moses Horton, q.v.). The memoir, by Margaretta Matilda Odell, "a collateral descendant of Mrs. Wheatley," is the chief primary source on Phillis Wheatley's life. "Mrs. Wheatley," it should be noted, is John Wheatley's wife, not Phillis.

THE POEMS OF PHILLIS WHEATLEY, AS THEY WERE ORIGINALLY PUBLISHED IN LONDON, 1773. Philadelphia: R.R. and C.C. Wright, 1909. 88 p.

POEMS AND LETTERS. 1st collected ed. Ed. Charles F. Heartman, with an Appreciation by Arthur A. Schomburg. New York: C.F. Heartman, 1915. 111 p.

In Chapman IBP.

LIFE AND WORKS OF PHILLIS WHEATLEY; CONTAINING HER COMPLETE
POETICAL WORKS, NUMEROUS LETTERS, AND A COMPLETE BIOGRAPHY
OF THIS FAMOUS POET OF A CENTURY AND A HALF AGO, BY G. HER-
BERT RENFRO. Also, a Sketch of the Life of Mr. Renfro by Leila Amos
Pendleton. Washington, D.C.: R.L. Pendleton, 1916. 112 p.

THE POEMS OF PHILLIS WHEATLEY. Ed. Charlotte Ruth Wright. Philadelphia:
The Wrights, 1930. 104 p.

THE POEMS OF PHILLIS WHEATLEY. Ed. Julian D. Mason, Jr. Chapel Hill:
Univ. of North Carolina Press, 1966. 113 p.

    In Chapman IBP.

Bibliographies

Heartman, Charles F. "Bibliography of the Poetical Works of Phillis Wheatley."
In A BIBLIOGRAPHICAL CHECKLIST OF AMERICAN NEGRO POETRY. Comp.
Arthur A. Schomburg. New York: Charles F. Heartman, 1916, pp. 47-57.

Porter, Dorothy B. "Early American Negro Writers: A Bibliographical Study."
PAPERS OF THE BIBLIOGRAPHICAL SOCIETY OF AMERICA, 39 (1945), 192-270.

    For Wheatley see pages 261-67.

Additional bibliographic information is in Julian Mason's edition of THE POEMS
OF PHILLIS WHEATLEY (1966, see above), and in the books by Heartman and
Robinson listed below.

Biography and Criticism

Brown NPD; Jackson BPA; Loggins NA; Redding TMPB; Rollins FANP; Whitlow
BAL; Williams TAS.

Allen, William G. WHEATLEY, BANNEKER, AND HORTON; WITH SELEC-
TIONS FROM THE POETICAL WORKS OF WHEATLEY AND HORTON, AND
THE LETTER OF WASHINGTON TO WHEATLEY, AND OF JEFFERSON TO
BANNEKER. Boston: Laing, 1849. 48 p.

Borland, Kathryn Kilby, and Helen Ross Speicher. PHILLIS WHEATLEY:
YOUNG COLONIAL POET. Indianapolis: Bobbs-Merrill, 1968. 200 p.

    A biography for children.

Collins, Terence. "Phillis Wheatley: The Dark Side of the Poetry." PHYLON,
36 (1975), 78-88.

Costanzo, Angelo. "Three Black Poets in Eighteenth Century America." SSC

REVIEW (Shippenburg State College, Pa.), 1973, pp. 89-101.

Davis, Arthur. "Personal Elements in the Poetry of Phillis Wheatley." PHYLON, 14 (1953), 191-98.

Deane, Charles, ed. LETTERS OF PHILLIS WHEATLEY, THE NEGRO SLAVE POET OF BOSTON. Boston: Privately Printed, 1864. 19 p. Also in PRO-CEEDINGS OF THE MASSACHUSETTS HISTORICAL SOCIETY, 7 (1864), 267-79.

Fuller, Miriam Morris. PHILLIS WHEATLEY: AMERICA'S FIRST BLACK POETESS. Champaign, Ill.: Garrard Publishing Co., 1971. 94 p.

A biography for children.

Graham, Shirley. THE STORY OF PHILLIS WHEATLEY. New York: Messner, 1949. 176 p.

Gregoire, Henri. AN ENQUIRY CONCERNING THE INTELLECTUAL AND MORAL FACULTIES, AND LITERATURE OF NEGROES; FOLLOWED WITH AN ACCOUNT OF THE LIFE AND WORKS OF FIFTEEN NEGROES AND MULAT-TOES, DISTINGUISHED IN SCIENCE, LITERATURE AND THE ARTS. Trans. D.B. Warden. Brooklyn, N.Y.: Printed by Thomas Kirk, 1810. 253 p.

Originally published in French as DE LA LITTERATURE DES NE-GRES. . . . Paris: Maradan, 1808.

Gregory, Montgomery. "The Spirit of Phillis Wheatley." OPPORTUNITY, 1 (1923), 374-75.

Heartman, Charles F. PHILLIS WHEATLEY (PHILLIS PETERS): A CRITICAL AT-TEMPT AND A BIBLIOGRAPHY OF HER WRITINGS. New York: Published by the author, 1915. 47 p.

Contains ten facsimiles.

Holmes, Wilfred. "Phillis Wheatley." NEGRO HISTORY BULLETIN, 6 (1943), 117-18.

Kuncio, R.C. "Some Unpublished Poems of Phillis Wheatley." NEW ENGLAND QUARTERLY, 43 (1970), 287-99.

Mason, R. Lynn. "Phillis Wheatley--Soul Sister." PHYLON, 33 (1972), 222-30.

Renfro, G. Herbert. "A Discourse on the Life and Poetry of Phillis Wheatley." A.M.E. CHURCH REVIEW, 7 (1891), 76-109.

Richmond, Merle A. BID THE VASSAL SOAR: INTERPRETATIVE ESSAYS ON THE LIFE AND POETRY OF PHILLIS WHEATLEY (CA. 1753-1784) AND GEORGE MOSES HORTON (CA. 1797-1883). Washington, D.C.: Howard Univ. Press, 1974. 216 p.

> Pages 3-83 deal with Wheatley.

Robinson, William H. PHILLIS WHEATLEY IN THE BLACK AMERICAN BE-GINNINGS. Detroit: Broadside, 1975. 95 p.

> Includes a few previously unpublished poems.

Seeber, Edward D. "Phillis Wheatley." JOURNAL OF NEGRO HISTORY, 24 (1939), 259-62.

Shurtleff, N.B. "Phillis Wheatley, The Negro-Slave Poet." BOSTON DAILY ADVERTISER, 21 Dec. 1863. Also in PROCEEDINGS OF THE MASSACHUSETTS HISTORICAL SOCIETY, 7 (1864), 270-72.

Silverman, Kenneth. "Four New Letters by Phillis Wheatley." EARLY AMERI-CAN LITERATURE, Winter 1974, pp. 257-72.

Slattery, J.R. "Phillis Wheatley, the Negro Poetess." CATHOLIC WORLD, 39 (1884), 484-98.

Thatcher, Benjamin B. MEMOIR OF PHILLIS WHEATLEY. Boston: n.p., 1834. 36 p.

Wegelin, Oscar. "Was Phillis Wheatley America's First Negro Poet?" LITER-ARY COLLECTOR, Aug. 1904, pp. 117-18.

Weight, Glenn S. "The Anniversary of Phillis Wheatley Remains an Inspiration to All." NEGRO HISTORY BULLETIN, 25 (1962), 91-92.

Yeocum, William H. "Phillis Wheatley--The First African Poetess." A.M.E. CHURCH REVIEW, 6 (1890), 329-33.

WHITFIELD, JAMES MONROE (1822-71)

AMERICA AND OTHER POEMS. Buffalo, N.Y.: James S. Leavitt, 1853. 85 p.

> Twenty-three poems.

"A Poem Written for the Celebration of the Fourth Anniversary of President Lincoln's Emancipation Proclamation." In EMANCIPATION ORATION . . . AND

POEM . . . , by Ezra Rothschild Johnson. San Francisco: Elevator Office, 1867, pp. 23-32.

Biography and Criticism

Brawley NG; Loggins NA; Sherman IP; Wagner BPUS; Williams TAS.

Sherman, Joan R. "James Monroe Whitfield, Poet and Emigrationist: A Voice of Protest and Despair." JOURNAL OF NEGRO HISTORY, 52 (1972), 169-76.

WHITMAN, ALBERY ALLSON (1851-1901)

LEELAH MISLED: A POEM. Elizabethtown, Ky.: Richard LaRue, 1873. 33 p.

NOT A MAN, AND YET A MAN. Springfield, Ohio: Republic Printing Co., 1877. 254 p. Rpt. Miami, Fla.: Mnemosyne Publishing Co., 1969.

Nineteen poems.

THE RAPE OF FLORIDA. St. Louis, Mo.: Nixon-Jones Printing Co., 1884. 95 p.

TWASINTA'S SEMINOLES; OR, RAPE OF FLORIDA. Rev. ed. St. Louis, Mo.: Nixon-Jones Printing Co., 1885. 97 p.

TWASINTA'S SEMINOLES; OR, RAPE OF FLORIDA. 3rd ed., carefully revised. St. Louis, Mo.: Nixon-Jones Printing Co., 1890. 96 p.

Includes NOT A MAN, AND YET A MAN; and DRIFTED LEAVES, twenty-three short poems, two of them in dialect.

WORLD'S FAIR POEM. By Dr. Alberry [sic] A. Whitman. Read in Memorial Art Palace, Chicago, Illinois, September 22nd, 1893. Atlanta: Holsey Job Printery, [1893?]. 9 p.

AN IDYL OF THE SOUTH: AN EPIC POEM IN TWO PARTS. New York: Metaphysical Publishing Co., 1901. 126 p.

Biography and Criticism

Brawley NG; Brown NPD; Loggins NA; Sherman IP; Wagner BPUS; Williams TAS.

Braithwaite, William Stanley. "Rev. Whitman's Idyl." COLORED AMERICAN, Jan.-Feb. 1902, p. 206.

Sherman, Joan R. "Albery Allson Whitman: Poet of Beauty and Manliness."
CLA JOURNAL, 15 (1971), 126–43.

WILLIAMS, EDWARD W. (1863-91)

VIEWS AND MEDITATIONS OF JOHN BROWN. Washington, D.C.: n.p.,
1893. 16 p.

WILLIAMS, PETER

"Hymns Composed by Peter Williams and Sung on the Occasion of the Delivery
of an Address to the New York African Society for Mutual Relief." In AN
ADDRESS TO THE NEW YORK AFRICAN SOCIETY FOR MUTUAL RELIEF, DE-
LIVERED IN THE UNIVERSALIST CHURCH, JANUARY 2, 1809, by William
Hamilton. New York: n.p., 1809, p. 4.

> Williams' hymns are also in Dorothy Porter, EARLY NEGRO WRIT-
> ING (Boston: Beacon Press, 1971), pp. 568–70.

WILSON, JOSEPH THOMAS (1836-91)

VOICE OF A NEW RACE: ORIGINAL SELECTION OF POEMS, WITH A TRIL-
OGY AND ORATION. Hampton, Va.: Normal School Steam Press, 1882.
43 p.

2. 1901-45

Paul Laurence Dunbar died in 1906 at the age of thirty-three. The subsequent
decade saw the advent of such poets as Fenton Johnson, James Weldon Johnson,
and Claude McKay, but black poetry generally received little recognition until
the mid-twenties when Alain Locke's anthology THE NEW NEGRO (1925) and
the first books of Countee Cullen and Langston Hughes signaled the beginning
of the Harlem Renaissance. Sterling Brown's SOUTHERN ROAD (1932) is a
unique tour de force of folk and dialect expression whose time-bomb effect has
not yet been fully felt.

Jean Wagner's BLACK POETS is the best critical and biographical guide for the
early years of the period; the Renaissance and subsequent years are discussed in
Brown NPD, Davis FDT, and many other works.

In this section, primary works are listed first, in chronological order, followed
by secondary works, in alphabetical order. Works indexed in Chapman IPB are
so indicated.

ADAMS, WELLINGTON ALEXANDER

LYRICS OF AN HUMBLE BIRTH. Washington, D.C.: Murray Bros., 1914. 48 p.

ALDEBARAN. See BYER, D.P., below, this section.

ALLEN, JUNIUS MORDECAI (1875-1906)

RHYMES, TALES AND RHYMED TALES. Topeka, Kans.: Monotyped by Crane and Co., 1906. 153 p.
> Four prose tales and nineteen poems sketching black life.

Biography and Criticism

Brown NPD; Wagner BPUS.

ANDERSON, ANITA TURPEAU

PENPOINTS: GROUP OF POEMS AND PROSE WRITINGS. Fairmont Heights, Md.: Campbell Press, 1943. 20 p.

ANDREWS, HENRY H.

VICIOUS YOUTH. Boston: Popular Poetry Publishers, 1940. 34 p.

IDLE MOMENTS. New York: Poets Press, 1941. 50 p.

ANDUZE, AUBREY A. (Born in St. Thomas, Virgin Islands)

REMINISCENCE. St. Thomas, V.I.: Art Shop, 1940. 89 p.

ARTIS, DALE ANNE

SONGS OF CIRCUMSTANCE. Philadelphia: Dorrance, 1944. 71 p.

ATHENS, IDA GERDING

BRETHREN. Cincinnati: Talaria Publication Co., 1940. 70 p.

ATKINS, THOMAS

THE EAGLE. St. Louis, Mo.: Argus, 1936. 87 p.

AUDAIN, GEORGE E. (Born in St. Thomas, Virgin Islands)

SAINT THOMAS IN PROSE AND VERSE. Charlotte Amalie: Mail Notes Printing Co., n.d. 68 p.

BAILEY, WILLIAM EDGAR

THE FIRSTLING. No imprint. [1914?].

BANKS, WILLIAM AUGUSTUS

BEYOND THE ROCKIES AND OTHER POEMS. Philadelphia: Dorrance, 1926. 64 p.

"LEST WE FORGET." Chattanooga: Central High Press, 1930. 11 p.

"GATHERING DUSK." Chattanooga: Wilson Printing Co., 1935. 8 p.

BATIPPS, PERCY OLIVER

LINES OF LIFE. Media, Pa.: American Publishing Co., 1924. 118 p.

BATTLE, EFFIE T.

GLEANINGS FROM DIXIE-LAND IN TEN POEMS. Okolona, Miss.: Published by the author, 1914. 28 p.

BAXTER, JOSEPH HARVEY LOWELL

THAT WHICH CONCERNETH ME: SONNETS AND OTHER POEMS. Roanoke, Va.: Magic City Press, 1934. 87 p.

SONNETS FOR THE ETHIOPIANS AND OTHER POEMS. Roanoke, Va.: Magic City Press, 1936. 113 p.

BEADLE, SAMUEL ALFRED. See section for 1760-1900, above.

BELL, JAMES MADISON. See section for 1760-1900, above.

BERRY, LLOYD ANDREW

"UNEXPECTED." Dayton, Ohio: Published by the author, 1914. 38 p.

HEART SONGS AND BYGONES. Dayton, Ohio: Published by the author, 1926. 40 p.

BIRD, JESSIE CALHOUN

AIRS FROM THE WOOD-WINDS. Introd. Arthur Huff Fauset. Philadelphia: Alpress, 1935. 23 p.

BLADES, WILLIAM C.

NEGRO POEMS, MELODIES, PLANTATION PIECES, CAMP MEETING SONGS, ETC. Boston: Badger, 1921. 168 p.

BLAKELEY, AL ETHELRED

POETIC FACTS AND PHILOSOPHY. New York: Published by the author, 1936. 23 p.
> Nineteen poems and two prose pieces urging black pride and unity.

BONTEMPS, ARNA. See section for 1946-1975, below.

BORDERS, WILLIAM HOLMES

THUNDERBOLTS. Atlanta: Morris Brown College Press, 1942. 50 p.

BOYD, RAVEN FREEMONT (1901-)

HOLIDAY STANZAS. New York: Fortuny's, 1940. 93 p.

BRADLEY, HENRY T.

EFFUSIONS OF THE SOUL. New York: Broadway Publishing Co., 1917. 26 p.

OUT OF THE DEPTHS. New York: Avondale Press, 1928. 113 p.

BRAITHWAITE, WILLIAM STANLEY BEAUMONT (1878-1962)

LYRICS OF LIFE AND LOVE. Boston: Herbert Turner and Co., 1904. 80 p.
  In Chapman IBP.

THE HOUSE OF FALLING LEAVES, WITH OTHER POEMS. Boston: John W. Luce and Co., 1908. 112 p.
  In Chapman IBP.

SELECTED POEMS. New York: Coward-McCann, 1948. 96 p.
  In Chapman IBP.

Biography and Criticism

Brawley NG; Brown NPD; Redding TMPB.

Braithwaite, William S. "The House Under Arcturus: An Autobiography." PHYLON, 2 (1941), 9-26, 121-36, 250-59.

Butcher, Philip. "W.S. Braithwaite's Southern Exposure: Resumé and Revelation." SOUTHERN LITERARY JOURNAL, 3 (Spring 1971), 3-17.

_____. William S. Braithwaite and the College Language Association." CLA JOURNAL, 15 (1971), 117-25.

_____, ed. THE WILLIAM STANLEY BRAITHWAITE READER. Ann Arbor: Univ. of Michigan Press, 1972. 322 p.

Spellman, Fronzell. "The Twentieth Century's Greatest Negro Anthologist." NEGRO HISTORY BULLETIN, 26 (1963), 137.

Braithwaite edited the annual ANTHOLOGY OF MAGAZINE VERSE for the years 1913-29 and 1958, as well as some ten other general poetry anthologies.

BRAWLEY, BENJAMIN (1882-1939)

A PRAYER. Atlanta: Atlanta Baptist College, 1899. 6 p.
  Music by A.H. Ryder.

A TOAST TO LOVE AND DEATH. Atlanta: Published by the author, 1902. 29 p.

THE PROBLEM AND OTHER POEMS. Atlanta: Atlanta Baptist College, 1905. 18 p.

THE DESIRE OF THE MOTH FOR THE STAR. Atlanta: Published by the author, 1906. 10 p.

THE DAWN AND OTHER POEMS. N.p.: 1912. [12] p.

HOWARD UNIVERSITY SONGS. No imprint. [1912?]. 10 p.

THE SEVEN SLEEPERS OF EPHESUS: A LYRICAL LEGEND. Atlanta: Foote and Davies, 1917.

POEMS. No imprint. [20] p.

BREWER, JOHN MASON (1896-)

ECHOES OF THOUGHT. Fort Worth, Tex.: Progressive Printing, 1922. 54 p.

NEGRITO: NEGRO DIALECT POEMS OF THE SOUTHWEST. San Antonio, Tex.: Naylor Printing Co., 1933. 97 p.

THE LIFE OF JOHN WESLEY ANDERSON IN VERSE. Dallas: C.C. Cockrell and Son, 1938. 108 p.

BROOKS, WALTER HENDERSON (1851-)

ORIGINAL POEMS. Washington: Sunday School of the Rev. W.H. Brooks's Church, 1932. 40 p.

THE PASTOR'S VOICE. Washington, D.C.: Associated Publishers, 1945. 391 p.

BROWN, MATTYE JEANETTE

ORIGINAL POEMS AND BIBLICAL INFORMATION. Nashville, Tenn.: Published by the author, 1945. 40 p.

BROWN, SAMUEL E.

LOVE LETTERS IN RHYME. New York: Published by the author, 1930. 29 p.

BROWN, STERLING ALLEN (1901-   )

SOUTHERN ROAD. Introd. James Weldon Johnson. New York: Harcourt, 1932. 135 p.

 In Chapman IBP.

THE LAST RIDE OF WILD BILL AND ELEVEN NARRATIVE POEMS. Introd. Dudley Randall. Detroit: Broadside, 1975. 53 p.

Biography and Criticism

Brawley NG; Davis FDT; Redding TMPB; Wagner BPUS.

Henderson, Stephen. "A Strong Man Called Sterling Brown." BLACK WORLD, 19 (Sept. 1970), 5-12.

Locke, Alain. "Sterling Brown, the New Negro Folk Poet." In NEGRO ANTHOLOGY. Ed. Nancy Cunard. London: Wishart, 1933, pp. 111-15.

O'Meally, Robert G. "An Annotated Bibliography of the Works of Sterling A. Brown." CLA JOURNAL, 19 (1975), 268-79.

Rowell, Charles A. "Sterling A. Brown and the Afro-American Tradition." STUDIES IN THE LITERARY IMAGINATION, 3 (Fall 1974), 131-52.

STERLING A. BROWN: A UMUM TRIBUTE. Ed. Black History Museum Committee. Philadelphia: Black History Museum UMUM Publishers, 1976. 106 p.

 Includes tributes by some thirty writers, poems and essays by Brown, and a "Bibliography of Works by and about Sterling A. Brown," pages 89-101.

BROWNLEE, JULIUS PINKNEY (1886-   )

RIPPLES. Anderson, S.C.: Cox Stationery Co., 1914. 48 p.

BRYANT, FRANKLIN HENRY

BLACK SMILES, OR THE SUNNY SIDE OF SABLE LIFE. Nashville, Tenn.: Blackport Studio, 1903. 56 p. Later ed. Nashville, Tenn.: Southern Missionary Society, 1909. 57 p.

 "Grandpa's fireside stories in six poems, being a recital of humorous incidents characteristic of Negro life 'befo' du War.'" The book includes Paul Laurence Dunbar's poem "The Ninety and Nine."

BRYANT, JOSEPH G.

STEPPING BACK. Philadelphia: A.M.E. Book Concern, [191-?). 16 p.

A verse tale written between 1909 and 1914 to provide financial support for Bethel Institute, Cape Town, South Africa.

BURRELL, LOUIS V.

THE PETALS OF THE ROSE: POEMS AND EPIGRAMS. Morton, Pa.: Published by the author, 1917. 55 p.

BUSH, OLIVIA WARD (1869-)

DRIFTWOOD. Providence, R.I.: Atlantic Printing Co., 1914. 86 p.

Poetry and prose.

BUTLER, JAMES ALPHEUS. See section for 1946-75, below.

BYER, D.P.

CONQUEST OF COOMASSIE: AN EPIC OF THE MASHANTI NATION. By Aldebaran (pseud.). Long Beach, Calif.: Worth While Publishing Co., 1926. 123 p.

CANNON, DAVID WADSWORTH, JR. (1911-38)

BLACK LABOR CHANT AND OTHER POEMS. New York: National Council on Religion in Higher Education, 1939. 56 p.

CARMICHAEL, WAVERLEY TURNER

FROM THE HEART OF A FOLK. Introd. James Holly Hanford. Boston: Cornhill Co., 1918. 60 p.

Fifty-four poems, mostly in dialect, characterized by rich emotion and individual humor, on personal, religious, and political themes. In Chapman IBP.

CARRIGAN, NETTIE W.

RHYMES AND JINGLES FOR THE CHILDREN'S HOUR. Boston: Christopher, 1940. 57 p.

CARTER, HERMAN J.C.

THE SCOTTSBORO BLUES. Nashville, Tenn.: Mahlon Publishing Co., 1933. 32 p.

CASON, P. MARTIN

BOOK OF FIFTY POEMS: OUR BRAVE HEROES. No imprint. [ca. 1920]. 64 p.

CHERIOT, HENRI

VARIANT VERSE. Orlando, Fla.: Published by the author, [ca. 1915].

BLACK INK. Orlando, Fla.: Published by the author, 1917. 44 p.
> About forty poems in dialect, on racial and miscellaneous themes.

CLARK, MAZIE EARHART

GARDEN OF MEMORIES. Cincinnati: Eaton Publishing Co., 1932. 62 p.

LYRICS OF LOVE, LOYALTY AND DEVOTION. Cincinnati: Eaton Publishing Co., 1935. 112 p.

LIFE'S SUNSHINE AND SHADOWS. Cincinnati: Eaton Publishing Co., 1940. 112 p.

CLEM, CHARLES DOUGLAS (1876-1934)

RHYMES OF A RHYMSTER. Edmond, Okla.: Published by the author, [1901?]. 52 p.
> Thirty-four poems.

A LITTLE SOUVENIR. N.p.: Published by the author, 1908. 8 p.
> Six poems.

THE UPAS TREE OF KANSAS. Chanute, Kans.: Tribune Publishing Co., 1917. 24 p.
> Prose and poetry.

Biography and Criticism

Sherman IP.

Mather, Frank L., ed. WHO'S WHO OF THE COLORED RACE. Chicago: n.p., 1915, p. 68.

Sherman, Joan R. "Poet with a Purpose: Charles Douglas Clem." NEGRO HISTORY BULLETIN, 34 (1971), 163-64.

CLIFFORD, CARRIE WILLIAMS (1862-1934)

RACE RHYMES. Washington, D.C.: Printed by R.L. Pendleton, 1911. 28 p.

THE WIDENING LIGHT. Boston: Walter Reid Co., 1922. 65 p. New ed., introd. Rosemary Clifford Wilson. New York: Crowell, 1971. 98 p.

    About sixty poems on personal, political, and occasional topics.

COFFIN, FRANK BARBOUR. See section for 1760-1900, above.

COLLINS, HARRY JONES

FROM SHADOW TO SUNSHINE. Cleveland: Published by the author, 1918. 47 p.

COLLINS, LESLIE MORGAN (1914-)

EXILE. Atlanta: B.F. Logan Press, 1938. 39 p.

CONNER, NELLIE VICTORIA

ESSENCE OF GOOD PERFUME. Burbank, Calif.: Ivan Deach, Jr., 1940. 169 p.

COOKE, AMOREL E. O'KELLY

FADED FOLIAGE AND FRAGRANT FLOWERS FROM THE HEART OF BETHANY. Newark, N.J.: Published by the author, 1922. 96 p.

    Poetry and prose.

CORBETT, MAURICE NATHANIEL (1859- ?)

THE HARP OF ETHIOPIA. Introd. John C. Dancy. Nashville, Tenn.: National Baptist Publishing Board, 1914. 276 p.

A 7,500-line epic on the Negro in America.

COTTER, JOSEPH SEAMON, SR. (1861-1949)

A RHYMING. Louisville, Ky.: New South Publishing Co., 1895. 32 p.

In Chapman IBP.

LINKS OF FRIENDSHIP. Introd. Thomas G. Watkins. Louisville, Ky.: Bradley and Gilbert Co., 1903. 64 p. New ed. 1918. 29 p.

Fifty-four poems. In Chapman IBP.

CALEB, THE DEGENERATE: A PLAY IN FOUR ACTS. A STUDY OF THE TYPES, CUSTOMS AND NEEDS OF THE AMERICAN NEGRO. Louisville, Ky.: Bradley and Gilbert Co., 1903. 57 p. New ed. New York: Henry Harrison, 1940. 67 p.

A drama in verse.

A WHITE SONG AND A BLACK ONE. Louisville, Ky.: Bradley and Gilbert Co., 1909. 64 p. Rpt. New York: AMS Press, 1974.

Forty-eight poems. In Chapman IBP.

COLLECTED POEMS. New York: Henry Harrison, 1938. 78 p. Rpt. Freeport, N.Y.: Books for Libraries, 1974.

Seventy-three poems. In Chapman IBP.

SEQUEL TO THE "PIED PIPER OF HAMELIN" AND OTHER POEMS. New York: Henry Harrison, 1939. 93 p.

Sixty-nine poems. In Chapman IBP.

Biography and Criticism

Brawley NG; Sherman IP.

Kerlin, Robert T. "A Poet from Bardstown." SOUTH ATLANTIC QUARTERLY, 20 (1921), 213-21.

Townsend, John Wilson. "Kentucky's Dunbar: Joseph Seamon Cotter." In LORE OF THE MEADOWLANDS. Lexington, Ky.: Press of J.L. Richardson and Co., 1911, pp. 23-27.

COTTER, JOSEPH SEAMON, JR. (1895-1919)

THE BAND OF GIDEON AND OTHER LYRICS. Introd. C.Y. Rice. Boston: Cornhill Co., 1918. 29 p.

In Chapman IBP.

COWDERY, MAE V.

WE LIFT OUR VOICES AND OTHER POEMS. Introd. William Stanley Braithwaite. Philadelphia: Alpress, 1936. 68 p.

In Chapman IBP.

CREQUE, CYRIL (1899-   , born in St. Thomas, Virgin Islands)

TRADE WINDS. Newport, R.I.: Franklin Printing House, 1934. 110 p.

ST. THOMAS, VIRGIN ISLANDS: PANORAMA. Wauwatosa, Wis.: Kenyon Press, 1947. 81 p.

CULLEN, COUNTEE (1903-46)

NOTE: All Cullen titles listed here are in Chapman IBP, except THE LOST ZOO.

COLOR. New York: Harper, 1925. 108 p.

THE BALLAD OF THE BROWN GIRL: AN OLD BALLAD RETOLD. New York: Harper, 1927. 11 p.

COPPER SUN. New York: Harper, 1927. 89 p.

THE BLACK CHRIST AND OTHER POEMS. New York: Harper, 1929. 110 p.

THE MEDEA AND SOME POEMS. New York: Harper, 1935. 97 p.

THE LOST ZOO (A RHYME FOR THE YOUNG BUT NOT TOO YOUNG). By Christopher Cat and Countee Cullen. New York: Harper, 1940. 72 p.

ON THESE I STAND: AN ANTHOLOGY OF THE BEST POEMS OF COUNTEE CULLEN, SELECTED BY HIMSELF AND INCLUDING SIX NEW POEMS NEVER BEFORE PUBLISHED. New York: Harper, 1947. 197 p.

Biography and Criticism

Brawley NG; Davis FDT; Jackson BPA; Jahn NAL; Redding TMPB; Rollins FANP; Wagner BPUS; Whitlow BAL; Williams TAS; Young BW30s.

Baker, Houston A., Jr. A MANY-COLORED COAT OF DREAMS: THE PO-ETRY OF COUNTEE CULLEN. Detroit: Broadside, 1974. 60 p.

Bontemps, Arna. "Countee Cullen, American Poet." PEOPLE'S VOICE, 5 (26 Jan. 1946), 52-53.

Bronz, Stephen H. ROOTS OF NEGRO RACIAL CONSCIOUSNESS. New York: Libra, 1964. 101 p.

Canaday, Nicholas, Jr. "Major Themes in the Poetry of Countee Cullen." In THE HARLEM RENAISSANCE REMEMBERED. Ed. Arna Bontemps. New York: Dodd, Mead, 1972, pp. 103-26.

Daniel, Walter C. "Countee Cullen as Literary Critic." CLA JOURNAL, 14 (1971), 281-90.

Davis, Arthur P. "The Alien-and-Exile Theme in Countee Cullen's Racial Poems." PHYLON, 14 (1953), 390-400.

Dinger, Helen Josephine. "A Study of Countee Cullen." Master's thesis, Columbia University, 1953.

Dodson, Owen. "Countee Cullen (1903-1946)." PHYLON, 7 (1946), 19-21.

Dorsey, David F. "Countee Cullen's Use of Greek Mythology." CLA JOUR-NAL, 13 (1969), 68-77.

Ferguson, Blanche. COUNTEE CULLEN AND THE NEGRO RENAISSANCE. New York: Dodd, Mead, 1966. 213 p.

Huggins, Nathan Irvin. HARLEM RENAISSANCE. New York: Oxford Univ. Press, 1971. 343 p.

Lash, John S. "The Anthologist and the Negro Author." PHYLON, 8 (1947), 68-76.

Perry, Margaret. A BIO-BIBLIOGRAPHY OF COUNTEE P. CULLEN, 1903-1946. Westport, Conn.: Greenwood, 1971. 135 p.

Indispensable for reference; includes a fifty-five-page bibliography of works by and about Cullen.

Reimherr, Beulah. "Countee Cullen: A Biographical and Critical Study." Master's thesis, University of Maryland, 1960.

_____. "Race Consciousness in Countee Cullen's Poetry." SUSQUEHANNA UNIVERSITY STUDIES, 7 (1963), 65-82.

Smith, Robert A. "The Poetry of Countee Cullen." PHYLON, 11 (1950), 216-21.

Turner, Darwin T. "Countee Cullen: The Lost Ariel." In his IN A MINOR CHORD: THREE AFRO-AMERICAN WRITERS AND THEIR SEARCH FOR IDENTITY. Carbondale: Southern Illinois Univ. Press, 1971, pp. 60-88.

Webster, Harvey. "A Difficult Career." POETRY, 70 (1947), 220-25.

Woodruff, Bertram L. "The Poetic Philosophy of Countee Cullen." PHYLON, 1 (1940), 213-23.

CUTHBERT, MARION VERA

APRIL GRASSES. New York: Woman's Press, 1936. 30 p.

SONGS OF CREATION. New York: Woman's Press, 1949. 46 p.

> In Chapman IBP.

DANCER, WILLIAM E.

TODAY AND YISTIDAY: POEMS IN DIALECT. Tuskegee, Ala.: Tuskegee Institute, 1914.

FACTS, FUN AND FICTION. 4th ed. Jacksonville, Fla.: Published by the author, 1917.

DANDRIDGE, RAYMOND GARFIELD (1882-1930)

PENCILED POEMS. Cincinnati: Powell and White, Printers, 1917. 51 p.

> Fifty poems by a half-paralyzed poet, acclaimed by his local admirers as the "Paul Laurence Dunbar of Cincinnati." In Chapman IBP.

THE POET AND OTHER POEMS. Cincinnati: Powell and White, Printers, 1920. 64 p.

> Fifty-six poems; some are reprinted in ZALKA PEETRUZA (1928, below). In Chapman IBP.

ZALKA PEETRUZA AND OTHER POEMS. Introd. Calvin Dill Wilson. Cincinnati: McDonald Press, 1928. 107 p.

> Eighty-six poems, many in dialect, on a wide variety of subjects. In Chapman IBP.

DANGERFIELD, ABNER WALKER (1833-)

MUSINGS. Washington, D.C.: Triangle Printing Co., 1914. 39 p.

DAVIS, FRANK MARSHALL (1905-)

BLACK MAN'S VERSE. Chicago: Black Cat Press, 1935. 83 p.

I AM THE AMERICAN NEGRO. Chicago: Black Cat Press, 1937. 69 p.

THROUGH SEPIA EYES. Chicago: Black Cat Press, 1938. 10 p.

47TH STREET. Prairie City, Ill.: Press of James Decker, 1948. 105 p.

Biography and Criticism

Brawley NG; Brown NPD; Davis FDT; Jackson BPA; Wagner BPUS; Young BW30s.

Kloder, Helena. "The Film and Canvas of Frank Marshall Davis." CLA JOURNAL, 15 (1971), 59-63.

Randall, Dudley. "An Interview with Frank Marshall Davis." BLACK WORLD, 23 (Jan. 1974), 37-48.

DAVIS, STANFORD E.

PRICELESS JEWELS. New York: Knickerbocker Press, 1911. 138 p.

DEAS, KATHERINE

LIFE LINE POEMS. Chicago: Edward C. Deas, n.d. 32 p.

DETT, ROBERT NATHANIEL (1882-1943)

THE ALBUM OF A HEART. Jackson, Tenn.: Published by the author, 1911. 69 p.

DICKERSON, NOY JASPER

ORIGINAL POETRY. Bluefield, W. Va.: Published by the author, n.d. 33 p.

A SCRAP BOOK. Boston: Christopher, 1913. 48 p.

DINKINS, CHARLES ROUNDTREE

LYRICS OF LOVE. Introd. John W. Gilbert. Columbia, S.C.: State Co., 1904. 230 p.

DISMOND, BINGA (1891-1956)

WE WHO WOULD DIE AND OTHER POEMS. New York: W. Malliet, 1943. [93] p.

DOUGLASS, PRENTICE PERRY

LEAVES IN THE WIND. New York: Exposition, 1944. 62 p.

DUBOIS, WILLIAM EDWARD BURGHARDT (1868-1963)

DARKWATER: VOICES FROM WITHIN THE VEIL. New York: Harcourt, Brace and Howe, 1920. 276 p. Rpts. New York: Schocken Books, 1969; New York: AMS Press, 1969; the original ed. was also issued as DARKWATER: THE TWENTIETH CENTURY COMPLETION OF "UNCLE TOM'S CABIN." Washington, D.C.: Austin Jenkins, 1920. 276 p.

Prose essays, interspersed with eleven poems.

SELECTED POEMS. Foreword by Kwame Nkrumah, exposition by Shirley Graham. Accra: Ghana Universities Press, 1965. 42 p. Also in FREEDOMWAYS, 5 (Winter 1965), 88-102; and in BLACK TITAN: W.E.B. DUBOIS: AN ANTHOLOGY BY THE EDITORS OF FREEDOMWAYS. Boston: Beacon Press, 1970, pp. 286-303.

Eleven poems.

Bibliography

Aptheker, Herbert. ANNOTATED BIBLIOGRAPHY OF THE PUBLISHED WRIT-INGS OF W.E.B. DUBOIS. Millwood, N.Y.: Kraus-Thomson Organization, 1973. 626 p.

> See Aptheker's Subject Index, p. 625, "poetry [by DuBois]."

Biography and Criticism

Brown NPD; Redding TMPB.

Broderick, Francis L. W.E.B. DUBOIS: NEGRO LEADER IN A TIME OF CRISIS. Stanford, Calif.: Stanford Univ. Press, 1959. 259 p.

Clarke, John Henrik, Esther Jackson, Ernest Kaiser, and J.H. O'Dell, eds. BLACK TITAN: W.E.B. DUBOIS: AN ANTHOLOGY BY THE EDITORS OF FREEDOMWAYS. Boston: Beacon Press, 1970. 333 p.

> "This book is an extension of the special W.E.B. DuBois Memorial issue of FREEDOMWAYS magazine (Vol. 5, No. 1, Winter 1965)." Includes Ernest Kaiser's "A Selected Bibliography of the Published Writings of W.E.B. DuBois, pp. 309-30.

Graham, Shirley. HIS DAY IS MARCHING ON: A MEMOIR OF W.E.B. DUBOIS. Philadelphia: Lippincott, 1971. 384 p.

> The author is DuBois' widow.

Hamilton, Virginia. W.E.B. DUBOIS: A BIOGRAPHY. New York: Crowell, 1972. 218 p.

> For children.

Lacy, Leslie Alexander. CHEER THE LONESOME TRAVELER: THE LIFE OF W.E.B. DUBOIS. New York: Dial, 1970. 183 p.

Logan, Rayford W., ed. W.E.B. DUBOIS: A PROFILE. New York: Hill & Wang, 1971. 324 p.

Rudwick, Elliott M. W.E.B. DUBOIS: A STUDY IN MINORITY GROUP LEADERSHIP. Philadelphia: Univ. of Pennsylvania Press, 1970. 382 p. New ed. Published as W.E.B. DUBOIS: PROPAGANDIST OF THE NEGRO PROTEST. New York: Atheneum, 1968. 390 p.

Tuttle, William M., ed. W.E.B. DUBOIS. Englewood Cliffs, N.J.: Prentice-Hall, 1973. 186 p.

DUNGEE, JOHN RILEY (1860-)

RANDOM RHYMES. Norfolk, Va.: Guide Publishing Co., 1929. 101 p.

EASTMOND, CLAUDE T.

LIGHT AND SHADOWS. Boston: Christopher, 1934. 66 p.

EDWIN, WALTER LEWIS

SONGS IN THE DESERT. London: Frank Morland, 1909. 31 p.

EPPERSON, ALOISE BARBOUR

THE HILLS OF YESTERDAY AND OTHER POEMS. Introd. Fannie M. Jones. Washington: Printed by James Brown, 1944. 74 p.

UNTO MY HEART AND OTHER POEMS. Boston: Christopher, 1953. 201 p.

FERNANDIS, SARAH COLLINS (1863-)

VISION. Boston: Gorham, 1925.

FIELDS, MAURICE C. (1915-38)

THE COLLECTED POEMS OF MAURICE C. FIELDS. New York: Exposition, 1940. 64 p.

TESTAMENT OF YOUTH. New York: Pegasus, 1940. 32 p.

FIGGS, CARRIE LAW MORGAN

POETIC PEARLS. Jacksonville, Fla.: Edward Waters College Press, 1920. 32 p.

NUGGETS OF GOLD. Chicago: Jaxon Printing Co., 1921. 31 p.

FISHER, GERTRUDE ARQUENE

ORIGINAL POEMS. Parsons, Kans.: Foley Railway Printing Co., 1910. 11 p.

FLANAGAN, THOMAS JEFFERSON (1890-)

THE HARVEST HYMN. Atlanta: Published by the author, n.d. 12 p.

BY THE PINE KNOT TORCHES. Atlanta: Dicker Co., 1921. 64 p.

THE ROAD OF MOUNT McKEITHAN. Atlanta: Independent Publishers Corp., 1927. 46 p.

SMILIN' THROUGH THE CORN, AND OTHER VERSE. Atlanta: Independent Publishers Corp., 1927. 63 p.

THE CANYONS AT PROVIDENCE (THE LAY OF THE CLAY MINSTREL). Atlanta: Morris Brown College Press, 1940. 21 p.

FLEMING, SARAH LEE BROWN

CLOUDS AND SUNSHINE. Boston: Cornhill Co., 1920. 53 p.

FORD, NICK AARON (1904-)

SONGS FROM THE DARK. Boston: Meador, 1940. 40 p.
> In Chapman IBP.

FORD, ROBERT EDGAR

BROWN CHAPEL: A STORY IN VERSE. Baltimore: Published by the author, 1905. 307 p.

FORTSON, BETTIOLA HELOISE (1890-)

MENTAL PEARLS: ORIGINAL POEMS AND ESSAYS. Chicago: Published by the author, 1915. 62 p.

FORTUNE, TIMOTHY THOMAS (1856-1928)

DREAMS OF LIFE. New York: Fortune and Peterson, 1905. 192 p.

FULTON, DAVID BRYANT (1863-)

MOTHER OF MINE: ODE TO THE NEGRO WOMAN. New York: August V. Bernier, 1923. 10 p.

GAIRY, RICHARDSON A.

THE POET'S VISION, AND THE NOBLEST STRUGGLE. New York: New York Age Publishing Co., 1909. 38 p.

Two poems.

GARDNER, BENJAMIN FRANKLIN (1900-)

BLACK. Introd. Glen Perrins. Caldwell, Idaho: Caxton Printers, 1933. 79 p.

GARVEY, MARCUS (1887-1940, born in Jamaica, West Indies)

SELECTIONS FROM THE POETIC MEDITATIONS OF MARCUS GARVEY. New York: Amy Jacques Garvey, 1927. 30 p.

THE TRAGEDY OF WHITE INJUSTICE. New York: Amy Jacques Garvey, 1927. 22 p. Rpt. New York: Haskell House, 1969.

GHOLSON, EDWARD (1889-)

MUSINGS OF A MINISTER. Boston: Christopher, 1943. 101 p.

GIBSON, POWELL WILLARD (1875-)

GRAVE AND COMIC RHYMES. Alexandria, Va.: Murray Bros., Printers, 1904. [46] p.

AIDA. Winchester, Va.: Published by the author, [1929?]. 5 p.

GILBERT, MERCEDES (?-1952)

SELECTED GEMS OF POETRY, COMEDY AND DRAMA. Boston: Christopher, 1931. 89 p.

First thirty-nine pages are poetry.

GILMORE, F. GRANT

MASONIC AND OTHER POEMS. N.p.: Published by the author, 1908. 20 p.

"PRINCE HALL." "THE CANDIDATE." "SIGN OF DISTRESS . . . ." N.p.: [Published by the author?], 1918. [18] p.

GIMENEZ, JOSEPH PATRICK (Born in St. Thomas, Virgin Islands)

VIRGIN ISLANDS FOLKLORE AND OTHER POEMS. New York: Harding, 1933. 100 p.

CARIBBEAN ECHOES. New York: Galleon Press, 1934. 62 p.

DEEP WATERS. St. Thomas, V.I.: Art Shop, 1939. 72 p.

VOICE OF THE VIRGIN ISLANDS. Philadelphia: Dorrance, 1952. 50 p.

GOODWIN, RUBY BERKLEY (1903-)

FROM MY KITCHEN WINDOW. Introd. Margaret Widdemer. New York: Wendell Malliet, 1942. 66 p.

A GOLD STAR MOTHER SPEAKS. Fullerton, Calif.: Orange County Printing Co., 1944. [17] p.

Biography and Criticism

Goodwin, Ruby Berkley. ITS GOOD TO BE BLACK. New York: Doubleday, 1953. 256 p.

Ruby Goodwin's autobiography.

GORDON, SELMA

POEMS. No imprint. 19 p.

SPECIAL POEMS. No imprint. 19 p.

GOVERN, RENA GREENLEE

DEMOCRACY'S TASK. New York: Published by the author, 1945. 36 p.

GRAVES, LINWOOD D.

POEMS OF SIMPLICITY AND THE LIVING DEAD, A SHORT TRUE STORY. Kingsport, Tenn.: Kingsport Press, 1938. 116 p.

MOTHER; ALSO "THE HIDDEN FLOWER." No imprint.

GUYTON, MATILDA

THE BLACK WOMAN. Cleveland: Published by the author, 1939. 35 p.

HANDY, OLIVE LEWIS

MY DEEPLY SOLEMN THOUGHTS. N.p.: 1939. 35 p.

HANDY, WILLIAM HENRY (1852-)

TRUTHS IN RHYME, AND MISCELLANEOUS PROSE COMPOSITIONS. New York: Caxton Press, 1928. 66 p.

HARLESTON, EDWARD NATHANIEL (1869-)

THE TOILER'S LIFE. Introd. L.S. Crandall. Philadelphia: Jenson Press, 1907. 238 p.

HARRIS, HELEN C., LUCIA MAE PITTS, and TOMI CAROLYN TINSLEY

TRIAD. Washington, D.C.: Plymouth Press, 1945. 95 p.

HARRIS, LEON R. (1886-)

THE STEEL MAKERS AND OTHER WAR POEMS . . . NUMBER ONE. Portsmouth, Ohio: T.C. McConnell Printery, 1918. 15 p.

LOCOMOTIVE PUFFS FROM THE BACK SHOP. Boston: Bruce Humphries, 1946. 56 p.

HARRISON, JAMES MINNIS (1873-)

SOUTHERN SUNBEAMS. Richmond, Va.: Saint Luke Press, 1926. 100 p.

HART, ESTELLE PUGSLEY

THOUGHTS IN POETRY. New York: Tobias Press, 1911. 143 p.

HATCHETTE, WILFRED IRWIN (Born in St. Thomas, Virgin Islands)

YOUTH'S FLIGHT. St. Thomas, V.I.: Art Shop Press, 1938. 38 p.

BLOOD, SWEAT AND TEARS. Wauwotosa, Wis.: Kenyon Press, 1947. 93 p.

HAWKINS, WALTER EVERETTE (1886-)

CHORDS AND DISCORDS. Washington, D.C.: Murray Brothers Press, 1909. New ed. Boston: R.G. Badger, 1920. 100 p.

PETALS FROM THE POPPIES. New York: Fortuny's, 1936.

Biography and Criticism

Brown NPD.

HAYDEN, ROBERT E. See section for 1946-75, below.

HAYSON, MAXWELL NICY

SAMUEL COLERIDGE-TAYLOR: AN ODE OF WELCOME. Washington, D.C.: Published by the author, 1906. 10 p.

HENDERSON, ELLIOT BLAINE (1877-1944)

PLANTATION ECHOES: A COLLECTION OF ORIGINAL NEGRO DIALECT POEMS. Introd. E.G. Burkram. Columbus, Ohio: Press of F.J. Heer, 1904. 95 p.

THE SOLILOQUY OF SATAN AND OTHER POEMS. Springfield, Ohio: Published by the author, 1907. 64 p.

"DIS, DAT AN' TUTTER." Springfield, Ohio: Published by the author, 1908. 51 p.

HUMBLE FOLKS. Introd. E.G. Burkram. Springfield, Ohio: Published by the author, 1909. 65 p.

DARKY MEDITATIONS. Springfield, Ohio: Published by the author, 1910. 68 p.

UNEDDEEKAYTED FO'KS. Springfield, Ohio: Published by the author, 1911. 61 p.

JES' PLAIN BLACK FO'KS. Springfield, Ohio: Published by the author, [1912?]. 51 p.

OLD FASHIONED BLACK FO'KS. Columbus, Ohio: Published by the author, 1913. 54 p.

DARKEY [sic] DITTIES. Columbus, Ohio: Published by the author, 1915. 54 p.

POLISHED AND UNPOLISHED DIAMONDS: THE NEGRO. No imprint. [191-?]. [20] p.

HENDERSON, GEORGE S.

POETICAL REPORTS OF LIFE. New York: Printed for the author, Gunther Press, 1938. 136 p.

HENDERSON, S.S.

RELIGIOUS POETRY AND CHRISTIAN THOUGHT. Newark, N.J.: J.M. Stoute, Printer, 1920. 96 p.

HENRY, THOMAS MILLARD

THE OPTIMIST. New York: Hebbons Press, 1928. 49 p.

HILL, JOHN CALHOUN

PICCOLO. Vol. 1. Meridian, Miss.: Tell Framer, Printer, [19-?]. 140 p.

HILL, JULIOUS C.

A SOONER SONG. New York: Empire Books, 1935. 63 p.

A SONG OF MAGNOLIA. Boston: Meador Publishing Co., 1937. 88 p.

HILL, LESLIE PINCKNEY (1880-1960)

THE WINGS OF OPPRESSION AND OTHER POEMS. Boston: Stratford Co., 1921. 124 p.

TOUSSAINT LOUVERTURE, A DRAMATIC HISTORY. Boston: Christopher, 1928. 137 p.

HILL, MILDRED MARTIN

A TRAIPSIN' HEART. New York: Wendell Malliet, 1942. 61 p.

HILL, VALDEMAR A. (Born in St. Thomas, Virgin Islands)

RIPPLES. St. Thomas, V.I.: Art Shop, 1935. 33 p.

HOLDER, JAMES ELLIOTT

BALLAD, A CHRISTMAS INCIDENT. No imprint. [1905?]. 7 p.

THE COLORED MAN'S APPEAL TO WHITE AMERICANS. Atlantic City, N.J.: Published by the author, 1906. [8] p.

HOLLOWAY, JOHN WESLEY (1865-1935)

BANDANAS. No imprint. 119 p.

FROM THE DESERT. Introd. H.H. Proctor. New York: Neale Publishing Co., 1919. 147 p.

HOLMES, B.L.

TWILIGHT REFLECTIONS. Edgefield, S.C.: n.p., 1942. 54 p.

THE IDOL HOUR. Edgefield, S.C.: n.p., n.d. 47 p.

HOWARD, ALICE HENRIETTA

ONION TO ORCHARD. New York: William-Frederick Press, 1945. 32 p.

HUGHES, LANGSTON (1902-67)

THE WEARY BLUES. Introd. Carl van Vechten. New York: Knopf, 1926. 109 p.
    In Chapman IBP.

FINE CLOTHES TO THE JEW. New York: Knopf, 1927. 89 p.
    In Chapman IBP.

DEAR LOVELY DEATH. Amenia, N.Y.: Troutbeck Press, 1931. [16] p.

Limited edition of 100 signed copies.

THE NEGRO MOTHER AND OTHER DRAMATIC RECITATIONS. New York: Golden Stair Press, 1931. 20 p.

THE DREAM KEEPER AND OTHER POEMS. New York: Knopf, 1932. 77 p.

SCOTTSBORO LIMITED: FOUR POEMS AND A PLAY IN VERSE. New York: Golden Stair Press, 1932. [18] p.

A NEW SONG. Introd. Michael Gold. New York: International Workers Order, 1938. 31 p.

Includes "Song of Spain," published in DEUX POEMES par Federico Garcia Lorca et Langston Hughes (N.p.: Nancy Cunard and Pablo Neruda, 1937). [8] p.

SHAKESPEARE IN HARLEM. New York: Knopf, 1942. 124 p.

In Chapman IBP.

FREEDOM'S PLOW. New York: Musette Publishers, 1943. 14 p.

JIM CROW'S LAST STAND. Atlanta: Negro Publication Society of America, 1943. 30 p.

LAMENT FOR DARK PEOPLES AND OTHER POEMS. Ed. and Introd. H. Driessen. Amsterdam: H. van Krimpen, 1944. 48 p.

FIELDS OF WONDER. New York: Knopf, 1947. 114 p.

In Chapman IBP.

ONE-WAY TICKET. New York: Knopf, 1949. 136 p.

In Chapman IBP.

MONTAGE OF A DREAM DEFERRED. New York: Henry Holt, 1951. 75 p.

THE LANGSTON HUGHES READER. New York: George Braziller, 1958. 501 p.

Poetry and prose.

SELECTED POEMS OF LANGSTON HUGHES. New York: Knopf, 1959. 297 p.

Contains 198 poems in thirteen sections.

ASK YOUR MAMA: 12 MOODS FOR JAZZ. New York: Knopf, 1961. 92 p.

THE PANTHER AND THE LASH: POEMS OF OUR TIMES. New York: Knopf, 1967. 191 p.

In Chapman IBP.

DON'T YOU TURN BACK. New York: Knopf, 1969. 78 p.

In Chapman IBP.

GOOD MORNING REVOLUTION: UNCOLLECTED SOCIAL PROTEST WRITINGS. Ed. Faith Berry. New York: Lawrence Hill, 1973. 145 p.

Poetry and prose.

Bibliographies

Babb, Inez Johnson. "Bibliography of Langston Hughes, Negro Poet." Master's thesis, Pratt Institute Library School, 1947.

Dickinson, Donald C. A BIO-BIBLIOGRAPHY OF LANGSTON HUGHES, 1902-1967. Hamden, Conn.: Archon Books, 1967. 267 p. Rev. ed. Hamden, Conn.: Shoestring Press, 1972.

Kaiser, Ernest. "Selected Bibliography of the Published Writings of Langston Hughes." FREEDOMWAYS, 8 (1968), 185-91.

Mandelik, Peter, and Stanley Schatt. A CONCORDANCE TO THE POETRY OF LANGSTON HUGHES. Detroit: Gale Research Co., 1975. 296 p.

Using the most recent appearance of a poem as the standard edition, "An Index to Poem Titles," pp. xiii-xv, lists 572 poems, with each located in one of fifteen of Hughes's books.

O'Daniel, Therman B. "Langston Hughes: A Selected Classified Bibliography." In LANGSTON HUGHES, BLACK GENIUS: A CRITICAL EVALUATION. Ed. Therman B. O'Daniel. New York: Morrow, 1971, pp. 211-41.

Section 26, pp. 227-39, lists almost 200 books and articles about Hughes.

Tate, Allen. "Langston Hughes, 1902--." In his SIXTY AMERICAN POETS. Rev. ed. Washington, D.C.: Library of Congress, 1954, pp. 52-55.

Woodress, James. "(James) Langston Hughes (1902-1967)." In his AMERICAN

FICTION, 1900-1950: A GUIDE TO INFORMATION SOURCES. Detroit: Gale Research Co., 1974, pp. 131-33.

Biography and Criticism

Brawley NG; Brown NPD; Davis FDT; Gibson MBP; Jackson BPA; Jahn NAL; Redding TMPB; Rollins FANP; Wagner BPUS; Whitlow BAL; Williams TAS; Young BW30s.

Bontemps, Arna. "Langston Hughes: He Spoke of Rivers." FREEDOMWAYS, 8 (1968), 140-43.

Carmen, Y. "Langston Hughes: Poet of the People." INTERNATIONAL LITERATURE, No. 1 (1939), pp. 192-94.

Carrington, Glenn. "The Harlem Renaissance--A Personal Memoir." FREEDOMWAYS, 3 (1963), 307-11.

Davis, Arthur P. "The Harlem of Langston Hughes' Poetry." PHYLON, 13 (1952), 276-83. Also in IMAGES OF THE NEGRO IN AMERICAN LITERATURE. Ed. Seymour Gross and John Hardy. Chicago: Univ. of Chicago Press, 1966, pp. 194-203.

Emanuel, James. "Christ in Alabama: Religion in the Poetry of Langston Hughes." In Gibson MBP, pp. 57-68.

_____. LANGSTON HUGHES. New York: Twayne, 1967. 192 p.

Farrison, W. Edward. "Langston Hughes, Poet of the Negro Renaissance." CLA JOURNAL, 15 (1972), 401-10.

Garber, E.D. "Form as a Complement to Content in Three of Langston Hughes' Poems." NEGRO AMERICAN LITERATURE FORUM, 5 (1971), 137-39.

Holmes, Eugene C. "Langston Hughes: Philosopher Poet." FREEDOMWAYS, 8 (1968), 144-51.

"Hommage a Langston Hughes." PRESENCE AFRICAINE. N.s., No. 64 (1967), pp. 33-58.

Hudson, Theodore R. "Technical Aspects of the Poetry of Langston Hughes." BLACK WORLD, 22 (Sept. 1973), 24-45.

Hughes, Langston. THE BIG SEA: AN AUTOBIOGRAPHY. New York: Knopf, 1940. 335 p.

_____. I WONDER AS I WANDER: AN AUTOBIOGRAPHICAL JOURNEY. New York: Rinehart, 1956. 405 p.

Isaacs, Harold R. "Five Writers and Their African Ancestors." PHYLON, 21 (1960), 247-54. Also in his THE NEW WORLD OF NEGRO AMERICANS. New York: John Day, 1963, pp. 231-87.

Jemie, Onwuchekwa. LANGSTON HUGHES: AN INTRODUCTION TO THE POETRY. New York: Columbia Univ. Press, 1976. 234 p.

Kent, George E. "Langston Hughes and Afro-American Folk and cultural Tradition." In his BLACKNESS AND THE ADVENTURE OF WESTERN CULTURE. Chicago: Third World, 1972, pp. 53-75.

Kramer, Aaron. "Robert Burns and Langston Hughes." FREEDOMWAYS, 8 (1968), 159-66.

Meltzer, Milton. LANGSTON HUGHES: A BIOGRAPHY. New York: Crowell, 1968. 281 p.

For young readers.

Myers, Elisabeth P. LANGSTON HUGHES: POET OF HIS PEOPLE. Champaign, Ill.: Garrard, 1970. 144 p.

For children.

O'Daniel, Therman B., ed. LANGSTON HUGHES, BLACK GENIUS: A CRITICAL EVALUATION. New York: Morrow, 1971. 245 p.

Piquion, Rene. LANGSTON HUGHES: UN CHANT NOUVEAU. Introd. Arna Bontemps. Port-au-Prince, Haiti: Imprimerie de l'Etat, 1940. 159 p.

Prowle, Allen D. "Langston Hughes." In Bigsby BAW2, pp. 77-87.

Rive, Richard. "Taos in Harlem: Interview with Langston Hughes." CONTRAST, 14 (1967), 33-39.

Rollins, Charlemae. BLACK TROUBADOUR: LANGSTON HUGHES. Chicago: Rand McNally and Co., 1970. 143 p.

For children.

Taylor, Patricia. "Langston Hughes and the Harlem Renaissance." In THE HARLEM RENAISSANCE REMEMBERED. Ed. Arna Bontemps. New York: Dodd, Mead, 1972, pp. 90-102.

Wagner, Jean. "Langston Hughes." INFORMATIONS ET DOCUMENTS, No. 135 (15 Jan. 1961), pp. 30-35.

Waldron, Edward E. "The Blues Poetry of Langston Hughes." NEGRO AMERICAN LITERATURE FORUM, 5 (1971), 140-49.

Walker, Alice. LANGSTON HUGHES, AMERICAN POET. New York: Crowell, 1974.

    For children.

JACKSON, LAURA F.

PARADISE (CLEVELAND PARK) AND OTHER POEMS. Washington, D.C.: R.L. Pendleton, Printer, 1920. [16] p.

JAMISON, ROSCOE CONKLIN (1888-1918)

NEGRO SOLDIERS ("THESE TRULY ARE THE BRAVE") AND OTHER POEMS. South St. Joseph, Mo.: William McNeil, 1918. [16] p. 2nd ed. Kansas City, Kans.: Gray Printing Co., 1918. [16] p.

    Published posthumously by Charles Bertram Johnson.

JARVIS, JOSE ANTONIO (1901- , born in St. Thomas, Virgin Islands)

FRUITS IN PASSING. St. Thomas, V.I.: Art Shop, 1932. 99 p.

BAMBOULA DANCE AND OTHER POEMS. St. Thomas, V.I.: Art Shop, 1935. 57 p.

BLUEBEARD'S LAST WIFE. Charlotte Amalie, St. Thomas, V.I.: Published by the author, 1951. 26 p.

JEFFERSON, WILSON JAMES (1879-)

VERSES. Boston: R.G. Badger, 1909. 32 p.

BLACK ANNALS. Philadelphia: Published by the author, 1929. 8 p.

JENKINS, WELBORN VICTOR (1879-)

TRUMPET IN THE NEW MOON AND OTHER POEMS. Introd. E.H. Webster. Boston: Peabody Press, 1934. 62 p.

THE "INCIDENT" AT MONROE: A REQUIEM FOR THE VICTIMS OF JULY 25TH, 1946. Written at the scene of the tragedy. Atlanta: Printed by Robinson Printing Co.: Published by United Negro Youth of America for the Malcolm–Dorsey Memorial Committee, 1948. 46 p.

JENKINS, WILLIAM H.

BLOSSOMS. Princess Anne, Md.: Princess Anne Academy Press, [192?]. 35 p.

JETER, G. TROY

THE VOLGA WHISPERS. N.p.: n.p., 1936. 46 p.

JOHNSON, ADOLPHUS

THE SILVER CHORD. Philadelphia: Published by the author, [1915?]. 48 p.

JOHNSON, CHARLES BERTRAM (1880-)

WIND WHISPERINGS. No imprints. [1900?].

THE MANTLE OF DUNBAR AND OTHER POEMS. No imprint. [1918?]. 32 p.

SONGS OF MY PEOPLE. Boston: Cornhill, 1918. 55 p.

 In Chapman IBP.

JOHNSON, EMMA MAE DORA

POEMS. Introd. J.W. Scott and Alice Moore Dunbar. Huntington, W. Va.: Published by the author, 1914. 20 p.

JOHNSON, FENTON (1888-1958)

A LITTLE DREAMING. Chicago: Peterson Linotyping Co., 1913. 80 p.

VISIONS OF THE DUSK. New York: Published by the author, 1915. 71 p.

SONGS OF THE SOIL. New York: Published by the author, 1916. 39 p.

Biography and Criticism

Brawley NG; Brown NPD; Redding TMPB; Wagner BPUS.

JOHNSON, FRANK A. (1905-32)

FIRESIDE POEMS. New York: Standard Printing Co., 1931. 37 p. Rev. memorial ed., comp. and ed. Sarah L. Johnson Swint. Foreword by A.C. Powell, Sr. New York: Printed by Theo Gaus's Sons, 1953. 47 p.

JOHNSON, GEORGIA DOUGLAS (1886-1966)

THE HEART OF A WOMAN AND OTHER POEMS. Introd. William Stanley Braithwaite. Boston: Cornhill, 1918. 62 p.

> In Chapman IBP.

BRONZE. Introd. W.E.B. DuBois. Boston: B.J. Brimmer, 1922. 101 p.

AN AUTUMN LOVE CYCLE. Introd. Alain Locke. New York: Harold Vinal, 1928. 70 p.

SHARE MY WORLD. Washington, D.C.: Published by the author, 1962. 32 p.

Biography and Criticism

Brawley NG.

Dover, Cedric. "The Importance of Georgia Douglas Johnson." CRISIS, 59 (1952), 633-36, 674.

JOHNSON, HENRY THEODORE (1857-1910)

WINGS OF EBONY. Philadelphia: A.M.E. Book Concern, 1904. 51 p.

JOHNSON, HERBERT CLARK (1911-)

POEMS FROM FLAT CREEK. Francestown, N.H.: Marshall Jones Co., 1943. 64 p.

JOHNSON, JAMES WELDON (1871-1938)

FIFTY YEARS, A POEM. Atlanta: Atlanta Univ. Press, [1913?]. 8 p.

FIFTY YEARS AND OTHER POEMS. Introd. Brander Matthews. Boston: Cornhill, 1917. 92 p.

> In Chapman IBP.

GOD'S TROMBONES: SEVEN NEGRO SERMONS IN VERSE. New York: Viking, 1927. 56 p.

In Chapman IBP.

SAINT PETER RELATES AN INCIDENT OF THE RESURRECTION DAY. New York: Viking, 1930. 14 p.

Limited edition of 200 signed copies.

SAINT PETER RELATES AN INCIDENT: SELECTED POEMS. New York: Viking, 1935. 105 p.

Biography and Criticism

Brawley NG; Brown NPD; Davis FDT; Jackson BPA; Jahn NAL; Redding TMPB; Rollins FANP; Wagner BPUS; Whitlow BAL; Williams TAS.

Auslander, Joseph. "Sermon Sagas." OPPORTUNITY 5, (1927), 274-75.

Baxter, Harvey L. "James Weldon Johnson." CRISIS, 45 (1938), 291.

Bronze, Stephen. ROOTS OF NEGRO RACIAL CONSCIOUSNESS. New York: Libra, 1964, pp. 18-46.

Carroll, R.A. "Black Racial Spirit: An Analysis of James Weldon Johnson's Critical Perspective." PHYLON, 32 (1971), 365-73.

Collier, Eugenia. "James Weldon Johnson, Mirror of Change." PHYLON, 21 (1960), 351-59.

Copeland, George Edward. "James Weldon Johnson: A Bibliography." M.A. thesis, Pratt Institute, Brooklyn, N.Y., 1951.

Egypt, Ophelia Settle. JAMES WELDON JOHNSON. New York: Crowell, 1974. 40 p.

A biography for children.

Felton, Harold W. JAMES WELDON JOHNSON. N.Y.: Dodd, Mead, 1972. 91 p.

A biography for children.

Fullinwider, S.P. THE MIND AND MOOD OF BLACK AMERICA: 20TH CENTURY THOUGHT. Homewood, Ill.: Dorsey Press, 1969, pp. 85-92.

JAMES WELDON JOHNSON. Nashville, Tenn.: Department of Publicity, Fisk Univ., [1914?]. [35] p.

Johnson, James Weldon. ALONG THIS WAY. New York: Viking, 1933. 418 p.

    Autobiography.

Levy, Eugene. JAMES WELDON JOHNSON, BLACK LEADER, BLACK VOICE. Chicago: Univ. of Chicago Press, 1973. 288 p.

Tarry, Ellen. YOUNG JIM: THE EARLY YEARS OF JAMES WELDON JOHNSON. New York: Dodd, Mead, 1967. 230 p.

    For young readers.

Tate, Allen. "James Weldon Johnson 1871-1938." In his SIXTY AMERICAN POETS. Rev. ed. Washington, D.C.: Library of Congress, 1954, pp. 59-61.

    A detailed bibliographical listing of Johnson's books and pamphlets; GOD'S TROMBONES is described as "perhaps the highest imaginative achievement of Negro literature in our time."

Tate, Ernest C. "Sentiment and Horse Sense: James Weldon Johnson's Style." NEGRO HISTORY BULLETIN, 25 (1962), 152-54.

_____. THE SOCIAL IMPLICATIONS OF THE WRITINGS AND THE CAREER OF JAMES WELDON JOHNSON. New York: American Press, 1968. 186 p.

JOHNSON, JESSIE DAVIS

CHRISTMAS POEMS. Washington, D.C.: Published by the author, 1937. 12 p.

JOHNSON, MAGGIE POGUE

VIRGINIA DREAMS: LYRICS FOR THE IDLE HOUR. TALES OF THE TIME TOLD IN RHYME. N.p.: John Leonard, 1910. 64 p.

THOUGHTS FOR IDLE HOURS. Roanoke, Va.: Stone Printing and Mfg. Co., 1915. 55 p.

FALLEN BLOSSOMS. [Parkersburg?], W. Va.: n.p., 1951. 151 p.

JONES, ANNA ARMSTRONG

A MOTHER'S MUSINGS. Edwardsville, Ill.: Published by the author, 1933. [11] p.

JONES, CHARLES PRICE (1865-1949)

AN APPEAL TO THE SONS OF AFRICA: A NUMBER OF POEMS, READINGS, ORATIONS AND LECTURES DESIGNED ESPECIALLY TO INSPIRE YOUTH OF AFRICAN BLOOD WITH SENTIMENTS OF HOPE AND TRUE NOBILITY AS WELL AS TO ENTERTAIN AND INSTRUCT ALL CLASSES OF READERS AND LOVERS OF REDEEMED HUMANITY. Jackson, Miss.: Truth Publishing Co., 1902. 131 p.

JONES, EDWARD SMYTH (1881-)

SOUVENIR POEM: OUR GREATER LOUISVILLE. Louisville, Ky.: Published by the author, 1908. [8] p.

THE ROSE THAT BLOOMETH IN MY HEART AND OTHER POEMS. By Invincible Nad. Louisville, Ky.: [Published by the author], 1908. 53 p.

THE SYLVAN CABIN: A CENTENARY ODE ON THE BIRTH OF LINCOLN: AND OTHER VERSE. Introd. William Stanley Braithwaite. Boston: Sherman, French, 1911. 96 p.

JONES, HAROLD R.

BROADWAY AND OTHER POEMS. No imprint. 59 p.

JONES, JOSHUA HENRY, JR. (1876-)

THE HEART OF THE WORLD AND OTHER POEMS. Boston: Stratford, 1919. 83 p.

POEMS OF THE FOUR SEAS. Boston: Cornhill, 1921. 52 p.

JONES, YORKE (1860-)

GOLD AND INCENSE. Fort Wayne, Ind.: Glad Tidings, 1925.

KING, JEFFERSON

DARKY PHILOSOPHY TOLD IN RHYME. Chicago: Smith Jubilee Music Co., 1906. 61 p.

KIRTON, ST. CLAIR

POETIC CREATIONS. Boston: Lester Benn, 1943. 36 p.

KNOX, JACQUELINE LLOYD

BITTERSWEETS. Philadelphia: Dorrance, 1938. 50 p.

KNOX, JEAN LINDSAY

A KEY TO BROTHERHOOD. New York: Paebar, 1932. [24] p.

LAINE, HENRY ALLEN (1870-)

FOOT PRINTS. Richmond, Ky.: Cut Rate Printing Co., 1914. 54 p. New ed. Richmond, Ky.: Daily Register Press, 1924. 80 p. Published as FOOT-PRINTS: New York: Hobson Book Press, 1947. 144 p.

Poetry and prose.

LATIMER, LEWIS HOWARD (1848-1929)

POEMS OF LOVE AND LIFE. Published by his friends and advisers, 1925. [22] p.

LA VAN, MAUDE PEARL

COLORED BOYS IN KHAKI. N.p.: Cosmo-Advocate Publishing Co., 1918. 13 p.

LEE, ERICA B. (Born in St. Thomas, Virgin Islands)

REFLECTIONS. San Juan, Puerto Rico: Padilla Printing Works, 1939. 50 p.

LEE, FRANCIS COLE (1883-)

FAITH OF OUR FATHERS. 2nd ed. Alpine, Colo.: Handset by Sand Dune Sage, 1939. [10] p.

OPAL DUST.

LEE, JOHN FRANCIS (1873-1930)

POEMS. Norfolk, Va.: Burk and Gregory, Printers, 1905. 54 p.

THE PRINCE IN EBONY. N.p.: n.p., 1907. 112 p.

LEVY, FERDINAND NORTHCUT CONSTANTINE

FLASHES FROM THE DARK. Dublin, Ireland: Printed at the Sign of the Three Candles, 1941. 45 p.

LINDEN, CHARLOTTE E. (1859-)

SCRAPS OF TIME. Springfield, Ohio: Published by the author, n.d. 16 p.

AUTOBIOGRAPHY AND POEMS. 3rd ed. Springfield, Ohio: Published by the author, [1907?]. 64 p.
> Cover title: SCRAPS OF TIME.

LONG, NAOMI C. See MADGETT, NAOMI L., in section for 1946–75, below.

LOVE, ROSE LEARY

NEBRASKA AND HIS GRANNY. Tuskegee, Ala.: Tuskegee Institute Press, 1936. 69 p.

LYNCH, CHARLES ANTHONY (1890-)

GLADYS KLYNE AND MORE HARMONY. Boston: Gorham Press, 1915. 75 p.

LYNN, EVE. See section for 1946–75 below.

McBROWN, GERTRUDE PARTHENIA

THE PICTURE-POETRY-BOOK. Washington, D.C.: Associated Publishers, 1935. 73 p.
> For children.

McCLELLAN, GEORGE MARION. See section for 1760–1900, above.

McCORKLE, GEORGE WASHINGTON

POEMS OF THOUGHT AND CHEER. Petersburg, Va.: N.p., n.d. 16 p. Washington, D.C.: National Bureau of Negro Writers and Entertainers, n.d. 21 p.

POEMS OF PERPETUAL MEMORY. No imprint. 35 p.

POEMS OF PERPETUAL MEMORY AND . . . RHYMES FROM THE DELTA.
High Point, N.C.: Published by the author, n.d. 119 p.

RHYMES FROM THE DELTA. 2nd ed., rev. High Point, N.C.: Published by
the author, 1948. 155 p.

McDONALD, SAMUEL E.

THE OTHER GIRL, WITH SOME FURTHER STORIES AND POEMS. New York:
Broadway Publishing Co., 1903. 79 p.

McGEE, PERRY HONCE

MY VALUED RUBY. Washington, Pa.: Published by the author, 1920. 90 p.

McKANE, ALICE WOODBY (1865-)

CLOVER LEAVES. Boston: Still and Still, 1914. 32 p.

McKAY, CLAUDE (1890-1948, born in Jamaica, West Indies)

SONGS OF JAMAICA. Kingston, Jamaica: Aston W. Gardner, 1912. 140 p.
>   Reprinted in THE DIALECT POETRY OF CLAUDE McKAY (1972,
>   see below).

SONGS FROM JAMAICA. London: Augener, 1912. 11 p.
>   Six poems set to music.

CONSTAB BALLADS. London: Watts & Co., 1912. 94 p.
>   Reprinted in THE DIALECT POETRY OF CLAUDE McKAY (1972,
>   see below).

SPRING IN NEW HAMPSHIRE AND OTHER POEMS. Introd. I.A. Richards.
London: Grant Richards, 1920. 40 p.

HARLEM SHADOWS. Introd. Max Eastman. New York: Harcourt, Brace,
1922. 95 p.
>   In Chapman IBP.

SELECTED POEMS. Introd. John Dewey; biographical note by Max Eastman.

New York: Bookman Associates, 1953. 112 p. Rpt. New York: Harcourt, Brace, 1969.

> In Chapman IBP.

THE DIALECT POETRY OF CLAUDE McKAY. Freeport, N.Y.: Books for Libraries, 1972.

> Reprints SONGS OF JAMAICA and CONSTAB BALLADS (both cited above).

THE PASSION OF CLAUDE McKAY: SELECTED POETRY AND PROSE, 1912-1948. Ed. Wayne F. Cooper. New York: Schocken, 1973. 363 p.

> Includes twenty-six poems, important letters and articles, and a ten-page bibliography.

Biography and Criticism

Davis FDT; Jackson BPA; Jahn NAL; Redding TMPB; Wagner BPUS; Whitlow BAL.

Bronz, Stephen. ROOTS OF NEGRO RACIAL CONSCIOUSNESS. New York: Libra, 1964, pp. 69-89.

Collier, Eugenia. "The Four-Way Dilemma of Claude McKay." CLA JOURNAL, 15 (1972), 345-53.

Conroy, Mary. "The Vagabond Motif in the Writings of Claude McKay." NEGRO AMERICAN LITERATURE FORUM, 5 (1971), 15-23.

Cooper, Wayne. "Claude McKay and the New Negro of the 1920's." PHYLON, 25 (1964), 297-306. Also in Bigsby BAW2, pp. 53-67.

Drayton, Arthur D. "McKay's Human Pity: A Note on His Protest Poetry." BLACK ORPHEUS (Ibadan), No. 17 (June 1965), pp. 39-48. Also in INTRODUCTION TO AFRICAN LITERATURE. Ed. Ulli Beier. London: Longmans, 1967, pp. 76-88.

Gayle, Addison, Jr. CLAUDE McKAY: THE BLACK POET AT WAR. Detroit: Broadside, 1972. 46 p.

Jackson, Blyden. "The Essential McKay." PHYLON, 14 (1953), 216-17.

Kent, George E. "The Soulful Way of Claude McKay." BLACK WORLD, 20 (Nov. 1970), 37-51. Also in BLACKNESS AND THE ADVENTURE OF WESTERN CULTURE. Chicago: Third World, 1972, pp. 36-52.

McFarlane, J.E. Clare. "Claude McKay." In A LITERATURE IN THE MAK-

ING. Kingston, Jamaica: Pioneer Press, 1956, pp. 84-91.

McKay, Claude. A LONG WAY FROM HOME. New York: Lee Furman, 1937. 354 p.

Autobiography.

Smith, Robert A. "Claude McKay: An Essay in Criticism." PHYLON, 9 (1948), 270-73.

Stoff, Michael B. "Claude McKay and the Cult of the Primitive." In THE HARLEM RENAISSANCE REMEMBERED. Ed. Arna Bontemps. New York: Dodd, Mead, 1972, pp. 124-46.

Tolson, Melvin B. "Claude McKay's Art." POETRY, 83 (1954), 287-90.

MAJORS, MONROE ALPHEUS (1864-)

EPIC POEM TO HON. FREDERICK DOUGLASS. Chicago: Published by the author, 1917. 12 p.

MARGETSON, GEORGE REGINALD (1888- , born in St. Kitts, West Indies)

ENGLAND IN THE WEST INDIES; A NEGLECTED AND DEGENERATING EMPIRE. Boston: R.H. Blodgett & Co., 1906. 35 p.

ETHIOPA'S FLIGHT. THE NEGRO QUESTION; OR, THE WHITE MAN'S FEAR. Cambridge, Mass.: Published by the author, 1907. 22 p.

A plea for justice and equality in white America.

SONGS OF LIFE. Boston: Sherman, French and Co., 1910. 57 p.

THE FLEDGLING BARD AND THE POETRY SOCIETY. Boston: R. Badger, 1916. 111 p.

MARSHALL, FLORENCE E.

ARE YOU AWAKE? Lansing, Mich.: Shaw Publishing Co., 1936. 96 p.

MASK, W.E.

WHISPERS FROM HEAVEN AND MELODIES OF THE HEART. Washington, D.C.: Published by the author, [191-?]. 27 p.

MASON, MONROE

THOUGHTS OF AN AMERICAN SOLDIER AND A BRIEF HISTORY OF THE 372ND U.S. INFANTRY. N.p.: n.p., 1919. [43] p.

Poetry and prose.

MEANS, ST. ELMO

REV. ST. ELMO MEANS' POEMS, ESSAYS, MUSINGS AND QUOTATIONS. N.p.: n.p., 1920. 97 p.

MEANS, STERLING M.

THE DESERTED CABIN AND OTHER POEMS. Atlanta: A.B. Caldwell, 1915. 96 p.

THE BLACK DEVILS AND OTHER POEMS. Louisville, Ky.: Pentecostal Publishing Co., 1919. 56 p.

MERRITT, ALICE HADEN (1905-)

DREAM THEMES AND OTHER POEMS. Philadelphia: Dorrance, 1940. 57 p.

PSALMS AND PROVERBS: A POETICAL VERSION. Philadelphia: Dorrance, 1941. 64 p.

WHENCE WATERS FLOW: POEMS FOR ALL AGES "FROM OLD VIRGINIA." Richmond, Va.: Dietz Press, 1948. 69 p.

MERRIWEATHER, CLAYBRON WILLIAM

THE PLEASURES OF LIFE, LYRICS OF THE LOWLY, ESSAYS AND OTHER POEMS. Hopkinsville, Ky.: New Era Printing Co., 1931. 156 p.

GOOBER PEAS. Boston: Christopher, 1932. 174 p.

SUN FLOWER; LYRICS OF SUNSHINE AND OTHER POEMS. Hopkinsville, Ky.: New Era Printing Co., 1938. 152 p.

MIDDLETON, HENRY DAVIS

DREAMS OF AN IDLE HOUR. Chicago: Advocate Publishing Co., 1908. 70 p.

Poetry and prose.

MILLS, THELMA

A BOOK OF COMMONSENSE POEMS. Book No. 1. No imprint. 10 p.

A BOOK OF SIX COMMON SENSE POEMS. New York: Gaillard Press, n.d. 10 p.

SIX POEMS. BOOK THREE. New York: Type-Art Press, 1942. 8 p.

MOODY, CHRISTINA [CHRISTINA MOODY BRIGGS]

A TINY SPARK. Washington, D.C.: Murray Brothers, 1910. 43 p.

THE STORY OF THE EAST ST. LOUIS RIOT. N.p.: n.p., 1917. [5] p.

MOORER, LIZELIA AUGUSTA JENKINS

PREJUDICE UNVEILED AND OTHER POEMS. Boston: Roxburgh Publishing Co., 1907. 170 p.

MORRIS, JOHN DAVID

NATURE'S MEDITATIONS. Toledo, Ohio: Published by the author, 1922. 32 p.

MORRISON, WILLIAM LORENZO

DARK RHAPSODY. New York: H. Harrison, 1945. 62 p.
In Chapman IBP.

NAILOR, ALEXANDER J.

DIVINELY INSPIRED MESSAGE POEMS. N.p.: Published by the author, 1922. 59 p.

NEWSOME, EFFIE LEE (1885-)

GLADIOLA GARDEN: POEMS OF OUTDOORS AND INDOORS FOR SECOND GRADE READERS. Washington, D.C.: Associated Publishers, 1940. 167 p.

COME YE APART. Indianapolis: Inter-Racial Missionary Association, [195-?].

PAISLEY, JOHN WALTER

THE VOICE OF MIZRAIM. New York: Neale, 1907. 122 p.

RAS BRAVADO. Boston: Christopher, 1938.

PATTERSON, HARRY WILSON

GEMS OF THE SOUL; A BOOK OF VERSE AND POETIC PROSE. Washington, D.C.: Murray Brothers, 1935. 40 p.

PEKTOR, IRENE MARI

WAR--OR PEACE? Oceano, Calif.: Harbison and Harbison, 1939. 60 p.

GOLDEN BANNERS. Boston: Christopher, 1941. 211 p.

PENDLETON, LEILA AMOS

FRAGMENTS OF RHYME. Washington, D.C.: Published by the author, 1921. 8 p.

PERKINS, MINNIE LOUISE

A STRING OF PEARLS. Chicago: Published by the author, 1945. 17 p.

PETERS, ETHEL PAULINE, and ADA TRESS

WAR POEMS. No imprint. [194-?]. 83 p.

PITTS, LUCIA MAE. See HARRIS, HELEN C., above, this section.

POOHL, HENRY HARDY

STRIKE BACK. N.p.: n.p., 1924. 74 p.

POPEL, ESTHER A.W. [ESTHER POPEL SHAW]

THOUGHTLESS THINKS BY A THINKLESS THOUGHTER. No imprint. [192-?]. 16 p.

A FOREST POOL. Washington, D.C.: Modernistic Press, 1934. 42 p.

PORTER, GEORGE WELLINGTON

RACE POEMS . . . INTENDED TO INSPIRE HOPE IN THE NEGRO PEOPLE. Clarksville, Tenn.: Published by the author, [1910?]. 48 p.

STREAMLETS OF POETRY. Philadelphia: A.M.E. Book Concern, 1912. 87 p.

POSEY, EDWIN

THE VOICE OF THE NEGRO IN SOUTH CAROLINA. Columbia, S.C.: Crescent Printing Co., 1917. 54 p.

PRYOR, PHILIP LOUILLE

BROKEN STRINGS AND OTHER THINGS. No imprint. [194-?]. [14] p.

LYRICS OF LIFE, LOVE, AND LAUGHTER. Toledo, Ohio: Pioneer Publishing Co., 1945. 23 p.

QUILLIAN, W.A.

BLACK MOTHERS OF THE SOUTH AND TWENTY OTHER POEMS. East Point, Ga.: Published by the author, 1937. 24 p.

RAGLAND, JAMES FARLEY (1904-)

LYRICS AND LAUGHTER. Lawrenceville, Va.: Brunswick Times-Gazette Press, 1939. 90 p.

THE HOME TOWN SKETCH BOOK: "IT HAPPENED HERE:" A SOUVENIR OF BRUNSWICK INCIDENTS, OF DALE AND HILL IN LAWRENCEVILLE, AND ST. PAUL SCHOOL EVENTS. Lawrenceville, Va.: Brunswick Times-Gazette Press, 1940. 76 p.

RHYMES OF THE TIMES. Introd. Arthur P. Davis. New York: W. Malliet, 1946. 110 p.

A SLICE OF LIVING. Richmond, Va.: Published by the author, 1953. 47 p.

STEPPING STONES TO FREEDOM: POEMS OF PRIDE AND PURPOSE. Richmond, Va.: Quality Printing Co., 1960. 30 p.

RATCLIFFE, THEODORE P.

BLACK FOREVER MORE. Okolona, Miss.: Okolona Industrial School, 1939. 36 p.

RAY, HENRIETTA. See section for 1760-1900, above.

REYNOLDS, EVELYN CRAWFORD. See LYNN, EVE, in section 1946-75, below.

REYNOLDS, JAMES RICHARD (1870-)

THE WOLF BROTHERS AND POEMS. New York: Published by the author, [192-?]. 63 p.

RICHARDS, ELIZABETH DAVIS (1884-)

THE PEDDLER OF DREAMS AND OTHER POEMS. New York: W.A. Broder, 1928. 96 p.

RICHARDSON, WILLIS YOUNG (1889-)

ECHOES FROM THE NEGRO SOUL. San Antonio, Tex.: Alamo Printing Co., 1926. 99 p.

RICKS, WILLIAM NAUNS (1876-)

THE WHISTLE MAKER AND OTHER POEMS. San Francisco: Althof and Bahls, 1914. 16 p.

RIDOUT, DANIEL LYMAN

VERSES FROM A HUMBLE COTTAGE. Hampton, Va.: Hampton Institute Press, 1924. 28 p.

RILEY, JAMES W.

IN MEMORY OF DEPARTED FRIENDS. Washington, D.C.: Murray Brothers, 1914. 48 p.

ROWLAND, IDA

LISPING LEAVES. Philadelphia: Dorrance, 1939. 55 p.

SAMUEL, AARON

A HELPING HAND. New York: n.p., 1905. 75 p.

SAVAGE, EUDORA W.

VIBRATIONS OF MY HEART STRINGS. New York: Exposition, 1944. 94 p.

SCOTT, EMORY ELRAGE

LYRICS OF THE SOUTHLAND. Chicago: Wilton Press, 1913. 93 p.

SCOTT, RALEIGH ALONZO

SCOTT'S POETIC GEMS . . . A CHOICE COLLECTION OF HIS BEST POEMS
. . . . Opelika, Ala.: J.B. Ware, 1918. 44 p.

SEWARD, WALTER EDDIE (1891-)

NEGROES CALL TO THE COLORS AND SOLDIERS CAMP-LIFE POEMS. Athens,
Ga.: Knox Institute Press, 1919. 112 p.

SEYMOUR, ALEXANDER

BRIGHTER CHRISTMAS: CHRISTMAS POEMS. New York: Crest Publishing
Co., 1945. 15 p.

LOVE LIGHTERS: LOVE POEMS. New York: Crest Publishing Co., 1945. 15 p.

SHACKELFORD, OTIS M. (1871-)

SEEKING THE BEST. DEDICATED TO THE NEGRO YOUTH. Kansas City,
Mo.: Franklin Hudson, 1909. 177 p. 12th ed. 1922. 192 p.

> Prose and poetry including "Bits of History, or a Dream of Freedom
> Realized," which was modeled on "Hiawatha."

SHACKELFORD, THEODORE HENRY (1887- , born in Canada)

MAMMY'S CRACKLIN' BREAD AND OTHER POEMS. Philadelphia: I.W.
Klopp, 1916. 58 p.

MY COUNTRY AND OTHER POEMS. Introd. Charles H. Dodd. Philadelphia:
I.W. Klopp, 1918. 216 p.

SHACKELFORD, WILLIAM HENRY (1878-)

PEARLS IN PROSE AND POETRY. Nashville, Tenn.: National Baptist Publishing Board, 1907. 82 p.

POEMS. Nashville, Tenn.: African Methodist Episcopal Sunday School Union Press, [1915?].

SHAW, ESTHER POPEL. See POPEL, ESTHER A.W., above, this section.

SHIELDS, ANNA E.

ETHIOPIA'S PETITION. Cambridge, Mass.: Published by the author, 1918. 8 p.

PASSION WEEK. Cambridge, Mass.: Published by the author, 1924. 13 p.

UNPOLISHED TRUTHS. Cambridge, Mass.: Published by the author, [192-?]. 28 p.

SHOKUNBI, MAE GLEATON

SONGS OF THE SOUL. Philadelphia: Dorrance, 1945. 76 p.

SILCOTT, W. LLEWELLYN

BUDS AND BLOSSOMS. N.p.: n.p., 1940. 38 p.

SIMMONS, VIRGINIA LEE

WHITECAPS. Yellow Springs, Ohio: Antioch Press, 1942. 79 p.

SIMPKINS, THOMAS V. See section for 1946-75, below.

SMITH, J. PAULINE

"EXCEEDING RICHES" AND OTHER VERSE. Detroit: n.p., 1922. 89 p.

SMITH, S.P.

OUR ALMA MATER AND OTHER POEMS. Washington, D.C.: A.C. Garner, 1904. [25] p.

STANFORD, THEODORE ANTHONY

DARK HARVEST. Introd. Joseph V. Baker. Philadelphia: Bureau on Negro Affairs, 1936. 32 p.

STEED, OPHELIA DUDLEY

"AMERICA'S NEGRO" SUB-TITLED "THIS IS OUR COUNTRY." Cleveland, Ohio: Published by the author, 1944. 18 p.

TANNER, BENJAMIN TUCKER (1835-1923)

STRAY THOUGHTS. No imprint. 20 p.

TATUM, LAURENCE CARLYLE

LOG CABIN LYRICS. Los Angeles: n.p., 1918.

TEMPLE, GEORGE HANNIBAL. See section for 1760-1900, above.

THOMAS, CHARLES CYRUS (1909-)

A BLACK LARK CAROLING. Dallas: Kaleidograph Press, 1936. 73 p.

SWEET LAND OF LIBERTY. Ravenna, Ohio: Published by the author, 1937. 6 p.

YOUNG BOUGH BLOSSOMING. Hollywood, Calif.: n.p., [1954?]. 33 p.

THOMAS, JAMES HENRY

SENTIMENTAL AND COMICAL POEMS. Nashville, Tenn.: National Baptist Publishing Board, 1913. 171 p.
   Poetry and prose.

THOMPSON, AARON BELFORD. See section for 1760-1900, above.

THOMPSON, CLARA ANN

SONGS FROM THE WAYSIDE. Rossmoyne, Ohio: Published by the author, 1908. 96 p.

A GARLAND OF POEMS. Boston: Christopher, 1926. 96 p.

THOMPSON, JOSEPH

SONGS OF CAROLINE. Chicago: Published by the author, 1936. 30 p.

THOMPSON, PRISCILLA JANE

ETHIOPE LAYS. Rossmoyne, Ohio: Published by the author, 1900. 95 p.

GLEANINGS OF QUIET HOURS. Rossmoyne, Ohio: Published by the author, 1907. 100 p.

THORNE, J. ALBERT

THE DEW OF HERMON; OR, DWELLING TOGETHER IN UNITY. Toronto: Methodist Book and Publishing House, 1920. 15 p.

THORNE, JACK. See FULTON, DAVID BRYANT, above, this section.

THORNTON, GEORGE BENNETT. See section for 1946–75, below.

THURMAN, HOWARD (1900-)

THE GREATEST OF THESE. Mills College, Calif.: Eucalyptus Press, 1944. 25 p.

TINDLEY, CHARLES ALBERT

BEST POEMS OF THE LATE REVD. CHARLES ALBERT TINDLEY. Ed. Mrs. J.C. Tindley. Philadelphia: n.p., 1934. 38 p.

TINSLEY, TOMI CAROLYN. See HARRIS, HELEN C., above, this section.

TODD, WALTER E.

YOUNG MEN'S CHRISTIAN ASSOCIATION, A POEM. Washington, D.C.: Oscar Morris, 1905. 4 leaves.

PARSON JOHNSON'S LECTURE. Washington, D.C.: Murray Brothers, 1906. 45 p.

FIRESIDE MUSINGS. Washington, D.C.: Murray Brothers, 1908. 52 p.

GATHERED TREASURES. Washington, D.C.: Murray Brothers, 1912. 39 p.

A LITTLE SUNSHINE. Washington, D.C.: Murray Brothers, 1917. 61 p.

TODMAN, GERWYN (Born in St. Thomas, Virgin Islands)

ST. THOMAS: A RETROSPECTION. St. Thomas, V.I.: George E. Audain, Printer, 1921. 58 p.

TOLSON, MELVIN B. See section for 1946-75, below.

TOMAS, BENITO LUCIANO

HARLEMITTA DREAMS. New York: East End Printing Co., 1934. 95 p.

TOMLIN, J. HENRI

VARIED VERSES. N.p.: Published by the author, 1937. 92 p.

TOOMER, JEAN (1894-1967)

CANE. Introd. Waldo Frank. New York: Boni & Liveright, 1923. 239 p. Rpt. New York: University Place Press, 1967. New ed., introd. Arna Bontemps. New York: Harper, 1969. New ed., introd. Darwin Turner, New York: Liveright, 1975. 116 p.

"Blue Meridian." In THE NEW CARAVAN. Ed. Alfred Kreymborg, et al. New York: Norton, 1936, pp. 633-54. Also in BLACK WRITERS OF AMERICA. Ed. Richard Barksdale and Keneth Kinnamon. New York: Macmillan, 1972, pp. 507-14. Published as "The Blue Meridian" in THE POETRY OF THE NEGRO 1746-1970. Ed. Langston Hughes and Arna Bontemps. New York: Doubleday, 1970, pp. 107-13.

Biography and Criticism

Davis FDT; Redding TMPB; Wagner BPUS; Whitlow BAL.

Ackley, Donald G. "Theme and Vision in Jean Toomer's Cane." STUDIES IN BLACK LITERATURE, 1 (Spring 1970), 45-65.

Bell, Bernard. "A Key to the Poems in CANE." CLA JOURNAL, 14 (1971), 251-58.

Bontemps, Arna. "The Negro Renaissance: Jean Toomer and the Harlem Writers of the 1920's." In ANGER AND BEYOND. Ed. Herbert Hill. New York: Harper, 1966, pp. 20-36.

Chase, Patricia. "The Women in CANE." CLA JOURNAL, 14 (1971), 259-73.

Duncan, Bowie. "Jean Toomer's CANE: A Modern Black Oracle." CLA JOURNAL, 15 (1972), 323-33.

Durham, Frank, ed. THE MERRILL STUDIES IN "CANE." Columbus, Ohio: Charles E. Merrill Co., 1971. 113 p.

Farrison, W. Edward. "Jean Toomer's CANE again." CLA JOURNAL, 15 (1972), 295-302.

Fischer, William C. "The Aggregate Man in Jean Toomer's CANE." STUDIES IN THE NOVEL, 3 (1971), 190-215.

Fullinwider, S.P. "Jean Toomer: Lost Generation or Negro Renaissance." PHYLON, 27 (1966), 396-403. Also in THE MIND AND MOOD OF BLACK AMERICA. Homewood, Ill.: Dorsey Press, 1969, pp. 133-43.

Grant, Sister Mary Kathryn. "Images of Celebration in CANE." NEGRO AMERICAN LITERATURE FORUM, 5 (1971), 32-36.

Holmes, Eugene. "Jean Toomer: Apostle of Beauty." OPPORTUNITY, 3 (1925), 252-54, 260.

Innes, Catherine. "The Unity of Jean Toomer's CANE." CLA JOURNAL, 15 (1972), 306-23.

Lieber, Todd. "Design and Movement in CANE." CLA JOURNAL, 13 (1969), 35-50.

McKeever, Benjamin F. "CANE as Blues." NEGRO AMERICAN LITERATURE FORUM, 4 (1970), 61-63.

Mason, Clifford. "Jean Toomer's Black Authenticity." BLACK WORLD, 20 (Nov. 1970), 70-76.

Munson, Gorham. "The Significance of Jean Toomer." OPPORTUNITY, 3 (1925), 262-63.

Nower, Joyce. "Fooling Master." SATIRE NEWSLETTER, 7 (Fall, 1969), 5-10.

Reilly, John M. "Jean Toomer: An Annotated Checklist of Criticism." RE-SOURCES FOR AMERICAN LITERARY STUDY, (Spring 1974), 27-54.

_____. "The Search for Black Redemption: Jean Toomer's Cane." STUDIES IN THE NOVEL, 2 (1970), 312-24.

Rosenfeld, Paul. "Jean Toomer." In his MEN SEEN: TWENTY-FOUR MODERN AUTHORS. New York: Dial Press, 1925, pp. 227-33.

Scruggs, C.W. "Mark of Cain and the Redemption of Art: A Study in Theme and Structure of Jean Toomer's CANE." AMERICAN LITERATURE, 44 (1972), 276-91.

Thompson, Larry E. "Jean Toomer: As Modern Man." In THE HARLEM RE-NAISSANCE REMEMBERED. Ed. Arna Bontemps. New York: Dodd, Mead, 1972, pp. 51-62.

Toomer, Jean. "Chapters from EARTH-BEING, an Unpublished Autobiography." BLACK SCHOLAR, 2 (Jan. 1971), 3-13.

_____. ESSENTIALS: DEFINITIONS AND APHORISMS. Private ed. Chicago: Lakeside Press, 1931. 64 p.

_____. THE FLAVOR OF MAN. William Penn Lecture, 1949. Philadelphia: Young Friends Movement of the Philadelphia Yearly Meetings, 1949. 32 p. Rpt. Philadelphia: Wider Quaker Fellowship, 1974.

Turner, Darwin T. "Jean Toomer: Exile." In IN A MINOR CHORD: THREE AFRO-AMERICAN WRITERS AND THEIR SEARCH FOR IDENTITY. Carbondale: Southern Illinois Univ. Press, 1971, pp. 1-59.

_____. "Jean Toomer's CANE: Critical Analysis." NEGRO DIGEST, 18 (Jan. 1969), 54-61.

Waldron, Edward E. "The Search for Identity in Jean Toomer's 'Esther.'" CLA JOURNAL, 14 (1971), 277-80.

Watkins, Patricia. "Is There a Unifying Theme in CANE?" CLA JOURNAL, 15 (1972), 303-6.

Westerfield, Hargis. "Jean Toomer's 'Fern': A Mythical Dimension." CLA JOURNAL, 14 (1971), 274-76.

TOOMEY, RICHARD E.S.

THOUGHTS FOR TRUE AMERICANS: A BOOK OF POEMS DEDICATED TO THE LOVERS OF AMERICAN IDEALS. Introd. Paul Laurence Dunbar. Washington, D.C.: Neale, 1901. 80 p.

Twenty-eight poems on racial and political subjects.

TURNER, A. JOHN (1914-)

INTERLUDE. St. Louis, Mo.: Cathrell Printing Co., 1934.

THE DARK SINGER. East St. Louis, Ill.: Published by the author, 1940.

SEVEN SACRED POEMS. St. Louis, Mo.: Published by the author, 1946.

THE SONG I SING. New York: Exposition, 1964. 64 p.

TURNER, LUCY MAE

'BOUT CULLUD FOLKSES. New York: H. Harrison, 1938. 64 p.

In Chapman IBP.

TYLER, EPHRAIM DAVID

TYLER'S POEMS: POEMS OF EVERYDAY LIFE. Shreveport, La.: Published by the author, [193-?]. 44 p. 12th ed. [1940?]. 81 p.

TYNES, BERYL EWEL

PENPOINT DRIPPINGS. Lynchburg, Va.: Published by the author, 1935. 16 p.

Twelve poems on love, ambition, race.

UNDERHILL, IRVIN W. (1868-)

DADDY'S LOVE AND OTHER POEMS. Philadelphia: A.M.E. Book Concern, [1905?]. 87 p.

THE BROWN MADONNA AND OTHER POEMS. Philadelphia: [Published by the author?]. 1929. 95 p.

USSERY, AMOS A.

THE NEGRO SAYS. Little Rock, Ark.: Published by the author, n.d. 10 p.

VANCE, HART

CUI BONO? N.p.: n.p., 1919. 12 p.

WALKER, JAMES ROBERT. See section for 1946–75, below.

WALKER, MARGARET. See section for 1946–75, below.

WALKER, WILLIAM

WALKER'S EVERY DAY LIFE POETRY BOOK. Chicago: S.L. White, 1936. 69 p.

WALKER'S BOOK OF ORIGINAL POEMS. Chicago: Jones and Co., 1939. 25 p.

POEM BOOK OF INSPIRATIONAL THOUGHTS. Chicago: Published by the author, 1940. 16 p.

WALKER'S HUMOROUS POEMS BOOK. Chicago: Published by the author, 1940. 16 p.

WALKER'S NO. 1 ALL OCCASIONS POEM BOOK. New York: Exposition, 1940. 32 p.

MOTHER'S DAY SPECIAL POEMS BOOK. Chicago: Published by the author. 1941. 32 p.

WALKER'S NO. 8 POEM BOOK. Chicago: Published by the author, 1942. 16 p.

WALKER'S NO. 9 POEM BOOK. Chicago: Published by the author, 1943. 20 p.

POEM BOOK NUMBER TEN OF EVERY DAY LIFE POETRY. Chicago: Published by the author, 1943. 20 p.

WALKER'S NO. 2 ALL OCCASIONS POEM BOOK: EVERY DAY LIFE POETRY. Chicago: Published by the author, 1944. 206 p.

WALLER, EFFIE

SONGS OF THE MONTHS. Introd. Mary Elliot Flanery. New York: Broadway Publishing Co., 1904. 175 p.

> Contains 109 poems, mostly on nature.

RHYMES FROM THE CUMBERLAND. New York: Broadway Publishing Co., 1909. 53 p.

> Sixteen poems on nature.

WARD, ELLA J. MAYO

PURPLE WINGS. Charlottesville, Va.: Michie Co., 1941. 87 p.

BOUGAINVILLEA AND DESERT SAND. Charlottesville, Va.: Michie Co., 1942. 72 p.

WARRICK, CALVIN HORATIO

THE TRUE CRITERIA AND OTHER POEMS. Kansas City, Mo.: Sojourner Press, 1924. 120 p.

WATKINS, LUCIAN BOTTOW (1878-1921)

VOICES OF SOLITUDE. Chicago: Donohue and Co., 1903. 128 p.

WHISPERING WINDS. [Published before 1920?].

WEAVER, EDWIN EARL

THE AMERICAN. New York: Exposition, 1945. 63 p.

WESTFIELD, CHESTER J.

THE EXPERIENCES OF COMPANY "L," 368TH INFANTRY, A UNIT OF THE BLACK BUFFALO DIVISION, TOLD IN VERSE TYPICAL OF A SOLDIER'S LIFE IN FRANCE. Nashville, Tenn.: Hemphill Press, 1919. 8 p.

WHITE, CHARLES FREDERICK (1876-)

PLEA OF THE NEGRO SOLDIER AND A HUNDRED OTHER POEMS. Easthampton, Mass.: Enterprise Printing Co., 1908. 170 p.

    In Chapman IBP.

WHITE, JAMES WILSON

WHITE'S POEMS. Washington, D.C.: Published by the author, 1925. 94 p.

WHITMAN, ALBERY A. See section for 1760-1900, above.

WHITNEY, SALEM TUTT (1879-1934)

MELLOW MUSINGS. Introd. Thomas G.L. Oxley. Boston: Colored Poetic League of the World, 1926. 126 p.

WHYTE, THOMAS HENRY

POETICAL INSPIRATION. Toronto: Rowen Press, 1934. 40 p.

WIGGINS, BERNICE LOVE (1897-)

TUNEFUL TALES. Introd. William Coleman. El Paso, Tex.: Published by the author, 1925. 174 p.

    Contains 103 poems, mostly on religious themes.

WILDS, MYRA VIOLA

THOUGHTS OF IDLE HOURS. Nashville, Tenn.: National Baptist Publishing Board, 1915. 81 p.

WILKINSON, HENRY BERTRAM (1889-)

IDLE HOURS. New York: F. Hitchcock, 1927. 86 p.

SHADY-REST. New York: F. Hitchcock, 1928. 69 p.

DESERT SANDS. London: A. Stockwell, 1933. 108 p.

TRANSITORY. Boston: Popular Poetry Publishers, 1941. 20 p.

WILLIAMS, FRANK B.

FIFTY YEARS OF FREEDOM. Washington, D.C.: Hamilton Printing Co., 1913. 8 p.

A poem of fourteen eight-line stanzas tracing to 1913 the history of the Afro-American from the shores of Africa.

WILLIAMS, HENRY ROGER (1869-1929)

THE CHRIST IS A NEGRO. Mobile, Ala.: Published by the author, 1923. [19] p.

HEART THROBS: POEMS OF RACE INSPIRATION. Mobile, Ala.: Gulf City Printing Co., 1923. 80 p.

ARE WE FREE? AN EMANCIPATION DAY ADDRESS WRITTEN IN CADENCED VERSES. Mobile, Ala.: Published by the author, 1928. 26 p.

WITHERS, ZACHARY

POEMS AFTER SLAVERY. San Francisco: Pacific Coast Appeal Publishing Co., 1905. 47 p.

In Chapman IBP.

WITHERSPOON, JAMES WILLIAM

A BREATH OF THE MUSE: A VOLUME OF POETIC BROWSINGS CONTAINING SEVERAL PROSE WRITINGS. Columbia, S.C.: Hampton Publishing Co., 1927. 132 p.

WOOD, ODELLA PHELPS

RECAPTURED ECHOES. New York: Exposition, 1944. 64 p.

WRIGHT, BRUCE McMARION (1918-)

FROM THE SHAKEN TOWER. Cardiff, Wales: W. Lewis, 1944. 38 p.

WRIGHT, JULIUS C. (1886?-)

POETIC DIAMONDS, WRITTEN FOR THE INTEREST OF THE AFRO-AMERICANS AND ALL CONCERNED. By Julius C. Wright, a youth of twenty who never spent a day in College. Montgomery, Ala.: W.E. Allred Printing Co., 1906. 64 p.

YANCEY, BESSIE WOODSON (1882-)

ECHOES FROM THE HILLS. Washington, D.C.: Associated Publishers, 1939. 62 p.

YEISER, IDABELLE

MOODS. Philadelphia: Colony Press, 1937. 88 p.

LYRIC AND LEGEND. Boston: Christopher, 1947. 77 p.

3. 1946-75

With the rise of black consciousness in the 1960s a new generation of poets found a huge new audience, and at least the potential technical and economic means of reaching it, ranging from mimeograph machines in friends' cellars to the most professional Broadside Press productions. While the commercial publishers and vanity presses for the most part continued publishing clothbound volumes, many of the first works of the new poets--Nikki Giovanni, LeRoi Jones, Don L. Lee, Audre Lorde, Clarence Major, to name a few of the best known-- came out in pamphlet form. To help researchers locate volumes we have, therefore, added the annotation "Paper" to the entries for those volumes which we know originally appeared only in paper covers.

Particularly for the most recent years, we have been unable to locate copies, or even accurate listings of some volumes; thus some entries are incomplete, and other titles have no doubt escaped us altogether. Nevertheless, about a thousand titles are listed in this section; almost twice as many as appeared in all of the years preceding.

Critical material on the new poets has been slight and widely scattered; since the compilation of this section Eugene B. Redmond's DRUMVOICES (see above, part 1, under Critical Studies) has appeared, with a long and useful chapter covering this period.

In this section, primary works are listed first, in chronological order, followed by secondary works, in alphabetical order. Works indexed in Chapman IPB are so indicated.

ABDULLAH, JAMAL

BLACK VIEWS: POETRY AND PROSE CORNER. New York: United Brothers Communication System, 1975. 25 p. Paper.

ABDULLAH of New York. See MUHAMMED, Abdullah, below, this section.

ABDUS-SALAM, MUSTAFA J.

"VISIONS OF TODAY:" NEW PROJECTIONS. New York: Published by the author, 1974. [12] p. Paper.

ABRAM, THERESA WILLIAMS (1903-)

ABRAM'S TREASURES. New York: Vantage, 1967. 80 p.

RHYTHM AND ANIMALS. Oklahoma City, Okla.: Best Way, 1971.

ACQUAAH, DANIEL KOFI (Born in Ghana)

EACH MAN IS WITHIN HIMSELF. Boston: Gemini Press, 1973. 43 p. Paper.

AFRICAN SHORT STORIES AND OTHER POEMS. Roxbury, Mass.: Scoham Bookshelf, 1974. [15] p. Paper.

   Poetry and prose.

ADAMS, DAISIE HASSON

MERCHANT OF DREAMS. New York: Exposition, 1947. 32 p.

ADAMS, DORIS B.

LONGING AND OTHER POEMS. Philadelphia: Dorrance, 1962. 30 p.

ADDISON, LLOYD (1931-)

THE AURA & THE UMBRA. Heritage series, no. 8. London: Breman, 1970. 24 p. Paper.

AHEART, ANDREW NORWOOD (1921-)

FIGURES OF FANTASY. New York: Exposition, 1949. 54 p.

AI [FLORENCE ANTHONY] (1947-)

CRUELTY. Boston: Houghton Mifflin, 1973. 46 p.

ALBA, NANINA (1917-68)

THE PARCHMENTS. N.p.: n.p., 1962.

THE PARCHMENTS II. N.p.: n.p., 1967.

ALEXANDER, ELRETA MELTON

WHEN IS A MAN FREE? Philadelphia: Dorrance, 1967. 43 p.

ALEXANDER, LEWIS (1900-)

ENCHANTMENT.

ALHAMISI, AHMED AKINWOLE [LE GRAHAM] (1940-)

THE BLACK NARRATOR: POEMS BY LE GRAHAM. Detroit: Black Arts, 1966. 16 p. Paper.

BLACK SPIRITUAL GODS: NEW POMES. Detroit: Black Arts, 1968. 16 p. Paper.

GUERILLA WARFARE: NEWER POMES. Detroit: Black Arts, 1970. 16 p. Paper.

> In Chapman IBP.

HOLY GHOSTS. Detroit: Black Arts, 1972. 62 p. Paper.

ALI, NATHANIEL

EXCERPTS FROM THE DIARY OF A YOUNG BLACK SLOWLY GOING MAD. San Francisco: Shabbaz Publishing Co., 1970. 44 p.

ALI, YUSEF HAKIM (1923-)

SPIRIT, SOUL, CONSCIOUSNESS AND REALIZATION. Detroit: Agascha Productions, 1975. 67 p. Paper.

ALLEN, SAMUEL W. [PAUL VESEY] (1917-)

ELFENBEINZAHNE. IVORY TUSKS. Gedichte eines Afroamerikaners. Ed. and trans. Janheinz Jahn. Heidelberg, Germany: Wolfgang Rothe Verlog, 1956. 47 p.

> Twenty poems in English, with German translations.

IVORY TUSKS AND OTHER POEMS. Millbrook, N.Y.: Printed at Kriya Press, 1968. [32] p. Paper.

Twenty-two poems, most of them not in ELFENBEINZAHNE.

PAUL VESEY'S LEDGER. Heritage series, no. 27. London: Breman, 1975. 20 p. Paper.

ALLISON, MARGARET M.

THE SUN LOOK UPON ME AND I AM BLACK. Madison, Wis.: Published by the author, 1970. 28 p. Paper.

ALLMAN, REVA WHITE

I'VE KNOWN LOVE. New York: Vantage, 1975. 39 p.

AMINI, JOHARI. See LATIMORE, JEWEL C., below, this section.

AMOS, WINSOM

LIKE A DREAM. Detroit: Harlo Press, 1971. 15 p. Paper.

ORIOLE TO BLACK MOOD. Westerville, Ohio: Published by the author, 1973. 24 p. Paper.

AMUNGO, SONEBEYATTA [ROOSEVELT HAGAN] (1956-)

THE YOUTH MAKES THE REVOLUTION. Detroit: Black Arts, 1971. 16 p. Paper.

ANDERSON, CHARLES L. (1938-)

FRUSTRATION: A NEGRO POET LOOKS AT AMERICA. Puebla, Mexico: El Grupo Literario of the "United Nations" School, [1960?]. [20] p. Paper.

ANDERSON, EDNA L.

THROUGH THE AGES. Philadelphia: Dorrance, 1946. 58 p.

ANDERSON, GLORIA EDWARDS

PEARLS OF BLACK. Detroit: Harlo Press, 1975. 63 p.

ANDERSON, ODIE (1943-)

TRIAL OF GOD. New York: Exposition, 1970. 49 p.
Verse play.

ANGELOU, MAYA (1928-)

JUST GIVE ME A COOL DRINK OF WATER 'FORE I DIIIE. New York: Random House, 1971. 48 p.
In Chapman IBP.

O PRAY MY WINGS ARE GONNA FIT ME WELL. New York: Random House, 1975. 67 p.

ANONYMOUS

THE SOUL DELIGHT. By Anonymous. Boston: Christopher, 1961. 91 p.

ANTHONY, FLORENCE. SEE AI, above, this section.

ANTHONY, JAMES K.

THREE SHADES OF BLUE. New York: Vantage, 1956. 63 p.

ARMSTRONG, HENRY (1912-)

TWENTY YEARS OF POEM, MOODS AND MEDITATION. Los Angeles: Published by the author, 1954. 80 p. Paper.

ARMSTRONG, NAOMI YOUNG

A CHILD'S EASTER. N.p.: Published by the author, 1971. [13] p. Paper.

ARNEZ, NANCY L. See MURPHY, BEATRICE M., below, this section.

ARNOLD, WALTER G.

IN QUEST OF GOLD, THE NEGRO IN AMERICA AND OTHER POEMS. New York: William-Frederick, 1947. 35 p.

ARTHUR, BARBARA

COMMON SENSE POETRY. Berkeley, Calif.: Respect International, 1969.

ASHBURN, GENE HOLMES (1926-)

DARK GODS. New York: William-Frederick, 1952. 26 p.

ASTWOOD, ALEXANDER CARL

BEAUTY AND THE UNIVERSE. Boston: Humphries, 1950. 72 p.

ATKINS, RUSSELL (1927-)

A PODIUM PRESENTATION. Brooklyn Heights, Ohio: Poetry Seminar Press, 1960. [8] p. Paper.

PHENOMENA. Wilberforce, Ohio: Free Lance Poets and Prose Workshop, Wilberforce Univ. Press, 1961. 79 p.

TWO BY ATKINS: THE ABORTIONIST AND THE CORPSE + TWO POETIC DRAMAS TO BE SET TO MUSIC. Cleveland: Free Lance Press, 1963. 32 p. Paper.

OBJECTS. Eureka, Calif.: Hearse Press, 1963. [20] p. Paper.

OBJECTS, 2. 2nd printing. Cleveland: Renegade Press, 1964. [18] p. Paper.

HERETOFORE. Heritage series, no. 7. London: Breman, 1968. 32 p. Paper.

HERE IN THE. Cleveland Poets series, no. 13. Cleveland: Cleveland State Univ. Poetry Center, 1976. 52 p. Paper,

ATKINSON, WILLIAM HENRY, SR.

THINKING ALOUD IN VERSE. N.p.: Published by the author, 1963. 40 p. Paper.

LITTLE RAYS FOR THE DARK PLACES. N.p.: Published by the author, 1968. 102 p. Paper.

AUBERT, ALVIN (1930-)

AGAINST THE BLUES. Detroit: Broadside, 1972. 30 p. Paper.
In Chapman IBP.

Biography and Criticism

Rowell, Charles H. "An Interview with Alvin Aubert: The Black Poet in the Afternoon." BLACK WORLD, 22 (Aug. 1973), 34-48, 72.

AVERY, CHARLES E.

BLACK TRACES. New York: Carlton, 1973. [79] p.
Photographs and poems.

AVINGTON, RONALD BERNARD

EXPRESSIONS FROM INNER SPACE. New York: Vantage, 1974. 48 p.

AWEUSI, ALLI and MACHEWEO

WORDS NEVER KILL. Oakland, Calif.: Deep Black Writers' Workshop, 1974. 74 p. Paper.

AYERS, VIVIAN

SPICE OF DAWNS. New York: Exposition, 1953. 39 p.

HAWK. Houston: Hawk Press, 1957. 64 p. Paper.

BACON, MARY ALBERTA

POEMS OF COLOR. New York: Exposition, 1948. 61 p.

BAGLEY, JOYCE M.

JOTS OF THOUGHTS. New York: Vantage, 1974. 64 p.

BAILEY, GERTRUDE BLACKWELL

IF WORDS COULD SET US FREE. Jericho, N.Y.: Exposition, 1974. 59 p.

BAILEY, RICHARD

SOUL BLOOD POEMS. Indianapolis: Published by the author, 1969.

BAKER, ROBERT MILUM. See JOHNSON, HOMER PRESTON, below, this section.

BANG, BILLY

MAGIC LIVES ON THE LOWER EASTSIDE. New York: Ghazal Productions, 1974. 19 p. Paper.

BARAKA, (IMAMU) AMIRI. See JONES, LEROI, below, this section.

BARLOW, GEORGE (1948-)

GABRIEL. Detroit: Broadside, 1974. 63 p.

BARRAX, GERALD W. (1933-)

ANOTHER KIND OF RAIN. Pittsburgh: Univ. of Pittsburgh Press, 1970. 86 p.
　　In Chapman IBP.

BARRETT, NATHAN (1933-)

FLOATING WORLD. No imprint. [New York. 1962?]. [24] p. Paper.

BEACH, MARION ["TUMBLEWEED"]

COME RIDE WITH ME. Chicago: D.M.A.A.H. Press, 1970. 31 p. Paper.

BEANUM, ROLAND LEWIS

THE KOLLECTOR: POEMS AND ETCHINGS. No imprint. [ca. 1970]. 27 p. Paper.

BEAVER, JOSEPH T.

AFRICA IN PERSPECTIVE. Washington, D.C.: Published by the author, 1966. [24] p. Paper.

BEGELEUS, ANDRE EMILE III

WE ARE BETRAYED AND OTHER POEMS. Hicksville, N.Y.: Exposition, 1975. 48 p.

BENJAMIN, JOSEPH LOUIS

AND THE TRUTH SHALL MAKE US FREE. New York: Carlton, 1964. 67 p.
Written with Anita Honis.

RUN WHITE MAN, RUN! New York: Vantage, 1970. 69 p.
Poetry and prose.

BENSKINA, PRINCESS ORELIA (Born in Panama)

NO LONGER DEFEATED AND OTHER POEMS. New York: Carlton, 1972. 64 p.

THE INFLAMMABLE DESIRE TO REBEL. New York: Vantage, 1973. 44 p.

I HAVE LOVED YOU ALREADY. Hicksville, N.Y.: Exposition, 1975. 47 p.

BERRI, WILHELM C.

THE WEANING YEARS BEYOND. New York: Vantage, 1969. 144 p.

BESS, OLEAN

MIXED FEELINGS. St. Albans, N.Y.: Published by the author, 1972. [24] p. Paper.

BEST, MARGARET S.

SERENITY. N.p.: Published by the author, 1969. Paper.

BETHUNE, LEBERT (1937- , born in Jamaica, West Indies)

JUJU OF MY OWN. Paris: Imprimerie Union, 1965. 47 p. Paper.

BETTS, CHARLOTTE

I SEE A BLACK DAWN. Introd. Mildred F. Cross. Fort Smith, Ark.: South and West, 1974. 43 p. Paper.

BIBBINS, RICHARD E.

BRIDGE FROM HELL. Detroit: Agascha Productions, 1972. 58 p. Paper.

BIBBS, HART LEROY (1930-)

POLY RYTHMS TO FREEDOM. New York: Mac McNair, 1964. 40 p. Paper. Another ed. published as POLY RHYTHMS TO FREEDOM. Paris: Imprimerie Fact, [196-?]. 38 p. Paper, mimeographed.

BIRCH, McLANE (1942-)

THE KANDI MAN. Detroit: Broadside, 1970. 27 p. Paper.

BIRMINGHAM, JOHN

SHADOWS AND THE LIMELIGHT. Kansas City, Mo.: Published by the author, 1972. 12 p. Paper, mimeographed.

BLACK, AUSTIN (1928-)

THE TORNADO IN MY MOUTH. New York: Exposition, 1966. 80 p.

BLAKE, JAMES W.

BEHIND THE MASK. Introd. Michael S. Harper. San Francisco: Julian Richardson Associates, 1974. 74 p. Paper.

BLAKELY, HENRY (1916-)

WINDY PLACE. Introd. Gwendolyn Brooks. Detroit: Broadside, 1974. 71 p.

BLANTON, KATHRYN FRANKLIN (1921-)

A DICTIONARY OF POETRY. VOLUME I. New York: Vantage, 1974. 70 p.

BOGUS, DIANE

I'M OFF TO SEE THE GODDAMN WIZARD, ALRIGHT! Chicago: Published by the author, 1971. 45 p. Paper.

BOHANON, MARY

POEMS AND CHARACTER SKETCHES. New York: Greenwich, 1967. 47 p.

EARTH BOSOM AND COLLECTED POEMS. New York: Carlton, 1973. 48 p.

BONTEMPS, ARNA WENDELL (1902-73)

PERSONALS. Heritage series, no. 4. London: Breman, 1963. 44 p. Paper.

Biography and Criticism

Davis FDT; O'Brien IBW; Rollins FANP.

Baker, Houston A., Jr. "Arna Bontemps: A Memoir." BLACK WORLD, 22 (Sept. 1973), 4-9.

Brown, Sterling A. "Arna Bontemps: Co-Worker, Comrade." BLACK WORLD, 22 (Sept. 1973), 11, 91-97.

BOWEN, ROBERT T.

FOURTEENTH OF JUNE. [Los Angeles?]: n.p., 1968.

BOYCE, ARNOLD (1921- , born in West Indies)

THE TURN OF THE CENTURY. New York: Published by the author, 1970. 79 p. Paper.

BOYD, SUE ABBOTT

HOW IT IS: SELECTED POEMS, 1952-1968. Homestead, Fla.: Olivant Press, 1968. 172 p.

A PORTION OF THE FORT ROOT POEMS, VOLUME 1, ACT 1. Fort Smith, Ark.: South and West, 1973. 22 p. Paper.

BOYD, TOM

THOUGHTS OF THE SILENT MINORITY. Brooklyn, N.Y.: Caridad Printing, 1971. [36] p. Paper.

BOYER, JILL WITHERSPOON (1947-)

DREAM FARMER. Detroit: Broadside, 1975. 24 p. Paper.

BOZE, ARTHUR (1945-)

BLACK WORDS. Detroit: Broadside, 1972. 22 p. Paper.
   In Chapman IBP.

LOVING YOU. Kansas City, Mo.: Hallmark Editions, 1972.

IN LOVE WITH YOU. Los Angeles: Poetry Co., 1973. [57] p. Paper.

BRAGG, LINDA BROWN (1939-)

A LOVE SONG TO BLACK MEN. Detroit: Broadside, 1974. 32 p. Paper.

BRAITHWAITE, WILLIAM S. See section for 1901–45, above.

BRISBY, STEWART

URINATING IN THE POOL. Syracuse, N.Y.: Pulpartforms Unltd., 1974. [24] p. Paper.

BRITT, NELLIE

MY MASTER AND I: POEMS THAT WILL ENCOURAGE, INSPIRE AND STRENGTHEN. New York: Carlton, 1964. 48 p.

BROOKS, GWENDOLYN (1917-)

A STREET IN BRONZEVILLE. New York: Harper, 1945. 57 p.

ANNIE ALLEN. New York: Harper, 1949. 60 p.
   In Chapman IBP.

BRONZEVILLE BOYS AND GIRLS. New York: Harper, 1956. 40 p.

THE BEAN EATERS. New York: Harper, 1960. 71 p.

SELECTED POEMS. New York: Harper, 1963. 127 p.

IN THE MECCA. New York: Harper, 1968. 54 p.

   In Chapman IBP.

RIOT. Detroit: Broadside, 1969. 22 p. Paper.

FAMILY PICTURES. Detroit: Broadside, 1970. 23 p. Paper.

ALONENESS. Detroit: Broadside, 1971. [16] p. Paper.

THE WORLD OF GWENDOLYN BROOKS. New York: Harper, 1971. 426 p.

   Contains ANNIE ALLEN, A STREET IN BRONZEVILLE, MAUD
   MARTHA (novel), THE BEAN EATERS, and IN THE MECCA.

THE TIGER WHO WORE WHITE GLOVES, OR: WHAT YOU ARE YOU ARE.
Chicago: Third World, 1974. [36] p.

   A poem for children.

BECKONINGS. Detroit: Broadside, 1975. 16 p. Paper.

Bibliographies

Hoff, Jon N. "Gwendolyn Brooks: A Bibliography." CLA JOURNAL, 17
(1973), 21-32.

Mahoney, Heidi L. "Selected Checklist of Material by and about Gwendolyn
Brooks." NEGRO AMERICAN LITERATURE FORUM, 8 (1974), 210-11.

Biography and Criticism

Davis FDT; Jackson BPA; Rollins FANP; Whitlow BAL.

Baker, Houston A., Jr. "The Achievement of Gwendolyn Brooks." CLA JOURNAL
16 (1972), 23-31. Also in SINGERS OF DAYBREAK: STUDIES IN BLACK AMERI-
CAN LITERATURE. Washington, D.C.: Howard Univ. Press, 1974, pp. 43-51.

Bird, Leonard G. "Gwendolyn Brooks: Educator Extraordinaire." DISCOURSE,
12 (1969), 158-66.

Brooks, Gwendolyn. REPORT FROM PART ONE. Introd. Don L. Lee and
George Kent. Detroit: Broadside, 1972. 215 p.

   Autobiography.

Brooks, Gwendolyn, et al. A CAPSULE COURSE IN BLACK POETRY WRITING.
Detroit: Broadside, 1975. 64 p.

Brown, Frank London. "Chicago's Great Lady of Poetry." NEGRO DIGEST, 11 (Dec. 1961), 53-57.

Crockett, J. "An Essay on Gwendolyn Brooks." NEGRO HISTORY BULLETIN, 19 (1955), 37-39.

Cutler, B. "Long Reach, Strong Speech." POETRY, 13 (1964), 388-89.

Davis, Arthur P. "The Black and Tan Motif in the Poetry of Gwendolyn Brooks." CLA JOURNAL, 6 (1962), 90-97.

_____. Gwendolyn Brooks: A Poet of the Unheroic." CLA JOURNAL, 7 (1963), 114-25.

Furman, Marva Riley. "Gwendolyn Brooks: The 'Unconditioned' Poet." CLA JOURNAL, 17 (1973), 1-10.

Garland, Phyllis. "Gwendolyn Brooks: Poet Laureate." EBONY, 23 (July 1968), 48-50.

Hansell, William H. "Aestheticism versus Political Militancy in Gwendolyn Brooks's 'The Chicago Picasso' and 'The Wall.'" CLA JOURNAL, 17 (1973), 11-15.

Harriott, F. "Life of a Pulitzer Poet." NEGRO DIGEST, 8 (Aug. 1950), 14-16.

Hudson, Clenora F. "Racial Themes in the Poetry of Gwendolyn Brooks." CLA JOURNAL, 17 (1973), 16-20.

Jaffe, Dan. "Gwendolyn Brooks: An Appreciation from the White Suburbs." In Bigsby BAW 2, pp. 89-98.

Kent, George E. "The Poetry of Gwendolyn Brooks." Part 1 in BLACK WORLD, 20 (Sept. 1971), 30-43; part 2 in BLACK WORLD, 20 (Oct. 1971), 36-48, 68-71. Also in BLACKNESS AND THE ADVENTURE OF WESTERN CULTURE. Chicago: Third World, 1972, pp. 104-38.

Kunitz, Stanley. "Bronze by Gold." POETRY, 76 (1950), 52-56.

Lee, Don L. "The Achievement of Gwendolyn Brooks." BLACK SCHOLAR, 3 (June-Summer 1972), 32-41.

McCluskey, John. "To the Mecca." STUDIES IN BLACK LITERATURE, 4 (Autumn 1973), 25-30.

Miller, Jeanne-Marie A. "Poet Laureate of Bronzeville, U.S.A." FREEDOM-WAYS, 10 (1970), 63-75.

Rivers, Conrad Kent. "Poetry of Gwendolyn Brooks." NEGRO DIGEST, 13 (June 1964), 67-69.

Stavros, George. "An Interview with Gwendolyn Brooks." CONTEMPORARY LITERARY 12 (Winter 1970), 1-20.

BROOKS, HELEN MORGAN

AGAINST WHATEVER SKY. Provincetown, Mass.: Advocate Press, 1955. 30 p.

FROM THESE MY YEARS.

BROOKS, JONATHAN HENDERSON (1904-45)

THE RESURRECTION & OTHER POEMS. Dallas: Kaleidograph Press, 1948. 55 p.

BROWN, CHARLES E.

SURGING. Terre Haute, Ind.: Afro American Cultural Center, 1973. 29 p. Paper.

BROWN, HERBERT G.

INTO THE LIGHT. New York: Comet, 1959. 38 p.

BROWN, HERMAN. See MUMBA, below, this section.

BROWN, JOE C. (1908-)

BUT NOT LIKE YESTERDAY. Detroit: Broadside, 1968. [8] p. Paper.

BROWN, ROBERT HARVEY

WINE OF YOUTH. New York: Exposition, 1949. 46 p.

BROWN, STERLING A. See section for 1901-45, above.

BROWNING, ALICE C.

BLACK N' BLUE. Chicago: Browning Publications, 1973. 34 p. Paper.

BRYANT, FREDERICK JAMES, JR. (1942-)

SONGS FROM RAGGED STREETS. Greenfield Center, N.Y.: Greenfield Review Press, 1974. 39 p. Paper.

BUFORD, ELMER. See FELTON, B., below, this section.

BUFORD, LORENZO NEIL

MEN DON'T CRY. Alton, Ill.: Dan Merkle Printing Co., 1972. 76 p. Paper.

TO BE HEARD. Alton, Ill.: Published by the author, 1972. [52] p. Paper.

BURLEIGH, BENNY [Pseud. of THOMAS HILDRED ODEN]

TWO GUN BILL. New York: Comet, 1957. 44 p.

BURNETT, DENISE. See DAMALI, below, this section.

BURROUGHS, MARGARET TAYLOR GOSS (1917-)

WHAT SHALL I TELL MY CHILDREN WHO ARE BLACK? Chicago: M.A.A.H. Press, 1968. 32 p.

AFRICA, MY AFRICA! Chicago: DuSable Museum Press, 1970. 23 p. Paper.

BUTLER, ANNA LAND (1901-)

ALBUM OF LOVE LETTERS--UNSENT. Vol. 1: MORNING 'TIL NOON. New York: Margent Press, 1952.

TOUCHSTONE. Provincetown, Mass.: Advocate Press, 1961. 29 p.

HIGH NOON. Charleston, Ill.: Prairie Press Books, 1971.

BUTLER, JAMES ALPHEUS (1905-)

MAKE WAY FOR HAPPINESS. Boston: Christopher, 1932. 133 p.

SEPIA VISTAS. New York: Exposition, 1941. 68 p.

PHILOSOPHER AND SAINT: SONNETS AND OTHER POEMS. New York: Exposition, 1951. 64 p.

20TH CENTURY SONG SONNETS: SPHERE OF THE SPRITE AND THE SAGE. Tampa, Fla.: Laurel, 1973.

BYRON, ASAMAN B.W. (Born in Trinidad, West Indies)

LORD I'M GONNA TAKE FREEDOM. New York: Published by the author, 1968. Paper.

TO BE BLACK IS TO BE EQUAL (=) TO GOD. New York: Published by the author, 1971. 26 p. Paper.

CAIN, JOHNNIE MAE

DO YOU REMEMBER. . . . Philadelphia: Dorrance, 1972. 100 p.

CANADA, JAMES L.

IF I WERE TO TELL YOU. Philadelphia: Dorrance, 1973. 91 p.

REALITY IS MY AWARENESS SENSE. East Weymouth, Mass.: Gemini Book Village, 1974. 49 p.

CANNON, CHARLES E. (1946-)

SAINT NIGGER. Detroit: Broadside, 1972. 24 p. Paper.

CARRINGTON, HAROLD (1938-64)

DRIVE SUITE. Heritage series, no. 14. London: Breman, 1972. 12 p. Paper.

CARTER, BRUCE WAYNE

ODES TO THE IMMORTALS--THE 1972 OLYMPIANS. New York: Carlton, 1974. 47 p.

CARTER, LILLIE BLAND

WHISPERING LEAVES. Toledo, Ohio: Marcella's Stenographic Service, 1953. 13 p. Paper.

CASEY, BERNIE

LOOK AT THE PEOPLE. Illus. by the author. New York: Doubleday, 1969. 92 p.

In Chapman IBP.

CASEY, RAYMOND O. See SHABAZZ, TURHAN ABDUL, below, this section.

CHAMBERS, STEPHEN A.

FORMS, ON #3. New York: Afro-Arts, 1968. [27] p. Paper.

CHANCELLOR, JACK

I AM CURIOUS (BLACK). New York: Exposition, 1973. 30 p.

CHASE-RIBOUD, BARBARA

FROM MEMPHIS & PEKING. New York: Random House, 1974. 112 p.

CHENAULT, JOHN

BLUE BLACKNESS. Cincinnati: Seven Hills Neighborhood Houses, 1969. 32 p. Paper.

CHIRI, RUWA (1943-74, born in Rhodesia)

AN ACKNOWLEDGEMENT OF MY AFRO-AMERICAN BROTHER. Chicago: Free Black Press, 1968. 36 p. Paper.

CHISHOLM, WILLIAM MASON

SPLINTERED DARKNESS. Brooklyn, N.Y.: Trilon Press, 1953. 86 p.

CHRISTIAN, MARCUS BRUCE (1900-)

IN MEMORIAM, FRANKLIN DELANO ROOSEVELT, 1882-1945. New Orleans: Published by the author, [194-?].

THE COMMON PEOPLES' MANIFESTO OF WORLD WAR II. New Orleans: Les Cenelles Society of Arts and Letters, 1948. 28 p. Paper.

HIGH GROUND: A COLLECTION OF POEMS PUBLISHED IN COMMEMORATION OF THE UNITED STATES SUPREME COURT'S DECISION OF MAY 17, 1954, AND ITS FINAL DECREE OF MAY 31, 1955, ABOLISHING RACIAL SEGREGATION IN THE NATION'S PUBLIC SCHOOLS. New Orleans: Southern Publishing Co., 1958. 20 p. Paper.

CLARK, CHINA (1949-)

POEMS FROM CHINA. No imprint. [1971?]. [15] p. Paper.

CLARKE, JOHN HENRIK (1915-)

REBELLION IN RHYME. Prairie City, Ill.: Decker Press, 1948. 105 p.

CLARKE, LEROY (1938- , born in Trinidad, West Indies)

TASTE OF ENDLESS FRUIT: LOVE POEMS AND DRAWINGS. Brooklyn, N.Y.: Published by the author, 1974. [64] p. Paper.

CLEMMONS, VINCENT

SKETCHES BY VINCE. Flushing, N.Y.: New Voices, 1973. 36 p. Paper.

CLIFTON, LUCILLE (1936-)

GOOD TIMES. New York: Random House, 1969. [83] p.

THE BLACK BC'S. New York: Dutton, 1970. 46 p.
    Poetry and prose, for children.

SOME OF THE DAYS OF EVERETT ANDERSON. New York: Holt, 1970. [32] p.
    For children.

EVERETT ANDERSON'S CHRISTMAS COMING. New York: Holt, 1971. [32] p.
    For children.

AN ORDINARY WOMAN. New York: Random House, 1974. 94 p.

THE TIMES THEY USED TO BE. New York: Holt, 1974.]48] p.
For children.

COBB, CHARLIE (1944-)

FURROWS. Tougaloo, Miss.: Flute Publications, 1967. 59 p. Paper.

EVERYWHERE IS YOURS. Chicago: Third World, 1971. 16 p. Paper.

COBB, PAMELA (1950-)

INSIDE THE DEVIL'S MOUTH: FIRST POEMS. Detroit: Lotus Press, 1975.
44 p. Paper.

COFFEY, JOHN

A NEGRO SPEAKS OF LIFE. Karlsruhe, Germany: Printed by Engelhardt and
Bauer, 1961. 31 p. Paper.

COFFIN, FRANK BARBOUR. See section for 1760-1900, above.

COLLIER, MAXIE

POEMS OF THE SOULMATES: THE WARMTH AND THE SOUL OF TRUE
BLACK LOVE. By Maxie and Betty Collier. Washington, D.C.: NuClassics
and Science Publishing Co., [1972?]. 53 p. Paper.

COLLINS, BOOKER T. See WHITE, JESSIE, below, this section.

CONLEY, CYNTHIA. See ZUBENA, SISTER, below, this section.

CONLEY, EVERETT N.

A SLICE OF BLACK LIVING. Berlin, N.J.: Conlam Enterprises, 1970. 8 p.
Paper.

COOPER, ALVIN CARLOS

STROKE OF MIDNIGHT. Counterpoise Series, 2. Nashville, Tenn.: Hemphill Press, 1949. 18 p. Paper.

COOPER, LULA

A MURMER OF ESSENCE. Wilmington, Del.: Published by the author, 1972. 24 p. Paper.

CORNISH, SAM (1935-)

IN THIS CORNER: SAM CORNISH AND VERSES. Baltimore, Md.: Fleming-McAllister Press, 1964. [42] p. Paper.

PEOPLE BENEATH THE WINDOW. Foreword by Mike Walters. Baltimore, Md.: Sacco Publishers, [1965?]. [48] p. Paper.

GENERATIONS. Cambridge, Mass.: Published by the author, 1966. [12] p. Paper.

THE SHABBY BREATH OF YELLOW TEETH. No imprint. [1967?]. Paper.

ANGLES. Baltimore, Md.: Published by the author, [1967?]. [12] p. Paper.

WINTERS. Cambridge, Mass.: Sans Souci Press, 1967. 18 p. Paper.

FLEMING/McALLISTER PRODUCTIONS PRESENTS "A REASON FOR INTRUSION." AN OMNIBUS OF MUSINGS FROM THE FILES OF SAM CORNISH, PAMELA WILLIAMS, PAUL D. McALLISTER. Baltimore, Md.: Fleming/McAllister Publisher, 1969. [48] p. Paper.

SHORT BEERS. Cambridge, Mass.: Beanbag Press, [1969?]. [8] p. Paper.

GENERATIONS. Introd. Ruth Whitman. Boston: Beacon Press, 1971. 81 p.

SOMETIMES: TEN POEMS. Cambridge, Mass.: Pym-Randall Press, 1973. [20] p. Paper.

CORTEZ, JAYNE (1936-)

PISSSTAINED STAIRS AND THE MONKEY MAN'S WARES. New York: Phrase Text, 1969. [52] p. Paper.

FESTIVALS AND FUNERALS. New York: Phrase Text, 1971. [43] p. Paper.

SCARIFICATIONS. New York: Bola Press, 1973. 64 p. Paper.

COX, JOSEPH MASON ANDREW

THE COLLECTED POETRY OF JOSEPH MASON ANDREW COX. Francestown, N.H.: Golden Quill Press, 1970. 120 p.

LAND DIMLY SEEN. New York: Cox and Hopewell, 1975. 187 p.

COX, OLLIE

LAST CALL FOR PEACE. New York: Arlain Printing Co., 1959. 87 p. Paper.

CRAWFORD, ISAAC

MEDITATIONS OF SOLITUDE. Hixson, Tenn.: n.p., 1916. 67 p.

WEEDS AND OTHER POEMS. Brooklyn, N.Y.: Published by the author, 1952. 61 p.

CROUCH, STANLEY (1945-)

AIN'T NO AMBULANCES FOR NO NIGGUHS TONIGHT. New York: Richard W. Baron, 1972. 87 p.

CRUMP, PHYLLIS (1955-)

POETIC VIBRATIONS. New York: Ja-Mac Publishing Co., 1971. 53 p. Paper.

CRUZ, VICTOR HERNANDEZ (1949- , born in Puerto Rico)

PAPO, GOT HIS GUN AND OTHER POEMS. New York: Calle Once Publications, 1966. 28 p. Paper, mimeographed.

SNAPS. New York: Random House, 1969. 135 p.

   In Chapman IBP.

MAINLAND. New York: Random House, 1973. 83 p.

TROPICALIZATION. New York: Reed, Cannon and Johnson, 1976. 83 p. Paper.

CULLEN, COUNTEE. See section for 1901-45, above.

CULVER, ELOISE CROSBY (1915-72)

GREAT AMERICAN NEGROES IN VERSE, 1723-1965. Washington, D.C.: Associated Publishers, 1966. 80 p.

In Chapman IBP.

CUNEY, WILLIAM WARING (1906-)

PUZZLES. Selected and introd. Paul Breman. Utrecht, Netherlands: De Roos, 1960. 79 p.

STOREFRONT CHURCH. Heritage series, no. 23. London: Breman, 1973. 20 p. Paper.

CUNNINGHAM, JIM. See OLUMO, below, this section.

CURRIER, RAYMOND

HALF-DARK HOUSE. Crescent City, Fla.: New Atheneum Press, 1962. 60 p.

CURRY, ANDREW (1931-)

17TH TRACTATUS ON WORDS: SELECTED POEMS. Paradise, Calif.: DUST-books, 1969. 45 p. Paper.

CUTHBERT, MARION VERA. See section for 1901-45, above.

DAMALI [DENISE BURNETT]

I AM THAT WE MAY BE. Chicago: Third World, 1974. 21 p. Paper.

DANNER, MARGARET (1915-)

IMPRESSIONS OF AFRICAN ART FORMS. Introd. Emilie A. Newcomb and Broadus N. Butler. Detroit: Contemporary Studios, 1960. 19 p. Paper. Rpt. Detroit: Broadside, 1968.

TO FLOWER. Counterpoise Series, 4. Nashville, Tenn.: Hemphill Press, 1963. 30 p. Paper.

POEM COUNTERPOEM. With Dudley Randall. Detroit: Broadside, 1966. 24 p. Paper.

IRON LACE. Millbrook, N.Y.: Printed at Kriya Press, 1968. [32] p. Paper. Limited edition of 200 copies.

THE DOWN OF A THISTLE. Waukesha, Wis.: Country Beautiful, 1975. 144 p.

DANTE. See GRAHAM, DONALD L., below, this section.

DAVIS, CHERYL

IMANI. Madison, Wis.: Published by the author, [1969?].

WE ALL GONNA GO TOGETHER. Madison, Wis.: Published by the author, 1971.

DAVIS, DORIS

LIVE WIRES. With Dorothy Davis. New York: Vantage, 1975. 94 p.

DAVIS, FRANK MARSHALL. See section for 1901-45, above.

DAVIS, JOE

THE SOUND OF THUNDER. New York: Carlton, 1971. 47 p.

DEAN, BARBARA

THE KEY. Chicago: Free Black Press, 1970. Paper.

DEASE, RUTH ROSEMAN (1911-)

SCAN-SPANS. New York: Vantage, 1967. 79 p.

DESHANDS, LOTTIE BELLE

GOLDEN GEMS OF A NEW CIVILIZATION. New York: Exposition, 1955. 95 p.

DEVEAUX, ALEXIS (1950-)

SPIRITS IN THE STREETS. Illus. by the author. New York: Doubleday, 1973.
192 p.

> Poetry and prose.

DICKERSON, JAMES WARDFUL

THE RHYTHM OF LAUGHTER AND OTHER POEMS. New York: New Voices,
1958. 85 p.

REFLECTIONS OF A POET. Hicksville, N.Y.: Exposition, 1975. 64 p.

DIGGS, ALFRED [BROTHER]

THE PLAIN POET. Chicago: Ja Lal Hassen Press, 1968. 10 p. Paper.

NATURALLY BLACK. Chicago: Published by the author, 1968. 27 p. Paper.

BLACK CHILDREN BLACK AND BEAUTIFUL. Chicago: Published by the
author, 1969. 16 p. Paper.

DODSON, OWEN (1914-)

POWERFUL LONG LADDER. New York: Farrar, 1946. 103 p.

> In Chapman IBP.

THE CONFESSION STONE: A SONG CYCLE BY MARY ABOUT JESUS.
Washington, D.C.: Published by the author, 1960. 8 p. Paper.

THE CONFESSION STONE: SONG CYCLES. Heritage series, no. 13. London: Breman, 1970. 28 p. Paper.

Biography and Criticism

There is an interview with Dodson in O'Brien IBW.

DOMINIQUE, OTIS G.

POEMS FOR BOYS AND GIRLS. Philadelphia: Dorrance, 1966. 39 p.

DOOLEY, THOMAS. See EBON, below, this section.

DOUGLAS, RODNEY K. (Born in Grenada, West Indies)

HOPE AND REFLECTION. New York: Carlton, 1973. 47 p.

DRAFTS, C. EUGENE

BLOODWHISPERS/BLACK SONGS. Detroit: Broadside, 1974. 14 p. Paper.

DRAYTON, THOMAS

LOOKING IT OVER. No imprint. [1967?]. [25] p. Paper.

A GRAIN OF SAND. New York: Little Hut, 1970. 75 p. Paper.

DU BOIS, W.E.B. See section for 1901-45, above.

DUCKETT, ALFRED (1918-)

RAPS. Chicago: Nelson-Hall Co., 1973. 68 p.

DUDLEY, JOAN C. See TOKUNBO, below, this section.

DUMAS, AARON

THE STRANGER. Seattle: Black Arts/West, 1971. 114 p.

DUMAS, HENRY (1934-68)

POETRY FOR MY PEOPLE. Ed. Hale Chatfield and Eugene Redmond. Introd. Imamu Ameer Baraka (LeRoi Jones). Carbondale: Southern Illinois Univ. Press, 1970. 183 p.

PLAY EBONY PLAY IVORY. Introd. Eugene Redmond. New York: Random House, 1974. 135 p.

DUREM, RAY (1915-63)

TAKE NO PRISONERS. Heritage series, no. 17. London: Breman, 1971. 24 p. Paper.

DUST [Pseud. of WELVIN STROUD] (1937-)

POEMS BY DUST. San Francisco: Julian Richardson Associates, 1969. [24] p. Paper.

EADDY, FELTON

IF I HOLD MY TONGUE. Orangeburg, S.C.: Peaceweed Press, [1974?].

EATON, ESTELLE ATLEY

OUT OF MY DREAMS AND OTHER VERSES. Boston: Christopher, 1959. 105 p.

EBERHARDT, JUANITA BURLESON

THE WORLD HAS MANY DOORS THAT I ENTER. Chicago: Du Sable Museum of African American History Press, 1975. 106 p.

EBON [THOMAS DOOLEY] (1942-)

REVOLUTION. Chicago: Third World, 1968. 31 p. Paper.

ECKELS, JON

BLACK DAWN. Berkeley, Calif.: Printed by Wuerth Letter Shop, 1966. 27 p.

THIS TIME TOMORROW. San Francisco: Success Printers, [1966?]. Paper.

BLACK RIGHT ON. San Francisco: J. Richardson, 1969. 44 p. Paper.

HOME IS WHERE THE SOUL IS. Detroit: Broadside, 1969. 25 p. Paper.

OUR BUSINESS IN THE STREETS. Detroit: Broadside, 1971. 32 p. Paper.

FIRESIGN: POETRY FOR THE FREE & WILL BE. San Jose, Calif.: Firesign Press, 1973. 60 p.

ELDER, ELEANOR HARDEE (1868-)

ME N' DE CHILLUN. New York: Paebar, 1948. 77 p.

ELDRIDGE, STANLEY

RETURN ME TO MY MIND. New York: Fortune Society, 1970. [32] p. Paper.

ELLETT, M. DEBORAH (1949-)

FROM THEM I COME. A Free Will Publication, 1973.

ELLIOTT, EMILY

STILL WATERS AND OTHER POEMS. Cambridge, Mass.: Published by the author, 1949.

ELLISTON, MAXINE HALL. See JAMILA-RA, below, this section.

EMANUEL, JAMES (1921-)

THE TREEHOUSE AND OTHER POEMS. Detroit: Broadside, 1968. 24 p. Paper.

PANTHER MAN. Detroit: Broadside, 1970. 32 p. Paper.

EMERUWA, LEATRICE

BLACK GIRL, BLACK GIRL (VARIATIONS ON A THEME). [Cleveland, 1973?].

BLACK VENUS IN GEMINI.

ENNIS, WILLIE, JR.

POETICALLY SPEAKING. New York: Exposition, 1957. 56 p.

EUBANKS, CALLIE MILES

I WANT TO GO HOME. New York: Vantage, 1971. 46 p.

EVANS, BENNIE

DENIM AND LACE AND THE ROSARY IS THE LANGUAGE OF TODAY. Los Angeles: Published by the author, 1950. 32 p. Paper.
    Poetry and prose.

EVANS, EMMERY (1943-)

EMMERY THE LOVE POET. Long Beach, Calif.: Published by the author, 1971.

EVANS, MARI (1927-   )

WHERE IS ALL THE MUSIC? Heritage series, no. 6. London: Breman, 1968. 24 p. Paper.

I AM A BLACK WOMAN. New York: Morrow, 1970. 95 p.
> Reviewed by Stephen E. Henderson in BLACK WORLD, 20 (July 1971), 51-52, 88-92; and by Johari M. Amini in the same issue, 92-94. In Chapman IBP.

EVANS, MARILYN [Pseud.]

AFRICA, ONCE MORE WITH FEELING. New York: Vantage, 1971. 64 p.

FABIO, SARAH WEBSTER (1928-   )

A MIRROR: A SOUL; A TWO-PART VOLUME OF POEMS. San Francisco: J. Richardson, 1969. 44 p. Paper.

BLACK BACK: BACK BLACK. Introd. Don L. Lee. Oberlin, Ohio: New Media Workshop, 1973. 56 p. Paper.

BOSS SOUL. Oberlin, Ohio: New Media Workshop, 1973. 21 p. Paper.

JUJUS/ALCHEMY OF THE BLUES. Oberlin, Ohio: New Media Workshop, 1973. 62 p. Paper.

JUJUS AND JUBILEES: CRITICAL ESSAYS IN RHYME ABOUT POETS/MUSICIANS/BLACK HEROES, WITH INTRODUCTORY NOTES. Oberlin, Ohio: New Media Workshop, 1973. 56 p. Paper.

MY OWN THING. Oberlin, Ohio: New Media Workshop, 1973. 47 p. Paper.

SOUL AIN'T: SOUL IS--THE HURT OF IT ALL. Oberlin, Ohio: New Media Workshop, 1973. 31 p. Paper.

TOGETHER / TO THE TUNE OF COLTRANE'S EQUINOX. Oberlin, Ohio: New Media Workshop, 1973. 54 p. Paper.

FAIR, RONALD (1932-   )

EXCERPTS. Heritage series, no. 26. London: Breman, 1975. 20 p. Paper.

FATISHA

SAPPHIRE LONGING IN THE BLUE DUST. No imprint. [1975?]. [24] p.
Paper.

FALKNER-LASHLEY, JACQUELINE [OLUBAYO]

THE HIGHEST JOY. St. John's, Antigua, West Indies: Antigua Printing &
Publishing Co., 1974. [52] p. Paper.

FAUST, NAOMI

SPEAKING IN VERSE. Boston: Branden Press, 1974. 87 p. Paper.

FELTON, B. [ELMER BUFORD] (1934-)

CONCLUSIONS. Introd. Russell Atkins. Cleveland: Monarch Printing Service, 1971. [44] p. Paper.

FENNELL, ROBERT E.

SECOND MOVEMENT. Introd. Georgia Douglas Johnson. Hawkins, Tex.:
Published by the author, 1962. 15 p. Paper.

FERDINAND, VAL III [KALAMU YA SALAAM] (1947-)

THE BLUES MERCHANT. Introd. Adam Weber. New Orleans: BlkArtSouth,
1969. 20 p. Paper.

HOFU NI KWENU. MY FEAR IS FOR YOU. New Orleans: Ahidiana, 1973.
24 p. Paper.

PAMOJA TUTASHINDA. TOGETHER WE WILL WIN. New Orleans: Ahidiana,
1974. [24] p. Paper.

FERNANDEZ, RONALD

THE IMPATIENT REBEL. New Orleans: BlkArtSouth, 1969. 20 p. Paper.

FIELDS, JULIA (1938-)

POEMS. Millbrook, N.Y.: Printed at Kriya Press, 1968. [32] p. Paper.

EAST OF MOONLIGHT. Charlotte, N.C.: Red Clay Books, 1973. 52 p. Paper.

FIGUEROA, JOSE-ANGEL (1946- , born in Puerto Rico)

EAST 110TH STREET. Detroit: Broadside, 1973. 45 p. Paper.

FISHER, JAMES A., JR.

EBONY WORDS OF POETRY. Appalachia, Va.: Young Publications, 1965.

FISHER, JOHN

SUITE FOR CYNTHIA: A LONG POEM. San Francisco: Humanessence Publishing Co., 1973. [16] p. Paper.

TWO LONG POEMS: SISYPHUS AT ABADDON; FOR BOB KAUFMAN. San Francisco: Humanessence Publishing Co., 1974. [16] p. Paper.

FISHER, RANDOLPH

THE TREASURY OF LIFE. New York: Exposition, 1947. 92 p.

FITZ, A.W., SR.

POEMS OF PROTEST. Council Bluffs, Iowa: Published by the author, 1949.

FITZPATRICK, LORENZO

TO SEE, TO FEEL, TO CARE. San Antonio, Tex.: Naylor Co., 1972. 36 p.

FLEMING, ROBERT

MELONS. Introd. Russell Atkins. Cleveland: Melon Press, 1974. [32] p. Paper.

STARS. Cleveland: Printed by International Graphics and Printing Co., 1975. [56] p. Paper.

FORBES, CALVIN (1945-)

BLUE MONDAY. Middletown, Conn.: Wesleyan Univ. Press, 1974. 63 p.

FRANKLIN, CARL

PORTRAIT OF MAN: A LOVE POEM. New York: Exposition, 1952. 47 p.

FRAZIER, ERIC (1947-)

BLACK GOLD AND YOU. Bronx, N.Y.: Universal Messengers Publication Co., 1971. [20] p. Paper.

FRAZIER, MAX YERGAN

FIFTEEN FAMILIAR FACES IN VERSE. New York: Vantage, 1959. 44 p.

BLACK AND UNEQUALED. New York: Exposition, 1971. 63 p.

FRAZIER, RUBY PRIMUS

RUBY'S BLACK EMERALDS. New York: Rannick Playwrights Co., 1971. [32] p. Paper.

FREDRICK, HELEN BURLESON

WHERE DID YOU LAST FIND ME: AN ANTHOLOGY OF PROSE, POETRY AND SONGS. Chicago: DuSable Museum of African American History Press, 1975. 112 p.

FUDGE, ANTHONY R.

MIGRATION. Introd. Norman Jordan. Cleveland: ARF Press, 1972. 43 p. Paper.

FULANI, RICHARD

DARK REFLECTIONS AND SOULDIERS. Brooklyn, N.Y.: Published by the author, 1973. 35 p. Paper.

DISCOVERY, REVOLUTION & UNDERSTANDING. Brooklyn, N.Y.: Published by the author, 1973. 31 p. Paper.

SECOND THE EMOTION. Brooklyn, N.Y.: Published by the author, 1974. 41 p. Paper.

FULGER, WILLIE E.

TRUTH IS BEAUTY. New York: Vantage, 1963. 68 p.

FULLER, CHESTER

SPEND SAD SUNDAYS SINGING SONGS TO SASSY SISTERS. Chicago: Third World, 1974. 20 p. Paper.

FULLER, STEPHANY JEAN DAWSON. See STEPHANY, below, this section.

GABUGAH, O.O. See YOUNG, AI, below, this section.

GARRISON, PAUL J.

ASK ME BETWEEN DRINKS. N.p.: Mays Printing Co., 1971. Paper.

GATES, EDDIE

THE POET'S DOORWAY. New York: Carlton, 1964. 64 p.

GATES, JEANNETTE McPHERSON

REFLECTIONS. Portland, Oreg.: Press-22, 1971. 57 p.

SILHOUETTES. Sandy, Oreg.: St. Paul's Press, 1972. Paper.

RELEVANCE AND REALITY: POETRY AND PHOTOGRAPHY. Sandy, Oreg.: St. Paul's Press, 1973. 35 p. Paper.

GEARY, EFTON F.

REFLECTIONS OF A BLACK MAN. San Antonio, Tex.: Naylor Co., 1970. 36 p.

GEX, QUO VADIS (1950-)

DARK WATERS. New Orleans: BlkArtSouth, 1969. 20 p. Paper.

GIBBS, RUTH DUCKETT

BLACK IS THE COLOR. Introd. Rev. Jesse Louis Jackson. Great Neck,

N.Y.: Center for Media Development, 1973. 38 p. Paper.

GIBSON, RUFUS

LYRICS OF LIFE AND LOVE. New York: Carlton, 1964. 96 p.

GILBERT, ZACK (1925-)

MY OWN HALLELUJAHS. Chicago: Third World, 1971. 40 p. Paper.

GIMENEZ, JOSEPH PATRICK. See section for 1901-45, above.

GINN, HENRY

THE HALF TREE. Savannah, Ga.: Published by the author, 1967.

GIOVANNI, NIKKI (1943-)

BLACK FEELING BLACK TALK. Introd. Barbara Crosby. Wilmington, Del.: Privately Printed, 1968. 19 p. Paper. 2nd ed., enl. New York: Published by the author, 1969. 26 p. Paper. Rpt. Detroit: Broadside, 1970.

> The first edition contains nineteen poems; the second contains twenty-five poems.

BLACK JUDGEMENT. Detroit: Broadside, 1968. 36 p. Paper.

BLACK FEELING BLACK TALK BLACK JUDGEMENT. New York: Morrow, 1970. 98 p.

> In Chapman IBP.

RE:CREATION. Detroit: Broadside, 1970. 48 p. Paper.

SPIN A SOFT BLACK SONG: POEMS FOR CHILDREN. New York: Hill & Wang, 1971. [64] p.

MY HOUSE. Introd. Ida Lewis. New York: Morrow, 1972. 69 p.

> In Chapman IBP.

EGO-TRIPPING AND OTHER POEMS FOR YOUNG PEOPLE. New York: Lawrence Hill, 1973. 37 p.

THE WOMEN AND THE MEN. New York: Morrow, 1975. [64] p.
Forty-two poems written from 1970 to 1975.

Biography and Criticism

Lee DV; Whitlow BAL.

Bailey, P[eter]. "Nikki Giovanni: I Am Black, Female, Polite." EBONY, Feb. 1972, pp. 48-50, 52, 54, 56.

Giovanni, Nikki. GEMINI: AN EXTENDED AUTOBIOGRAPHICAL STATE-MENT ON MY FIRST TWENTY-FIVE YEARS OF BEING A BLACK POET. Indianapolis: Bobbs-Merrill, 1971. 149 p.

Giovanni, Nikki, and Margaret Walker. A POETIC EQUATION: CONVER-SATIONS BETWEEN NIKKI GIOVANNI AND MARGARET WALKER. Washington, D.C.: Howard Univ. Press, 1974. 148 p.

Murphy, Frederick B. "Nikki." ENCORE, 5 May 1975, pp. 30-34.

Palmer, R. Roderick. "The Poetry of Three Revolutionists: Don L. Lee, Sonia Sanchez, and Nikki Giovanni." CLA JOURNAL, 15 (1971), 25-36. Also in Gibson MBP, pp. 135-46.

Thompson, M. Cordell. "Nikki Giovanni: Black Rebel with Power in Poetry." JET, 25 May 1972, pp. 18-24.

GIPSON, RALPH E.

FOR BLACKS ONLY: POEMS AND ESSAYS. Jericho, N.Y.: Exposition, 1974. 96 p.

GOMILLION, E. SHARON

FORTY ACRES AND A MULE. Baltimore, Md.: Diana Press, 1973. 27 p. Paper.

GOODE, JACQUES

RAW MILK. New York: Kioka Productions, 1972. 48 p. Paper.

GOODWIN, LEROY

"INSIDE POEMS"--BUT NOT JOKES. Introd. Will Inman. Los Angeles: Bean

Bag Press, 1967. 18 p. Paper.

GOUGH, EUGENE S.

ONLY TO LIVE LIFE. New York: Vantage, 1975. 39 p.

GOWARD, GLADYS McFADDEN

SEE HOW THEY PLAY: A PICTORIAL TOUR THROUGH THE ORCHESTRA. New York: Exposition, 1953. 50 p.

GRAHAM, DONALD L. [DANTE] (1944-70)

BLACK SONG. Introd. John O. Killens. Nashville Tenn.: Division of Cultural Research, Fisk Univ., 1966. [12] p. Paper.

SOUL MOTION I. Nashville, Tenn.: Division of Cultural Research, Fisk Univ., 1969. Paper.

SOUL MOTION II. Nashville, Tenn.: Division of Cultural Research, Fisk Univ., 1970. 19 p. Paper.

GRAHAM, J. RODNEY

NATION. Chicago: New Era Theatre Concept, [1971?]. 14 p. Paper.

GRAHAM, LE. See ALHAMISI, AHMED AKINWOLE, above, this section.

GRAHAM, LORENZ (1902-)

HOW GOD FIX JONAH. Introd. W.E.B. DuBois. New York: Reynal, 1946. 171 p.
> "Stories from the bible . . . in the idiom of the West African native" retold for children.

EVERY MAN HEART LAY DOWN. New York: Crowell, 1970. [48] p.
> Text extracted from HOW GOD FIX JONAH (1946, above).

DAVID HE NO FEAR. New York: Crowell, 1971. [47] p.
> Text extracted from HOW GOD FIX JONAH (1946, above).

GOD WASH THE WORLD AND START AGAIN. New York: Crowell, 1971. [40] p.

Text extracted from HOW GOD FIX JONAH (1946, above).

A ROAD DOWN IN THE SEA. New York: Crowell, 1971.

Text extracted from HOW GOD FIX JONAH (1946, above).

HONGRY CATCH THE FOOLISH BOY. New York: Crowell, 1973. [40] p.

Text extracted from HOW GOD FIX JONAH (1946, above).

GRAYSON, EDWARD D. III

WHOSE MIND IS THE MIND OF MINE. No imprint. [1970?]. [18] p. Paper.

GREEN, ULYSSES

A NIGGER'S THOUGHTS. Carbondale, Ill.: Published by the author, [1972?].

GREENE, EMILY JANE

IN THE GREEN PASTURES. Los Angeles: Published by the author, 1966. 64 p.

GREENIDGE, JOHN

THOUGHT SPASMS. New York: Published by the author, 1968. [14] p. Paper, mimeographed. Rev. ed. 1973. 39 p. Paper.

GREENLEE, SAM (1930-)

BLUES FOR AN AFRICAN PRINCESS. Introd. Nikki Giovanni. Chicago: Third World, 1971. 36 p. Paper.

AMMUNITION! Introd. Andrew Salkey. London: Bogle L'Ouverture Publications, 1975. 84 p.

GREENWOOD, THERESA (1936-)

PSALMS OF A BLACK MOTHER. Anderson, Ind.: Warner Press, 1970. 96 p. Paper.

GREGG, ERNEST

AND THE SUN GOD SAID: THAT'S HIP. New York: Harper and Row, 1972. [24] p.

GRIMES, NIKKI [NAOMI] (1950-)

POEMS. Introd. James Sneed. New York: Celebrated Blackness, 1970. [18] p. Paper.

GROSVENOR, KALI (1960-)

POEMS BY KALI. Introd. William Melvin Kelley. New York: Doubleday, 1970. 62 p.

    In Chapman IBP.

HAGAN, ROOSEVELT. See AMUNGO, SONEBEYATTA, above, this section.

HAINES, CORRIE and ROBERTA

AS I SEE IT (PROSE--POETRY--FREE VERSE). By Corrie and Roberta Haines. Washington, D.C.: NuClassics and Science Publishing Co., 1974. 40 p. Paper.

HALL, IRMA P. (1935-)

POLE MOTO (GENTLE FIRE). Dallas: Akini Isi Publishing Co., 1973. 32 p. Paper.

HAMILTON, SARAH B. EDMONDS

OUT OF MY HEART. New York: Exposition, 1961. 96 p.

HAMMOND, BASIL CALVIN

SOMETHING TO REMEMBER. New York: Exposition, 1960. 87 p.

HAMMOND, DOUG

IN THIS MAZE OF SEEMING WONDERS. New York: A Jodgoa Publication, 1974. 21 p. Paper.

HARDEMAN, BEAUREGARD ANDREW, JR. (1944-)

REVOLUTION IS: A BOOK OF POEMS. By B. Rap. San Francisco: Published by the author, 1971. 69 p. Paper.

METAMORPHOSIS OF SUPERNIGGER: TEN POEMS. By B. Rap. San Francisco: Published by the author, 1973. 42 p. Paper.

HARDING, PHILIP M.

HARLEM INTERIOR: 3 POEMS. Teaneck, N.J.: Blockprint Press, [1947?]. [17] p. Paper.

HARDING, VINCENT (1931-)

TO THE GALLANT BLACK MEN NOW DEAD. Atlanta: Published by the author, 1967. 13 p. Paper, mimeographed. Also in NEGRO DIGEST, 16 (Nov. 1966), 54-75.

HARPER, MICHAEL S. (1938-)

DEAR JOHN, DEAR COLTRANE. Pittsburgh: Univ. of Pittsburgh Press, 1970. 88 p.

In Chapman IBP.

HISTORY IS YOUR OWN HEARTBEAT. Urbana: Univ. of Illinois Press, 1971. 95 p.

PHOTOGRAPHS: NEGATIVES: HISTORY AS APPLE TREE. San Francisco: Scarab Press, 1972. [29] p.

Limited edition of 500 signed copies.

SONG: I WANT A WITNESS. Pittsburgh: Univ. of Pittsburgh Press, 1972. 63 p.

Reviewed by R. Roderick Palmer in CLA JOURNAL, 16 (1973), 529-31.

DEBRIDEMENT. New York: Doubleday, 1973. 110 p.

NIGHTMARE BEGINS RESPONSIBILITY. Urbana: Univ. of Illinois Press, 1975. 97 p.

Biography and Criticism

There is an interview with Harper in O'Brien IBW.

HARRELD, CLAUDIA WHITE

REMEMBERED ENCOUNTERS. Atlanta: Logan Press, 1951. 44 p.

HARRIS, BILL

PRAISESONGS. Detroit: Allone Press, [1972?]. Paper.

HARRIS, GENETHEL

THOUGHTS TO SHARE. Bronx, N.Y.: Published by the author, 1972. 31 p. Paper.

HARRIS, LEON. See section for 1901-45, above.

HARRIS, NEIL (1936-)

STRAIGHT FROM THE GHETTO. New York: Printed by Saphrograph Co., 1971. [56] p. Paper.

HARRIS, WENDELL W.

ECHOES AND SHADOWS. Philadelphia: Dorrance, 1968. 41 p.

HARRIS, WILLIAM J. (1942-)

HEY FELLA, WOULD YOU MIND HOLDING THIS PIANO A MOMENT. Ithaca, N.Y.: Ithaca House, 1974. 42 p.

HARRISON, EUNICE B.

HERE IS MY HEART. New York: Carlton, 1962. 55 p.

HARRISON, JAMES S.

CHARRED WOOD. New York: Vantage, 1971. 64 p.

HARRISON, JERRY

COOLHEAD. San Francisco: Published by the author, 1968. 53 p.

HAVARD, HARRISON

BLACK LOVE'S/BLACK WEALTH: A COLLECTION OF POEMS. By Harrison Havard, Barbara Townsley, and T.J. Whitaker. Vicksburg, Miss.: Javekcher Press, 1974. 24 p. Paper.

HAWKINS, ODIE (1937-)

ME AND THEM. Los Angeles: Published by the author, 1969. 48 p. Paper.

HAYDEN, ROBERT EARL (1913-)

HEART-SHAPE IN THE DUST. Detroit: Falcon Press, 1940. 63 p.
>   Forty-seven poems; in Chapman IBP.

THE LION AND THE ARCHER. Counterpoise Series, 1. Nashville, Tenn.: Hemphill Press, 1949. [20] p. Paper.
>   Contains "The Lion" by Hayden and "The Archer" by Myron O'Higgins.

FIGURE OF TIME. Counterpoise Series, 3. Nashville, Tenn.: Hemphill Press, 1955. 20 p. Paper.

A BALLAD OF REMEMBRANCE. Heritage series, no. 1. London: Breman, 1962. 72 p. Paper.
>   In Chapman IBP.

SELECTED POEMS. New York: October House, 1966. 79 p.
>   Forty-one poems; includes most of A BALLAD OF REMEMBRANCE, (see above). In Chapman IBP.

WORDS IN THE MOURNING TIME. New York: October House, 1970. 64 p.
>   Twenty poems.

THE NIGHT BLOOMING CEREUS. Heritage series, no. 20. London: Breman, 1972. 16 p. Paper.

ANGLE OF ASCENT: NEW AND SELECTED POEMS. New York: Liveright, 1975. 131 p.

> Contains nine new poems, as well as seven of the eight in THE NIGHT BLOOMING CEREUS, all of WORDS IN THE MOURNING TIME, and thirty-nine of the forty-one in SELECTED POEMS (all cited above).

Biography and Criticism

Davis FDT; Jackson BPA; O'Brien IBW; Whitlow BAL; Young BW30s.

Davis, Charles T. "Robert Hayden's Use of History." In Gibson MBP, pp. 96-111.

Fetrow, Fred M. "Robert Hayden's 'Frederick Douglass': Form and Meaning in a Modern Sonnet." CLA JOURNAL, 17 (1973), 79-84.

O'Sullivan, Maurice J., Jr. "The Mask of Allusion in Robert Hayden's 'The Diver.'" CLA JOURNAL, 17 (1973), 85-92.

Pool, Rosey. "Robert Hayden, Poet Laureate." NEGRO DIGEST, 15 (June 1966), 39-43.

HELLSTROM, GERRY (1937-)

FLOWER AND STONE. Gothenburg, Sweden: Calecarlia Press, 1958. 71 p. Paper.

HENDERSON, DAVID (1942-)

FELIX OF THE SILENT FOREST. Introd. LeRoi Jones. New York: Poets Press, 1967. [48] p. Paper.

DE MAYOR OF HARLEM. New York: Dutton, 1970. 128 p.

HERNTON, CALVIN C. (1934-)

THE COMING OF CHRONOS TO THE HOUSE OF NIGHTSONG: AN EPICAL NARRATIVE OF THE SOUTH. New York: Interim Books, 1964. [40] p. Paper.

MEDICINE MAN: COLLECTED POEMS. Introd. Joe Johnson. New York: Reed, Cannon, and Johnson, 1976. 115 p. Paper.

HERRING, MEL

BLACK COFFEE. New York: Published by the author, 1969.

HERRINGTON, RICHARD

WHERE I'M COMING FROM. Houston: Published by the author, [1971?]. Paper.

HERSHAW, FAY McKEENE

VERSE ALONG THE WAY. New York: Exposition, 1954. 48 p.

HIGGS, OLIVER F.

INTO THE REALM. Waterbury, Conn.: Poets Press, 1954. 37 p.

HILL, ANNE K.

AURORA. New York: Published by the author, 1948. 53 p.

HILL, ROY L. (1925-)

CORRIE J. CARROLL AND OTHER POEMS. Introd. Paul Jen-su Lin. Philadelphia: Dorrance, 1962. 35 p.

FORTY-NINE POEMS. Manhattan, Kans.: Ag Press, 1968. 71 p.

TRAFFIC LIGHTS AND OTHER POEMS. Absecon, N.J.: McDaniel and Hall Press, 1969. 48 p. Paper.

HOAGLAND, EVERETT (1942-)

TEN POEMS. Lincoln University, Pa.: American Studies Institute, [1969?].

BLACK VELVET. Pomona, Calif.: Published by the author, 1970. [14] p. Paper. Rev. ed. Detroit: Broadside, 1970. 32 p. Paper.

HOBBS, STERLING. See STERLING X, below, this section.

HODGES, FRENCHY JOLENE (1940-)

BLACK WISDOM. Detroit: Broadside, 1971. 30 p. Paper.
In Chapman IBP.

FOR MY GUY. Detroit: Tibi Productions, 1975. 37 p. Paper.

PIECE DE WAY HOME. Detroit: Tibi Productions, 1975. 30 p. Paper.

HODGES, GEORGE WASHINGTON

MY SOUVENIRS: POEMS AND STORIES. New York: n.p., 1951. 36 p.

HOLDEN, ADELE V.

FIGURINE AND OTHER POEMS. Philadelphia: Dorrance, 1961. 88 p.

HOLDER, J.N.

NOVEL AFMERLAND: VERSE TO REMEMBER. New York: n.p., 1953. Paper.

HOLLOWAY, ARIEL (1905-)

SHAPE THEM INTO DREAMS. New York: Exposition, 1955. 48 p.

HONIS, ANITA. See BENJAMIN, JOSEPH LOUIS, above, this section.

HOOKER, MICHAEL CRAIG

HONOR AWAKENS AGAIN FOR WE ARE ALL GIFTED AND REAL. Berkeley, Calif.: Oyez, 1973. 34 p. Paper.

HORD, FRED

AFTER H(OURS). Chicago: Third World, 1974. 28 p. Paper.

HORNE, FRANK (1899-1974)

HAVERSTRAW. Heritage series, no. 3. London: Breman, 1963. 40 p. Paper.

HOWARD, BEATRICE THOMAS

POEMS AND QUOTATIONS. New York: Published by the author, 1956. 36 p.

HOWARD, VANESSA (1955-)

A SCREAMING WHISPER. New York: Holt, 1972. 59 p.

HOWELL, GENE

CLIMACTIC INSIGHTS. Illus. by the author. N.p.: Published by the author, 1975. 28 p. Paper.
    Cover title: CLIMATIC INSIGHTS.

HOWELL, WILBERT R.

THE RHYME OF THE DEVIL-GERMS. New York: Pageant, 1963. 28 p.

HUFF, WILLIAM HENRY

SOWING AND REAPING, AND OTHER POEMS. Avon, III.: Hamlet Press, 1950. 77 p.

FROM DEEP WITHIN. Chicago: Dierkes Press, 1951. 40 p. Paper.

HUGGINS, ERICA. See NEWTON, HUEY P., below, this section.

HUGHES, LANGSTON. See section for 1901-45, above.

HUGHES, RONNIE (1945-)

RAPPIN. Brooklyn, N.Y.: Published by the author, 1971. 32 p. Paper.

HUMPHREY, MYRTLE "MOSS" (1934-)

BE A MAN BOY AND OTHER POEMS. Los Angeles: Capricorn House West, 1973.

AS MUCH AS I AM. Los Angeles: Capricorn House West, 1973.

HUTCHINSON, SYLVESTER

BRIDE OF WHITENESS AND OTHER POEMS. New York: Vantage, 1967. 72 p.

IFETAYO, FEMI FUNMI [REGINA MICOU] (1954-)

WE THE BLACK WOMAN. Detroit: Black Arts, 1970. 16 p. Paper.

IMAN, YUSEF

SOMETHING BLACK. Newark, N.J.: Jihad, 1967. 46 p. Paper.

POETRY FOR BEAUTIFUL BLACK WOMEN. Newark, N.J.: Jihad, 1969. [28] p. Paper.

ISMAIL, IBRAHIM IBN

POEMS FOR NIGGERS AND CRACKERS. With James V. Hatch. Introd. David DuBois. Cairo, Egypt: Published by the authors, 1965. 54 p. Paper.

BLACK NO SUGAR. Cairo, Egypt: Published by the author, [1966?].

JACKMON, MARVIN. See MARVIN X, below, this section.

JACKSON, ANGELA

VOO DOO / LOVE MAGIC. Chicago: Third World, 1974. 23 p. Paper.

JACKSON, AURILDA. See JONES, AURILDA JACKSON, below, this section.

JACKSON, BOOKER T. (1929-)

GOD LOOKS DOWN. Fort Smith, Ark.: South and West, 1968. 32 p. Paper.

NEEDS WORLD THE. Fort Smith, Ark.: South and West, 1972. 40 p. Paper.

JACKSON, JOHN R.

SOULFUL SOUNDS. New York: Exposition, 1973. 64 p.

JACKSON, JOHN ROBERT. See JOHNSON, HOMER PRESTON, below, this section.

JACKSON, MAE (1946-)

CAN I POET WITH YOU. Introd. Nikki Giovanni. New York: Black Dialogue Publishers, 1969. [16] p. Paper.

JACKSON, WILLIAM B.

POEMS I. New York: Rannick Playwrights Co., 1971. [32] p. Rev. ed. published as I HAVE CHANGED THE WORLD. New York: Rannick Playwrights Co., 1971. [32] p. Paper.

JACOBSON, HARRIET PRICE

SONGS IN THE NIGHT. New York: Exposition, 1947. 63 p.

JAMILA-RA [MAXINE HALL ELLISTON] (1945-)

THE GOOD BOOK. Introd. Yaki Yakubu. Chicago: Jamaa Scenes, 1971. 41 p. Paper.

JEFFERS, LANCE (1919-)

MY BLACKNESS IS THE BEAUTY OF THIS LAND. Detroit: Broadside, 1970. 24 p. Paper.

WHEN I KNOW THE POWER OF MY BLACK HAND. Introd. Eugene B. Redmond. Detroit: Broadside, 1974. 62 p.

JEFFERSON, ANITA GOMEZ

MAZES. Cleveland: Ramekha Press, 1972. 44 p. Paper.

JEFFERSON, KEITH

THE HYENA READER. Introd. Eugene Redmond. East St. Louis, Ill.: Black River Writers, 1975. 34 p. Paper.

JENKINS, WELBORN VICTOR. See section for 1901-45, above.

JENNINGS, H.A. See WOLDE, HABTE, below, this section.

JENRETTE, CORINNE McLEMORE (1903-)

JUST FOR FUN AND PLEASURE. New York: Carlton, 1970. 128 p.

JERROD

TO PAINT A BLACK PICTURE. Chicago: Free Black Press, 1969. 20 p.
Paper.

JEWELL, AANDER

THERE IS A SONG. New York: Pageant, 1967. 31 p.

JIGGETTS, BESS (1933-)

SOFT SOULS. New York: Baker Enterprises, n.d.

JOANS, TED (1928-)

"FUNKY" JAZZ POEMS. Introd. Robert George Reisner. New York: Rhino
Review, 1959. [20] p. Paper.

ALL OF TED JOANS AND NO MORE: POEMS AND COLLAGES. Introd.
Ilizabeth D. Klar. New York: Excelsior-Press, 1961. 93 p. Paper.

THE TRUTH: A POEM. Amsterdam, Netherlands: Surrealistisch Kabinet,
1968. [40] p. Paper.

> English text, with translations into thirty-six languages. The En-
> glish text appears also in "FUNKY" JAZZ POEMS (above) and
> BLACK POW-WOW (below).

BLACK POW-WOW: JAZZ POEMS. New York: Hill & Wang, 1969. 130 p.

> In Chapman IBP.

PROPOSITION POUR UN MANIFESTE BLACK POWER POUVOIR NOIR. Trans.
Jeannine Cimet and Robert Benayoun. Paris: Losfeld, 1969. 75 p. Paper.

AFRODISIA: NEW POEMS. New York: Hill & Wang, 1970. 150 p.

> In Chapman IBP.

A BLACK MANIFESTO IN JAZZ POETRY AND PROSE. London: Calder and
Boyars, 1971. 92 p.

A BLACK POW-WOW OF JAZZ POEMS. London: Calder and Boyars, 1973. 159 p.

Biography and Criticism

CONTEMPORARY AUTHORS. Detroit: Gale Research, 1974. Vols. 45–48, p. 262.

Gates, Skip. "Ted Joans: Tri-Continental Poet." TRANSITION (Accra), No. 48 (Apr.-June 1975), pp. 4-12.

An interview with Joans.

JOHNSON, ALICIA LOY (1944-)

REALITIES VS. SPIRITS. Carbondale, Ill.: Published by the author, 1969. [48] p. Paper.

JOHNSON, B.J. (1944-)

FROGS' HOLLOW AND OTHER POEMS. Philadelphia: Dorrance, 1973. 32 p.

MAN ON FIRE. Philadelphia: Dorrance, 1975. 32 p.

JOHNSON, DORIS J.

A CLOUD OF SUMMER AND OTHER NEW HAIKU. Chicago: Follet, 1967. 48 p.

JOHNSON, GEORGIA DOUGLAS. See section for 1901-45, above.

JOHNSON, HOMER PRESTON

TWILIGHT DREAMS: THE POETRY OF HOMER PRESTON JOHNSON, JOHN ROBERT JACKSON AND ROBERT MILUM BAKER. New York: Exposition, 1950. 63 p.

JOHNSON, HUGH G.

POEMS. New York: Comet, 1961. 41 p.

JOHNSON, OSCAR L.

JESUS WAS A FREAK. N.p.: Books Plus, 1972. 80 p. Paper.

JOHNSTON, PERCY EDWARD (1930-)

"CONCERTO FOR GIRL & CONVERTIBLE," OPUS NO. 5 AND OTHER POEMS. Washington, D.C.: Murray Bros., 1960. 24 p. Paper.

CONTINENTAL STREAMLETS. With Leroy Stone. Washington, D.C.: Continental Press, 1960. Paper.

SEAN PENDRAGON REQUIEM. New York: Dasein-Jupiter Hammon, 1964. 27 p. Paper.

SIX CYLINDER OLYMPUS. New York: Jupiter Hammon, 1964. 36 p. Paper.

JOHNSTON, STANLEY FIELDS

JOHNSTON'S JINGLES: FOR LIFETIME ENJOYMENT AND THOUGHT STIMULATION. . . . 400 POEMS AND SUBPOEMS . . . IN LITERARY ENGLISH, AND IN NORTH AMERICAN NEGRO DIALECT AND SLANG. 1st gen. abr. ed. Boston: Popular Publishers, 1955. 256 p.

JOHNSTONE, FREDERICK ADOLPHUS (1906-)

EMBERS. New York: Warwick Book Press, 1948. 100 p.

JONAS, STEPHEN (1921-70)

LOVE, THE POEM, THE SEA & OTHER PIECES EXAMINED. San Francisco: White Rabbit, 1957. [9] p. Paper.

TRANSMUTATIONS. Introd. John Wieners. London: Ferry Press, 1966. [66] p. Paper.

EXERCISES FOR EAR: BEING A PRIMER FOR THE BEGINNER IN THE AMERICAN IDIOM. Introd. Gerrit Lansing. London: Ferry Press, 1968. 80 p.

MORPHOGENESIS (BEING A CONVENTIONALIZATION OF "MORPHEMES" BY JACK SPICER). Cambridge, Mass.: Restau Press, 1970. [11] p. Paper.

SELECTED POEMS. Introd. Raffael de Gruttold. Boston: Stone Soup, 1973. [44] p. Paper.

TWO FOR JACK SPICER. South San Francisco, Calif.: ManRoot Books, 1974. [16] p. Paper.

JONES, ABIGAIL ROBERTS (1932-)

WHERE I HAVE WALKED. Philadelphia: Dorrance, 1974. 71 p.

JONES, AURILDA JACKSON

UNTANGLED. New York: Vantage, 1956. 40 p.

ECHO CALLS OF LAUGHTER OVER GREENER YEARS. Los Angeles: Trident Shop, 1975. 16 p. Paper.

LOVE TOUCHES THE EARTH (LOVE POEMS). Los Angeles: Trident Shop, 1975. 15 p. Paper.

JONES, E.H. (1925-)

A PLEASANT ENCOUNTER AND OTHER POEMS. New York: Vantage, 1964. 59 p.

JONES, GLADYS B.

TIMES, THINGS AND STUFF. Montclair, N.J.: Lewis Business Service, 1972. 106 p. Paper.

JONES, JYMI (1940-)

GUERILLA WARFARE IN PHILLY. Elkins Park, Pa.: Uhuru Publications, 1970. 18 p. Paper.

THE FRUIT THEORY. Philadelphia: Dorrance, 1973. 86 p.

JONES, [EVERETT] LEROI [IMAMU AMIRI BARAKA] (1934-)

PREFACE TO A TWENTY VOLUME SUICIDE NOTE. New York: Totem Press and Corinth Books, 1961. 47 p. Paper.

    Twenty-six poems.

THE DEAD LECTURER. New York: Grove, 1964. 79 p.

    Forty-two poems.

BLACK ART. Newark, N.J.: Jihad, 1966. [10] p. Paper, mimeographed.

The second edition (13 pages, mimeographed) and the third edition (20 unnumbered pages, offset), both labeled "Second Printing 1967," have the cover title BLACK ARTS. Contents included in BLACK MAGIC (1969, below).

BLACK MAGIC: SABOTAGE: TARGET STUDY: BLACK ART: COLLECTED POETRY, 1961-1967. Indianapolis: Bobbs-Merrill, 1969. 225 p.

> Contains 171 poems. "This book contains three books, SABOTAGE (1961-63), TARGET STUDY (1963-65), and BLACK ART (1965-66). The first, SABOTAGE, picks up just after THE DEAD LECTURER, which picked up right after PREFACE TO A TWENTY VOLUME SUICIDE NOTE." In Chapman IBP.

IN OUR TERRIBLENESS (SOME ELEMENTS AND MEANING IN BLACK STYLE). By Imamu Amiri Baraka (LeRoi Jones) and Fundi (Billy Abemathy). Indianapolis: Bobbs-Merrill, 1970. [171] p.

IT'S NATION TIME. By Imamu Amiri Baraka (LeRoi Jones). Chicago: Third World, 1970. 24 p. Paper.

SPIRIT REACH. By Imamu Amiri Baraka (LeRoi Jones). Newark, N.J.: Jihad, 1972. 25 p. Paper.

AFRIKAN REVOLUTION: A POEM. By Imamu Amiri Baraka. Newark, N.J.: Jihad, 1973. [8] p. Paper.

HARD FACTS (EXERPTS) [sic]. By Amiri Baraka. Newark, N.J.: Congress of Afrikan People, 1976. 39 p. Paper.

> Twenty-seven poems. The second and third printings were published in Newark by Revolutionary Communist League (MLM) and People's War, respectively.

Bibliographies

Dace, Leticia. LEROI JONES (IMAMU AMIRI BARAKA): A CHECKLIST OF WORKS BY AND ABOUT HIM. London: Nether Press, 1971. 196 p.

> Lists over 1,700 books and articles by and about Jones, as well as reviews of his works; substantially complete to mid-1969.

Biography and Criticism

See also the section on Jones under Drama, Part 2: Individual Authors, 1951-75.

Axios, Costas, and Nikos Syvriotis. PAPA DOC BARAKA FASCISM IN NEW-

ARK. New York: National Caucus of Labor Committees, 1973. 36 p.

A violent attack on Jones's politics, poetry, and personality.

Benston, Kimberly W. BARAKA: THE RENEGADE AND THE MASK. New Haven, Conn.: Yale Univ. Press, 1976. 290 p.

Coleman, Larry. "Comic-strip Heroes: LeRoi Jones and the Myth of American Innocence." JOURNAL OF POPULAR CULTURE, 3 (1969), 191-204.

Collins, Douglas. "LeRoi Jones as Poet." LANGUES MODERNES, 60 (1966), 336-38.

Dippold, Mary Diane. LEROI JONES: TRAMP WITH CONNECTIONS. Ann Arbor, Mich.: University Microfilms, 1972. 410 p.

A detailed critical biography, with a useful "Selected Bibliography," pp. 388-410.

Fischer, W.C. "Pre-revolutionary writing of Imamu Amiri Baraka." MASSACHUSETTS REVIEW, 14 (1973), 259-305.

Gallagher, Kathleen. "The Art(s) of Poetry: Jones and MacLeish." MIDWEST QUARTERLY, 12 (1971), 383-92.

Gottlieb, Saul. "They Think You're an Airplane and You're Really a Bird." EVERGREEN REVIEW, No. 50 (Dec. 1967), pp. 50-53, 96-97.

An interview.

Harris, Norman. "A Recurring Malady: Imamu Baraka's Move to the 'Left.'" ENDARCH, 1 (Fall 1974), 5-20.

Hudson, Theodore R. FROM LEROI JONES TO AMIRI BARAKA: THE LITERARY WORKS. Durham, N.C.: Duke Univ. Press, 1973. 225 p.

"Interview: Imamu Amiri Baraka." BLACK COLLEGIAN, 3 (Mar.-Apr. 1973), 30-31, 33.

Jackson, Esther M. "LeRoi Jones (Imamu Amiri Baraka): Form and the Progression of Consciousness." CLA JOURNAL, 17 (1973), 33-56.

Jacobus, Lee A. "Imamu Amiri Baraka: The Quest for Moral Order." In Gibson MBP, pp. 112-26.

Levertov, Denise. "Poets of the Given Ground." NATION, 192 (14 Oct. 1961), 251-52.

Major, Clarence. "The Poetry of LeRoi Jones." NEGRO DIGEST, 14 (Mar. 1965), 54-56.

Munro, C. Lynn. "LeRoi Jones: A Man in Transition." CLA JOURNAL, 17 (1973), 57-78.

Otten, Charlotte F. "LeRoi Jones: Napalm Poet." CONCERNING POETRY, 3 (Spring 1970), 5-11.

Pennington-Jones, Paulette. "From Brother LeRoi Jones through THE SYSTEM OF DANTE'S HELL to Imamu Ameer Baraka." JOURNAL OF BLACK STUDIES, 4 (1973), 195-214.

Russell, Charlie. "LeRoi Jones Will Get Us All in Trouble." LIBERATOR, 4 (Aug. 1964), 18.

Taylor, Clyde. "Baraka as Poet." In Gibson MBP, pp. 127-34.

Velde, Paul. "LeRoi Jones: Pursued by the Furies." COMMONWEAL, 88 (1968), 440-41.

Watkins, Mel. "Talk with LeRoi." NEW YORK TIMES BOOK REVIEW, 27 June 1971, p. 4.

JONES, ROSIE LEE LOGAN

TENDER CLUSTERS. San Antonio, Tex.: Naylor Co., 1969. 108 p.

JORDAN, JUNE (1936-)

WHO LOOK AT ME. New York: Crowell, 1969. 97 p.

SOME CHANGES. Introd. Julius Lester. New York: Dutton, 1971. 86 p.
    In Chapman IBP.

NEW DAYS: POEMS OF EXILE AND RETURN. New York: Emerson Hall, 1974. 131 p.

JORDAN, NORMAN (1938-)

DESTINATION ASHES (FOUR YEARS WITH A BLACK POET IN THE GHETTO). Cleveland: Jordan Press, 1967. [26] p. Paper, mimeographed. 4th ed. published as DESTINATION: ASHES. Introd. Don L. Lee. Cleveland: Vibration

Press, 1969. 54 p. Paper. 5th ed. Chicago: Third World, 1971. 72 p. Paper.

The first edition contained eighteen poems; the fourth contains thirty-seven poems; the fifth contains fifty-two poems.

ABOVE MAYA (TO A HIGHER CONSCIOUSNESS). Introd. Russell Atkins. Cleveland: Jordan Press, 1971. 50 p. Paper.

Biography and Criticism

Lee DV.

JOSEPH, FITZROY G. (Born in Trinidad, West Indies)

A LIVING EXPRESSION. New York: Pageant, 1958. 60 p.

KAI, NUBIA

PEACE OF MY MIND. Introd. Ade Olatunji. Detroit: Pamoja Press, 1975. 26 p. Paper.

KALI, MUMBA [CORNELIUS MAYS] (1949-)

JUST TRYIN' TO BE BLACK! Washington, D.C.: Temple of the Black Messiah, [1972?]. 21 p. Paper.

KAUFMAN, BOB (1935-)

SOLITUDES CROWDED WITH LONELINESS. New York: New Directions, 1965. 87 p. Paper.

Includes texts of "Second April" and "Abomunist Manifesto," previously published as folding broadsides by City Lights, San Francisco, in 1959.

GOLDEN SARDINE. Pocket Poets Series, 21. San Francisco: City Lights, 1967. 81 p. Paper.

Biography and Criticism

Christian, Barbara. "What Ever Happened to Bob Kaufman." BLACK WORLD, 21 (Sept. 1972), 20-29.

KELLY, ARNOLD J.

FROM THE DEPTHS OF MY SOUL. Hicksville, N.Y.: Exposition, 1974. 64 p.

KENDRICK, DOLORES (1927-)

THROUGH THE CEILING. Heritage series, no. 24. London: Breman, 1975. 20 p. Paper.

KENNEDY, BEATRICE BURTON

DEEP WITHIN. Philadelphia: Dorrance, 1975. 25 p.

KGOSITSILE, KEORAPETSE (1938- , born in South Africa)

SPIRITS UNCHAINED. Detroit: Broadside, 1969. 23 p. Paper.

FOR MELBA. Chicago: Third World, 1970. 24 p. Paper.

MY NAME IS AFRIKA. Introd. Gwendolyn Brooks. New York: Doubleday, 1971. 89 p.

THE PRESENT IS A DANGEROUS PLACE TO LIVE. Introd. George Kent. Chicago: Third World, 1974. 34 p. Paper.

PLACES AND BLOODSTAINS (NOTES FOR IPELENG). Introd. Chinua Achebe. Oakland, Calif.: Achebe Publications, 1975. 30 p. Paper.

KILGORE, JAMES C. (1928-)

THE BIG BUFFALO AND OTHER POEMS. Cleveland: Cuyahoga Community College Press, 1970. Paper.

MIDNIGHT BLAST AND OTHER POEMS. Cleveland: Printed by King Publishing and Printing Corp., 1970. 33 p. Paper.

A TIME OF BLACK DEVOTION. Ashland, Ohio: Ashland Poetry Press, 1971. 55 p. Paper.

KILPATRICK, GEORGE A. (1941-)

A VOICE IN THE COSMOS. New York: Carlton, 1972. 32 p.

KING, BERT ROSCOE

THE WISE FOOL AND OTHER POEMS. New York: Exposition, 1959. 79 p.

KING, MONTGOMERY WORDSWORTH

BORN NUDE AND MODERN. New York: Vantage, 1974. 86 p.

KING, THURMAN W.

AWAKEN YOUR THOUGHTS. Philadelphia: Dorrance, 1973. 46 p.

KNIGHT, ETHERIDGE (1933-)

POEMS FROM PRISON. Introd. Gwendolyn Brooks. Detroit: Broadside, 1968. 31 p. Paper.

BELLY SONG AND OTHER POEMS. Detroit: Broadside, 1973. 62 p.

Biography and Criticism

Lee DV.

KNOWLES, EDMOND and EDMOND A.

AT THE THRESHOLD. New York: Vantage, 1974. 86 p.

KOGER, EARL

EARL KOGER'S MOTHER GOOSE: JINGLES AND RHYMES. Baltimore, Md.: Earl Koger Co., 1970. [16] p. Paper.

LA GRONE, OLIVER (1915-)

FOOTFALLS: POETRY FROM AMERICA'S BECOMING. Detroit: Darel Press, 1949. 37 p. Paper.

THEY SPEAK OF DAWNS. Detroit: Brinkley Printers, 1963. [18] p. Paper.

LAKIN, MATTIE T. (1917-)

PORTICO OF THE TEMPLE. Gastonia, N.C.: Minges Printers, 1970. 42 p. Paper.

LAMARRE, HAZEL WASHINGTON (1917-)

BREATH IN THE WORLDWIND. Los Angeles: Print Rite Printing Co., 1955. 47 p.

IL SILENZIO. Hollywood, Calif.: Swordsman Press, 1972.

HALF-PAST TOMORROW. Hollywood, Calif.: Swodsman Press, 1973.

LANE, PINKIE GORDON (1923-)

WIND THOUGHTS. Fort Smith, Ark.: South and West, 1972. 59 p. Paper.

LASHLEY, JACQUELINE FALKNER. See FAULKNER-LASHLEY, JACQUELINE, above, this section.

LATIMORE, JEWEL C. [JOHARI AMINI] (1935-)

IMAGES IN BLACK. 2nd ed. Chicago: JC Press, 1967. 13 p. Paper, mimeographed. Rev. ed. Chicago: Third World, 1969. 13 p. Paper.

BLACK ESSENCE. Introd. Don L. Lee. Chicago: Third World, 1968. 17 p. Paper, mimeographed.

LET'S GO SOME WHERE. By Johari Amini (Jewel C. Latimore). Introd. Gwendolyn Brooks. Chicago: Third World, 1970. 31 p. Paper.

LAW, JOHN

FRANKLIN DELANO ROOSEVELT, A FRIEND TO MAN. New York: William-Frederick, 1946. Paper.

A NATION IN DISTRESS. New York: William-Frederick, 1972.

LEE, DON L. [MWALIMU HAKI R. MADHUBUTI] (1942-)

THINK BLACK! Introd. Eugene P.R. Feldman. Chicago: NuAce Social Printers, 1967. 26 p. Paper. Rev. ed. Detroit: Broadside, 1967. 24 p. Paper.

BLACK PRIDE. Introd. Dudley Randall. Detroit: Broadside, 1968. 34 p. Paper.

DON'T CRY, SCREAM. Introd. Gwendolyn Brooks. Detroit: Broadside, 1969. 64 p.

In Chapman IBP.

WE WALK THE WAY OF THE NEW WORLD. Detroit: Broadside, 1970. 71 p. Paper.

In Chapman IBP.

DIRECTIONSCORE: SELECTED AND NEW POEMS. Detroit: Broadside, 1971. 208 p. Paper.

Includes most of BLACK PRIDE, DON'T CRY, SCREAM, and THINK BLACK; all of WE WALK THE WAY OF THE NEW WORLD; and five new pieces. In Chapman IBP.

BOOK OF LIFE. By Mwalimu Haki R. Madhubuti (Don L. Lee). Detroit: Broadside, 1973. 80 p.

Biography and Criticism

Giddings, Paula. "From a Black Perspective: The Poetry of Don L. Lee." In AMISTAD 2. Ed. John A. Williams and Charles F. Harris. New York: Random House, 1971, pp. 297-318.

"Interview: The World of Don L. Lee." BLACK COLLEGIAN, 1 (Feb.-Mar. 1971), 24-27, 29, 33-34.

Llorens, David. "Black Don Lee: Writer-in-Residence at Cornell University." EBONY, 24 (Mar. 1969), 72-78, 80.

Miller, Eugene E. "Some Black Thoughts on Don Lee's THINK BLACK! Thunk by a Frustrated White Academic Thinker." COLLEGE ENGLISH, 34 (May 1973), 1094-1102.

Mosher, Marlene. NEW DIRECTIONS FROM DON L. LEE. Hicksville, N.Y.: Exposition, 1975. 148 p.

A critical study; includes "A Selected Bibliography of Published Works by and about Don L. Lee," pp. 121-36.

Palmer, R. Roderick. "The Poetry of Three Revolutionists. Don L. Lee, Sonia Sanchez, and Nikki Giovanni." CLA JOURNAL, 15 (1971, 25-36. Also in Gibson MBP, pp. 135-46.

Serwaa, Amma. "How Don L. Lee Treats his Sisters." TRANSITION (Howard Univ.), 1, No. 2 (1972), 107-22.

Shands, Annette Oliver. "The Relevancy of Don L. Lee as a Contemporary Black Poet." Black World, 21 (June 1972), 35-48.

LEE, HARRISON EDWARD

POEMS FOR THE DAY. New York: Comet, 1954. 23 p.

LEIA, SANDI

THE SILHOUETTE OF A PEN. Milwaukee, Wis.: Shore Publishing Co., 1971. 96 p. Paper.

LESTER, JULIUS (1939-)

THE MUD OF VIETNAM: PHOTOGRAPHS AND POEMS. New York: Folklore Center, 1967. [12] p. Paper.

WHO I AM. New York: Dial, 1974. [55] p.

LEVY, LYN. See LYN, below, this section.

LEWIS, CARRIE LOUISE

POLISHED PEBBLES. New York: Exposition, 1960. 48 p.

LEWIS, IOLA ELIZABETH

LIFE CAN BE BEAUTIFUL AND OTHER POEMS AND SONGS. Bethesda, Md.: Published by the author, 1966. 70 p.

LEWIS, LARRY. See MOGUMBO, VAJAVA, below, this section.

LIGHTNIN' ROD (1944-)

HUSTLERS CONVENTION. New York: Harmony Books, 1973. 125 p. Paper.

LIGHTS, RIKKI

DOG MOON. New York: Sunbury Press, 1976. 50 p. Paper.

LILLY, OCTAVE, JR. (1908-75)

CATHEDRAL IN THE GHETTO AND OTHER POEMS. New York: Vantage, 1970. 96 p.

Biography and Criticism

"Interview with Octave Lilly, Jr." NKOMBO, No. 9 (June 1974), pp. 27-36.

Interviewers are Tom Dent and Keorapetse Kgositsile.

LINSON, RASHAAN CONNEL

POEMS OF THE PART AND THE WHOLE. N.p.: n.p., 1972.

LOCKE, EDWARD

PAUSE, AND OTHER POEMS. New York: Exposition, 1954. 64 p.

LOCKHART, THEODORE

IN SEARCH OF ROOTS. Philadelphia: Dorrance, 1970. 40 p.

LOFTIN, ELOUISE (1950-)

JUMBISH. New York: Emerson Hall, 1972. 40 p. Paper.

BAREFOOT NECKLACE. Brooklyn, N.Y.: Jamima House Press, 1975. 78 p. Paper.

Includes contents of JUMBISH (1972), above.

LOFTIS, NORMAN JOHN (1943-)

EXILES AND VOYAGES. New York: Black Market Press, 1970. 63 p. Paper.

BLACK ANIMA. New York: Liveright, 1973. 116 p.

LOMAX, PEARL CLEAGUE (1948-)

WE DON'T NEED NO MUSIC. Detroit: Broadside, 1972. 16 p. Paper.

LONG, DOUGHTRY (1942-)

BLACK LOVE BLACK HOPE. Introd. Dudley Randall. Detroit: Broadside, 1971. 30 p. Paper.

SONG FOR NIA: A POETIC ESSAY IN THREE PARTS. Detroit: Broadside, 1971. 38 p. Paper.

LONG, NAOMI C. See MADGETT, NAOMI LONG, below, this section.

LORDE, AUDRE (1934-)

THE FIRST CITIES. Introd. Diane di Prima. New York: Poets Press, 1968. [32] p. Paper.

CABLES TO RAGE. Heritage series, no. 9. London: Breman, 1970. 28 p. Paper.

FROM A LAND WHERE OTHER PEOPLE LIVE. Detroit: Broadside, 1973. 46 p. Paper.

NEW YORK HEAD SHOP AND MUSEUM. Detroit: Broadside, 1974. 56 p. Paper.

BETWEEN OUR SELVES. Point Reyes, Calif.: Eidolon Editions, 1976. 22 p. Paper.

COAL. New York: Norton, 1976. 70 p.

Biography and Criticism

CONTEMPORARY AUTHORS. Detroit: Gale Research Co., 1971. Vols. 25–28, p. 457.

LOUISE, FANNIE

ALLOW ME TO SAY. Washington, D.C.: Published by the author, [1972?].

LOVE, MELVIN

WAR IN HEAVEN AND OTHER POEMS. New York: Exposition, 1954. 64 p.

LOVE, ROSE LEARY

NEBRASKA AND HIS GRANNY. Tuskegee, Ala.: Tuskegee Institute Press, 1966.

LOVING, WINIFRED "OYOKO"

REMEMBER WHEN. Christiansted, St. Croix, Virgin Islands: Printed by JET Printing Service, 1974. 24 p. Paper.

LOVINGOOD, PENMAN

POEMS OF A SINGER. Compton, Calif.: Lovingood Co., 1963. 68 p.

LUTOUR, LOU

THE POWER AND THE GLORY. Charleston, Ill.: Prairie Press, 1967. 33 p. Paper.

I DREAMED A DREAM. Charleston, Ill.: Prairie Press, 1969. 31 p. Paper.

TREASURE HOUSE. Charleston, Ill.: World Resource Books, 1970. 47 p. Paper.

FREEDOM TRAIN. No imprint. [1971?].

LYLE, K. CURTIS (1944-)

DRUNK ON GOD & FROM OUT OF NOWHERE. Los Angeles: Blind Joe Death Editions, 1975. 45 p.

LYN [LYN LEVY] (1946-)

SINGING SADNESS HAPPY. Detroit: Broadside, 1972. 32 p. Paper.

LYNN, EVE [Pseud. of EVELYN CRAWFORD REYNOLDS]

NO ALABASTER BOX AND OTHER POEMS. Introd. Gene Rhodes. Philadelphia: Alpress, 1936. 37 p.

TO NO SPECIAL LAND. Introd. Mary McLeod Bethune. New York: Exposition, 1953. 64 p.

PUT A DAISY IN YOUR HAIR. Introd. Marian Anderson. Philadelphia: Dorrance, 1963. 31 p.

LYONS, CHARLES [IS SAID] (1935-)

IS SAID. Columbus, Ohio: Lyons Productions, 1973. 96 p. Paper.

"MASTER PLAN." Columbus, Ohio: Lyons Productions, 1974. 100 p. Paper.

"SECRET PRAYER." Columbus, Ohio: Lyons Productions, 1975. 32 p. Paper.

LYONS, W.T. (1919-)

SOUL IN SOLITUDE. New York: Exposition, 1970. 54 p.

THE HEARTBEAT OF SOUL. Hicksville, N.Y.: Exposition, 1975. 79 p.

McALPIN, NEAL, JR.

FROM BROTHERMAN WITH LOVE. Nashville, Tenn.: Published by the author, 1973. 32 p. Paper.
    At top of cover: "An Open Letter to Black Women."

McCAIN, W. CALVIN

A SWORD IN TRUTH. Tremont, Ill.: Award Poets Paperbacks, 1970. 25 p. Paper.

PIECES OF PEACE: CONCEPTS OF A POET. Jericho, N.Y.: Exposition, 1974. 80 p.

McCLANE, KENNETH A. (1951-)

OUT BEYOND THE BAY. Ithaca, N.Y.: Ithaca House, 1975. 70 p. Paper.

McCLAURIN, IRMA

POEMS I. New York: Rannick Playwrights Co., 1971. [32] p. Paper. Rev. ed. published as BLACK CHICAGO. New York: Rannick Playwrights Co., 1971. [32] p. Paper.

SONG IN THE NIGHT. Chicago: Pearl Press, 1974. [32] p. Paper.

McCORKLE, GEORGE WASHINGTON. See section for 1901-45, above.

McDANIELS, EUGENE

THE GOSPEL BLUES AND POETRY OF EUGENE McDANIELS. New York: Charles Hansen Music and Books, 1971. 88 p. Paper.

McELROY, COLLEEN (1935-)

THE MULES DONE LONG SINCE GONE. Seattle: Harrison-Madrona Center, 1973. Paper.

MUSIC FROM HOME. Introd. John Gardner & Knute Skinner. Carbondale: Southern Illinois Univ. Press, 1976. 100 p.

McFARLAND, HARRY STANLEY (1900- , Jamaica, West Indies)

EXPERIENCES OF A HEART, ITS JOYS, ITS SORROWS. Boston: Meador, 1931. 68 p.
This title was published anonymously.

PASSING THRU. New York: Wendell Malliet, 1950. 120 p.

COLUMBIA SPEAKS. No imprint. [1953]. [7] p. Paper.

TO MY COUNTRY. No imprint. [1953].]7] p. Paper.

GROWING UP. Boston: Meador, 1956. 88 p.

MISSING PAGES. Boston: Forum, 1962. 72 p.

UNION. No imprint. [1963]. [17] p. Paper.

MORE MISSING PAGES. New York: Carlton, 1966. 56 p.

SOME MORE MISSING PAGES. New York: Vantage, 1969. 102 p.

TRILOGY. New York: Vantage, 1971. 81 p.

CREST. New York: Vantage, 1975. 42 p.

McGAUGH, LAWRENCE (1940-)

A FIFTH SUNDAY. Berkeley, Calif.: Oyez, 1965. [26] p. Paper.

VACUUM CANTOS. Berkeley, Calif.: Oyez, 1969. [32] p. Paper.

McGHEE, MAUDE

TO GET MY NAME IN THE KINGDOM BOOK. Atlanta: Published by the author, 1963. 42 p.

McKAY, CLAUDE. See section for 1901–45, above.

McLEARY, EDNA TUBBS

TOMORROW'S YESTERDAY. No imprint. [196–?].

McMORRIS, THOMAS

STRIVING TO WIN. Boston: Christopher, 1949. 144 p.

McNAIR, JOSEPH (1948–)

EARTHBOOK. Menlo Park, Calif.: Thoth, 1972. 36 p. Paper.

McNEAL, JAMES HARRISON

THOUGHTS IN THE NEGRO EXPERIENCE. Philadelphia: Russell Press, 1967. 60 p. Paper.

McNEIL, DEE DEE (1943–)

DEE DEE DOODLES: RIDDLES, POETRY AND PICTURES TO COLOR. Los Angeles: Al-Bait Haram Publishing Co., 1972. [43] p. Paper.

MADGETT, NAOMI LONG [NAOMI CORNELIA LONG] (1923–)

SONGS TO A PHANTOM NIGHTINGALE. By Naomi Cornelia Long. New York: Fortuny's, 1941. 30 p.

ONE AND THE MANY. New York: Exposition, 1956. 64 p.

STAR BY STAR. Detroit: Harlo Press, 1965. 64 p. Paper.

PINK LADIES IN THE AFTERNOON: NEW POEMS 1965–1971. Detroit: Lotus Press, 1972. 63 p. Paper.

MADHUBUTI, MWALIMU HAKI R. See LEE, DON L., above, this section.

MAHONE, BARBARA (1944-)

SUGARFIELDS. Introd. Hoyt W. Fuller. No imprint. [1970]. 32 p. Paper.

MAJOR, CLARENCE (1936-)

THE FIRES THAT BURN IN HEAVEN. Chicago: Published by the author, 1954. Paper.

LOVE POEMS OF A BLACK MAN. Omaha: Coercion Press, 1964. 14 p. Paper.

HUMAN JUICES. Omaha: Coercion Press, 1965. 12 p. Paper.

SWALLOW THE LAKE. Middletown, Conn.: Wesleyan Univ. Press, 1970. 64 p.

PRIVATE LINE. Heritage series, no. 15. London: Breman, 1971. 24 p. Paper.

SYMPTOMS & MADNESS. New York: Corinth, 1971. 76 p.
   In Chapman IBP.

THE COTTON CLUB: NEW POEMS. Detroit: Broadside, 1972. 22 p. Paper.

THE SYNCOPATED CAKEWALK. New York: Barlenmir House, 1974. 53 p.

Biography and Criticism

Interview in O'Brien IBW.

MALCOM, BARBARA. See NAYO, below, this section.

MANNAN, LAILA. See SANCHEZ, SONIA, below, this section.

MARKS, JIM (1934-)

VIBRATIONS IN SANCTUARY. Palo Alto, Calif.: Jamal Publishing Co., 1970. 49 p. Rev. ed. published as VIBRATIONS IN SANCTUARY, ONE

MORE TIME. Palo Alto, Calif.: Jamal Publishing Co., 1970. 64 p. Paper.

JAZZ WOMEN SOUL. Introd. Al Young. Millbrae, Calif.: Celestial Arts, 1974. [128] p. Paper.

MARSH, CLIFTON E. (1946-)

JOURNEY TO SHANARA: A LOVE STORY AND A PROPOSAL TO FREEDOM. Syracuse, N.Y.: Shanara Publishers, 1974. 24 p. Paper.

MARSHALL, ULYSSES S. (1950-)

THOUGHTS FROM THE ASYLUM. Detroit: Agascha Productions, 1974. 24 p. Paper.

MARTIN, HERBERT WOODWARD (1933-)

NEW YORK THE NINE MILLION AND OTHER POEMS. Grand Rapids, Mich.: Abracadabra Press, 1969. 25 p. Paper.

THE SHIT-STORM POEMS. Grand Rapids, Mich.: Pilot Press, 1973. 40 p. Paper.

THE PERSISTENCE OF THE FLESH. Detroit: Lotus Press, 1976. 67 p. Paper.

MARTIN, ROSE HINTON

ENDEARING ENDEAVOURS. New York: Pageant, 1960. 56 p.

MARVIN X [MARVIN JACKMON, EL MUHAJIR] (1944-)

BLACK MAN LISTEN: POEMS AND PROVERBS. Detroit: Broadside, 1969. 28 p. Paper.

FLY TO ALLAH. Fresno, Calif.: Al Kitab Sudan, 1969. 24 p. Paper.

WOMAN--MAN'S BEST FRIEND (PROVERBS, PARABLES, POEMS, SONGS). By El Muhajir. San Francisco: Al Kitab Sudan, 1973. 88 p. Paper.

Includes complete texts of BLACK MAN LISTEN and FLY TO ALLAH.

MASSEY, JOE C.

SINGING STARS. New York: Greenwich, 1961. 57 p.

MAST, VERNETTA (1955-)

CHAINED. Introd. E.R. Fowlks. Dallas: Akini Isi Publishing Co., 1973. 34 p. Paper.

MATANAH [DOROTHY JUNE WATKINS]

BITS AND PIECES. Ed. and Introd. Delores F. Ridge. Rev. ed. Dallas: Published by the author, 1974. 25 p. Paper.

LOVE BONES. Arranged and ed. Delores F. Ridge. Dallas: Published by the author, 1974. 75 p. Paper.

MBEMBE [MILTON SMITH] (1946-)

TO GO ON. Shawnee Mission, Kans.: BkMk Press, 1973. 20 p. Paper.

MELANCON, NORMAN (1939-)

I'LL JUST BE ME: POEMS FOR YOUNG AND OLD. New York: Exposition, 1967. 32 p.

BIRTH OF A SLAVE CHILD. Los Angeles: National Poetry Press, 1968.

MENKITI, IFEANYI (1940- , born in Nigeria)

AFFIRMATIONS. Chicago: Third World, 1971. 24 p. Paper.

MERRITT, ALICE HADEN. See section for 1901-45, above.

MICOU, REGINA. See IFETAYO, FEMI FUNMI, above, this section.

MILLER, CLIFFORD LEONARD

THE HAUNTING VOICE. Introd. Rolfe Cobleigh. Boston: Lavalle Press, 1924. 19 p. Paper.

YOUR BROTHER'S BROTHER. Introd. Ralph O. Jackson. Boston: Lavalle Press, 1948. 16 p. Paper.

IMPERISHABLE THE TEMPLE. Mexico City: Published by the author, [1963?]. [86] p.

MILLER, HENRY JEFFERSON (1877-)

BLASTED BARRIERS: VIEWS OF A REPORTER IN STORY AND SONG. Boston: Christopher, 1950. 140 p.

MILLER, MAY

INTO THE CLEARING. Washington, D.C.: Charioteer Press, 1959. 24 p.

POEMS. Thetford, Vt.: Cricket Press, 1962. [13] p. Paper.

NOT THAT FAR. San Luis Obispo, Calif.: Solo Press, 1973. [24] p. Paper.

THE CLEARING AND BEYOND. Washington, D.C.: Charioteer Press, 1974. 49 p.
> "Part 1 of this book is a reissue of the poems in the volume IN-TO THE CLEARING. . . . Part 2, titled 'Beyond,' is a selection of later poems."

DUST OF UNCERTAIN JOURNEY. Detroit: Lotus Press, 1975. 67 p. Paper.

MISSICK, RUPERT (Born in Bahama Islands)

NAKED MOON. New York: Graham Publications, 1970. 30 p. Paper.

MITCHELL, JOE H.

BLACK ODYSSEY. Markham, Ill.: Natural Resources Unlimited, 1974. 36 p. Paper.

BLACKLASH BLUES. Markham, Ill.: Natural Resources Unlimited, 1974. 34 p. Paper.

LOVIN' YOU. Markham, Ill.: Natural Resources Unlimited, 1974. 37 p. Paper.

NATURE'S CHILD. Markham, Ill.: Natural Resources Unlimited, 1974. 37 p. Paper.

O WOMAN. Markham, Ill.: Natural Resources Unlimited, 1974. 77 p. Paper.

ONE ROOM SHACK. Markham, III.: Natural Resources Unlimited, 1974. Paper.

VIGNETTES. Markham, III.: Natural Resources Unlimited, 1974. 37 p. Paper.

TAPESTRY. Markham, III.: Natural Resources Unlimited, 1975. 40 p. Paper.

MOBLEY, EVELYN

SOMETHING FOR EVERYONE. Philadelphia: Dorrance, 1974. 24 p.

MOGUMBO, VAJAVA [LARRY LEWIS]

ASSASSIN POEMS. By Vajava Mogumbo and Brothers. Introd. Obagun Omar Mogumbo (Sidney Van Lewis). Detroit: Black Graphics International, 1970. 22 p. Paper.

MONROE, REGINALD (1938-)

BLACK FLOWERS. New York: Lyle Stuart, 1971. 72 p.

MOORE, DAVID. See MOR, AMUS, below.

MOORE, LANESE B.

CAN I BE RIGHT? New York: Vantage, 1971. 48 p.

MOORE, RAYMOND L.

VISIONS OF REALITY AND OTHER POEMS. Chicago: Free Black Press, 1969. 33 p. Paper.

MOORE, ROBERT E. (1950-)

HOLMES & OTHER POEMS. Introd. Linda Baron Dudley. New York: Published by the author, 1974. [24] p. Paper.

MOR, AMUS [DAVID MOORE]

THE COMING OF JOHN. Introd. Abd-al Hakimu Ibn Alkalimat. Chicago: 21st Century Atoma, 1969. 23 p. Paper.

MORELAND, JOHN

ONLY THE PEN WAS MINE. Los Angeles: Lyric Publishing Co., 1966.
25 p. Paper.

MORGAN, JAMES H. (1916-)

POEMS BY CANDLELIGHT AND THE FLARE OF A MATCH: POEMS COM-
POSED AND WRITTEN FOR ENCOURAGEMENT AND ENTERTAINMENT.
New York: Vantage, 1967. 152 p.

MORRIS, JAMES CLIFTONNE (1920-)

CLEOPATRA AND OTHER POEMS. New York: Exposition, 1955. 64 p.

FROM A TIN-MOUTH GOD TO HIS BRASS-EARED SUBJECTS. New York:
Greenwich, 1966. 141 p.

MUHAJIR, EL. See MARVIN X, above, this section.

MUHAMMAD, UMAR AHMAD ABDULLAH

WE WILL ALWAYSSSS BE HERE. Brooklyn, N.Y.: EAST Publications, 1973.
42 p. Paper.

MUHAMMED, ABDULLAH

CONSCIOUS BLACK COMMUNICATION. By Abdullah of New York: Brooklyn, N.Y.: EAST Publications, 1972. 34 p. Paper.
    Poetry and prose.

MUJAHADA, SAYIF [BRUCE C. GEARY] (1941-)

GET BACK INSANITY. Introd. Samuel Allen. Boston: Afrikan Heritage
Press, 1975. 32 p. Paper.

MUNGIN, HORACE

DOPE HUSTLER JAZZ. New York: Brothers Distributing Co., 1968. 31 p.
Paper.

NOW SEE HERE, HOMES! New York: Brothers Distributing Co., 1969.
33 p. Paper.

MURPHY, BEATRICE M. (1908-)

LOVE IS A TERRIBLE THING. New York: Hobson Book Press, 1945. 65 p.

THE ROCKS CRY OUT. With Nancy L. Arnez. Detroit: Broadside, 1969. 24 p. Paper.

MURPHY, RUTH

JORDAN GET BACK. N.p.: Published by the author, 1964. 48 p.

MURRAY, HENRY CLIFFORD

THE SIGHT OF DAWN. New York: Exposition, 1959. 61 p.

MURRAY, PAULI (1910-)

DARK TESTAMENT AND OTHER POEMS. Norwalk, Conn.: Silvermine, 1970. 106 p.

MURRELL, VIRGINIA

BURNT ICARUS. Whittier, Calif.: Stockton Trade Press, 1962. 94 p.

MUUMBA [HERMAN BROWN]

SOME POETRY AND THINGS. No imprint. [196-?]. [40] p. Paper.

MYLES, GLENN (1933-)

DOWN & COUNTRY. Berkeley, Calif.: Artman's Press, 1974. Paper.

NALL, HIRAM

UP FROM THE DEAD LEVEL. Madison, Wis.: Printed by FAS Publishing, 1974. 35 p. Paper.

NAYO [BARBARA MALCOM]

I WANT ME A HOME. New Orleans: BlkArtSouth, 1969. 20 p. Paper.

NEAL, LARRY (1937-)

BLACK BOOGALOO (NOTES ON BLACK LIBERATION). Introd. LeRoi Jones. San Francisco: Journal of Black Poetry Press, 1969. 60 p. Paper.

HOODOO HOLLERIN' BEBOP GHOSTS. Washington, D.C.: Howard Univ. Press, 1974. 87 p.

> Neal says " a rough cross-section of my most publishable poems . . . written between 1964 and 1973."

NELSON, DAVID (1939-)

BLACK IMPULSE. New York: Drum Publications, 1968. [16] p. Paper.

NELSON, RHOBENA

JUS' BLACK. Detroit: 5 Points Printers, 1966. Paper.

NEWTON, HUEY P. and ERICA HUGGINS

INSIGHTS & POEMS. Introd. Richard Baker. San Francisco: City Lights, 1975. 84 p.

NICHOLAS, MICHAEL (1941-)

WATERMELONS INTO WINE. Honolulu: Published by the author, 1968. [19] p. Paper.

NICHOLES, MARION (1944-)

LIFE STYLES. Introd. Don L. Lee. Detroit: Broadside, 1971. 22 p. Paper.

> In Chapman IBP.

NICHOLS, JAMES EMANUEL

VERSE FRAGMENTS. New York: Vantage, 1958. 77 p.

ODEN, GLORIA (1923-)

THE NAKED FRAME: A LOVE POEM AND SONNETS. New York: Exposition, 1952. [35] p.

ODEN, THOMAS HILDRED. See BURLEIGH, BENNY, above, this section.

O'HIGGINS, MYRON. See THE LION AND THE ARCHER under HAYDEN, ROBERT, above, this section.

OJI, ABAYOME [JACQUES WAKEFIELD]

LUB. New York: Brothers Hue Man Publications, 1971. [24] p. Paper.

OLATUNJI, ADE

PAMOJA: THE BEGINNING, THE EARLY YEARS/POEMS 1969-1971. Detroit: Pamoja Press, 1974. 27 p. Paper.

PRAISE SONG. Detroit: Pamoja Press, 1975. 24 p. Paper.

OLIVER, SMITH

GOD-CHILD. 2nd ed. New York: H. Wolff Book Manufacturing Co., 1966. 51 p.

> "First edition printed in Madras, India. Second edition printed in New York."

OLOGBONI, TEJUMOLA. See TAYLOR, ROCKIE D., below, this section.

OLUBAYO. See FALKNER-LASHLEY, JACQUELINE, above, this section.

OLUMO [JIM CUNNINGHAM] (1936-)

THE BLUE NARRATOR. Chicago: Third World, 1974. 26 p. Paper.

PALMER, VERNON U. (1930-)

THE NEW GRAND ARMY. New York: Vantage, 1965. 64 p.

PAMOJA, IMANI

GITTIN OUR MINDS, OUR SHIT, OUR PEOPLE TOGETHER. Dallas: Akini Isi Publishing Co., 1971. 34 p. Paper.

PARKER, J.W.

MY HEART'S DESIRE. Oakland, Calif.: Published by the author, [195-?]. 83 p.

PARKER, PAT

CHILD OF MYSELF. San Lorenzo, Calif.: Shameless Hussy Press, 1972. [36] p. Paper.

PIT STOP. Oakland, Calif.: Women's Press Collective, 1975. [44] p. Paper.

PARKS, GORDON (1912-)

A POET AND HIS CAMERA. New York: Viking, 1968. [92] p.

WHISPERS OF INTIMATE THINGS. Introd. Philip B. Kunhardt, Jr. New York: Viking, 1971. 96 p.

IN LOVE. Philadelphia: Lippincott, 1971. [80] p.

MOMENTS WITHOUT PROPER NAMES. New York: Viking, 1975. 172 p.

PATTERSON, LUCILLE J.

SAPPHIRE. Chicago: Published by the author, 1972. 17 p. Paper.

PATTERSON, RAYMOND R. (1929-)

26 WAYS OF LOOKING AT A BLACK MAN AND OTHER POEMS. New York: Award Books, 1969. 185 p. Paper.

PATTERSON, VIVIAN

CRIES FROM THE CHICAGO GHETTO. Chicago: N.p., [1973?]. Paper.

PENNY, ROB (1940-)

BLACK TONES OF TRUTH. Introd. August Wilson. Pittsburgh: Oduduwa Productions, [1970?]. 33 p. Paper.

PERKINS, EUGENE (1932-)

AN APOLOGY TO MY AFRICAN BROTHER. Chicago: Adams Press, 1965. 24 p. Paper.

BLACK IS BEAUTIFUL. Chicago: Free Black Press, 1968. 30 p. Paper.

WEST WALL. Chicago: Free Black Press, 1969. [20] p. Paper.

SILHOUETTE. Chicago: Free Black Press, 1970. 74 p. Paper.

PERRY, JOHN SINCLAIR

VOICE OF HUMANITY: SONG OF THE NEW WORLD. Boston: Christopher, 1952. 46 p.

PFISTER, ARTHUR (1949-)

BEER CANS, BULLETS, THINGS & PIECES. Introd. Imamu Amiri Baraka. Detroit: Broadside, 1972. 30 p. Paper.

PHILLIPS, WALDO

POETRY IN PROFLECTION. Los Angeles: Compton Counseling Center, 1965. 38 p.

PINSON, DAVE

STUDIES IN BLACK AND WHITE. New York: Vantage, 1966. 65 p.

PITCHER, OLIVER (1924-)

DUST OF SILENCE. Introd. Robert Grantham. New York: Troubador Press, 1958. 30 p. Paper.

PLUMPP, STERLING D. (1940-)

PORTABLE SOUL. Chicago: Third World, 1969. 21 p. Paper.

HALF BLACK HALF BLACKER. Introd. Don L. Lee. Chicago: Third World, 1970. 32 p. Paper.

STEPS TO BREAK THE CIRCLE. Introd. Keorapetse Kgositsile. Chicago: Third World, 1974. 28 p. Paper.

> Kgositsile's introduction also appears in BLACK WORLD, 23 (Sept. 1974), 30-34.

CLINTON: Detroit: Broadside, 1976. 23 p. Paper.

POLK, ELAINE D.R.

DREAMS AT TWILIGHT: RELIGIOUS MEDITATIONS IN VERSE AND PROSE.
New York: Exposition, 1957. 96 p.

PORTER, JOHN THOMAS

IN SPITE OF HANDICAPS. New York: Comet, 1959. 50 p.

PORTER, WELLINGTON

THE ETERNITY OF THOUGHT . . . WITH THE PATH OF LIGHT: THE WISDOM
OF THE ETHIOPIANS. New York: Vantage, 1974. 80 p.

Poetry and prose.

POSEY, CECIL JAMES

A MESSAGE FROM NOAH AND OTHER POEMS. New York: Henry Harrison,
1946. 47 p.

POWELL, RAPHAEL P.

THE PRAYER FOR FREEDOM. New York: Published by the author, 1957.
15 p.

PRATHER, JOHN L.

PRATHER'S PROVERBS. New York: Greenwich, 1967. 104 p.

Poetry and prose.

PRESTWIDGE, KATHLEEN J. (1927-)

WISDOM TEETH. Introd. Sy King. New York: Published by the author,
1973. 59 p. Paper.

PRICE, E. CURMIE

THE STATE OF THE UNION. Surrey, British Columbia: Sono Nis Press,
1970. 70 p.

PRIME, CYNTHIA JUDY (Born in Trinidad, West Indies)

THE SOUR AND THE SWEET: A COLLECTION OF POEMS ON ASPECTS OF

THE BLACK EXPERIENCE. New York: William-Frederick, 1972. 85 p.

PRITCHARD, GLORIA CLINTON

TREES ALONG THE HIGHWAY. New York: Comet, 1953. 26 p.

PRITCHARD, NORMAN H. (1939-)

THE MATRIX: POEMS, 1960-1970. New York: Doubleday, 1970. 203 p.

EECCHHOOEESS. New York: New York Univ. Press, 1971. [62] p.

RA, SUN. See SUN RA, below, this section.

RAGLAND, JAMES FARLEY. See section for 1901-45, above.

RAHMAN, YUSUF [RONALD STONE; TAR LEE SUN]

TWO POEMS: TRANSCENDENTAL BLUES, ACCELERATION. Philadelphia: Am God Publishing Co., [1966?]. 23 p. Paper.
    Cover title: ALHOMDULLILAH!

RAINS, OLLIE F.

ORIGINAL POEMS OF NATURE AND ALL WALKS OF LIFE. Los Angeles: Privately printed, 1946. 40 p.

RANDALL, DUDLEY (1914-)

POEM COUNTERPOEM. With Margaret Danner. Detroit: Broadside, 1966. 24 p. Paper.

CITIES BURNING. Detroit: Broadside, 1968. 16 p. Paper.

LOVE YOU. Heritage Series, no. 10. London: Breman, 1970. 16 p. Paper.
    In Chapman IBP.

MORE TO REMEMBER: POEMS OF FOUR DECADES. Chicago: Third World, 1971. 77 p.

AFTER THE KILLING. Chicago: Third World, 1973. 16 p. Paper.

Biography and Criticism

NICHOLAS, A.X. "A Conversation with Dudley Randall." BLACK WORLD, 21 (Dec. 1971), 26–34.

An interview.

RANDALL, JAMES, JR. (1938-)

DON'T ASK ME WHO I AM. Detroit: Broadside, 1970. 16 p. Paper.

CITIES AND OTHER DISASTERS. Detroit: Broadside, 1973. 30 p. Paper.

RANDALL, JON C. (1942-)

INDIGOES. Detroit: Broadside, 1975. 15 p. Paper.

RANDOLPH, JEREMY

POEMS I. New York: Rannick Playwrights Co., 1971. [32] p. Paper.
Rev. ed. published as FIGHT TO BE FREE! New York: Rannick Playwrights Co., 1971. [32] p. Paper.

POEMS II. New York: Rannick Playwrights Co., 1971. [32] p. Paper.
Rev. ed. published as SEZ ME, A SOUTHERN NIGGER. New York: Rannick Playwrights Co., 1971. [32] p. Paper.

RAP, B. See HARDEMAN, BEAUREGARD ANDREW, JR., above, this section.

RAVEN, JOHN (1936-)

BLUES FOR MOMMA AND OTHER LOW DOWN STUFF. Detroit: Broadside, 1971. 31 p. Paper.

In Chapman IBP.

REASON, ARTHUR WESLEY

POEMS OF INSPIRATION FOR BETTER LIVING. New York: Exposition, 1959. 97 p.

REDDY, T.J. (1945-)

LESS THAN A SCORE, BUT A POINT. New York: Vintage, 1974. 97 p. Paper.

REDMOND, EUGENE B. (1937-)

A TALE OF TIME & TOILET TISSUE. East St. Louis, Ill.: Published by the author, 1969. 12 p. Paper.

SENTRY OF THE FOUR GOLDEN PILLARS. East St. Louis, Ill.: House of Truth, 1970. 32 p. Paper.

RIVER OF BONES AND FLESH AND BLOOD. East St. Louis, Ill.: Black River Writers, 1971. 64 p. Paper.

SONGS FROM AN AFRO/PHONE: NEW POEMS. East St. Louis, Ill.: Black River Writers, 1972. 63 p. Paper.

IN A TIME OF RAIN & DESIRE: NEW LOVE POEMS. East St. Louis, Ill.: Black River Writers, 1973. 103 p.

CONSIDER LONELINESS AS THESE THINGS. Rome, Italy: Centro Studi e Scambi Internazionali, 1974. 16 p. Paper.

REED, CLARENCE

NOT FOREVER TEARS. Newark, N.J.: Jihad, 1967. 17 p. Paper, mimeographed. 2nd ed. Newark: Jihad, 1969. 23 p. Paper.

REED, ISHMAEL (1938-)

CATECHISM OF D NEOAMERICAN HOODOO CHURCH. Heritage series, no. 11. London: Breman, 1970. 28 p. Paper.

CONJURE: SELECTED POEMS, 1963-1970. Amherst: Univ. of Massachusetts Press, 1972. 83 p.

CHATTANOOGA. New York: Random House, 1973. 55 p.

Biography and Criticism

O'Brien IBW.

Beauford, Fred. "Conversation with Ishmael Reed." BLACK CREATION, 4 (1973), 12-15.

"When State Magicians Fail: An Interview with Ishmael Reed." NICKEL RE-

VIEW, 28 Aug. 1968; reprinted with an afterword by Joe Goncalves in JOURNAL OF BLACK POETRY, No. 12 (1969), pp. 72-77.

REEVES, HENRY

IN A MEADOW'S CALM. Peterborough, N.H.: Windy Row Press, 1971. 111 p.

REYNOLDS, EVELYN CRAWFORD. See LYNN, EVE, above, this section.

RICE, DAVID (1947-)

OM. Lincoln, Neb.: Gazette Collective, 1974. 36 p. Paper.

LIFE DEATH AND LOVE. Eugene, Oreg.: Coalition Press, 1975. 68 p. Paper.

EROGENOUS ZONE: SENSUAL POETRY. Washington, D.C.: King Publications, 1975. 28 p. Paper.

RICHARDSON, BEULAH

A BLACK WOMAN SPEAKS OF WHITE WOMANHOOD, OF WHITE SUPREMACY, OF PEACE. New York: American Women for Peace, 1951. 9 p. Paper.

RICHARDSON, NOLA (1936-)

WHEN ONE LOVES: THE BLACK EXPERIENCE IN AMERICA. Millbrae, Calif.: Celestial Arts, 1974. 95 p. Paper.

EVEN IN A MAZE. Introd. Dorothy Sayles. Los Angeles: Crescent Publications, 1975. 54 p. Paper.

RIOS, CARLOS ROBERT

BOOK I. New York: Rannick Playwrights Co., 1971. [31] p. Paper. Rev. ed. published as THE VOICE OF PUERTO RICAN HARLEM. New York: Rannick Playwrights Co., 1971. [32] p. Paper.

RIVERS, CONRAD KENT (1933-68)

PERCHANCE TO DREAM, OTHELLO. Wilberforce, Ohio: Wilberforce Univ. Press, 1959. 17 p. Paper.

THESE BLACK BODIES AND THIS SUNBURNT FACE. Cleveland: Free Lance Press, 1962. 28 p. Paper.

DUSK AT SELMA. Cleveland: Free Lance Press, 1965. 20 p. Paper, mimeographed.

THE STILL VOICE OF HARLEM. Heritage series, no. 5. London: Breman, 1968. 24 p. Paper.

    In Chapman IBP.

THE WRIGHT POEMS. Heritage series, no. 18. Introd. Ronald Fair. London: Breman, 1972. 19 p. Paper.

Biography and Criticism

Lee DV. See also Ronald Fair's introduction to Rivers' THE WRIGHT POEMS (1972, above).

ROBBIN, WILLIAM ALLSTON

ELBOWROOM! ELBOWROOM! New York: Vantage, 1965. 68 p.

ROBERSON, ED (1939-)

WHEN THY KING IS A BOY. Pittsburgh: Univ. of Pittsburgh Press, 1970. 75 p.

ETAI-EKEN. Pittsburgh: Univ. of Pittsburgh Press, 1975. 84 p. Paper.

ROBERTS, D.L. (1927-)

TREMOLO. Illus. by the author. New York: Exposition, 1956. 40 p.

ROBINSON, EUGENE E.

INSPIRATIONS. New York: Vantage, 1958. 90 p.

ROBINSON, JERRILYN

UP TIGHT. Gary, Ind.: Kutana Publishing Co., 1972. 32 p. Paper.

RODGERS, CAROLYN M. (1943-)

PAPER SOUL. Introd. Hoyt W. Fuller. Chicago: Third World, 1968. [20] p. Paper.

SONGS OF A BLACKBIRD. Introd. David Llorens. Chicago: Third World, 1969. [34] p. Paper, mimeographed.

HOW I GOT OVAH: NEW AND SELECTED POEMS. Introd. Angela Jackson. New York: Doubleday, 1975. 81 p.

> Rodgers says, "I want my work to interest as many people as possible; therefore, some words have been either altered or eliminated completely."

Biography and Criticism

Lee DV.

ROE, HELENE

TEACH ME TO LIVE. No imprint. [1963?]. 19 p. Paper.

ROGERS, J. OVERTON (1933-)

BLUES AND BALLADS OF A BLACK YANKEE: A JOURNEY WITH SAD SAM. Introd. Whitney M. Young, Jr. New York: Exposition, 1965. 63 p.

ROLLINS, BRYANT

POETRY FOR MY FRIENDS. New York: Published by the author, 1973. [24] p. Paper.

ROYSTER, PHILIP M. (1943-)

THE BACK DOOR. Chicago: Third World, 1971. 29 p. Paper.

ROYSTER, SANDRA

WOMAN TALK. Chicago: Third World, 1974. 23 p. Paper.

> Cover title: WOMEN TALK.

RUFF, ROBERT L.

ACCENT ON NEW GRASS (RATHER THAN PIGMENT). 1970. Paper.

RUSSELL, BETH DUVALL

ON EARTH AS IT IS. Boston: Christopher, 1963. 144 p.

RUTLEDGE, DORIS

THE WEEPING POET. New York: Carlton, 1975. 48 p.

SAGGITTARUS [sic]. See SHEARS, CARL L., below, this section.

ST. JOHN, PRIMUS

SKINS ON THE EARTH. Port Townsend, Wash.: Copper Canyon Press, 1976. 83 p. Paper.

SALAAM, KALAMU YA. See FERDINAND, VAL III, above, this section.

SALGADO, LIONEL

THE SONGS OF THE FLOWERS WITH NO NAMES.

SAMUELS, CALVIN HENRY McNEAL

ME. New York: Comet, 1954. 41 p.
    Poetry and prose.

SANCHEZ, SONIA [LAILA MANNAN] (1934-)

HOME COMING. Detroit: Broadside, 1969. 32 p. Paper.

WE A BADDDDD PEOPLE. Introd. Dudley Randall. Detroit: Broadside, 1970. 72 p. Paper.
    In Chapman IBP.

IT'S A NEW DAY (POEMS FOR YOUNG BROTHAS AND SISTUHS). Detroit: Broadside, 1971. 29 p. Paper.

LOVE POEMS. New York: Third Press, 1973. 101 p.

A BLUES BOOK FOR BLUE BLACK MAGICAL WOMEN. Detroit: Broadside, 1974. 62 p.

Biography and Criticism

Lee DV.

Clarke, Sebastian. "Sonia Sanchez and Her Work." NEGRO DIGEST, 20 (June 1971), 44-48, 96-98. Also in PRESENCE AFRICAINE, No. 78 (1971), pp. 253-61.

Palmer, R. Roderick. "The Poetry of Three Revolutionists: Don L. Lee, Sonia Sanchez, and Nikki Giovanni." CLA JOURNAL, 15 (Sept. 1971), 25-36. Also in Gibson MBP.

SARTEN, LAVON

MY POETRY STANDS TO CHALLENGE. New York: Paebar, 1950. 142 p.

SCOTT, LEWIS E.

THE COMING OF LEWIS E. SCOTT. Trenton, N.J.: Commercial Printing Co., 1972. 32 p. Paper.

SCOTT-HERON, GIL (1949-)

SMALL TALK AT 125TH AND LENOX. New York: World Publishing Co., 1970. 56 p.

SEUELL, MALCHUS M. (1911-)

THE BLACK CHRIST AND VERSE. Los Angeles: Published by the author, 1957. 77 p. Paper.

THE MAD PAGAN AND VERSE. Downey, Calif.: Printed by Elena Quinn, 1959. 72 p. Paper.

WILD FLOWER. Detroit: Harlo Press, 1965. 30 p. Paper.

SHABAZZ, JOMO DON

JOMO. Kansas City, Mo.: Krizna Publishers, 1971.

SHABAZZ, TURHAN ABDUL [RAYMOND O. CASEY] (1937-   )

BLACK POETRY FOR EVERY OCCASION. Introd. Curtiss Porter. Pittsburgh: Oduduwa Productions, [1970?]. 30 p. Paper.

SHABAZZ, ZAKARIAH H.

PORTRAIT OF A POET. N.p.: Pyramid Press, 1969. 2nd ed. San Francisco: Published by the author, 1970. 36 p. Paper.

SHANDS, ANNETTE OLIVER

BLACK VOLUME. Mount Vernon, N.Y.: A & J Press, 1973. 46 p. Paper.

SHANGE, NTOSAKE (NTOZAKE) [PAULETTE WILLIAMS] (1948-   )

FOR COLORED GIRLS WHO HAVE CONSIDERED SUICIDE/WHEN THE RAIN-BOW IS ENUF. San Lorenzo, Calif: Shameless Hussy Press, 1975. [27] p. Paper.

Poetry and prose.

SHARP, SAUNDRA (1942-   )

FROM THE WINDOWS OF MY MIND. New York: Togetherness Productions, 1970. 52 p. Paper.

IN THE MIDST OF CHANGE. New York: Togetherness Productions, 1972. 40 p. Paper.

SHEARS, CARL L. [SAGGITTARUS (sic)]

AMONG THE LIVING DEAD. Washington, D.C.: NuClassics and Science Publishing Co., 1968. 50 p. Paper.

THE BLACKNESS OF MY SKIN AND THE KINKINESS OF MY HAIR. Washington, D.C.: NuClassics and Science Publishing Co., 1972. 82 p.

SHELLEY, WILLIAM

FROM THIS DARK HOUSE: POEMS OF A BLACK TEACHER. New York: Paulist Press, 1970. [50] p. Paper.

SHEPERD, JOHN H.

POEMS TO REMEMBER ALWAYS. New York: Greenwich, 1965. 31 p.

SHIELDS, RUTH E.

WHEN GOD'S FIRE COMES. New York: Carlton, 1969. 63 p.

SHIPPS, CHARLES KADIA

BLACK NEMESIS. Detroit: Harlo Press, 1973. 40 p. Paper.

SIMMONS, GERALD L., JR. (1944-)

EX-POSURES IN BLACK. Detroit: Ulozi Photographics, 1968. 35 p. Paper.

SIMMONS, JAMES W.

THOUGHTS FROM THE MIND. New York: Exposition, 1962. 94 p.

POETICAL AND PHILOSOPHICAL EXPRESSIONS. With an appendix for students. New York: Exposition, 1971. 75 p.

BELLE ISLE. 1971.

SIMMONS, JUDY DOTHARD (1944-)

JUDITH'S BLUES. Detroit: Broadside, 1973. 22 p. Paper.

SIMMONS, RHOZA W.

STEEL, STONE AND SATIN. London: Mitre Press, 1968. 106 p.

SIMPKINS, THOMAS V. (1898-)

RHYMES OF PUPPY LOVE AND OTHERS, INCLUDING NEGRO DIALECT. Boston: Christopher, 1935. 60 p.

RHYME AND REASON. Boston: Christopher, 1949. 95 p.

ABC'S OF BIRDS AND BEASTS. New York: Vantage, 1965. 60 p.

RHYMES OF THE RING AND POTPOURRI. Brooklyn, N.Y.: Pageant-Poseidon, 1972. 94 p.

SIMS, LILLIAN

COLLECTION OF POEMS. Chicago: Published by the author, 1971. Paper.

SINGLETON, YATUNDE. See YATUNDE, below, this section.

SMITH, ARTHUR LEE (1942-)

THE BREAK OF DAWN. Philadelphia: Dorrance, 1964. 55 p.

SMITH, DAVID

LAWD SPOKE TO ME FROM A RED SKY. Recorded and ed. Sam Cornish. Introd. Allan Brick. No imprint. [196-?]. 24 p. Paper.

SMITH, DEMON

SLIDE ON. Detroit: Black Arts Publications, 1971. 22 p. Paper.

OUT IN THE STREET. Detroit: Project B.A.I.T., 1975. 24 p. Paper.

SMITH, FRANCES LAURENCE

WISHFUL THINKING. 2nd ed. Baltimore: Garland Press, 1953. 46 p.

SMITH, IVORY H.

LIFE LINES. A collection of Inspiring Poetry and Prose, by Ivory H. Smith and Isabelle Tolbert. Charlotte, N.C.: n.p., 1952. 141 p.

SMITH, LUCY

NO MIDDLE GROUND. Philadelphia: Philadelphia Council of the Arts, Sciences and Professions, 1952. 30 p. Paper.

GIVE ME A CHILD. With Sarah Wright. Philadelphia: Kraft Publishing Co., 1955. [34] p. Paper.

SMITH, MARGARET L.

CREATIVE POEMS. New York: Vantage, 1974. 47 p.

SMITH, MILTON. See MBEMBE, above, this section.

SMITH, SIDNEY R.

REFLECTIONS. New York: Published by the author, 1971. Paper.

SMITH, WELTON (1940-)

PENETRATION. San Francisco: Journal of Black Poetry Press, 1971. 54 p.
Paper.

SMITH, WILLIE WESLEY, SR.

OUT THERE WAS SILENCE, TOO. New York: Vantage, 1968. 48 p.

SNELLINGS, ROLLAND. See TOURE, ASKIA MUHAMMAD, below, this
section.

SOUTHERLAND, ELLEASE (1943-)

THE MAGIC SUN SPINS. Heritage series, no. 25. London: Breman, 1975.
20 p. Paper.

SPEARMAN, AURELIA L.P. CHILDS

WHAT CHRISTMAS MEANS TO US. New York: Carlton, 1964. 99 p.

SPELLMAN, A.B. (1935-)

THE BEAUTIFUL DAYS. Introd. Frank O'Hara. New York: Poets Press, 1965.
[39] p. Paper.

SPRUILL, ROBERT L.

LINES OF OUR TIMES. Philadelphia: Dorrance, 1974. 67 p.

STEPHANY [STEPHANY JEAN DAWSON FULLER] (1947-)

MOVING DEEP. Introd. Dudley Randall. Detroit: Broadside, 1969. 32 p.
Paper.

STERLING X [STERLING HOBBS] (1953-)

WE RIGHTEOUS BUILDERS OF BLACK NATIONS. Chester, Pa.: Pyramid Publications, 1971. 80 p. Paper.

STEWART, J.T.

NOMMO. Seattle: Harrison–Madrona Center, [1972?]. Paper.

STEWART, PORTER ELLIS

PASSING BY. Introd. D.G. Stewart. Stanton, Tenn.: Published by the author, 1970. 34 p. Paper.

STEWART, TOBIAS, JR.

TOBIAS RAPS. Atlanta: Published by the author, 1973. [14] p. Paper.

STONE, LEROY. See CONTINENTAL STREAMLETS under JOHNSTON, PERCY EDWARD, above, this section.

STOWERS, J. ANTHONY

THE ALIENS. San Francisco: White Rabbit Press, 1967. [26] p. Paper.

STROUD, WELVIN. See DUST, above, this section.

SUMMERS, LUCY COOPER

99 PATCHES. New York: Carlton, 1969. 64 p.

SUN RA

THE IMMEASURABLE EQUATION. Chicago: Ihnfinity Inc./Saturn Research, 1972. 60 p. Paper.

SWANCY, ANDRE D. (1935-)

REFLECTIONS. Kansas City, Mo.: NIEU, 1968. [35] p. Paper.

SWANN, DARIUS LEANDER

THE ANSWERS: A PIECE FOR A VERSE CHOIR. New York: Board of Foreign Missions of the Presbyterian Church in the USA, 1953. 15 p. Paper.

TALIAFERRO, JUNE C. WILLIAMS

MOODS INTERMINGLED. New York: Vantage, 1974. 60 p.

TASSIN, IDA MAE

PROUD MARY: POEMS FROM A BLACK SISTER IN PRISON. Buffalo, N.Y.: Buffalo Women's Prison Project, 1971. 15 p. Paper.

TAYLOR, GLORIA LEE

DREAMS FOR SALE. New York: Exposition, 1953. 64 p.

TAYLOR, ROCKIE D. [TEJUMOLA OLOGBONI] (1945-)

DRUM SONG. Introd. Gwendolyn Brooks. Milwaukee, Wis.: Published by the author, 1969. [44] p. Paper.

THEUS, MARGARET FULLER

MY FAVORITE THOUGHTS. Chicago: n.p., n.d.

THIBODEAUX, MARY ROGER

A BLACK NUN LOOKS AT BLACK POWER. New York: Sheed and Ward, 1972. 114 p.

THIGPEN, WILLIAM A., JR. (1948-71)

DOWN NIGGER PAVED STREETS. Detroit: Broadside, 1972. 28 p. Paper.

THOMAS, BENJAMIN

MORNING COMES TOO SOON. New York: Carlton, 1969. 150 p.

THOMAS, CHARLES COLUMBUS

THE BLACK BROTHER GOOSE: RINDS FOR REVOLUTION. New York: Wilhelmina Publications, 1971.

THOMAS, CHARLES CYRUS. See section for 1901-45, above.

THOMAS, JOYCE CAROL (1938-)

BITTERSWEET. San Jose, Calif.: Firesign Press, 1973. 59 p.

CRYSTAL BREEZES. Berkeley, Calif.: Firesign Press, 1974. 47 p.

BLESSING. Berkeley, Calif.: Jocato Press, 1975. 48 p. Paper.

THOMAS, LORENZO (1944-)

FIT MUSIC: CALIFORNIA SONGS, 1970. New York: Angel Hair Books, 1972. [21] p. Paper.

DRACULA. New York: Angel Hair Books, 1973. [8] p. Paper.

THOMPSON, DOROTHENIA TINSEY

THREE SLICES OF BLACK. Chicago: Free Black Press, 1971. 32 p. Paper.

THOMPSON, FILIAN

AN ATMOSPHERE OF LIGHT AND LOVE. New York: Greenwich, 1962. 32 p.

THOMPSON, JAMES W. (1935-)

FIRST FIRE: POEMS, 1957-1960. Heritage series, no. 12. London: Breman, 1970. 19 p. Paper.

THOMPSON, JULIUS ERIC (1946-)

HOPES TIED UP IN PROMISES. Philadelphia: Dorrance, 1970. 52 p.

THORNTON, GEORGE BENNETT

BEST POEMS OF GEORGE B. THORNTON. Orangeburg, S.C.: College Press, 1937. 28 p.

GREAT POEMS. 1946. 41 p. 2nd ed. Wilberforce, Ohio: Published by the author, 1948. 59 p.

BEST POEMS, CONTAINING ALL THE POETICAL WORKS OF GEORGE B. THORNTON. Wilberforce, Ohio: Published by the author, 1959. 86 p.

SELECTIONS FROM THORNTON (VERSE). Wilberforce, Ohio: Published by the author, 1954. Paper.

TILLMAN, LISE M. (1951-)

OF VIOLETS AND BLUES. Markham, Ill.: Natural Resources Unlimited, 1974. 35 p. Paper.

TIWONI, HABIB (1939- , born in St. Thomas, Virgin Islands)

ATTACKING THE MONCADA OF THE MIND. New York: El Pueblo News Service, 1970. [74] p. Paper.

ISLANDS OF MY MIND. New York: Casha Publications, 1975. 56 p. Paper.

TOKUNBO [JOAN C. DUDLEY]

A VOICE FROM THE DARK IS CALLING. St. Albans, N.Y.: Published by the author, 1971. 24 p. Paper.

TOLBERT, ISABELLE. See SMITH, IVORY H., above, this section.

TOLSON, MELVIN BEAUNORUS (1900-1966)

RENDEZVOUS WITH AMERICA. New York: Dodd, Mead, 1944. 121 p.
> In Chapman IBP.

LIBRETTO FOR THE REPUBLIC OF LIBERIA. Introd. Allen Tate. New York: Twayne, 1953. [60] p.
> In Chapman IBP.

HARLEM GALLERY: BOOK 1, THE CURATOR. Introd. Karl Shapiro. New York: Twayne, 1965. 173 p.
> In Chapman IBP.

Biography and Criticism

Davis FTD; Jackson BPA.

Fabio, Sarah Webster. "Who Speaks Negro." NEGRO DIGEST, 16 (Dec. 1966), 54-58.

Flasch, Neva Joy. "Humor and Satire in the Poetry of Melvin B. Tolson." SATIRE NEWSLETTER, 7 (1969), 29-36.

_____. MELVIN B. TOLSON. Twayne's U.S. Authors Series, no. 215. New York: Twayne, 1972. 175 p.

"In Memory of Melvin B. Tolson." NEGRO DIGEST, 15 (Oct. 1966), 55.

McCall, Dan. "The Quicksilver Sparrow of M.B. Tolson." AMERICAN QUARTERLY, 18 (1966), 538-42.

Randall, Dudley. "Melvin B. Tolson: Portrait of a Poet as Raconteur." NEGRO DIGEST, 15 (Jan. 1966), 54-57.

Shapiro, Karl. "Melvin B. Tolson, Poet." NEW YORK HERALD TRIBUNE BOOK WEEK, 10 Jan. 1965. Reprinted in NEGRO DIGEST, 14 (May 1965), 75-77.

THOMPSON, D.G. "Tolson's Gallery Brings Poetry Home." NEGRO HISTORY BULLETIN, 29 (1965), 69-70.

TOLSON, MELVIN B. "A Poet's Odyssey." In ANGER AND BEYOND. Ed. Herbert Hill. New York: Harper, 1966, pp. 181-203. Reprinted in Gibson MBP, pp. 84-95.

TONEY, IEDA MAI

THE YOUNG SCHOLAR AND OTHER POEMS. Introd. Charles Leander Hill. Boston: Meador, 1951. 32 p.

TO RAISE THE DEAD AND FORETELL THE FUTURE. New York: New Lafayette Theatre, 1970. [16] p. Paper.

TORREGIAN, SOTERE (1941-)

THE GOLDEN PALOMINO BITES THE CLOCK. New York: Angel Hair Books, 1967. [29] p. Paper.

THE WOUNDED MATTRESS. Berkeley, Calif.: Oyez, 1970. 64 p.

TOTTRESS, RICHARD E.

TRUTH SPEAKS. Hicksville, N.Y.: Exposition, 1975. 63 p.

TOURE, ASKIA MUHAMMAD [ROLLAND SNELLINGS] (1938-)

JUJU (MAGIC SONGS FOR THE BLACK NATION). Introd. Ben Caldwell. Chicago: Third World, 1970. 20 p. Paper.

SONGHAI! Introd. John Oliver Killens. New York: Songhai Press, 1972. 70 p. Paper.

> Reviewed by Addison Gayle, Jr., in BLACK WORLD, 23 (Sept. 1974), 20-29.

Biography and Criticism

Thomas, Lorenzo. "Askia Muhammad Toure: Crying Out the Goodness." OBISIDIAN, 1 (Spring 1975), 31-49.

TOWNSLEY, BARBARA. See HAVARD, HARRISON, above, this section.

TRENT, HELEN

MY MEMORY GEMS. Salisbury, N.C.: Rowan Printing Co., 1948. 87 p.

TROUPE, QUINCY (1943-)

EMBRYO. New York: Barlenmir House, 1972. 56 p.

TURNER, A. JOHN. See section for 1901-45, above.

TURNER, DARWIN T. (1931-)

KATHARSIS. Wellesley, Mass.: Wellesley Press, 1964. 20 p. Paper.

ONE LAST WORD. Greensboro, N.C.: n.p., 1964. Paper, Mimeographed.

TURNER, FAITH M.

GETTING TO KNOW ME. Washington, D.C.: Published by the author, 1975. 17 p. Paper.

TURNER, VERNON KITABU

KUNG FU: THE MASTER: THE BOOK OF KITABU. Introd. Bobbi Humphrey. Virginia Beach, Va.: Donning and Hirshfeld, 1975. 54 p. Paper.

TYLER, WILFRED E. (1924-)

POEMS AND THOUGHTS. New York: Carlton, 1968.

QUOTATIONS AND POEMS. New York: Carlton, 1974. 62 p.

TYNER, LARRY

RHYTHMS OF RESURRECTION. Nashville, Tenn.: L.T. Productions, 1974. 22 p. Paper.

VESEY, PAUL. See ALLEN, SAMUEL W., above, this section.

WAKEFIELD, JACQUES. See OJI, ABAYOME, above, this section.

WALKER, ALICE (1944-)

ONCE. New York: Harcourt, 1968. 81 p.

> Reviewed by Carolyn Rodgers in NEGRO DIGEST, 17 (Sept.-Oct. 1968), 52, 11-13. In Chapman IBP.

REVOLUTIONARY PETUNIAS AND OTHER POEMS. New York: Harcourt, 1973. 70 p.

> Reviewed by Mary Helen Washington in BLACK WORLD, 22 (Sept. 1973), 51-52, 89.

Biography and Criticism

O'BRIEN IBW.

WALKER, JAMES ROBERT

POETICAL DIETS. No imprint. [1921?]. 146 p.

> Contains 159 poems. Jahn and Sherman give date as "18- "; but one poem, "The Evangelistic Call" (p. 59), is dated 1920.

BE FIRM MY HOPE. New York: Comet, 1955. 114 p.

MENUS OF LOVE. New York: Carlton, 1963. 130 p.

SPEAK NATURE. New York: Carlton, 1965. 122 p.

WALKER, MARGARET (1915-)

FOR MY PEOPLE. New Haven, Conn.: Yale Univ. Press, 1942. 58 p.
   In Chapman IBP.

PROPHETS FOR A NEW DAY. Detroit: Broadside, 1970. 32 p. Paper.
   In Chapman IBP.

OCTOBER JOURNEY. Detroit: Broadside, 1973. 38 p. Paper.

Biography and Criticism

Rollins FANP; Whitlow BAL; Young BW30s.

Giddings, Paula. "A Shoulder Hunched Against a Sharp Concern: Themes in the Poetry of Margaret Walker." BLACK WORLD, 21 (Dec. 1971), 20-25.

Giovanni, Nikki, and Margaret Walker. A POETIC EQUATION: CONVERSATIONS BETWEEN. . . . Washington, D.C.: Howard Univ. Press, 1974. 148 p.

Rowell, Charles H. "An Interview with Margaret Walker." BLACK WORLD, 25 (Dec. 1975), 4-17.

Walker, Margaret. "Willing to Pay the Price." In MANY SHADES OF BLACK. Ed. Stanton L. Wormley and W.H. Fenderson. New York: Morrow, 1969, pp. 119-30.
   This is an autobiographical statement by Walker.

WALKER, WAYNE

LETTER TO THE BLIND. 1969.

WASHINGTON, BOB

S.N.C.C."ERS" THEY PROBE DOWN TO THE C.O.R.E. Newark, N.J.: Power Press, 1968. 43 p. Paper.

WASHINGTON, RAYMOND (1942-)

VISION FROM THE GHETTO. New Orleans: BlkArtSouth, 1969. 20 p. Paper.

WATERS, HUTCH

AFRICA IN BROOKLYN. New York: Rannick Playwrights Co., 1971. [32] p. Paper.

WATERS, SHIRLEY A. (1949-)

PSALMS OF A BLACK WOMAN. Los Angeles: Hopkins-Thomas, 1969. [19] p. Paper.

WATKINS, DOROTHY J. See MATANAH, above, this section.

WATKINS, VIOLET PEACHES

MY DREAM WORLD OF POETRY: POEMS OF IMAGINATIONS, REALITY AND DREAMS. New York: Exposition, 1955. 128 p.

WATSON, FRANKLIN DELANO. See GEOGRAPHY OF THE NEAR PAST, under YOUNG, AL, below, this section.

WATSON, FREIDA K.

FEELIN'S. Los Angeles: Krizna, 1971. Paper.

WATSON, NANA

REAP THE HARVEST. New York: William-Frederick, 1952. 31 p.

WEATHERLY, TOM (1942-)

MAUMAU AMERICAN CANTOS. New York: Corinth, 1970. 47 p. Paper.

THUMPRINT. New York: Telegraph Books, 1971. 36 p. Paper.

WEATHERS, GEORGE A.

TENDER IS THE POETRY. New York: Carlton, 1968. 47 p.

Poetry: Individual Authors

WEBBER, CLEVELAND

AFRICA AFRICA AFRICA. Introd. David Moore. Chicago: Artistic Press, 1969. 28 p. Paper.

WEBSTER, BURL (Born in St. Kitts, West Indies)

REVERIES. Markham, Ill.: Natural Resources Unlimited, 1975. 40 p. Paper.

WEEKS, RICARDO

FREEDOM'S SOLDIER AND OTHER POEMS. Introd. Lawrence D. Reddick. New York: W. Malliet, 1947. 64 p. Paper.

ACCORDING TO SONNETEER: A POETIC SERIES ON THE LIFE OF JESUS CHRIST. New York: Manida Press, 1967. 48 p. Paper.

WELBURN, RON (1944-)

PERIPHERIES: SELECTED POEMS 1966-1968. Vol. 1. Greenfield Center, N.Y.: Greenfield Review Press, 1972. 40 p. Paper.

WELCH, LEONA NICHOLAS

BLACK GIBRALTAR. San Francisco: Leswing Press, 1971. 75 p. Paper.

WEST, GARLAND F.

LECTURES IN NIGGER HISTORY (THOUGHTS ON THE NIGGER CONDITION). Vol. I. Brooklyn, N.Y.: Published by the author, 1969. [96] p. Paper.

TALKING SHIT--ABOUT A SNOW WHITE DOVE. Brooklyn, N.Y.: Amistad Publishers, 1972. 89 p. Paper.

WHALING, MARIETTA R.

RHYME AND REASON. Hicksville, N.Y.: Exposition, 1975. 62 p.

WHITAKER, CHRISTINE D.

THE SINGING TEAKETTLE: POEMS FOR CHILDREN. New York: Exposition, 1956. 40 p.

WHITAKER, T.J. See HAVARD, HARRISON, above, this section.

WHITE, JESSIE

WRITINGS OF THE MILWAUKEE 3. With Booker T. Collins. Milwaukee: Wisconsin Inmates Peoples Union, [1971?]. 12 p. Paper.

WHITE, PAULETTE C. (1948-)

LOVE POEM TO A BLACK JUNKIE. Detroit: Lotus Press, 1975. 37 p. Paper.

WHITEHEAD, ARCH

BALM. New York: Horizon 6, 1973. 67 p. Paper.

ONCE IN A GREENHOUSE--IF ONLY FOR A NIGHT. New York: Horizon 6, 1973. 63 p. Paper.

FOREVER FOR A WHILE--ROBIN. New York: Horizon 6, 1973. 66 p. Paper.

WILKERSON, JAMES CLIFTON, JR.

20TH CENTURY POETRY. Stockton, Calif.: Published by the author, 1974. 71 p. Paper.

WILKERSON, JOHN WILLIAM (1951-)

YOU CRIED. Washington, D.C.: King Publications, 1974. 28 p. Paper.

WILLIAMS, DONALD F.

MY BLACK FATHER'S STRUGGLE. Culver City, Calif.: Printing Service, 1968. 36 p. Paper.

WILLIAMS, FLORENCE

THE GUIDING LIGHT. Nashville, Tenn.: National Baptist Training School Board, 1963. 94 p.

WILLIAMS, JEANETTE MARIE (1946-)

SOUL OF A SAPPHIRE. Chicago: Free Black Press, 1970. [24] p. Paper.

WILLIAMS, JOAN

THOUGHTS OF LOVE AND LIFE. Milwaukee, Wis.: Shore Publishing Co., 1972. 24 p. Paper.

WILLIAMS, JOHN A. (1925-)

POEMS. Syracuse, N.Y.: Published by the author, 1951. Paper, mimeographed.

WILLIAMS, PAMELA. See FLEMING/McALLISTER PRODUCTIONS under CORNISH, SAM, above, this section.

WILLIAMS, PAULETTE. See SHANGE, NTOSAKE, above, this section.

WILLIAMS, SHIRLEY [SHERLEY ANNE WILLIAMS] (1944-)

THE PEACOCK POEMS. Middletown, Conn.: Wesleyan Univ. Press, 1975. 87 p.

WILSON, ALICE T. (1908-)

HOW AN AMERICAN POET MADE MONEY AND FORGET-ME-NOT. New York: Pageant, 1968. 68 p.
    Screenplay and poems.

WILSON, FLORA McCULLOUGH (1927-)

NOT BY BREAD ALONE. New York: Carlton, 1970. 64 p.

WILSON, WILBERT R.

TRAVELS OF THE TWENTIETH CENTURY AND BEYOND. New York: Carlton, 1971. 61 p.

WIMBERLI, SIGEMONDE KHARLOS (1938-)

GHETTO SCENES. Chicago: Free Black Press, 1968. 44 p. Paper.

WINDHAM, REVISH

SHADES OF BLACK. New York: Heritage-Afro-Media, 1970. 30 p. Paper.

SHADES OF ANGER. New York: African American Book Club, 1972. 23 p. Paper.

WINSTON, BESSIE BRENT

ALABASTER BOXES. Washington, D.C.: Review and Herald Publishing Association, 1947. 160 p.

LIFE'S RED SEA AND OTHER POEMS. Washington, D.C.: Review and Herald Publishing Association, 1950. 32 p.

WOLDE, HABTE [H.A. JENNINGS] (1945-)

ENOUGH TO DIE FOR. Detroit: Broadside, 1972. 46 p. Paper.

WOOD, DEBBIE

ON BEING. Washington, D.C.: Published by the author, 1976. [21] p. Paper.

WOOLDRIDGE, IRIS

A TOUCH . . . A SMILE . . . A MEMORY. New York: Vantage, 1975. 53 p.

WORRELL, LELIA E.

REFLECTIONS: PAST, PRESENT, FUTURE. New York: Carlton, 1972. 46 p.

WORTHAM, ANNE

SILENCE. New York: Pageant, 1965. 51 p.

WRIGHT, BEATRICE

COLOR SCHEME. New York: Pageant, 1957. 59 p.

WRIGHT, ETHEL WILLIAMS

OF MEN AND TREES. New York: Exposition, 1954. 64 p.

WRIGHT, JAY (1935-)

DEATH AS HISTORY. Millbrook, N.Y.: Printed at Kriya Press, 1967. [24] p. Paper.

THE HOMECOMING SINGER. New York: Corinth, 1971. 95 p.

DIMENSIONS OF HISTORY. Santa Cruz, Calif.: Kayak, 1976. 112 p. Paper.

WRIGHT, NATHAN

THE SONG OF MARY. Boston: Bruce Humphries, 1958. 89 p.

WRIGHT, SARAH E.

GIVE ME A CHILD. With Lucy Smith. Philadelphia: Kraft Publishing Co., 1955. [34] p. Paper.

WYATT, FARICITA

THE RIVER MUST FLOW. Berkeley, Calif.: Published by the author, 1965. 25 p. Paper.

X, MARVIN. See MARVIN X, above, this section.

X, STERLING. See STERLING X, above, this section.

YATUNDE [YATUNDE SINGLETON]

KING WINBURN. New York: United Brothers Communication Systems, 1975. 43 p. Paper.

> Poetry and prose.

YEISER, IDABELLE. See section for 1901-45, above.

YOUNG, AL (1939-)

DANCING. New York: Corinth, 1969. 63 p. Paper.

THE SONG TURNING BACK INTO ITSELF. New York: Holt, Rinehart and Winston, 1971. 87 p.

GEOGRAPHY OF THE NEAR PAST. New York: Holt, Rinehart and Winston, 1976. 84 p.

> Includes, on pages 76-84, four poems ascribed to one O.O.

Gabugah (Franklin Delano Watson), "a militant advocate of the oral tradition" who allegedly dictated these poems to Young.

Biography and Criticism

Interview in O'Brien IBW.

YOUNG, WES H.

RAMBLING AND THINGS. New York: Vantage, 1972. 48 p.

ZAYD

CORNBREAD AND POTATO SALAD. Elkins Park, Pa.: Uhuru Publications, 1971. 24 p. Paper.

ZUBENA, SISTER [CYNTHIA CONLEY] (?-1972)

CALLING ALL SISTERS. Chicago: Free Black Press, 1970. 24 p. Paper. 2nd printing published as CALLIN' ALL SISTERS. Chicago: Published by the author, 1970. 24 p. Paper.

OM BLACK. Chicago: Published by the author, 1971. 28 p. Paper.

ZU-BOLTON, AHMOS II

A NIGGERED AMEN. San Luis Obispo, Calif.: Solo Press, 1975. [48] p. Paper.

AFRO-AMERICAN DRAMA, 1850-1975

DRAMA: INTRODUCTION

The attention given to Afro-American theatre has led many people to think
that it has only recently come into existence. Yet, for 200 years black artists have struggled to get the opportunity of developing their talent on the
stage, to put an end to their invisibility and their exclusion, and to free themselves from the various restrictive roles that the white world of producers and
playwrights has cast for them.

When white American dramatists started writing plays with black characters, as
early as 1769, blacks were not allowed to perform such parts. The American
professional stage employed only white actors, even for black roles. The first
black characters that appeared in drama were stereotypes, played by white
actors who blackened their faces and gave caricatures, burlesque, or sentimental representations of black people. The image of the black Sambo gradually
invaded the stage in the nineteenth century and was reproduced as prototype
in the minstrels, where white entertainers mimicked Afro-American dance,
walk, and speech, and in the melodrama, in which "darkies" or "coons" intro-
duced an element of comedy and exoticism.

Although the origin of minstrels has often been attributed to whites, it is likely
that the idea and the very form and structure of the show were borrowed from
entertainments which the slaves themselves created. They performed on the
plantation, sometimes for the benefit of their masters--who encouraged such
pastimes because they thought they provided a necessary relief from work as
well as an incentive to work better--but most often for their own benefit.
These early minstrel shows that have been seen as self-satires were in fact
mostly parodies of the white plantocracy, full of innuendos and double meaning,
"puttin' down ole massa." To the masters, these performances were amusing.
They saw them as awkward efforts to duplicate their manners or as a dimension
of slave foolishness, and never gave much attention to their satirical intent.
Ironically, when the official minstrel developed in the 1820s and became in
the 1840s the most popular form of national theatre, it was performed by white
professional actors in black face, was presented to white audiences, and clearly
mimicked Afro-Americans. When blacks were later admitted in the professional
groups, they were required to blacken their faces and they usually conformed
to the images created by white performers. Paradoxically, the minstrel show

reached the peak of its success at the time of the antislavery campaign. After emancipation, the representation of the black as a harmless comic character helped relieve the fear induced by the sudden confrontation of the black presence.

Because blacks were excluded for so long as audience, actors, or playwrights, one tends to dismiss the existence of any theatrical life among them. Recent research in Afro-American culture has brought to attention the importance of the tradition of the play and dramatization of Afro-American parades and festivals, all highly structured performances, often displaying sacred and secret symbols; they all involved music, dance, and a selective stylization of motifs and patterns. Furthermore, blacks made several attempts at developing their own professional theatres--such as the African Grove--presenting plays for a black audience that they were not allowed to see in white-owned theatres.

Whereas white melodrama thrived during the nineteenth century, offering more stereotyped images of blacks as obedient, pathetic Uncle Toms, contrasting them with black villains, fugitive slaves, or rebels, black performers and, to some extent, authors were allowed to participate in the development of the musical drama that replaced the minstrel tradition at the end of the century. In fact, American musical comedy is largely indebted to black talent. There again, blacks played a double role: on the one hand, they helped perpetuate certain stereotypes; on the other, they brought the original stamp of their own inventiveness and creativity. Thanks to the initiative of Bob Cole, a new pattern was set, proposing a complete control of theatrical material: the management, the writing, and the performing. Although the experience lasted only two decades because of the pressures and competition of white ownership, it gives evidence of black people's desire and ability to create and produce their own theatre. In 1898, A TRIP TO COONTOWN presented a new prototype for the musical comedy and tried to do away with its most farcical, burlesque characteristics, whereas George Walker and Bert Williams proved that they could combine all the talents needed for theatre producers and at the same time be writers, song composers, and performers.

Black artists, nevertheless, had a hard time trying to break through on the American stage. Dramatists were still few. They strove desperately to have their plays produced, and conformed more or less to artistic standards set for them, while the white playwrights showed a growing interest in Negro character and continued to impose their own images. The stereotype that had appeared in the nineteenth century minstrel and melodrama was further diversified. The docile, funny-looking slave had henceforth to compete with the Tragic Mulatto, the Carefree Primitive, the Beast who threatened to corrupt the purity of the white race. These somewhat contradictory figures received particular dramatic emphasis in the work of Ridgely Torrence and Eugene O'Neill. In spite of the efforts made by a few playwrights, notably Paul Green, to give a more realistic and convincing representation of black characters, most "white" dramas (like DuBose Heyward's PORGY) concentrated on melodramatic or exotic aspects of black life. The white writer remained the authority on the professional stage, an authority with which no black playwright could really compete. Jean Toomer, one of the accomplished writers of the Harlem Renaissance, found it difficult to have his plays produced. Meanwhile, whites made frequent visits to Harlem to get inspiration for their own shows, appropriating material for which the original creators were never given credit.

The economic control maintained by whites in the production of plays, coupled with a more subtle form of control imposed on artistic treatment and choice of material, forced black artists to retreat to their community and to organize their own theatrical activities. Their growing awareness of their condition and of the discriminatory practices--exclusion, eviction, or various forms of appropriation-- that threatened to stifle their creativity is partly responsible for the theatrical renaissance that took place in the twenties. The dramatist brought his plays back to his community and probably drew much vitality from this renewed contact with black audiences. Community theaters were created in the black neighborhoods of the main cities--the Pekin Theatre in the Chicago South Side, the Howard Players in Washington, D.C., the Dunbar Players in Philadelphia, Morgan College in Baltimore, Lincoln and Lafayette theatres in Harlem, the Gilpin Players in Cleveland, the Krigwa Players in several towns. Alain Locke, W.E.B. DuBois, and Randolph Edmonds were instrumental in promoting this "Negro Theatre Movement." In the thirties, black theatres were established in more than fourteen states; some were running contests and tournaments to encourage the creation of plays. Among them, the New Orleans Little Theatre Guild, the Harlem Suitcase, the Rose McClendon Players, the Negro Playwright Company, and the American Negro Theatre gave many successful performances.

While these companies were trying to develop a greater interest in theatre within black communities and were training professional actors, a few blacks (like Paul Robeson and Charles Gilpin) were becoming prominent on the legitimate stage, mostly in parts devised by white authors. One is reminded of Ira Aldridge who established his reputation in the nineteenth century by his outstanding interpretation of Shakespearian characters. The emergence of the black actor and the success he won in performing in white plays, relegated the black dramatist, however, to a very secondary role. In spite of the outlet opened to them in community theatre, both black dramatist and black actor remained in a very ambivalent situation; the dramatist wrote simultaneously for two separate audiences.

The list of plays that follows gives an indication of the creative activity of dramatists in spite of the obstacles they encountered in having their plays produced or published, and in spite of their enduring competition with white playwrights.

The first known black playwright,[1] William Wells Brown, appears as a very isolated figure. His plays were never performed and became known only through his public readings. At the end of the nineteenth century, a few black dramatists[2] won recognition as authors in a popular genre, the musical comedy. However, the ambition of black playwrights was not the world of light entertainment but that of serious drama. The black artist had been regarded for too long as an entertainer, a role that had traditionally been more acceptable to whites. The reaction of black authors was to assert the legitimacy of their own vocation, to prove the quality of their craftsmanship, and to create for the actor roles that were more relevant and less alienating to his talent. They had to deal with a material that had often been handled inappropriately. Efforts were made to promote playwriting, either through the creation of writers' workshops or through the organization of contests. A new emphasis was put on the production as well as on the publication of plays. In 1916, the Drama Committee of the N.A.A.C.P. in Washington, D.C., produced the first successful drama by a black writer, RACHEL, by Angelina Grimke. In 1924, the Howard Players performed BALO by Jean Toomer. Frank Wilson, John Matheus, and Georgia Douglas Johnson won prizes in drama contests sponsored by OPPORTUNITY. Although Alain Locke's anthology, PLAYS OF NEGRO LIFE (1927), included plays by whites, it also gave many little-known black playwrights an opportunity to be published at a time when production was still problematic. Of all the writers of the twenties, Willis Richardson was probably the most fortunate. His play, A CHIPWOMAN'S FORTUNE, was produced in 1923 by the Colored Folk Theater (later called the Ethiopian Art Theatre), sponsored by Raymond O'Neill and Mrs. Sherwood Anderson, before it appeared on Broadway. Five plays by Richardson were produced within a few years, 1921-27. Several black plays enjoyed a run on Broadway: (1) MEEK MOSE by Frank Wilson in 1928; (2) Wallace Thurman's HARLEM in 1929; (3) Hall Johnson's RUN LITTLE CHILLUN in 1933; and (4) Langston Hughes's MULATTO, 1935-37. Yet, on the whole, the situation of the black playwright remained precarious. He had to accept the sponsorship of whites to get his plays produced; sometimes, in order to insure his success, he had to associate his name with that of a white writer, as Wallace Thurman did with William Rapp for HARLEM; and mostly, he had to compete with white dramatists whose plays on "Negro life" were highly successful in the twenties.

The Federal Theatre Project gave a new impetus to playwriting and to theatre production during its four years of existence, 1935-39. Although it gave a preference to proletarian art and to the depiction of the plight of the black worker, it revitalized the interest of black communities in theatre and encouraged writers to improve their dramatic techniques.

A quick look at the plays written by blacks between 1900 and 1950 testifies to the great diversity of themes and dramatic forms, and to the persistence of certain trends and preoccupations. A great many plays seem mainly concerned with documenting the condition of blacks during that period--the destitution of poor blacks in the south, their exploitation by white landowners, the difficult migration to northern ghettos, the racial violence that was constantly being leveled at them. In that perspective, blacks are represented as victims of oppression. The dramatist emphasizes the dire socioeconomic conditions of sharecroppers and laborers. The white landowner, a direct descendant of the plantation owner, appears as the enemy responsible for all the ills that befall the black man; the landowner is an evil figure against whom it is right to rebel. In one of Randolph Edmonds' plays, a sharecropper avenges himself on his landlord for having driven his wife to exhaustion through too much work. Occasionally a play hints at the possibility of a common fight uniting poor whites and poor blacks against their oppressor. DON'T YOU WANT TO BE FREE by Langston Hughes appeals to interracial unity against the exploiters. But most plays insist upon the distinct fate of blacks, submitted as they are to racial as well as to economic abuse. Bearing testimony to the upsurge of violence against blacks, some authors represent it in its most extreme form, lynching. BAD MAN, by Edmonds, shows the struggle and heroic death of a man trying to save his people from the lynching mob. RACHEL, by Angelina Grimke, offers another dramatization of lynching in the South and of the ensuing humiliation of a family.

Miscegenation emerges as another important theme in the drama of the period. (One bears in mind MOTHER AND CHILD and MULATTO by Langston Hughes, and plays by G.D. Johnson and M. Livingston.) However, interracial marriage, as in EXIT AN ILLUSION by Marita Bonner, offers no solution to the plight of blacks, and will not insure their integration in the white community. On the contrary, mixed unions often bring disaster or tragedy, are not willingly accepted by either community, and may force the sinful member into exile or inflict some punishment upon him. Often, the accusation of rape is raised, mostly against the black man. In Garland Anderson's APPEARANCES, for example, a bellhop is accused of having raped a white woman. Black theatre, exploring the dramatic implication of rape not so much for the alleged victim as for the man who is labeled a rapist, tries to give the lie to the stereotype. The case of the Scottsboro boys prompted black artists to have their say about the indictment and trial of black youths by white society. The mulatto also became the prototype of the tragic and suffering hero. He served as a metaphor of the ambivalence of most blacks, swaying between two identities and two worlds--a world of poverty and destitution they hope to escape, and the white world where they will never be unrestrictedly admitted.

As seen through the theatre of that period, the aspirations of most blacks were toward integration into the white world: plays alternately represent a desperate struggle towards acceptance by whites (in Countee Cullen and Owen Dodson's THIRD FOURTH OF JULY a family fights bravely to get accepted into a white neighborhood), or the painful disillusionment when the dream does not come true. These aspirations often follow the dictates of some black leader; in that respect, CALEB, by Cotter, is a dramatization of the ideas expressed by Booker T. Washington, which were very popular at the time.

On the whole, throughout this first half of the century, black theatre was mainly concerned with chronicling the oppression of black people through a realistic or, more rarely, a symbolic approach. It shows their plight in southern shacks or in northern ghettos, the difficulties met by a family (THEY THAT SIT IN DARKNESS, by Mary Burrill), the struggle of a mother to keep her family together (ENVIRONMENT, by Mercedes Gilbert). It presents the economic and social unrest in Harlem in the thirties (JOB HUNTERS, by H.V.F. Edward), the fate of coal miners and black laborers (in J.F. Matheus' plays), and the exploitation of Harlemites by Jewish landlords, Italian racketeers, and Irish cops (LITTLE HAM, by Langston Hughes). As black people moved gradually but in great numbers from the South to the North, the theatre tried to give its dramatic account of this exodus. In antislavery plays, the North had appeared as the gateway to freedom. Fugitive slaves had always fled northward. Black migrants, leaving the sharecropper world, were hoping to escape a fateful environment. However, in many plays, the South was still viewed as home, a place where, compared with the anonymity of the North, many roots had been planted. Conflict between the attraction to an idealized North and the nostalgia for the South is represented in such plays as Frank Wilson's SUGAR CANE and John Matheus' 'CRUITER, whereas other plays begin to accuse the North of furthering the ills suffered by blacks. Suspicion and disillusionment appear in Thurman and Rapp's HARLEM, in Edmonds' OLD MAN PETE, and in Eulalie Spence's THE STARTER.

Certain plays, however, do not focus so much on socioeconomic conditions as on life-styles and interactions between blacks, or on relationships between members of the same family. This interest has given rise to a specific and prolific genre, the domestic drama or the domestic comedy, presenting--in a dramatic or comic mode--the various conflicts that pit against each other two generations (THE SEER by J.W. Butcher) of parents and children: mother and son, for example, in SACRIFICE by Thelma M. Duncan, or father and son (SILAS BROWN by R. Edmonds).

The most popular theatrical form, which appeared at the time of the Harlem Renaissance and was later developed by both white and black playwrights, is the folk drama. It found its most successful expression in the theatre of Jean Toomer and of Langston Hughes. These plays dealing with "Negro life," with simple, genuine black people, appealed equally to white and black audiences. They attempted to show blacks as human beings, loving, suffering, laughing, involved in the process of living and surviving. They deliberately refused to present a one-sided view of black experience but insisted on its joys as well as on its pains, choosing to deal with it in a humorous or sometimes satiric way. Avoiding certain pitfalls and the stereotyped dramatizations of sociological drama, such plays fell into other traps, however. They yielded too easily to certain fashions that deliberately sought exoticism and primitivism, and that saw black people as the best embodiments of a life close to nature, immune from the corrupting influence of industrialization.

The first half of the century was also marked by several wars that drew the attention of black dramatists. Their plays endeavored either to celebrate the heroism of the black soldier or to demonstrate the country's indebtedness to him. Many showed the ambiguous nature of black people's involvement in the wars, the consequences for the community at large. J.S. Cotter's ON THE FIELDS OF FRANCE presents the conflicting allegiances of the black warrior; MINE EYES HAVE SEEN, by Alice M. Dunbar Nelson presents his loyalty. Randolph Edmonds dramatizes the death of two soldiers, black and white, on a French battlefield (EVERYMAN'S LAND); THE BALLAD OF DORIE MILLER, by O. Dodson, is a celebration of the black hero at Pearl Harbor.

These war plays can be related to a series of historical plays, much larger in scope, that attempt to testify to the black man's presence in world history and to his participation in some of its most important events. W. Richardson dramatizes the death of Crispus Attucks killed during the Boston Massacre; G.D. Johnson celebrates Frederick Douglass; other plays pay their tribute to Sojourner Truth, Harriet Tubman, and Father Devine. Significantly enough, dramatists do not deal exclusively with American history. Toussaint l'Ouverture is the hero of L.P. Hill's play; his daughter is the central character in H.W. Harris' GENEFREDE. May Miller wrote plays on the daughter of the king of Haiti and on an African chief's resistance to French colonization; Richardson himself wrote many historical plays presenting successfully a Cuban hero, Antonio Maceo; Massinissa, a king of Numidia; and life at the court of the king of Abyssinia in 1898.

The theatre thus bears testimony to black history, and to an ancient civilization with its courts and kings and warriors. It encourages the former slaves to view themselves as descendants of famous Africans and as members of a large community scattered over several continents, to link their fate to other black liberators who struggled in the African colonies or in the Caribbean. The resistance of American slaves, celebrated by the first black playwright William Wells Brown in THE ESCAPE: OR, A LEAP FOR FREEDOM (1858), thus assumes a greater significance. It is not an isolated fight but a meaningful participation in a more general struggle. The black man is seen as the bearer of a culture more ancient than that of the people who now oppress him. The values he embodies are a threat to the Western world. His mission is not only to liberate himself from the yoke of oppression but also to save the world from the destructiveness of Western man (NATURAL MAN by Theodore Browne). Black theatre thus draws largely upon history but also upon legend and myth. On the other hand, it also contributes to the creation of new myths and legends. Its mode is epic or allegoric. Its form is often that of a pageant extolling the accomplishments of the black race, like STAR OF ETHIOPIA by W.E.B. DuBois and HIGH COURT OF HISTORIA by R. Edmonds, or representing the spirit of Negro progress (TWO RACES: A PAGEANT by Inez M. Burke and OUT OF THE DARK by Dorothy C. Guinn).

On the whole, the production of these five decades bears the mark of the main ideological trends and of the artistic choices of the time. The theatre gave expression to the emphasis on ethnic material and on negritude during the Harlem Renaissance, and to the nationalistic drive given in the twenties by the Garvey movement and later by the development of Pan-Africanism, mainly on the impulse of W.E.B. DuBois. In the thirties the concern with social problems and messages was expressed in realistic or naturalistic modes. The growing interest in black experience and life-styles encouraged the development of a dramaturgy that borrowed its form and substance from the black ethos and drew the epic of a people who possess a history and a culture. The theatre thus committed itself to two tasks, that of social and racial protest and that of celebrating black experience. The first found its most articulate expression in the drama of the Federal Theatre and especially in the work of Theodore Ward and, a decade later, in that of Richard Wright. In the other perspective, oppression is viewed as only one aspect of the experience—

257

as is the tradition of endurance, rebellion, and resistance--but it is no longer the central focus of the playwright. The emphasis is more on giving the distinctiveness of black life and culture within the United States, as it evolved in the southern plantation and later in the ghettos. The theatre also depicts blacks in the larger context that links their fate to the fate and history of other blacks and mainly to their mother country, Africa. The stage was thus used with a double purpose: (1) a platform from which to launch protest against the ills inflicted upon black people by white society, and (2) a place where black life could be not simply duplicated, but also re-created, receiving its proper scope and depth. The theatre could thus offer and legitimize new images of black people in reaction to the stereotypes that still existed in the white psyche and had often been revitalized by white dramatists.

In 1950, the situation of the black dramatist was still ambiguous. On the one hand, he was striving to win a certain autonomy from the artistic tenets and ideological constructs set by whites, and to assert black dramaturgy as a distinct artistic expression. On the other hand, he accepted the patronage of white producers and of a still predominantly white audience.

This situation did not change radically in the mid-century. The fifties nevertheless saw the definite emergence of the black playwright. Plays were not only written but also produced, performed, and occasionally even directed by blacks. The most important event in that respect was, in the late fifties, the production of Lorraine Hansberry's A RAISIN IN THE SUN in which artists appeared whose names were to become famous: Lonne Elder, Robert Brooks, Douglas T. Ward, and Ossie Davis. The playwrights of that decade asserted themselves as professional writers who were able to produce full-length plays and to develop plot and character.

At a time when public opinion was more and more concerned with desegregation and when campaigns were being organized to defend civil rights, the theatre again became a platform. TAKE A GIANT STEP by Louis Peterson presented the difficulties met by a black youth brought up in a predominantly white neighborhood. A RAISIN showed the younger family eager to leave their Chicago ghetto and struggling against the schemes of white residents and realtors to keep them out of the area where they had hoped to move. Loften Mitchell's A LAND BEYOND THE RIVER dramatized the pressures endured by a minister in a rural area when he fought to obtain bus transportation for black children. In William Branch's A MEDAL FOR WILLIE, a mother rejects the medal offered posthumously to her son for his courage in the Korean War. Protest is voiced; but violence as a strategy is dismissed, although certain plays almost explicitly state that it may soon become the only possible outlet and means of action. These works attempt rather laboriously to remain hopeful about the future; but they reassert that the hope lies less in the long-awaited success of the integrationist campaign than in the fortitude and strength of black people. The characters are strong-willed and seem to give a positive answer to the question once set by Langston Hughes: "Don't You Want to Be Free?" Thus, we can say that even though the theatre reflects the ideology of the time, it does not do so unquestioningly. Furthermore, the old images and stereotypes created by

whites are being constantly reexamined and contrasted with a more irreducible
reality (as in Alice Childress' TROUBLE IN MIND). The mother in A MEDAL
FOR WILLIE refuses to perform the role assigned to her in the ceremony honor-
ing her son. Her challenge to the white world is symbolic of the black character's refusal to submit to the white playwright's images of him. She asserts
the right to act and speak freely on her own terms. In a similar manner
PURLIE VICTORIOUS ridicules some of the conventional myths and stereotypes
applied to southern blacks; however, Ossie Davis' ultimate purpose is more to
entertain than to indict and his satire is witty but never virulent. The most
eloquent protest against the white world and its well-meaning liberals was
raised in BLUES FOR MR. CHARLIE which was presented to downtown audiences
in the same year as LeRoi Jones's first plays. Baldwin's drama marked the end
of an era, Jones's, the emergence of a much more radical militant theatre,
more or less appropriately called "revolutionary theatre."

LeRoi Jones (Imamu Amiri Baraka) stands out as the most important dramatist
of the sixties, not only because his plays were often produced Off-Broadway
and in other theatres and exploded like bombs on the American stage, but
also because he evolved new dramatic structures. He was one of the most
articulate theoreticians of the new black theatre. His work was emulated by
many other playwrights and encouraged them to go beyond protest and plea to
a total indictment of the white world and of the Uncle Toms who had been
its accomplices. His plays present violent verbal and physical confrontation
between blacks and whites. They stage the trials of the various groups--white
liberals, blinded, brainwashed "niggers" who betray their brothers--and the
forthcoming revolution. Plays become rituals of vengeance, retribution, and
purification. They prophesy the destruction of white society but also the re-
birth of the black nation. After having been ruthlessly murdered by whites,
the black character arises as a new revolutionary hero, an "avenger," a
"righteous bomber" whose mission is to eliminate those who have participated
in his oppression.

Black drama does not deliver its message in mere agitprop form. It creates
a wide diversity of forms, from the one-act didactic skits and revolutionary
commercials to fables and morality plays. It uses satire (Ben Caldwell), farce,
parody or allegory (Archie Shepp); it integrates chant and pantomine, dance,
and music in its rituals. The dramaturgy thus moves freely beyond the standard
structures of political drama, between the world of reality and a fantasy world,
and it frequently resorts to symbolism or surrealism. Thus the militant drama
of the sixties should not be seen as a mere reflection of the events and the
spirit of the decade. True, the theatre was used as propaganda to plead for
the end of the oppression of black people, for their integration and equal
rights; just as it also served to denounce the fallacy of the civil rights movement and of white liberal benevolence, it called forth the revolution and the
coming together of black people. Some plays might echo one specific ideol-
ogy--integrationist or separatist, revolutionary or nationalist. Certain plays
went beyond this and attempted to expose the workings of white domination,
the contradictions underlying the black struggle and its strategies, the conflicting loyalties (WE RIGHTEOUS BOMBERS). The theatre thus manages to win a

certain autonomy from both the event and the ideological currents that inform it, and to achieve a distance that allows for critical assessment. The artist asserts his right to speak out, not only in the face of the white world which is summoned to hear his voice and often challenged to respond, but in the face of his own people, forcing them to reconsider their statements and acts and identity. The dramatist induces them to develop new forms of action and thinking; he confronts them with new images that often invert the old stereotypes and appeal both to the mind and to the imagination. Seeking at the same time to educate and to entertain, this political theatre uses comedy, satire, and broad humor. Some plays, however, remain straightforwardly didactic, unimaginatively realistic; others sometimes verge on pathos and melodrama. The black revolutionary theatre is not without its flaws; yet it manages to preserve a certain dynamism, and its vitality comes from the fact that some of its artists were concerned not only with carrying out a message but also with creating an art form.

In spite of the domination of the social and political drama, other theatrical forms developed in the sixties. They either resumed and transformed the existing traditions or took the theatre along more experimental lines. The domestic drama continued to thrive, from A RAISIN and THE AMEN CORNER to the plays of Ron Milner and the psychodramas and satires of William Wellington Mackey and Charles Russell. The black family became the central protagonist in plays that presented its heroic struggle to survive or the inner conflict that pits its men against its women, its youth against the older generations. Dramatists attempted to give the lie to the attack brought on the black family by the Moynihan Report[3] and to various stereotypes it had revitalized. A large number of plays pursue the exploration of the black experience beyond the limits of the family and shift the scene to the street corner, the barber shop, or the storefront church. Their heroes are the men on the block, the pimps and prostitutes, winos and gamblers who had been left out or indicted by the political drama. In this "theatre of reality" they are allowed to live regardless of their shiftlessness. The dramatist withdraws his judgment and expects the spectator-reader to do the same. He maintains that these characters are entitled to as much attention as the heroes and victims in the militant plays. This theatre, best exemplified through Ed Bullins' drama, has been criticized for presenting only negative images and for harping on the more seamy and less reputable aspects of black life. Doing away with the dichotomy established by revolutionary drama that so carefully designates its villains and its heroes, the theatre of black experience sets the spotlight on this underworld and explores its life-styles, language, and culture as well as its dreams and inspirations. The plot often becomes incidental. The dramatic structure consists mainly in an orchestration of moods and blues; love relationships are built and broken, loyalties alternate with betrayals, hope with disillusionment. The mode shifts constantly from realism to fantasy, and these variations are enhanced through the use of music and light. Certain scripts, as in Melvin Van Peebles' drama, are more like musical scores; they emphasize the performance and suggest a sort of choreography.

A number of playwrights carry on other experiments. Paul Carter Harrison occasionally tries to create a total theatre involving dance, music, narrative, and dramatic modes and pleads for a dramaturgy that would come close to African theatre. Adrienne Kennedy makes extensive use of symbolism and surrealism in her drama on racial identity and conflict. Edgar White resorts to humor and burlesque to create a black picaro in plays that show a close relationship to the theatre of the absurd.

Black theatre has developed in many directions during the last decades, and it seems difficult to predict its future. Yet, one can point out some significant trends and changes. The potential audience has changed. The theatre of the fifties was still written predominantly for a white public as were the first revolutionary plays of the early sixties. Then the drama addressed itself to members of the black community in order to educate them and urge them to analyze their situation with their own minds and see it with their own eyes. It turned away from whites once it had vented all its rage and hatred on them and had ceremoniously buried the "Great White Hope." After the ritualistic dramas enacting the destruction of America, the white man was dead symbolically. The theatre could then devote itself to the building of the black nation, the raising of consciousness. It celebrated the coming together of black people. The collective rituals performed at the New Lafayette Theatre with Robert Macbeth and the work of Barbara Ann Teer and Glenda Dickerson take place at this stage of the symbolic action. Simultaneously the theatre of black experience developed, exploring the various depths of the ethnic sensibility of a blues people; it makes greater use of the structures of black music, and of the black church--the call and response pattern--of oral narrative and poetry. It substitutes rhythms, beats, and movements for the more rational development of plot and character. The theatre has thus partly freed itself from propaganda, didacticism, from the demands and restrictions imposed by ideologies, revolutionary or nationalistic, from the necessity to provide a message and make explanatory statements. It also uses its material more freely. It articulates black experience through a multiplicity of modes, and reaches for a synthesis of various art forms. Spurning the tenets of Western theatrical tradition, it tries to create a dramaturgy that is distinctively black.

A radical change has also been brought to the production and distribution patterns. A great number of groups have come to existence not only in the main urban centers but in rural areas. Through the activity of these groups, many blacks have been exposed to the theatre for the first time. Community theater has appeared in neighborhoods, YMCA's, churches, schools, and universities. Such groups have also created workshops to encourage actors and playwrights and have tried to develop a larger audience. Both acting and playwriting have become more professional. Artists have set up organizations to defend their rights and ensure the production of their work. Furthermore, black directors and producers have emerged. What had long been a rare occurrence has now become more common practice: black actors perform roles written by black playwrights in front of black audiences, and black plays are now being directed or even produced by blacks. Black critics are reviewing plays and having a say in their success; they often question the judgments passed by whites. Information on, and criticism of, black theatre has also spread through such magazines as BLACK THEATRE, BLACK CREATION, and BLACK WORLD; anthologies are being published.

Yet, in spite of all the positive steps that have been taken, the development of black theatre has now reached a state of crisis. The reasons for this crisis cannot be ascribed exclusively to the difficulties that the theatre world at large has had to face under dire economic conditions or to the competition with other media. The present situation is mostly due to certain contradictions and ambiguities that are inherent in the choices and strategies black theatre was forced to adopt throughout its history--between legalized separation, limited integration and self-willed separatism, as well as between Western and African aesthetics. For a long time, black artists have fought to break through the great white way and to win recognition on the "legitimate" stage. Whenever black theatre tried to develop as a separate, autonomous black institution, it discovered the extent of its dependency upon white structures. Its survival has wholly depended upon white money, funds given by antipoverty programs first, then through foundations or government subsidies. Once this support is reduced or withdrawn, black theatre cannot sustain itself. Besides, black theatre has always wavered between its attraction to downtown legitimate theatre--the stardom system, the taste of a white middle-class audience--and the loyalty to its community. On the one hand lies the hope and means to survive and become less marginal, but also the danger of becoming commercialized, controlled, and manipulated by whites, and of losing ethnic identity. On the other hand is a vital bond, warranting authenticity and truth, but a more ascetic and less prestigious adventure. If some artists and groups have been able to make a choice, many are caught in contradictions that have not yet been solved and that affect not only socioeconomic conditions but the aesthetics and the ethics of their work.

II

Part 1 of this section consists of (1) a brief list of major library sources, (2) the most useful periodicals in the field of Afro-American drama, (3) a list of bibliographical works devoted to the subject (general "Negro" or "theatre" bibliographies being excluded), (4) a list of play collections and anthologies, and (5) a list of selected historical and critical studies of Afro-American theatre, and by extension, other aspects of the black performing arts. Each of these sections are subdivided chronologically under the following headings: General, followed by subdivisions such as 1850-1900, 1900-1950, 1950-75, as appropriate.

As a rule, no annotations are provided for secondary sources when the titles indicate their contents with sufficient precision. Recent and easily available editions are indicated as well as, and sometimes in preference to, earlier ones-- as in the case of BLACK DRAMA by Loften Mitchell, which includes many articles published previously. This list of secondary sources is not exhaustive by any means; in fact, a careful selection has eliminated minor pieces or articles which do not deal with essential aspects of the black stage, and selection is more stringent for critical studies, which sometimes tend to abound, than for reports and articles centering on lesser-known local, technical, or practical aspects and problems of contemporary theatre groups.

The second part of this section contains a list of the works of individual authors, listed alphabetically within three periods: 1850-1900, 1901-50, and 1951-75. This list is one of published black playwrights born and/or living primarily in the United States. Our definition excludes a few contemporary black authors who are often considered Afro-Americans because of their association with the American stage but who have not really established residence in the United States; such is the case of West Indians Errol Hill and Errol John, and the Canadian Lennox Brown. Because he spent his life in Great Britain, Henry Francis Downing, the nineteenth-century playwright, does not appear here. Neither does Victor Sejour, who wrote mostly in French and dealt with non-racial themes. One of Sejour's plays, THE BROWN OVERCOAT, was produced Off-Broadway on December 6, 1972, in a translation by Townsend Brewster. Its text can be found in BLACK THEATER USA, edited by James V. Hatch and Ted Shine, pages 25-35.

To be included in our list, an author must have published one play at least, which means that several authors of early twentieth-century musicals, for instance, whose produced plays appear only in the form of summaries in THE BEST PLAYS series are not included. On the other hand, unpublished plays (produced or not) by a published author are listed in order to provide an accurate idea of his total production, if not necessarily of his qualitative importance. Such unpublished plays are not annotated, both for lack of space in the scope of this guide and to avoid duplicating BLACK PLAYWRIGHTS, a bibliography by James V. Hatch and Omanii Abdullah.

The title and bibliographical references of each of the published plays listed are followed by the circumstances of its first production, when known, and by a summary and/or analysis of its contents. The total page numbers of monographs are given where discovered from inspection or bibliographical citation.

I should like to thank Professor James V. Hatch with whom I exchanged information when we were preparing our respective works. We thought it advisable, at the time, to make our books more complementary than competitive and, as a result, he emphasized unpublished plays while I emphasized secondary sources.

Genevieve E. Fabre

NOTES TO DRAMA INTRODUCTION

1. Some historians claim that a certain James Brown connected with the African Grove Theatre was probably the first author of plays. It is also true that the famous actor, Ira Aldridge, was a playwright.

2. Will Marion Cook, J. Rosamond Johnson, P.L. Dunbar, Bob Cole, J.W. Johnson.

3. [Daniel P. Moynihan], "The Black Family. The Case for National Action." Office of Policy Planning and Research, U.S. Department of Labor, 1965.

ABBREVIATIONS USED IN THE DRAMA DIVISION

The following abbreviations have been used for books frequently referred to.
Fuller listings will be found in part one of the Drama division, primarily in
sections 4 (Play Collections) and 5 (Critical Studies).

See also the Abbreviations Used in the Poetry Division, p. 5.

Abramson NP	Abramson, Doris E. NEGRO PLAYWRIGHTS IN THE AMERICAN THEATRE, 1925-1969. New York: Columbia Univ. Press, 1969.
Bigsby BAW2	Bigsby, C.W.E., ed. THE BLACK AMERICAN WRITER. Vol. 2. Baltimore: Penguin, 1971.
BQ	A BLACK QUARTET. Introd. Clayton Riley. New York: New American Library, 1970.
Brasmer BD	Brasmer, William, and Dominick Consolo, eds. BLACK DRAMA, AN ANTHOLOGY. Columbus, Ohio: Charles E. Merrill, 1970.
Brown NPD	Brown, Sterling A. NEGRO POETRY AND DRAMA. Washington, D.C.: Associates in Negro Folk Education, 1937.
Bullins NLTP	Bullins, Ed, ed. THE NEW LAFAYETTE THEATRE PRESENTS. New York: Anchor Press, Doubleday, 1974.
Bullins NPBT	Bullins, Ed, ed. NEW PLAYS FROM THE BLACK THEATRE. New York: Bantam, 1969.
Childress BIS	Childress, Alice, ed. BLACK SCENES. New York: Doubleday, 1971.
Couch, NBP	Couch, William, Jr., ed. NEW BLACK PLAYWRIGHTS. Baton Rouge: Louisiana Univ. Press, 1968. New York: Avon, 1970. (Page references in this guide are to the Avon edition.)

Dent FST	Dent, Tom, Gilbert Moses, and Richard Schechner, eds. THE FREE SOUTHERN THEATER BY THE FREE SOUTHERN THEATER. Indianapolis: Bobbs-Merrill, 1969.
Gayle BA	Gayle, Addison, Jr., ed. THE BLACK AESTHETIC. New York: Doubleday, 1971.
Gayle BE	Gayle, Addison, Jr., ed. BLACK EXPRESSION. New York: Weybright and Talley, 1969.
Harrison KD	Harrison, Paul C., ed. KUNTU DRAMA: PLAYS OF THE AFRICAN CONTINUUM. New York: Grove Press, 1973.
Hatch BTU	Hatch, James V., ed. BLACK THEATER, USA. New York: Free Press, 1974.
Johnson BM	Johnson, James Weldon. BLACK MANHATTAN. New York: Knopf, 1930.
Jones BF	Jones, LeRoi, and Larry Neal, eds. BLACK FIRE. New York: William Morrow, 1968.
King BDA	King, Woodie, and Ron Milner, eds. BLACK DRAMA ANTHOLOGY. New York: Columbia Univ. Press, Signet, New American Library, 1972.
Locke PNL	Locke, Alain, and Montgomery Gregory, eds. PLAYS OF NEGRO LIFE: A SOURCEBOOK OF NATIVE AMERICAN DRAMA. New York: Harper, 1927.
Mitchell BD	Mitchell, Loften. BLACK DRAMA: THE STORY OF THE AMERICAN NEGRO IN THE THEATRE. New York: Hawthorn Books, 1967.
Oliver CBD	Oliver, Clinton C., and Stephanie Sills, eds. CONTEMPORARY BLACK DRAMA. New York: Scribner's, 1971.
Patterson AANT	Patterson, Lindsay, ed. ANTHOLOGY OF THE AMERICAN NEGRO IN THE THEATRE: A CRITICAL APPROACH. New York: Publishers Co., 1967.
Reardon BTDA	Reardon, William, and Thomas D. Pawley. THE BLACK TEACHER AND THE DRAMATIC ARTS. A DIALOGUE, BIBLIOGRAPHY AND ANTHOLOGY. Westport, Conn.: Negro Universities Press, 1970.
Richardson NHTP	Richardson, Willis, and May Miller, eds. NEGRO HISTORY IN THIRTEEN PLAYS. Washington, D.C.: Associated Publishers, 1935.
Richardson PP	Richardson, Willis, ed. PLAYS AND PAGEANTS FROM THE LIFE OF THE NEGRO. Washington, D.C.: Associated Publishers, 1930.
Turner BDA	Turner, Darwin, ed. BLACK DRAMA IN AMERICA: AN ANTHOLOGY. Greenwich, Conn.: Fawcett, 1971.

Part 1
DRAMA: GENERAL STUDIES

1. LIBRARY RESOURCES

For specific authors and collections, consult the DIRECTORY OF AFRO-AMERICAN RESOURCES, edited by Walter Schatz (New York: Bowker, 1970) and guides to special archives and manuscript collections in the United States. The following libraries and centers have important holdings concerning black theatre:

Atlanta. Atlanta University, Morehouse-Spelman Players Archives, Fine Arts Building.

Theatre history and criticism.

Denver. Denver Public Library.

Black theatre and minstrels.

Detroit. Detroit Public Library, Azalia Hackley Collection.

Los Angeles. University of California at Los Angeles Library, George P. Johnson Negro Film Collection.

New Haven, Conn. Yale University, Beinecke Library, James Weldon Johnson Collection.

New York City. Columbia University, Butler Library.

New York City. Hatch-Billops Collection, 491 Broadway.

New York City. International Theatre Institute, U.S. Section.

New York City. New York Public Library, Lincoln Center.
Clippings and files.

New York City. New York Public Library, Schomburg Collection.

Books, files, and clippings.

2. PERIODICALS

Included below are periodicals devoted to black drama, periodicals devoted to black literature or to black studies that frequently publish material on drama, and special issues on black drama of periodicals of more general interest.

AFRO-ASIAN THEATRE BULLETIN. 1965-71; then BULLETIN OF BLACK THEATRE. 1971-- . Washington, D.C.

This is the newsletter of the A.T.A. Black Theatre Project, published by the American Educational Theatre Association in Washington, D.C.

BLACK CREATION. 1970-- . New York.

Drama reviews and interviews of playwrights.

BLACK THEATRE. 1968-72. New York.

Each of the six issues deals exclusively with contemporary black theatre, featuring interviews, plays, articles on playwrights and theatre groups, reports, and reviews. The emphasis is on the New Lafayette Theatre group; Ed Bullins, Marvin X, Robert Macbeth, and Amiri Baraka (Leroi Jones) are well represented.

BLACK WORLD. May 1970-April 1976. See NEGRO DIGEST, below.

BULLETIN OF BLACK THEATRE. 1971-- . See AFRO-ASIAN THEATRE BULLETIN, above.

THE CRISIS. 1910-- . New York:

Published a score of short plays and reviewed theatre events regularly up to 1940. See "Index to Literary Materials in THE CRISIS, 1910-1934," compiled by Jean Fagan Yellin, in CLA JOURNAL, 15 (June 1971), 452-65 and 16 (Dec. 1971), 197-234, which lists plays and drama reviews separately.

DRAMA CRITIQUE, 7 (Spring 1964).

Special issue on Negro theatre.

DRAMA REVIEW, 12 (Summer 1968). New York.

"Black Theatre Issue." A very important issue, edited by Ed

Bullins: includes plays, statements, reports on activities, articles, and a bibliography of plays.

DRAMA REVIEW, 16 (Dec. 1972), 5-62. New York.

"Black Theatre Issue." Includes articles by James V. Hatch ("200 Years of Black Drama"), Margaret Wilkerson on black theatre in California, Jessica Harris on the National Black Theatre, Lisbeth Gant on the New Lafayette, and James P. Murray on black movies and theatre.

ENCORE (June 1970). New York.

Devoted to the black dramatic arts.

FREEDOMWAYS. 1961-- . New York.

A few drama reviews and a couple of short plays.

LIBERATOR. 1960-- . New York.

Published a number of drama reviews in the 1960s.

NEGRO DIGEST. 1942-51; 1961-70; then BLACK WORLD. May 1970-April 1976. Chicago.

Important articles are listed in "Criticism" sections. This magazine, edited by Hoyt Fuller for the Johnson Publications, devotes an annual issue, generally in April, to black theatre in the United States. Among these special issues, one should note:

NEGRO DIGEST, 11 (July 1962), 52-58.

"Annual Theatre Issue." NEGRO DIGEST, 15 (Apr. 1966).

Features articles by Robert Brug, Ed Bullins, Ossie Davis, Floyd Gaffney, LeRoi Jones, Woodie King, Fred O'Neal.

"Annual Theater Issue." NEGRO DIGEST, 16 (Mar. 1967).

Features David Rambeau on Concept East, and articles by Ottillie Markholt, W.K. Kgositsile, Ron Milner.

"Annual Theater Issue." NEGRO DIGEST, 17 (Apr. 1968).

Articles by Ron Milner, Barbara Ann Teer, Dick Campbell, Owen Dodson, Peter Labrie, Loften Mitchell, Peter Bailey, Hoyt W. Fuller.

"Black Theater in America." NEGRO DIGEST, 18 (Apr. 1969).

Articles by Barbara Ann Teer, Frank Silvera, Mootry, Woodie King, Floyd Gaffney; reports by Sam Greenlee, Tom Dent et al.; interview of Ed Bullins.

"Annual Theater Issue." NEGRO DIGEST, 19 (Apr. 1970).

Articles by Woodie King, H.A. Johnson, Donald Evans; reports by Val Ferdinand and others; plays by Ed Bullins and Jean Smith.

"Situation of the Black Theater in America." BLACK WORLD, 20 (Apr. 1971).

Interview of Amiri Baraka; plays by Ed Bullins, Alice Childress, Ronald Milner; special reports on black theatre groups.

"Annual Theater Issue." BLACK WORLD, 21 (Apr. 1972).

Articles by Woodie King and Amiri Baraka; bibliography; black theatre round-up; play by Kalamu Ya Salaam.

"Annual Theater Issue." BLACK WORLD, 22 (Apr. 1973).

Interview with Lonne Elder III; reports on black theatre in the United States; article by Carlton Molette; play by Don Evans.

"Annual Theater Issue." BLACK WORLD, 23 (Apr. 1974).

Reports on black theatre around the world; articles on Ed Bullins; checklist of plays performed since 1960.

NEGRO HISTORY BULLETIN. 1937-- . Washington, D.C.

Published a few short plays and articles.

OPPORTUNITY: A JOURNAL OF NEGRO LIFE. 1923-46. New York.

Published important reviews and a few short plays in the 1920s and 1930s.

PHYLON. 1940-- . Atlanta.

A number of detailed articles. Regular annual review, "The Negro on Broadway" by Miles Jefferson. See 7 (1946), 185-96; 8 (1947),

146-59; 9 (1948), 99-107; 10 (1949), 103-11; 11 (1950), 105-13; 12 (1951), 128-36; 13 (1952), 199-208; 14 (1953), 268-79; 15 (1954), 253-60; 16 (1955), 303-12; 17 (1956), 227-37; 18 (1957), 286-95.

THEATRE TODAY (Fall 1968). New York.

Special issue on black theatre.

Reviews, reports and theatre round-ups and occasional articles concerning black theatre today also appear in the BLACK COLLEGIAN, BLACK ENTERPRISE, EBONY, EDUCATIONAL THEATRE JOURNAL, ESSENCE, JET, JOURNAL OF NEGRO EDUCATION, MUHAMMAD SPEAKS, NEW YORK AMSTERDAM NEWS, NEW YORK THEATRE CRITICS REVIEW, RACE RELATIONS REPORTER, THEATRE INFORMATION BULLETIN, THIRD WORLD, and TUESDAY.

3. BIBLIOGRAPHIES

a. General

Busacca, Basil. "Checklist of Black Playwrights: 1823-1970." BLACK SCHOLAR, 5 (Sept. 1973), 48-54.

Lists authors, titles, and dates of plays produced or not, published or not.

Hatch, James V. BLACK IMAGE ON THE AMERICAN STAGE: A BIBLIOGRAPHY OF PLAYS AND MUSICALS, 1770-1970. New York: Drama Book Specialists, 1970. 162 p.

A pioneer attempt to list all American plays dealing with black characters, whether by black or white authors.

Hatch, James V., and Omanii Abdullah. BLACK PLAYWRIGHTS, 1823-1977: AN ANNOTATED BIBLIOGRAPHY OF PLAYS. New York: Bowker, 1977. 319 p.

Entries contain titles of published and unpublished plays, genre, statement of theme, date and place of production and/or publication, acts, and characters.

Reardon, William, and Thomas D. Pawley. THE BLACK TEACHER AND THE DRAMATIC ARTS: A DIALOGUE, BIBLIOGRAPHY AND ANTHOLOGY. Westport, Conn.: Negro Universities Press, 1970. 487 p.

The bibliography (pp. 71-121) lists plays, theses, books, and articles by decades and year with full references, but it is largely selective.

Sumpter, Clyde G. "The Negro in 20th Century American Drama: A Bibliography." THEATRE DOCUMENTATION, 3 (Fall 1970-Spring 1971), 3-27.

Lists play collections, plays, books, and articles by twenty- and ten-year periods.

Turner, Darwin T. AFRO-AMERICAN WRITERS. New York: Appleton-Century-Crofts, 1970. 117 p.

"Drama" section, pp. 29-30; see also "Art, Journalism, Music, Theatre" section, pp. 15-18.

b. 1950-75

Fabre, Genevieve E. "A Checklist of Original Plays, Pageants, Rituals, and Musicals by Afro-American Authors Performed in the United States from 1960 to 1973." BLACK WORLD, 23 (Apr. 1974), 81-97.

Jurges, Oda. "Selected Bibliography: Black Plays, Books, and Articles Related to Black Theatre Published from January 1961 to February 1968." DRAMA REVIEW, 21 (Apr. 1972), 92-98.

Willis, Richard, and Hilda McElroy. "Published Works of Black Playwrights in the United States, 1960-1970." BULLETIN OF BLACK THEATRE, 1 (Spring 1971), 8-15. Also in BLACK WORLD, 21 (Apr. 1972), 92-98.

4. PLAY COLLECTIONS

a. General

Adams, Peter, et al., eds. AFRO-AMERICAN LITERATURE: DRAMA. Boston: Houghton Mifflin, 1969. 246 p.

Plays by Ossie Davis, Lorraine Hansberry, and Loften Mitchell.

Brasmer, William, and Dominick Consolo, eds. BLACK DRAMA, AN ANTHOLOGY. Columbus, Ohio: Charles E. Merrill, 1970. 393 p.

Introduction by Darwin T. Turner; plays by L. Hughes, Paul Green, Douglas T. Ward (2), Adrienne Kennedy, Ossie Davis, and Ted Shine (2).

Harrison, Paul C., ed. KUNTU DRAMA: PLAYS OF THE AFRICAN CONTINUUM. New York: Grove Press, 1973. 325 p.

Preface by Oliver Jackson on "The African Continuum" and "Kuntu Drama"; introduction by editor on "Black Theatre in Search of a

Source"; plays by Jean Toomer, Aimé Césaire, Amiri Baraka, Adrienne Kennedy, Lennox Brown, Clay Goss, and Paul Carter Harrison.

Hatch, James V., ed. BLACK THEATER, USA: 45 PLAYS BY BLACK AMERI-CANS. New York: Free Press, 1974. 886 p.

Foreword by Ted Shine; plays by Ira Aldridge, Victor Sejour, William Wells Brown, Joseph S. Cotter, Sr., Garland Anderson, Angelina Grimke, Alice Dunbar Nelson, Mary Burrill, Myrtle S. Livingston, Ruth Gaines-Shelton, Eulalie Spence, Marita Bonner, Georgia Douglas Johnson, Jean Toomer, John Matheus, Willis Richardson (2), Randolph Edmonds, H.F.V. Edward, Langston Hughes (3), Theodore Ward, Owen Dodson, May Miller, Theodore Browne, Richard Wright and Paul Green, Stanley Richards, Abram Hill, Thomas Pawley, James Baldwin, Louis Peterson, William Branch, Loften Mitchell, Charles Sebree, C. Bernard Jackson and James V. Hatch, Douglas Turner Ward, Lorraine Hansberry, Alice Childress, Adrienne Kennedy, Martie Charles, Imamu Amiri Baraka, Ed Bullins, Ted Shine, and Val Ferdinand; bibliography and sum-mary of important plays.

Patterson, Lindsay, ed. BLACK THEATER: A 20TH CENTURY COLLECTION OF THE WORK OF ITS BEST PLAYWRIGHTS. New York: Dodd, Mead, 1971. 493 p. New York: New American Library, 1973. 705 p.

Plays by Bontemps and Cullen, Louis Peterson, William Branch, Alice Childress, Langston Hughes, L. Hansberry, O. Davis, LeRoi Jones, J. Baldwin, Ed Bullins, and Charles Gordone.

Turner, Darwin T., ed. BLACK DRAMA IN AMERICA: AN ANTHOLOGY. Greenwich, Conn.: Fawcett, 1971. 630 p.

Plays by Willis Richardson, Langston Hughes, Theodore Ward, Owen Dodson, Randolph Edmonds, Ossie Davis, LeRoi Jones, and Kingsley B. Bass, Jr.

b. 1900-1950

Locke, Alain, and Montgomery Gregory, eds. PLAYS OF NEGRO LIFE: A SOURCEBOOK OF NATIVE AMERICAN DRAMA. New York: Harper, 1972. Rpt. Westport, Conn.: Negro Universities Press, 1970. 430 p.

Introduction; plays by Willis Richardson, Frank H. Wilson, John Matheus, Eulalie Spence, John William Rogers, Jean Toomer, Georgia Douglas Johnson, Thelma Duncan, and Richard Bruce.

Richardson, Willis, ed. PLAYS AND PAGEANTS FROM THE LIFE OF THE NEGRO. Washington, D.C.: Associated Publishers, 1930. 373 p.

Twelve plays by Thelma Duncan, Maud Cuney-Hare, John Matheus,

May Miller, Inez Burke, Dorothy Guinn, Frances Gunner, Edward McCoo, and the editor.

Richardson, Willis, and May Miller, eds. NEGRO HISTORY IN THIRTEEN PLAYS. Washington, D.C.: Associated Publishers, 1935. 333 p.

Five plays by Richardson, four by May Miller, one each by H.W. Harris and Georgia D. Johnson.

c. 1950-75

A BLACK QUARTET: FOUR NEW BLACK PLAYS. Introd. Clayton Riley. New York: New American Library, 1970. 158 p.

Plays by Ed Bullins, Ron Milner, LeRoi Jones, and Ben Caldwell.

Bullins, Ed, ed. THE NEW LAFAYETTE THEATRE PRESENTS: PLAYS WITH AESTHETIC COMMENTS BY 6 BLACK PLAYWRIGHTS. New York: Anchor Press, Doubleday, 1974. 301 p.

Plays by Ed Bullins, J.E. Gaines, Clay Goss, Oyamo, Sonia Sanchez, and Richard Wesley.

_____. NEW PLAYS FROM THE BLACK THEATRE. New York: Bantam, 1969. 304 p.

Interview of Bullins by Marvin X; plays by Amiri Baraka, Kingsley Bass, Sonia Sanchez, Marvin X, Herbert Stokes, Ben Caldwell (2), Ed Bullins, Salimu, N.R. Davidson, and Charles Fuller.

Childress, Alice, ed. BLACK SCENES. New York: Doubleday, 1971. 154 p.

Scenes from plays by Ossie Davis, Roger Furman, Floyd Barbour, Ted Shine, Ed Bullins, Abbey Lincoln, William Branch, Julian Mayfield, Ted Ward, Steve Carter, Lorraine Hansberry, Loften Mitchell, D.T. Ward, Theodore Browne, and the editor.

Couch, William, Jr., ed. NEW BLACK PLAYWRIGHTS. Baton Rouge: Louisiana State Univ. Press, 1968. 256 p. New York: Avon, 1970, 285 p. Note: Page references in this guide are to the Avon edition.

Two plays by Douglas T. Ward, one each by Ed Bullins, William W. Mackey, Adrienne Kennedy, and Lonne Elder III (replaced by Paul C. Harrison in Avon edition).

Jones, LeRoi, and Larry Neal, eds. BLACK FIRE: AN ANTHOLOGY OF AFRO-AMERICAN WRITING. New York: William Morrow, 1968. 670 p.

Contains a drama section, the plays of which are listed here under their authors' names, and important contributions expressing the black nationalist movement of the 1960s.

King, Woodie, and Ron Milner, eds. BLACK DRAMA ANTHOLOGY. New York: Columbia Univ. Press, 1972. 671 p. New York: Signet, New American Library, 1972. 671 p.

> Plays by Amiri Baraka (2), Archie Shepp, Ed Bullins, Ron Milner, Lonne Elder III, Clifford Mason, Douglas T. Ward, Oliver Pitcher, Donald Greaves, Philip H. Dean, William W. Mackey, Joseph Walker, Ben Caldwell, Langston Hughes, Charles Gordon, Ron Zuber, William Branch, Peter DeAnda, Martie Charles, Errol Hill, Loften Mitchell, and Elaine Jackson.

Oliver, Clinton C., and Stephanie Sills, eds. CONTEMPORARY BLACK DRAMA. New York: Scribner's, 1971. 452 p.

> Plays by Lorraine Hansberry, Ossie Davis, Adrienne Kennedy, LeRoi Jones, James Baldwin, Douglas Turner Ward, Ed Bullins, and Charles Gordone.

Reardon, William R., and Thomas D. Pawley, eds. THE BLACK TEACHER AND THE DRAMATIC ARTS: A DIALOGUE, BIBLIOGRAPHY AND ANTHOLOGY. Westport, Conn.: Negro Universities Press, 1970. 487 p.

5. CRITICAL STUDIES

a. General

Abramson, Doris E. NEGRO PLAYWRIGHTS IN THE AMERICAN THEATRE, 1925-1969. New York: Columbia Univ. Press, 1969. 335 p.

Archer, Leonard C. BLACK IMAGES IN THE AMERICAN THEATRE. Brooklyn, N.Y.: Pageant-Poseidon, 1973. 351 p.

> Also deals with radio and television.

Belcher, Fannin S., Jr. "The Negro Theatre: A Glance Backward." PHYLON, 11 (1950), 121-26.

Bigsby, C.W.E., ed. THE BLACK AMERICAN WRITER. Vol. 2. Deland, Fla.: Everett, Edwards, 1969. Baltimore, Md.: Penguin, 1971. 253 p.

> Contains eight essays on black theatre (pp. 113-240); also listed by name of author.

Bradley, Gerald. "Goodbye Mr. Bones: The Emergence of Negro Themes and Character in American Drama." DRAMA CRITIQUE, 7 (Spring 1964), 79-86. Also in Patterson AANT, pp. 13-20.

Butcher, Margaret Just. THE NEGRO IN AMERICAN CULTURE. New York: Knopf, 1956; Mentor Books, 1957. 294 p.

> Based on materials left by Alain Locke; deals with the history of black theatre.

Cotton, Lettie Jo. "The Negro in the American Theatre." NEGRO HISTORY BULLETIN, 23 (1960), 172-78.

Couch, William, Jr. "The Problem of Negro Character and Dramatic Incident." PHYLON, 11 (1950), 127-33.

Cruse, Harold. THE CRISIS OF THE NEGRO INTELLECTUAL. New York: William Morrow, 1967. 594 p.

> Several chapters deal with theatre in Harlem and New York City.

Drewry, Cecilia. "Black Theatre: An Evolving Force." In BLACK LIFE AND CULTURE IN THE UNITED STATES. Ed. Rhoda Goldstein. New York: Crowell, 1971, pp. 322-40.

Duberman, Martin. "History and Theatre." COLUMBIA UNIVERSITY FORUM, Fall 1964. Also in Patterson AANT, pp. 199-204.

Edmonds, Randolph. "Black Drama in American Theatre, 1700." In THE AMERICAN THEATRE, A SUM OF ITS PARTS. FIRST AMERICAN COLLEGE THEATRE FESTIVAL ADDRESSES. New York: Samuel French, 1971. pp. 379-424.

Fletcher, Tom. 100 YEARS OF THE NEGRO IN SHOW BUSINESS. New York: Burdge, 1954. 337 p.

Hicklin, Fannie. "The American Negro Playwright, 1920-1964." Ph.D. dissertation, Univ. of Wisconsin, 1965.

Hughes, Langston, and Milton Meltzer. BLACK MAGIC: A PICTORIAL HISTORY OF THE NEGRO IN AMERICAN ENTERTAINMENT. Englewood Cliffs, N.J.: Prentice-Hall, 1967. 375 p.

Lewis, Samella, and Ruth G. Waddy, eds. BLACK ARTISTS ON ART. Vol. 1. Los Angeles: Contemporary Crafts Publishers, 1969. 132 p.

> Includes views expressed by theatre people.

McIlrath, Patricia. "Stereotypes, Types and Characterization in Drama." EDUCATIONAL THEATRE JOURNAL, 7 (Mar. 1955), 1-10.

Mitchell, Loften. BLACK DRAMA: THE STORY OF THE AMERICAN NEGRO IN THE THEATRE. New York: Hawthorn Books, 1967. 284 p.

Includes many articles previously published by the author.

Morrison, Allan. "100 Years of Negro Entertainment." EBONY, 19 (1963), 122-28.

"The Negro on Broadway." EBONY, 19 (1964), 186-94.

Patterson, Lindsay, ed. ANTHOLOGY OF THE AMERICAN NEGRO IN THE THEATRE: A CRITICAL APPROACH. International Library of Negro Life and History, Vol. 1. New York: Publishers Co., 1967. 306 p.

Contains various studies and articles, the most important of which are also listed in this bibliography under author's name.

Ralph, George. THE AMERICAN THEATRE, THE NEGRO AND THE FREEDOM MOVEMENT. Chicago: City Missionary Society, 1964.

Rollins, Charlemae. FAMOUS NEGRO ENTERTAINERS. New York: Dodd, Mead, 1967. 122 p.

Sandle, Floyd L. THE NEGRO IN AMERICAN EDUCATIONAL THEATRE: AN ORGANIZATIONAL DEVELOPMENT, 1911-1964. Ann Arbor, Mich.: Edwards Bros., 1964.

Schechter, William. THE HISTORY OF NEGRO HUMOR IN AMERICA. New York: Fleet Press, 1970. 214 p.

Includes many references to the stage.

Schiffman, Jack. UPTOWN: THE STORY OF HARLEM'S APOLLO THEATRE. New York: Cowles Book Co., 1971. 210 p.

Selby, John. BEYOND CIVIL RIGHTS. Cleveland: World Publishing Co., 1966. 215 p.

The history of Karamu House and its theatrical activities.

Styan, J.L. DARK COMEDY: THE DEVELOPMENT OF MODERN COMIC TRAGEDY. Toronto: Macmillan, 1962. 303 p.

Thompson, Larry. "The Black Image in Early American Drama, 1760-1930." BLACK WORLD, 24 (Apr. 1975), 54-69.

Turner, Darwin T. "The Black Playwright in the Professional Theatre of the United States of America, 1858-1959." In Brasmer BD, pp. 11-18. Also in Bigsby BAW2, pp. 113-28.

_____. "The Negro Dramatist's Image of the Universe." CLA JOURNAL, 5 (1961), 106-20. Also in BLACK VOICES. Ed. Abraham Chapman, New York: New American Library, 1968, pp. 677-89; and in Patterson AANT, pp. 65-74.

_____. "Negro Playwrights and the Urban Negro." CLA JOURNAL, 12 (1968), 19-25.

Van Vechten, Carl. "How Is the Theatre Represented in the Negro Collection at Yale?" THEATRE ANNUAL, 1943, pp. 32-38.

b. 1850-1900

Bowen, Elbert R. "Negro Minstrels in Early Rural Missouri." MISSOURI HISTORICAL REVIEW, 47 (1953), 103-19.

Brown, Allston T. "Early History of Negro Minstrelsy." NEW YORK CLIPPER, 17 May 1913, and following issues until August 1913.

Harrison, A. Cleveland. "The Octoroon Reconsidered." PLAYERS, 45 (1970), 282-86.

Hutton, Laurence. "The Negro on the Stage." HARPER'S, 79 (1889), 131.

Johnson, James Weldon. BLACK MANHATTAN. New York: Knopf, 1930. Rpt. New York: Atheneum, 1968. 284 p.

Kaplan, Sidney. "The Octoroon: Early History of Drama of Miscegenation." JOURNAL OF NEGRO EDUCATION, 20 (1951), 547-57.

Kendall, J.S. "New Orleans Negro Minstrels." LOUISIANA HISTORICAL QUARTERLY, (Jan. 1947), pp. 128-48.

Matthews, Brander. "The Rise and Fall of Negro Minstrelsy." SCRIBNER'S, 57 (1915), 754-59.

Moody, Rich. "Negro Minstrelsy." QUARTERLY JOURNAL OF SPEECH, 30 (1964), 321-28.

Nathan, Hans. DAN EMMETT AND THE RISE OF EARLY NEGRO MINSTRELSY. Norman: Univ. of Oklahoma Press, 1962. 496 p.

Pawley, Thomas D. "The First Black Playwrights." BLACK WORLD, 21 (Apr. 1972), 16-24.

Wittke, Carl. TAMBO AND BONES. Durham, N.C.: Duke Univ. Press, 1930. 269 p.

On black comedy and minstrelsy.

c. 1900-1950

Belcher, Fannin S., Jr. "Negro Drama; Stage Center." OPPORTUNITY, 17 (1939), 292-95.

Bond, Frederick W. THE NEGRO AND THE DRAMA: THE DIRECT AND IN-DIRECT CONTRIBUTION WHICH THE NEGRO HAS MADE TO DRAMA AND THE LEGITIMATE STAGE, WITH THE UNDERLYING CONDITIONS RESPON-SIBLE. Washington, D.C.: Associated Publishers, 1940. Rpt. Washington, D.C.: McGrath, 1969. 213 p.

Brawley, Benjamin. THE NEGRO GENIUS. New York: Dodd, Mead, 1937. Rpt. New York: Apollo Paperback, 1966. 365 p.

See especially pages 239-316.

Brown, Sterling. "The Federal Theatre" and "The Negro Attempts Legitimate." In Patterson AANT, pp. 101-7.

_____. NEGRO POETRY AND DRAMA. Washington, D.C.: Associates in Negro Folk Education, 1937. 142 p. Reprinted with THE NEGRO IN AMERI-CAN FICTION. New York: Arno, 1969.

Cantor, Eddie. "The Best Teacher I Ever Had." EBONY, 13 (June 1958), 103-6.

CAROLINA MAGAZINE. Special Issue on Negro Literature. Vol. 59 (Apr. 1929).

Four black plays.

Charters, Ann. NOBODY: THE STORY OF BERT WILLIAMS. New York: Macmillan, 1970. 157 p.

Cline, Julia. "Rise of the American Stage Negro." DRAMA, 21 (Jan. 1931), 9-10, 14.

"The Colored Players and Their Plays." THEATRE ARTS, 1 (1917), 138.

Cunard, Nancy, ed. NEGRO ANTHOLOGY. London: Wishart, 1934.

See "Negro Stars" section (pp. 291-345).

Cuney-Hare, Maud. "Musical Comedy." In NEGRO MUSICIANS AND THEIR MUSIC. Washington, D.C.: Associated Publishers, 1936, pp. 157-77. Also in Patterson AANT, pp. 36-49.

DuBois, William E.B. "Opinion--The Negro and the American Stage." CRISIS, 28 (1924), 56-57.

Edmonds, Randolph. "Some Reflections on the Negro in American Drama." OPPORTUNITY, 8 (1930), 303-5.

Flanagan, Hallie. ARENA. New York: Duell, Sloan and Pearce, 1940. 475 p.

Deals with the part played by the Negro in the Federal Theatre Project. On this subject also see Willson Whitman, BREAD AND CIRCUSES (New York: Oxford Univ. Press, 1937); Jane Matthews, THE FEDERAL THEATRE 1935-1939 (Princeton, N.J.: Princeton Univ. Press, 1967); the unpublished research studies compiled by the New York City W.P.A. on the Negro Dramatists Writers' Program (1936-40) at the Schomburg Collection; and Morgan Himmelstein, DRAMA WAS A WEAPON (New Brunswick, N.J.: Rutgers University Press, 1963).

Grant, G.C. "The Negro in Dramatic Art." JOURNAL OF NEGRO HISTORY, 17 (1932), 19-29.

Gregory, Montgomery. "The Drama of Negro Life." In THE NEW NEGRO. Ed. Alain Locke. New York: Boni, 1925, pp. 153-60. Also in Gayle BE, pp. 128-33.

_____. "For a Negro Theatre." NEW REPUBLIC, 28 (26 Nov. 1921), 350.

Haddon, Archibald. "Centenary of Negro Drama." CRISIS, 41 (1934), 35-36.

Hamilton, Jack. "The American Negro Theatre." DRAMATICS, 17 (Mar. 1946), 3-4.

Hay, Samuel A. "Alain Locke and Black Drama." BLACK WORLD, 21 (Apr. 1972), 8-14.

Housman, John. RUN-THROUGH. New York: Curtis, 1972.

See pages 173-211 on the Federal Negro Theatre.

Huggins, Nathan Irvin. HARLEM RENAISSANCE. New York: Oxford Univ. Press, 1971. 343 p.

See pages 244-301.

Isaacs, Edith J.R. THE NEGRO IN THE AMERICAN THEATRE. New York: Theatre Arts, 1947. 143 p.

　　Originally published in THEATRE ARTS, 26 (1942), 492-543.

Jeliffe, Rowena W. "A Negro Community Theatre." NEW THEATRE AND FILM, July 1935, p. 13.

　　On Karamu House.

Jerome, V.J. THE NEGRO IN HOLLYWOOD FILMS. New York: Masses & Mainstream, 1950. 64 p.

Kimball, Robert, and William Bolcom. REMINISCING WITH SISSLE AND BLAKE. New York: Viking, 1973. 254 p.

Kornweibel, Theodore. "Theophilus Lewis and the Theatre of the Harlem Renaissance." In THE HARLEM RENAISSANCE REMEMBERED. Ed. Arna Bontemps. New York: Dodd, Mead, 1972, pp. 171-88.

"Krigwa Players Little Negro Theatre." CRISIS, 32 (1926), 135-36.

Leonard, Claire. "The American Negro Theatre." THEATRE ARTS, 38 (1944), 421-23.

_____. "Dark Drama." NEGRO DIGEST, 2 (Aug. 1944), 81-82.

Lewis, Lloyd. "Life with Uncle Eggs." NEGRO DIGEST, 4 (July 1946), 19-22.

　　On comedian Bert Williams.

Locke, Alain. "Broadway and the Negro Drama." THEATRE ARTS, 25 (1941), 745-52.

_____. "The Drama of Negro Life." THEATRE ARTS, 10 (1926), 701-6. Also in Gayle BE, pp. 123-28.

_____. "The Negro and the American Theatre." In THEATRE: ESSAYS ON THE ART OF THE THEATRE. Ed. Edith J.R. Isaacs. Boston: Little, Brown, 1927, pp. 290-303.

_____. "Steps toward the Negro Theatre." CRISIS, 25 (1922), 66-68.

Lowell, J. "Round-Up: the Negro in American Drama, 1946-47." CRISIS, 54 (1947), 212-17.

Lowrey, Flora. "The Dallas Negro Players." SOUTHWEST REVIEW, 16 (1931), 373-82.

MacDougald, J.F. "The Federal Government and the Negro Theatre." OPPORTUNITY, 14 (1936), 135-37.

Matthews, Ralph. "The Negro Theatre--A Dodo Bird." In NEGRO ANTHOLOGY. Ed. Nancy Cunard. London: Wishart, 1934, pp. 312-16.

Mitchell, Loften. "On the 'Emerging' Playwright." In Bigsby BAW2, pp. 129-36.

Morse, George C. "Broadway Rediscovers the Negro." NEGRO HISTORY BULLETIN, 9 (1946), 173-76, 189-91.

Nathan, George Jean. "Negro Drama." AMERICAN MERCURY, 17 (May 1929), 117-18.

Noble, Peter. THE NEGRO IN FILMS. London: S. Robinson, 1948. 288 p.

O'Neil, Raymond. "The Negro in Dramatic Art." CRISIS, 27 (1924), 155-57.

Overstreet, Harry. "Images and the Negro." SATURDAY REVIEW OF LITERATURE, 27 (26 Aug. 1944), 5-6.

Pawley, Thomas. "Dunbar as Playwright." BLACK WORLD, 26 (Apr. 1975), 70-79.

"Racial Discrimination in Washington, D.C." EQUITY, 32 (1947), 9-13.

Robeson, Eslanda Goode. PAUL ROBESON, NEGRO. New York: Harper, 1930. 178 p.

"The Role of Blacks in the Federal Theatre, 1935-1939." JOURNAL OF NEGRO HISTORY, 59 (1974), 38-50.

Rowland, Mabel, ed. BERT WILLIAMS--SON OF LAUGHTER. New York: English Crafters, 1923. 218 p.

Saunders, Doris. "Command Performance of Williams and Walker." NEGRO DIGEST, 11 (Mar. 1962), 16-21.

Seton, Marie. PAUL ROBESON. London: Dobson, 1958. 254 p.

Silvera, John D. "Still in Blackface." CRISIS, 46 (1939), 71-72, 89.

Smith, Augustus. "On the White Man's Stage." NEW THEATRE AND FILM, July 1935, pp. 10-15.

Spinks, William. "Bert Williams, Brokenhearted Comedian." PHYLON, 11 (1950), 59-65.

Tobin, Terrence. "Karamu Theatre." DRAMA CRITIQUE, 7 (Spring 1964), 86-91.

Vorhees, Lillian W. "The Drama in a College for Negroes." DRAMA, 15 (Mar. 1926), 224.

Ward, Theodore. "Negro Playwrights Company." In PEOPLE'S THEATRE IN AMERICA. Ed. Karen M. Taylor. New York: Drama Books Specialists, 1972, pp. 186-91.

Waters, Ethel. HIS EYE IS ON THE SPARROW: THE AUTOBIOGRAPHY OF ETHEL WATERS. New York: Doubleday, 1951. 278 p.

"Why Not a Negro Drama of Negroes for Negroes?" CURRENT OPINION, 72 (1922), 639-40.

Williamson, Harvey. "The Gilpin Players." CRISIS, 42 (1935), 205-6, 214.

Wyatt, Euphemia Van Rensselaer. "The Drama: The American Negro Theatre." CATHOLIC WORLD, 161 (1945), 432.

d. 1950-75

"The Advent of the Negro Actor on the Legitimate Stage." JOURNAL OF NEGRO EDUCATION, 35 (1966), 237-45.

Anderson, John Q. "New Orleans Voodoo Ritual Dance and Its 20th Century Survivals." SOUTHERN FOLKLORE QUARTERLY, 24 (June 1960), 135-43.

"Art of Racial Identity." THEATRE PROFILES, 1 (1973) 173-74.

Austin, G.E. "The Advent of the Negro Actor on the Legitimate Stage in America." JOURNAL OF NEGRO EDUCATION, 35 (1966), 237-45.

Bailey, Peter. "Black Theater." EBONY, 24 (Aug. 1969), 126-44.

_____. "The Importance of Being Black." NEWSWEEK, 24 Feb. 1969, pp. 102-3.

_____. "Is the Negro Ensemble Company Really Black Theatre?" NEGRO DIGEST, 17 (Apr. 1968), 16-20.

_____. "Woodie King Jr.: Renaissance Man of Black Theater." BLACK WORLD, 24 (Apr. 1975), 4-10.

Baldwin, James. "James Baldwin on the Negro Actor." URBANITE (Apr. 1961). Also in Patterson AANT, pp. 127-30.

_____. "Theatre: The Negro In and Out." NEGRO DIGEST, 15 (Apr. 1966), 37-44.

Barksdale, Richard. "White Tragedy, Black Comedy." PHYLON, 22 (1961), 226-33.

Barnett, Douglas Q. "Black Arts/West." BLACK WORLD, 21 (May 1972), 87-89.
> On black theatre in Seattle.

Barrow, William. "Introducing the Concept." NEGRO DIGEST, 12 (May 1963), 76-79.
> On Detroit Concept East Theatre.

Beauford, Fred. "The Negro Ensemble Company: Five Years against the Wall." BLACK CREATION, 3 (Winter 1972), 16-18.

Bernard, Sidney. "Poetry/Drama in Harlem." NATION, 204 (1967), 826.

Bigsby, C.W.E. "Black Drama in the Seventies." TEXAS QUARTERLY, 3 (Spring 1971), 10-20.

_____. "Three Black Playwrights: Loften Mitchell, Ossie Davis, Douglas Turner Ward." In Bigsby BAW2, pp. 137-55.

Billington, M. "A Question of Colour." PLAYS AND PLAYERS, Oct. 1965, pp. 8-12.

"Black Drama: A New Outlook." NEW YORK COURIER, 28 Mar. 1970, pp. 21-22.

"Black Magic." Special issue of AFTER DARK, Jan. 1974.
    On the black performing arts: theatre, film, and music.

"Black Theatre: A Bid for Cultural Identity." BLACK ENTERPRISE, Sept. 1971, pp. 30-34, 44.

"Black Theatre: A Need for the 70s." SOUL ILLUSTRATED, 5 (1970), 88-89, 92.

Boge, N.S. "Ethnic Literature. Replacing Old Stereotypes with Positive Concepts." CLEAR HOUSE, 44 (1970), 527-30.

Brock, Bertha. "Designing for Black Theatre." THEATRE CRAFTS, 4 (Mar. 1972), 8-11.

Brooks, A. Russell. "The Comic Spirit and the Negro New Look." CLA JOURNAL, 6 (1962), 35-43.

Brown, Lloyd W. "The Cultural Revolution in Black Theatre." NEGRO AMERICAN LITERATURE FORUM, 8 (1974), 159-64.

Bullins, Ed. "Black Theatre Notes." BLACK THEATRE, No. 1 (1968), pp. 4-7.

_____. "The So-Called Western Avant-Garde Drama." LIBERATOR, 7 (Dec. 1967), 16-18. Also in Gayle BE, pp. 143-46.

_____. "Theatre of Reality." NEGRO DIGEST, 18 (Apr. 1969), 60-66.

_____. "Up from Politics." PERFORMANCE, No. 2 (Apr. 1972), pp. 52-60.
    Interview with Bullins by Erika Munk.

Cade, Toni. "Black Theater." In Gayle BE, pp. 134-43.

Campbell, Dick. "Is There a Conspiracy against Black Playwrights?" NEGRO DIGEST, 17 (Apr. 1968), 11-19.

Childress, Alice. "For a Negro Theatre." MASSES AND MAINSTREAM, 4 (Feb. 1951), 61-64.

_____. "Why Talk about That?" NEGRO DIGEST, 16 (Mar. 1967), 17.

_____. "A Woman Playwright Speaks Her Mind." In Patterson AANT, 75-81.

Clarke, Sebastian. "Out of the Mainstream: Black Theatre and Street Theatre Are Two Relevant Developments on the American Scene." PLAYS AND PLAYERS, Dec. 1972, pp. 34-35.

Davis, Ossie. "The Flight from Broadway." NEGRO DIGEST, 15 (Apr. 1966), 14-19.

Dent, Tom, Gilbert Moses, and Richard Schechner. THE FREE SOUTHERN THEATER BY THE FREE SOUTHERN THEATER. Indianapolis: Bobbs-Merrill, 1969. 230 p.

  Includes articles previously published in NEGRO DIGEST, FREEDOMWAYS, and BLACK THEATRE. See also "Dialogue: The Free Southern Theatre," TULANE DRAMA REVIEW, 9 (Summer 1965), and articles by Gilbert Moses and John O'Neal, cited below.

Dixon, Melvin. "Black Theatre: The Aesthetics." NEGRO DIGEST, 18 (July 1969), 41-44.

Dodson, Owen. "Black King Oedipus in the USA at Howard University Theatre." WORLD THEATRE, 15 (1966), 432-34.

_____. "Playwrights in Dark Glasses." NEGRO DIGEST, 17 (Apr. 1968), 31-36.

Dyke, Marjorie. "Negro Actor vs. Desegregation." EDUCATIONAL THEATRE JOURNAL, 9 (Mar. 1959), 17-22.

Elder, Lonne III. "A Negro Idea Theater." AMERICAN DIALOG, 1 (July-Aug. 1964), 30-31.

Ellis, Eddie. "Is Revolutionary Theatre in Tune with the People?" LIBERATOR, 5 (Dec. 1965), 8-9.

Emeruwa, Leatrice. "Black Art and Artists in Cleveland." BLACK WORLD, 22 (Jan. 1973), 23-33.

Evans, Donald T. "Bring It All Back Home: Playwrights of the Fifties." BLACK WORLD, 20 (Feb. 1971), 41-45.

  On William Branch, Louis Peterson, Alice Childress, and Loften Mitchell.

Famechon, Isabelle. "Theatre Noir Revolutionnaire." TRAVAIL THEATRAL, 4 (July 1971), 21-48.

Feingold, Michael. "The Negro Ensemble Company." YALE/THEATRE, 3 (Winter 1968), 69-75.

Fletcher, W.L., et al. "Black Theatre in Midwestern Colleges and Universities, a Survey Conducted by W. Fletcher, A. Williams and P. Cooke." BULLETIN OF BLACK THEATRE, No. 3 (Winter 1973), pp. 1-12.

Fuller, Hoyt. "Black Theatre in America." NEGRO DIGEST, 17 (Apr. 1968), 83-93.

_____. "Black World Interviews Woodie King, Jr.: BLACK WORLD, 26 (Apr. 1975), 12-17.

Gaffney, Floyd. "Black Theatre: Commitment and Communication." BLACK SCHOLAR, 1 (June 1970), 10-15.

Gant, Lisbeth. "New Lafayette Theatre: Anatomy of a Community Art Institution." DRAMA REVIEW, 16 (Dec. 1972), 46-55.

Gardner, Bettye, and Bettye Thomas. "The Cultural Impact of the Howard Theatre on the Black Community." JOURNAL OF NEGRO HISTORY, 55 (1970), 253-65.

Garnett, Bernard. "New Developments in Black Theatre." RACE RELATIONS REPORTER, 3 (7 Feb. 1972), 8.

Goldin, Mary. "Harlem Out of Mind." ART NEWS, 68 (Mar. 1969), 52-53.

Goncalves, Joe. "The Mysterious Disappearance of Black Arts/West." BLACK THEATRE, No. 2 (1969), pp. 23-25.

"Green Pastures: Behind the Times." DRAMATICS, 42, No. 6, pp. 17, 20-21.

Gussow, Mel. "The New Playwrights." NEWSWEEK, 20 May 1968, pp. 114-15.

Hanau, D. "Ghetto Theatre: Vital Drama or Social Therapy?" COMMUNITY, 26 (Apr. 1967), 7-10.

Hansberry, Lorraine. "American Theatre Needs Desegregating Too." NEGRO DIGEST, 10 (June 1961), 22-23.

_____. "A Challenge to Artists." FREEDOMWAYS, 3 (1963), 31-35.

Harris, Henrietta. "Building a Black Theatre." DRAMA REVIEW, 16 (Dec. 1972), 39-45.

Harrison, Paul Carter. "Black Theatre and the African Continuum." BLACK WORLD, 21 (Aug. 1972), 42-48.

_____. THE DRAMA OF NOMMO. New York: Grove, 1972. 233 p.
References to contemporary black theatre, especially pp. 119-233 (on Harrison, Gordone, LeRoi Jones, A. Kennedy).

Hay, Samuel A. "African-American Drama, 1950-1970." NEGRO HISTORY BULLETIN, 36 (1973), 5-8.

Haynes, Hilda. "The Black Actor in America." EQUITY, 45 (June 1960), 4-9.

Hill, Errol, and W. Talbot. "Exchange of Letters on Black Face vs. White Face on Stage." BULLETIN OF BLACK THEATRE, No. 3 (Winter 1973), pp. 9-10.

Hilliard, Robert. "The Drama and American Negro Life." SOUTHERN THEATRE, 10 (Winter 1966), 9-14.

_____. "The Integration of the Negro Actor in the New York Stage." EDUCATIONAL THEATRE JOURNAL, 8 (1956), 97-108.

Hughes, Langston. "The Need for an Afro-American Theatre." CHICAGO DEFENDER, 12 June 1961. Also in Patterson AANT, pp. 163-64.

_____. "The Negro and American Entertainment." In THE AMERICAN NEGRO REFERENCE BOOK. Ed. John P. Davis. Englewood Cliffs, N.J.: Prentice-Hall, 1966, pp. 826-49.

"Interracial Romances Blossom in the Theatre." JET, 24 Dec. 1964, pp. 58-61.

Johnson, Helen A. "Playwrights, Audiences and Critics." NEGRO DIGEST, 19 (Apr. 1970), 17-24.

Jones, LeRoi. "Black (Art) Drama Is the Same as Black Life." EBONY, 26 (Feb. 1971), 74-82.

_____. "Communications Project." DRAMA REVIEW, 12 (Summer 1968), 53-57.

_____. "In Search of the Revolutionary Black Theater." NEGRO DIGEST, 15 (Apr. 1966), 20-24.

_____. "What is Black Theatre: An Interview." BLACK WORLD, 20 (Apr. 1971), 32-39.

_____. "What the Arts Need Now." NEGRO DIGEST, 16 (Apr. 1967), 5-6.

_____, ed. AFRICAN CONGRESS. New York: William Morrow, 1972. 493 p.

Includes "Statements, Proposals, Resolutions," concerning black theatre and arts, made by Larry Neal, Cheo Katibu, Don Lee, and the Free Southern Theatre in September 1970 (pp. 190-218).

Jones, Martha M. "Barbara Ann Teer's National Black Theatre." BLACK CREATION, 3 (Summer 1972), 18-20.

_____. "Theater Southern Style: The Free Southern Theatre." BLACK CREATION, 4 (Fall 1972), 12-13.

Kaufman, M.W. "The Delicate World of Reprobation: A Note on Black Revolutionary Theatre." EDUCATIONAL THEATRE JOURNAL, 23 (1971), 446-59.

Kgositsile, K.W. "Towards Our Theatre: A Definitive Act." NEGRO DIGEST, 16 (Apr. 1967), 14-16. Also in Gayle BE, pp. 146-48.

Killens, John O. "Broadway in Black and White." AFRICAN FORUM, 1 (Winter 1966), 66-70.

King, Woodie. "Black Theatre: Present Condition." DRAMA REVIEW, 12 (Summer 1968), 117-24.

_____. "Black Theatre, Weapon for Change." NEGRO DIGEST, 16 (Apr. 1967), 35-39.

_____. "The Dilemma of a Black Theatre." NEGRO DIGEST, 19 (Apr. 1970), 10-15, 86-87.

_____. "Educational Theatre and the Black Community." BLACK WORLD, 21 (Apr. 1972), 25-29.

_____. "Problems Facing Negro Actors." NEGRO DIGEST, 15 (Apr. 1966), 53-59.

Kingham, G.L. "The Free Southern Theater." WORLD THEATRE, 14 (Sept. 1965), 50-63.

Lazier, Gil. "The Next Stage: Youth Theatre for the Ghetto." RECORD, 69 (Feb. 1968), 465-67.

Lee, Maryatt. "Soul and Latin: Street Theatre in Harlem." THEATRE QUARTERLY, 2 (Oct. 1972), 35-43. Also in THEATRE 4: 1970-71. New York: International Theatre Institute, 1972, pp. 150-57.

Lewis, Claude. "The New Theatre: Players, Poets, People." TUESDAY, Feb. 1969, pp. 6, 8, 10, 23.

Lewis, Theophilus. "Integration on the Stage." AMERICA, 11 (1966), 213-14.

_____. "Negro Actors in Dramatic Roles." AMERICA, 11 (1966), 298-300.

Lindsay, Powell. "We Still Need Negro Theatre in America." NEGRO HISTORY BULLETIN, 27 (Feb. 1964), 112.

Loney, G. "The Negro and the Theatre." EDUCATIONAL THEATRE JOURNAL, 20 (1963), 231-33.

Long, Richard A. "A Crisis in Consciousness." NEGRO DIGEST, 17 (May 1968), 82-92.

Macbeth, Robert. "The Black Ritual Theatre." BLACK THEATRE, No. 3 (1969), pp. 20-24.
      Interview by Marvin X.

_____. "Robert Macbeth Speaks." BLACK THEATRE, No. 6 (1972), pp. 14-20.

McCarthy, J.D., and W.L. Yancey. "Uncle Tom and Mister Charlie; Metaphysical Pathos in the Study of Racism and Personal Disorganization." AMERICAN JOURNAL OF SOCIOLOGY, 76 (1971), 648-72.
      Deals at some length with the Afro-American stage.

Markholt, Ottilie. "White Critics, Black Playwrights." NEGRO DIGEST, 16 (Mar. 1967), 54-55.

Marshall, William. "Let My People Speak." THEATRE ARTS, 38 (1953), 456-63.

Marton, Sister Kathryn. "The Relationship of the Theatre of Revolution and the Theology of Revolution to the Black Experience." TODAY'S SPEECH, 19 (Spring 1971), 35-41.

Miller, Adam D. "It's a Long Way to Saint Louis: Notes on the Audience for Black Drama." DRAMA REVIEW, 12 (Summer 1968), 147-50.

Milner, Ron. "Black Magic, Black Art." NEGRO DIGEST, 16 (Apr. 1967), 8-12.

_____. "Black Theater--Go Home!" NEGRO DIGEST, 17 (Apr. 1968), 5-10. Also in Gayle BA, pp. 306-12.

Molette, Carlton. "Afro-American Ritual Drama: An Essay." In ATLANTA UNIVERSITY CENTER SAMPLER. Ed. Oliver Pitcher. Atlanta: Atlanta Univ., [1970?], pp. 99-104.

_____. "Black Theatre in Atlanta." PLAYERS, 45 (1970), 162-69.

Morton, Frederic. "The Audacity of Sidney Poitier." HOLIDAY, 31 (June 1962), 103.

Moses, Gilbert. "Interviews on the Free Southern Theatre." BLACK CREATION, 3 (Winter, 1972), 19-23.

_____. "A Theatre Piece in Seven Moods." In THEATRE 4: 1970-71. New York: International Theatre Institute, 1972, pp. 12-16.

Murray, James P. "Black Movies/Black Theatre." DRAMA REVIEW, 16 (Dec. 1972), 56-61.

Neal, Larry. "Black Art and Black Liberation." EBONY, 24 (Aug. 1969), 54-58.

_____. "The Black Arts Movement." DRAMA REVIEW, 12 (Summer, 1968), 29-39. Also in Bigsby BAW2, pp. 187-202.

_____. "Cultural Nationalism and Black Theatre." BLACK THEATRE, No. 1 (1968), pp. 8-10.

_____. "Free Southern Theatre, the Conquest of the South." DRAMA REVIEW, 14 (1970), 169-74.

_____. "Into Nationalism Out of Parochialism." PERFORMANCE, No. 2 (Apr. 1972), pp. 32-40.

_____. "The Negro in the Theatre." DRAMA CRITIQUE, 7 (Spring 1964).

_____. "Toward a Relevant Black Theatre." BLACK THEATRE, No. 4 (1969), pp. 14-15.

"Negro Playwrights." EBONY, 14 (Apr. 1959), 95-100.

O'Neal, Frederick. "Integration Report." EQUITY, 49 (Sept. 1964), 7 ff.

_____. "Integration Showcase." EBONY, 14 (Aug. 1959), 70-74.

_____. "The Negro in Today's Theatre: Problems and Prospects." In THE NEGRO HANDBOOK. Chicago: Johnson Publishing Co., 1966, pp. 356-59.

_____. "Problems and Prospects." NEGRO DIGEST, 15 (Apr. 1966), 4-12.

_____. "The Status of the Negro Actor." DRAMA CRITIQUE, 7 (Spring 1964), 96.

O'Neal, John. "Motion in the Ocean: Some Political Dimensions of the Free Southern Theatre." DRAMA REVIEW, 12 (Summer 1968), 70-77.

_____. "Performing in the South." PERFORMANCE, No. 2 (Apr. 1972), pp. 41-51.
On the Free Southern Theatre.

_____. "Theater in Yorubaland." BLACK WORLD, 19 (July 1970), 39-48.

Ormon, Roscoe. "The New Lafayette Theatre." BLACK THEATRE, No. 2 (1969), pp. 5-6.

Pace, Donald. "The Apollo Theatre: Where the Good Times Are." AFTER DARK, Jan. 1974, pp. 74-77.

Patterson, James E. "The Negro Ensemble Company: A Profile." PLAYERS, 47 (1972), 224-29, 256-57.

Pawley, Thomas D. "The Black Theatre Audience." PLAYERS, 46 (1971), 257-61.

Peavy, Charles D. "Satire in Contemporary Black Drama." SATIRE NEWS-
LETTER, 7 (1969), 40-49.

Perkins, Eugene. "The Black Arts Movement." In THE BLACK SEVENTIES.
Ed. Floyd L. Barbour. Boston: Porter Sargeant, 1970, pp. 85-97.

Deals largely with theatre in Chicago and elsewhere.

Pilikian, H.I. "Faces, Races, Spaces." DRAMA, 100 (Spring 1971), 52-59.

Potter, Vilma R. "New Politics, New Mothers." CLA JOURNAL, 16 (1972),
247-55.

On the changing image of black women in plays.

Primus, Marc. "The Afro-American Folkloric Troupe." FREEDOMWAYS, 6
(1966), 31-36.

_____, ed. BLACK THEATRE: A RESOURCE DIRECTORY. New York: Black
Theatre Alliance, 1973.

Reardon, William R., and Thomas D. Pawley, eds. THE BLACK TEACHER AND
THE DRAMATIC ARTS. Westport, Conn.: Negro Universities Press, 1970.
487 p.

"Dialogue" (pp. 1-64) deals with problems of black university
theatre and activities of the Summer 1968 Institute of Dramatic
Art at Santa Barbara, University of California campus (see Bibliography and Play Collections sections, above.

Ricah, W.A.D. "Telling It Like It Is: The Examination of Black Theatre as
Rhetoric." QUARTERLY JOURNAL OF SPEECH, 56 (1970), 179-86.

Riley, Clayton. "A Black Quartet." LIBERATOR, 9 (Sept. 1969), 21-22.

A review article.

_____. "Black Theatre." In THEATRE 5: 1971-72. New York: Interna-
tional Theatre Institute, 1973, pp. 60-65.

_____. "The Negro and the Theatre." LIBERATOR, 7 (June 1967), 20;
(July 1967), 20; (Aug. 1967), 21.

Review feature.

_____. "Negro Theatre." ENCORE, 7 (Nov. 1960), 11-15.

_____. "On Black Theatre." In Gayle BA, pp. 313-30.

"Robert Macbeth and the New Lafayette." THEATRE TODAY, 1 (Fall 1968), 3-6, 13.

Rogers, Ray. "The Negro Actor." FREEDOMWAYS, 2 (1962), 310-13.

Scheffer, I. "Black Theatre in America." NATION, 25 Aug. 1969, pp. 51-52.

Steele, Shelby. "White Port and Lemon Juice, Notes on the Ritual in New Black Theatre." BLACK WORLD, 22 (June 1973), 4-13, 78-84.

"The Street As a Theatrical Environment: Symposium." THEATRE DESIGN AND TECHNOLOGY, 26 (Oct. 1971), 14-21.
   Bears largely on black street theatre; illustrations.

Strick, Ann. "Tolerance in the Theatre." NEGRO DIGEST, 6 (Jan. 1948), 82.

"Talking of Black Art, Theatre, Revolution and Nationhood." BLACK THEATRE, No. 5, (1971), pp. 18-37.
   Interviews of black intellectuals and revolutionaries taken at the First Pan-African Cultural Festival in Algiers, 1970, and in Manhattan and Harlem.

Taubes, Susan. "The White Mask Falls." TULANE DRAMA REVIEW, 7 (Spring 1963), 85-92.

Teer, Barbara Ann. "Report on Black Theatre." In REPORT FROM THE FIRST ONYX CULTURAL CONFERENCE. New York: Onyx Publications, 1970, pp. 44-51.

Thompson, Thomas A. "Burst of Negro Drama." LIFE, 29 May 1964, pp. 62-70.

Trotta, Geri. "Black Theatre." HARPER'S BAZAAR, 101 (Aug. 1968), 150-53.
   On D.T. Ward, M. Schultz, Robert Hooks, and Ed Bullins.

Turner, Sherry. "An Overview of the New Black Arts." FREEDOMWAYS, 9 (1969), 156-63.
   On visual and performing arts.

Turpin, Waters E. "The Contemporary American Negro Playwright." CLA JOURNAL, 9 (1965), 12-24.

Walker, Barbara. "It Was a Very Good Year for Community Theatre." BLACK CREATION, 3 (Summer 1972), 21-23.

Ward, Douglas Turner. "Black Answers to White Questions." In THEATRE I. New York: International Theatre Institute, D.B.S. Publication, 1968, pp. 68-75.

Interview.

_____. "Needed: A Theater for Black Themes." NEGRO DIGEST, 17 (Dec. 1967), 34-39.

Ward, Francis, and Val Gray. "The Black Artist--His Role in the Struggle." BLACK SCHOLAR, 2 (Jan. 1971), 23-33.

_____. "Root Ritual: the Institutionalization of an Idea." BLACK POSITION, No. 1 (1971), pp. 14-15.

Weales, G. "The Negro Revolution." In THE JUMPING OFF PLACE: AMERICAN DRAMA IN THE 1960S. New York: Macmillan, 1969, pp. 107-51.

Weisman, John. GUERILLA THEATRE: SCENARIOS FOR REVOLUTION. Garden City, N.Y.: Doubleday, Anchor, 1973, pp. 129 ff.

Williams, Jim. "The Need for a Harlem Theatre." FREEDOMWAYS, 3 (1963), 307-11.

_____. "Pieces on the Black Theatre and the Black Theatre Worker." FREEDOMWAYS, 9 (1969), 146-55.

_____. "Survey of Afro-American Playwrights." FREEDOMWAYS, 10 (1970), 26-45.

Williams, Randy. "The Black Artist as Activist." BLACK CREATION, 3 (Winter 1972), 42-45.

"Women as Directors." ESSENCE, May 1972, pp. 76-77.

Part 2
DRAMA: INDIVIDUAL AUTHORS

1. 1850-1900

The dramatists are listed below alphabetically. Under each author, sequences of listings, wherever applicable, are as follows: published plays, unpublished plays, collected plays, and biography and criticism. Pagination for monographs is given if discovered in the course of work with primary or secondary sources.

ALDRIDGE, IRA (1807-67)

Published Plays

THE BLACK DOCTOR. Dick's Standard Plays, no. 460. London: [1870?]. New York: DeWitt Publishing House, [188-?]. Also in Hatch BTU, pp. 3-24.

> The romantic story of a black physician who cures and secretly marries the daughter of a French aristocrat in the Isle de Bourbon. Adapted from I.V. Bridgeman's translation of the 1846 play by Auguste Anicet-Bourgeois and Pinel Dumanoit. Written and read publicly in 1847. Four acts.

Unpublished Plays

"Titus Andronicus." Adapted from Shakespeare; performed November 1840.

Biography and Criticism

Johnson BM, pp. 78-87.

Lewis, C.L. "Black Night of the Theatre: Ira Aldridge." NEGRO DIGEST, 17 (Apr. 1968), 44-47.

Marshall, Herbert, and Mildred Stock. IRA ALDRIDGE, THE NEGRO TRAGE-

DIAN. London: Rockliff, 1958. 355 p. Carbondale: Southern Illinois Univ. Press, Arcturus Books, 1968. 355 p. Paper.

Detailed biography centering on Aldridge's stage career in Europe.

BROWN, WILLIAM WELLS (1815-84)

Published Plays

THE ESCAPE: OR, A LEAP FOR FREEDOM: A DRAMA IN FIVE ACTS. Boston: R.F. Walcutt, 1858. 52 p. Rpts. New York: Prologue Press, 1969 (Introd. Louis Phillips); Philadelphia: Rhistoric Publications, 1969 (Introd. Maxwell Whiteman). Also in Hatch BTU, pp. 34-58.

Abolitionist melodrama based on first-hand experience of slavery. Written 1856; read in public on February 4, 1857.

Unpublished Plays

"Experience, or, How to Give a Northern Man a Backbone" [other title: "Doughface"?].

Read in public on April 9, 1856.

"Life at the South." 185- ?

"Miralda." 1855.

Biography and Criticism

Abramson, Doris. "William Wells Brown, First American Negro Playwright." EDUCATIONAL THEATRE, 20 (1968), 371-75.

Farrison, W. Edward. "Brown's First Drama." CLA JOURNAL, 2 (1958), 104-10.

_____. WILLIAM WELLS BROWN, AUTHOR AND REFORMER. Chicago: University of Chicago Press, 1969. 482 p.

EASTON, WILLIAM EDGAR (1861- ?)

Published Plays

CHRISTOPHE; A TRAGEDY IN PROSE OF IMPERIAL HAITI. Los Angeles: Grafton Publishing Co., 1911. 122 p.

Four-act drama on the Haitian ruler.

DESSALINES, A DRAMATIC TALE; A SINGLE CHAPTER FROM HAITI'S HISTO-RY. Galveston, Tex.: J.W. Burson-Co., 1893. 138 p.

> Historical epic in four acts celebrating Dessalines, whose courage inspired his soldiers to defeat the French army in Haiti. First performed in Chicago, January 1893.

2. 1901-50

The dramatists are listed below alphabetically for the period 1901 to 1950. Under each author, sequences of listings, wherever applicable, are as follows: published plays, unpublished plays, collected plays, and biography and criticism. Pagination for monographs is given if discovered in the course of work with primary or secondary sources.

ANDERSON, GARLAND (1886-1939)

Published Plays

"Appearances." In Hatch BTU, pp. 102-34.

> The drama of a black bellhop falsely accused of rape by a white woman. First performed October 13, 1925, at the Frolic Theatre, New York City. Written in the early 1920s and first titled "Don't Judge by Appearances"; copyrighted in 1924 as "Judge Not According to Appearances."

Biography and Criticism

Abramson NP, pp. 27-32.

Anderson, Garland. FROM NEWSBOY AND BELLHOP TO PLAYWRIGHT. San Francisco: Published by the author, [1925?]. 30 p.

Johnson BM, pp. 202-05.

ASHBY, WILLIAM MOBILE (1889-)

Published Plays

THE ROAD TO DAMASCUS: A PLAY IN SEVEN EPISODES. Boston: Christopher, 1935. 97 p.

BOND, FREDERICK WELDON

Published Plays

FAMILY AFFAIR. Institute: West Virginia State College, 1939.

The story of a black family victimized by the Depression.

BONNER, MARITA (1905-)

Published Plays

"Exit an Illusion." CRISIS, 36 (1929), 335-36, 352.

One-act play on the moral and psychological problems of miscegenation.

"The Pot Maker." OPPORTUNITY, 5 (Feb. 1927), 43-46.

One-act play; the domestic drama of Elias, who is called to preach, and destroys his wife's lover.

"The Purple Flower." CRISIS, 35 (Jan. 1928), 9-11. Also in Hatch BTU, pp. 202-7.

A one-act allegory on the revolution against the "white devils."

BROWNE, THEODORE (1910-)

Published Plays

"THE NATURAL MAN" (BASED ON THE LEGEND OF JOHN HENRY); A PLAY IN NINE EPISODES. [Seattle]: n.p., 1936. In Hatch BTU, pp. 362-81. One scene is in Childress BIS, pp. 129-36.

The drama of the black epic hero, "a giant in a straight jacket," in conflict with the dehumanizing forces of industrial civilization. First performed on January 28, 1937, by the Federal Theatre Project in Seattle as a full-length opera; performed as a play by the American Negro Theatre in New York City on May 7, 1941.

Unpublished Plays

"Go Down Moses," or "A Black Woman Called Moses." 1937 (?).

On Harriet Tubman.

"The Gravy Train." 1940.

Full-length drama about an aspiring young black.

"Minstrel."

Biography and Criticism

Abramson NP, pp. 102-9.

BRUCE, RICHARD

Published Plays

"Sahdji--An African Ballet." In Locke PNL, pp. 389-400.

> One-act play based on a short-story sketch first published in THE NEW NEGRO, ed. Alain Locke. New York: Boni, 1925, under the name of Bruce Nugent.

BURKE, INEZ M.

Published Plays

"Two Races: A Pageant." In Richardson PP, pp. 295-302.

> One-act play with the Spirit of Negro Progress as chief allegorical character.

BURRILL, MARY

Published Plays

"They That Sit in Darkness." BIRTH CONTROL REVIEW, Sept. 1919. Also in Hatch BTU, pp. 179-83.

> One-act southern domestic drama. Lindy Jasper, the eldest of seven children, takes over when her mother dies of exhaustion.

Unpublished Plays

"Aftermath." 1919.

BURROUGHS, NANNIE HELEN (1883-1961)

Published Plays

THE SLABTOWN DISTRICT CONVENTION (REVISED). A COMEDY IN ONE ACT. 11th ed. Washington, D.C.: n.p., 1942. 84 p.

BUSH, OLIVIA WARD

Published Plays

MEMORIES OF CALVARY: AN EASTER SKETCH. Philadelphia: A.M.E. Book Concern Print., [191-?]. 16 p.

BUTCHER, JAMES W., JR. (1909-)

Published Plays

"The Seer." In THE NEGRO CARAVAN. Ed. Sterling Brown et al. New York: Dryden, 1941, pp. 520–34.

> A one-act domestic comedy. A young black wins his beloved from her superstitious father, who had been influenced into marrying her to a seer.

Unpublished Plays

"Milk and Honey." Written before 1940.

COOPER, ANNA JULIA (1859-1964)

Published Plays

CHRISTMAS BELLS. A ONE-ACT PLAY FOR CHILDREN. No imprint. 16 p.

> A play in verse.

COTTER, JOSEPH SEAMON, SR. (1861-1949)

Published Plays

"Caesar Driftwood." In NEGROES AND OTHERS AT WORK AND PLAY. New York: Paebar, 1947.

> One-act play.

CALEB, THE DEGENERATE, A PLAY IN FOUR ACTS: A STUDY OF THE TYPES, CUSTOMS, AND NEEDS OF THE AMERICAN NEGRO. Louisville, Ky.: Bradley & Gilbert, 1903. 57 p. New York: Henry Harrison, 1940. 67 p. Also in Hatch BTU, pp. 64–99.

> Domestic and racial drama in verse, urging the black man to follow Booker T. Washington's work ethics.

"The Chastisement." In NEGROES AND OTHERS AT WORK AND PLAY. New York: Paebar, 1947.

> One-act play.

Biography and Criticism

See also the section on Cotter under Poetry, part 2: Individual Authors, 1760–1900.

Abramson NP, pp. 15-21.

COTTER, JOSEPH SEAMON, JR. (1895-1919)

Published Plays

"On the Fields of France." CRISIS, 20 (June 1920), 77.

> One-act patriotic drama on the conflicting allegiances of the American Negro during the First World War.

"Paradox." SATURDAY EVENING QUILL (Boston), June 1913.

CULLEN, COUNTEE (1903-46)

Published Plays

"The Third Fourth of July, A One-Act Play." THEATRE ARTS MAGAZINE, 30 (1946), 488-93.

> Poetic dance drama. A black family moves into a white neighborhood on July 4 but has to battle for two years before being accepted. Written in collaboration with Owen Dodson. Produced in 1945.

Unpublished Plays

"Byword for Evil." 1936 (?).

> Stage version of Cullen's MEDEA (New York: Harper, 1935), first performed 1936 at the Hedgerow Theatre. Ms. at Yale University.

"One Way to Heaven." 193- ?.

> Stage adaptation written with Arna Bontemps from Cullen's novel of the same title. Typescript at Yale University Library.

"St. Louis Woman."

> First performed 1946. A musical dramatization of Arna Bontemps' GOD SENDS SUNDAY, written in collaboration with him.

Biography and Criticism

See also the section on Cullen under Poetry, part 2: Individual Authors, 1901-45.

Perry, Margaret. A BIO-BIBLIOGRAPHY OF COUNTEE P. CULLEN. Westport, Conn.: Greenwood, 1971. 135 p.

CUNEY-HARE, MAUD (1874-1936)

Published Plays

"Antar of Araby." In Richardson PP, pp. 27-74. Copyright 1926.

> A historical play in four acts on the famous African hero.

DODSON, OWEN (1914-   )

Published Plays

"The Ballad of Dorie Miller." THEATRE ARTS MAGAZINE, 27 (July 1943).

> Performed February 1943 at the Great Lakes Naval Training Base. A short dramatic celebration of the black hero at Pearl Harbor.

"Bayou Legend." In Turner BDA, pp. 205-95.

> Lyrical adaptation of Ibsen's PEER GYNT in a southern black setting designed to create the legend of a black hero.

"Divine Comedy." In THE NEGRO CARAVAN. Ed. Sterling Brown et al. New York: Dryden Press, 1941, pp. 543-60 [extract]. Complete version in Hatch BTU, pp. 322-49.

> Poetic drama on the theme of Father Divine and his religious movement.

Everybody Join Hands." THEATRE ARTS MAGAZINE, 27 (Sept. 1943).

> First performed in Spelman College, Atlanta, 1943. One-act play on the necessity of fighting the Axis powers and creating a united front with the Chinese.

"Someday We're Gonna Tear Them Pillars Down." In POWERFUL LONG LADDER. New York: Farrar, Straus, 1946, pp. 16-22.

>A chant in verse symbolizing the slaves' longing for freedom and their decision to regain it.

"The Third Fourth of July." See under Cullen, above, this section.

Unpublished Plays

"Amistad." 1939.

>On Cinque's rebellion.

"Black Mother Praying."

"The Christmas Miracle." 1955.

>One-act musical.

"Climbing to the Soil." Performed January 1943.

>On George Washington Carver.

"The Confession Stone." 1964.

>TV play; also a 1974 dance opera based upon verse booklet of the same title published by Paul Breman, London, 1970.

"Don't Give Up the Ship." Performed May 1943.

"Doomsday Tale." 1941.

"Freedom the Banner." 1942.

"The Garden of Time." 1939.

"Gargoyles in Florida." 1936.

"Including Laughter." 1936.

"Lord Nelson, Naval Hero." Performed January 1943.

"Medea in Africa." Performed 1959.

"New World a Coming." 1944.

>Pageant.

"Old Ironsides." Performed 1942.

"The Southern Star." 1940.

"Till Victory Is Won." 1967.
> Libretto for an opera.

Biography and Criticism

Greene, Marjorie. "Young Man of the Theatre and His Left Hand." OPPOR-
TUNITY, 24 (1946), 200-201.

DUBOIS, WILLIAM EDWARD BURGHARDT (1868-1963)

Published Plays

"The Christ of the Andes." HORIZON, 4 (Nov.-Dec. 1908), 1-14.

"George Washington and Black Folk." CRISIS, 39 (1932), 121-24.
> A pageant on black American history, 1732-1932.

Unpublished Plays

"Star of Ethiopia." Performed Oct. 25, 1913.
> Pageant on black history written for the National Emancipation Ex-
> position. Summary in "The People of Peoples and Their Gifts to
> the World." CRISIS, 6 (1913), 339.

DUNBAR NELSON, ALICE [RUTH] MOORE (1875-1935)

Published Plays

"Mine Eyes Have Seen." CRISIS, 15 (1918), 271-75. Also in Hatch BTU,
pp. 174-77.
> On the loyalty of black soldiers to the American nation.

DUNCAN, THELMA MYRTLE (1902-)

Published Plays

"Black Magic." In YEARBOOK OF SHORT PLAYS, FIRST SERIES. Ed. Wise
and Snook. Evanston, Ill.: Row, Peterson, 1931, pp. 215-32.
> One-act comedy about a husband who resorts to voodoo to regain
> his wife's faithfulness.

"The Death Dance." In Locke PNL, pp. 323-31.

> A one-act play on African themes: a woman bribes the medicine man when her lover has to stand trial by a magic test. First performed April 7, 1923, by Howard University Players.

"Sacrifice." In Richardson PP, pp. 3-24.

> One-act play on a mother's deep despair when her son steals the questions for a chemistry exam.

EDMONDS, RANDOLPH S. (1900-)

Published Plays

"Bad Man." In SIX PLAYS FOR A NEGRO THEATRE (see under Collected Plays, below). Also in THE NEGRO CARAVAN. Ed. Sterling Brown et al. New York: Dryden Press, 1941, pp. 506-19; and in Hatch BTU, pp. 243-51.

> One-act drama on life in a sawmill camp in Alabama; the hero dies to save a cabinful of black people from a lynch mob.

"Bleeding Hearts." In SIX PLAYS FOR A NEGRO THEATRE (see under Collected Plays, below).

> One-act drama on a sharecropper who swears to avenge himself on his landlord when his overworked wife dies of pneumonia.

"The Breeders." In SIX PLAYS FOR A NEGRO THEATRE (see under Collected Plays, below).

> One-act drama on slaves who resist being used as breeders in the antebellum South.

"The Devil's Price." In SHADES AND SHADOWS (see under Collected Plays, below).

> Four-act drama on the theme of a king's lust for power.

"Earth and Stars." Revised version in Turner BDA, pp. 381-463.

> A full-length drama on the aims and problems of southern black leadership after World War II; written 1946, revised to emphasize the civil rights movement in the late fifties.

"Everyman's Land." In SHADES AND SHADOWS (see under Collected Plays, below).

> One-act dialogue between two American soldiers, one white, one black, who died on a French battlefield in World War I.

"Gangsters over Harlem." In THE LAND OF COTTON AND OTHER PLAYS
(see under Collected Plays, below).

> One-act melodrama about the numbers racket. First performed in
> 1939, at Dillard University, New Orleans.

"Hewers of Wood." In SHADES AND SHADOWS (see under Collected Plays,
below).

> One-act symbolic drama about the fate of black people destined
> to work for the whites until God frees them.

"High Court of Historia." In THE LAND OF COTTON AND OTHER PLAYS
(see under Collected Plays, below).

> Pageant in which the accomplishments of the black race are ex-
> tolled, a thing which black historians are charged with not having
> done. First performed in 1939, at Dillard University, New Orleans.

"The Land of Cotton." In THE LAND OF COTTON AND OTHER PLAYS (see
under Collected Plays, below).

> Three-act racial and social drama about white and black sharecrop-
> pers fighting against the exploitation imposed by the landowners.
> Performed in 1941 by the People's Community Theatre, New Orleans.

"Nat Turner." In SIX PLAYS FOR A NEGRO THEATRE (see under Collected
Plays, below).

> One-act melodrama about the killing of a black bootlegger.

"The New Window." In SIX PLAYS FOR A NEGRO THEATRE (see under Collected Plays, below).

"Old Man Pete." In SIX PLAYS FOR A NEGRO THEATRE (see under Collected
Plays, below).

> One-act social drama centering on the conflict between children
> and parents in a Harlem family.

"The Phantom's Treasure." In SHADES AND SHADOWS (see under Collected
Plays, below).

> One-act play about two boys who discover a buried treasure, only
> to lose it again.

"Shades and Shadows." In SHADES AND SHADOWS (see under Collected Plays,
below).

> One-act detective mystery play.

"Silas Brown." In THE LAND OF COTTON AND OTHER PLAYS (see under Collected Plays, below).

> One-act domestic drama about a miserly father who drives his son away from home. First performed in 1927, at Oberlin High School, Ohio.

"The Tribal Chief." In SHADES AND SHADOWS (see under Collected Plays, below).

> One-act melodrama about a Tibetan priest who commits murder.

"Yellow Death." In THE LAND OF COTTON AND OTHER PLAYS (see under Collected Plays, below).

> One-act play on the role of the black soldier in the Spanish Civil War. First performed in 1935.

Unpublished Plays

"The Call of Jubah." 1935.

"Career of College." 1956.

> A one-act purpose play.

"Christmas Gift." 1923.

> One-act play.

"Denmark Vesey." 1929.

"Doom." 1924.

> One-act play.

"Drama Enters the Curriculum." 1930.

"Famu's Objective IV."

> One-act play.

"For Fatherland." 1934.

"G.I. Rhapsody." 1943.

"The Highwayman." 1925.

> One-act play.

"Illicit Love." 1927.

"Job Hunting." 1922.
    One-act play.

"The Man of God." 1931.

"A Merchant in Dixie." 1923.

"The Outer Room." 1935.

"Peter Smith." 1933.

"Prometheus and the Atom." 1955.

"Rocky Roads." 1936.

"The Shadow Across the Path." 1943.

"The Shape of Wars to Come." 1943.
    One-act play.

"Simon in Cyrene." Performed 1939.
    One-act play.

"Sirlock Bones." 1928.
    One-act play.

"Stock Exchange." 1927.
    Musical.

"Takazee, A Pageant of Ethiopia." 1928.

"The Trial and Banishment of Uncle Tom." 1945.
    One-act play.

"Wives and Blues." 1938.

Collected Plays

THE LAND OF COTTON AND OTHER PLAYS. Washington, D.C.: Associated Publishers, 1942. 267 p.

> Includes "Silas Brown," "Yellow Death," "High Court of Historia," "Gangsters over Harlem," and "The Land of Cotton."

SHADES AND SHADOWS. Boston: Meador, 1930. 171 p. Rpt. Ann Arbor, Mich.: University Microfilms, 1970.

> Includes "The Tribal Chief," "The Phantom's Treasure," "The Devil's Price," "Hewers of Wood," "Everyman's Land," and "Shades and Shadows."

SIX PLAYS FOR A NEGRO THEATRE. Boston: Walter Baker, 1934. 155 p. Rpt. Ann Arbor, Mich.: University Microfilms, 1970.

> Includes "Bad Man," "The Breeders," "Nat Turner," "The New Window," "Old Man Peter," and "Bleeding Hearts."

Biography and Criticism

Brown NPD, pp. 22-23.

Brown, Sterling. "Six Plays." OPPORTUNITY, 12 (1934), 280.
> Review.

EDWARD, H.F.V. (1898-1973)

Published Plays

"Job Hunters." CRISIS, 38 (1931), 717-20. Also in Hatch BTU, pp. 256-61.
> One-act drama on the economic depression and social unrest in Harlem at the end of the thirties.

GAINES-SHELTON, RUTH A. (1873-)

Published Plays

"The Church Fight." CRISIS, 32 (May 1926), 17-21. Also in Hatch BTU, pp. 189-91.
> A satirical comedy on church politics. Winner of the second prize in the 1925 CRISIS contest.

GILBERT, MERCEDES (?-1952)

"Environment." In SELECTED GEMS OF POETRY, COMEDY AND DRAMA. Boston: Christopher, 1931, pp. 53-89.

> Three-act domestic drama of black life, about a mother who fights to keep her family together.

Unpublished Plays

"In Greener Pastures."

GRAHAM, OTTIE

Published Plays

"Holiday." CRISIS, 26 (May 1923), 12-17.

> One-act melodrama about a mulatto actress who passes for white, and the ensuing conflict with her daughter.

GRAHAM, SHIRLEY [SHIRLEY GRAHAM DUBOIS (1907-77)

Published Plays

TRACK THIRTEEN. Boston: Expression Co., [1940?].

> A radio comedy about life in a Pullman car.

Unpublished Plays

"Dust to Earth." 1943.

"I Gotta Home." 1942.

"Tom-Tom." 1932.

GRIMKE, ANGELINA WELD (1880-1958)

Published Plays

RACHEL, A PLAY IN THREE ACTS. Boston: Cornhill, 1920. 96 p. Also in Hatch BTU, pp. 139-72.

> Three-act drama on the aftereffects of lynchings and the humiliations undergone by a black family in the South. First performed March 3, 1916, by the Washington, D.C. Drama Committee of the NAACP, directed by Nathaniel Guy.

GUINN, DOROTHY

Published Plays

"Out of the Dark, A Pageant." In Richardson PP, pp. 305-30.

> A four-episode pageant on Afro-American history. Copyrighted by the National Board of the YMCA and performed in 1924.

GUNNER, FRANCES

Published Plays

"The Light of the Women, A Ceremonial for the Use of Negro Groups." In Richardson PP, pp. 333-42.

HAMILTON, ROLAND T.

Published Plays

CRACK OF THE WHIP: A SOCIAL PROBLEM PLAY. Columbus, Ohio: Spring Street Branch YMCA, [193-?]. 35 p.

HARRIS, HELEN WEBB

Published Plays

"Genefrede." In Richardson NHTP, pp. 219-37.

> A one-act children's historical play about the daughter of Haitian liberator Toussaint L'Ouverture.

HAZZARD, ALVIRA

Published Plays

"Mother Liked It." SATURDAY EVENING QUILL, No. 1 (1928), 10-14.

"Little Heads." SATURDAY EVENING QUILL, No. 2 (1929), 42-44.

HILL, ABRAM (1911-)

Published Plays

"Walk Hard." In Hatch BTU, pp. 439-71.

> Three-act drama on the trials of a black boxer competing for the

world championship in 1939. First performed December 19, 1944,
by American Negro Theatre, New York City.

Unpublished Plays

"Hell's Half Acre." 1938.

"Liberty Deferred." 1936.
> A Living Newspaper for the Federal Theatre Project. Written with
> John Silvera.

"Miss Mabel." 1951.

"On Strivers' Row." 1940.
> A full-length comedy about sophisticated Harlem.

"Power of Darkness." 1958.

"So Shall You Reap." 1938.

"Split Down the Middle." 1970.

"Stealing Lightning." 1937.
> One-act play.

Biography and Criticism

Mitchell BD, pp. 125-26, 135-36.

HILL, LESLIE PINCKNEY (1880-1960)

Published Plays

TOUSSAINT L'OUVERTURE. Boston: Christopher, 1928. 137 p.
> A historical drama in blank verse on Haiti's liberator.

HIRSH, CHARLOTTE TELLER

Published Plays

"Hager and Ishmael." CRISIS, 6 (1913), 30-31.
> Short one-act play about the episode in the Bible.

HUGHES, LANGSTON (1902-67)

Published Plays

"Booker T. Washington in Atlanta." In RADIO DRAMA IN ACTION. Ed. Erik Barnow. New York: Farrar, 1945, pp. 283-94.

> Radio play performed in 1945.

"Don't You Want to Be Free?" ONE-ACT PLAY MAGAZINE, 2 (1938), 359-93. Also in Hatch BTU, pp. 263-77.

> One-act play on the economic plight of the Harlem ghetto with an appeal for interracial unity against the exploiters. First performed February 1937. Centennial version typescript written 1963 as "A Negro History Play."

"Drums of Haiti." In Turner BDA, pp. 41-114.

> A three-act historical tragedy on Haitian self-rule. First performed 1935; revised 1938 as "Emperor of Haiti"; further revised 1963. See "Troubled Island," below.

"The Gold Piece." BROWNIES' BOOK, July 1921, pp. 191-94. Also in SADSA ENCORE (1949), pp. 30-32.

> A one-act play for children: a couple with their first large amount of money give it away to a poor woman.

"Limitations of Life." In Hatch BTU, pp. 656-57.

> One-act skit written in 1938 satirizing the film IMITATION OF LIFE (1934).

"Little Ham." In FIVE PLAYS (see under Collected Plays, below), pp. 43-112. Also in Hatch BTU, pp. 777-811.

> A three-act satirical comedy on the exploitation of Harlemites by Jewish landlords, Italian racketeers, and Irish cops.

"Mother and Child." In SADSA ENCORE (1950), pp. 31-35. Also in King BDA, pp. 399-405.

> A tragicomic vignette on southern black life from a short story in THE WAYS OF WHITE FOLK. Deals with the courage of a black man who refuses to leave town when he has a child by a white girl. First performed in 1966 at the American Place Theatre.

"Mulatto." In FIVE PLAYS (see under Collected Plays, below), pp. 1-35. Also in Brasmer BD, pp. 19-68.

A three-act tragedy on the rivalries and conflicts which arise
when a mulatto son, reared in the North, comes to the plantation.
Copyright 1931; first performed October 1934 at the Vanderbilt
Theatre, New York City.

"Mule Bone." Act III published in DRAMA CRITIQUE, 7 (Spring 1964), 103-7.

A comedy on the rivalry between two black youths who are in
love with the same girl. Written in collaboration with Zora Neale
Hurston; first performed 1964.

"The Prodigal Son." PLAYERS, 43 (Oct.-Nov. 1967), 16-21.

A gospel play in one act retracing the biblical episode in song
and mime. Written 1965. First performed May 1965, Greenwich
Mews Theatre, New York City.

SCOTTSBORO LIMITED: FOUR POEMS AND A PLAY IN VERSE. New York:
Golden Stair Press, 1932. 18 p.

One-act militant drama on the trial of the Scottsboro boys, ending
with request for audience involvement. First performed 1933.

SIMPLY HEAVENLY. New York: Dramatists Play Service, 1959. 86 p. Also
in THE LANGSTON HUGHES READER. New York: Braziller, 1958, pp. 244-
313; and in FIVE PLAYS (see under Collected Plays, below), pp. 114-80.

Book and lyrics by Langston Hughes based upon his own book,
SIMPLE TAKES A WIFE. Copyrighted 1956. First performed May
21, 1957, at the 85th Street Playhouse, with music by David
Martin.

"Soul Gone Home." ONE-ACT PLAY MAGAZINE, 1 (1937), 196-200. Also
in THE LANGSTON HUGHES READER. New York: Braziller, 1958, pp. 239-
43; and in FIVE PLAYS (see under Collected Plays, below), pp. 37-42.

One-act dialogue between a middle-aged prostitute and her dead
son. First performed 1937.

STREET SCENE. New York: Chappell, 1948. 273 p.

Lyrics for an American folk opera based upon a play by Elmer Rice
and written in collaboration with him. First performed January 9,
1947, in New York City.

TAMBOURINES TO GLORY. New York: Chappell, 1963. Also in FIVE PLAYS
(see under Collected Plays, below), pp. 184-258.

A two-act gospel-singing play on the vicissitudes of a storefront
church due to black underworld influence. First performed Novem-

ber 2, 1963, at the Little Theatre, New York City, with music
by Joe Huntley. Written in 1949 as a play, then as a novel in
1958 and readapted for the stage.

"TROUBLED ISLAND." New York: Leeds Music Corp., 1949. 38 p.

A libretto based upon "Drums of Haiti" (see above) for an opera
in three acts. First performed March 31, 1949, with music by
William Grant Still.

Unpublished Plays

Angelo Herndon Jones

One-act militant social drama. First performed 1936 by New
York Theatre League.

"The Ballad of the Brown King." 1961.

A Christmas song play in two acts.

"The Barrier." 1950.

Libretto for a full-length opera based on MULATTO (see above)
with music by Jan Meyerowitz.

"Black Nativity." 1961.

A Christmas song play in two acts.

"The Em-Fuehrer Jones." 1938.

One-act caricature of O'Neill's play THE EMPEROR JONES.

"Esther." 1957.

Libretto for an opera by Jan Meyerowitz.

"For This we Fight." 1943.

"Gospel Glory." 1962.

A passion play with songs.

"Jericho Jim Crow." 1963.

A song play.

"Joy to My Soul." 1937.

A three-act comedy.

"Jubilee, A Cavalcade of the Negro Theatre." 1941.

    CBS radio play written with Arna Bontemps.

"Just around the Corner." 1951.

    Lyrics for a two-act musical by Abby Mann, Bernard Drew, and
    Joe Sherman.

"Little Eva's End." 1938.

    One-act satirical sketch on UNCLE TOM'S CABIN.

"The Organizer." 1938.

    A blues opera in one act with music by James P. Johnson.

"Outshines the Sun."

"Port Town." 1960.

    Libretto for a one-act opera with music by Jan Meyerowitz.

"The Prodigal Son." 1955.

    A gospel song.

"St. Louis Woman." 1936.

    Revision of the version by Arna Bontemps and Countee Cullen.
    See Unpublished Plays under Countee Cullen, above.

"Shakespeare in Harlem." 1959.

    In collaboration with Robert Glenn.

"Soul Yesterday and Today." 1969.

    In collaboration with Bob Teague.

"The Sun Do Move." 1941.

    Three-act historical drama concerning a black family split up by
    slavery, the father's repeated escapes, his return to his wife, and
    their flight to the North. Performed in 1941 as "Sold Away" by
    the Chicago Skyloft Players. Typescript of musical, Yale Univer-
    sity Library.

"The Weary Blues." 1966.

    Stage adaptation of Hughes's poetry.

"When the Jock Hollers." 1936.

Three-act comedy written with Arna Bontemps.

Collected Plays

FIVE PLAYS BY LANGSTON HUGHES. Ed. Webster Smalley. Bloomington: Indiana Univ. Press, 1963. 268 p.

Includes: "Mulatto," "Soul Gone Home," "Tambourines to Glory," "Little Ham," and "Simply Heavenly." Introduction by the editor.

Biography and Criticism

Also see the section on Hughes under Poetry, part 2: Individual Authors, 1901-45.

Abramson NP, pp. 67-79.

Davis, Arthur P. "The Tragic Mulatto Theme in Six Works of Langston Hughes." PHYLON, 15 (1955), 195-204. Also in FIVE BLACK WRITERS. Ed. Donald Gibson. New York: New York Univ. Press, 1970, pp. 167-77.

Dickinson, Donald C. A BIO-BIBLIOGRAPHY OF LANGSTON HUGHES. Hamden, Conn.: Archon Books, 1967. 267 p. Rev. ed. Hamden, Conn.: Shoestring Press, 1972.

Emanuel, James. LANGSTON HUGHES. New York: Twayne, 1967. 192 p.

Miles, William. "Isolation in Langston Hughes' SOUL GONE HOME." In FIVE BLACK WRITERS. Ed. Donald Gibson. New York: New York Univ. Press, 1970, pp. 178-82.

Mitchell BD, pp. 145-47, 197-98, 204.

Nichols, Lewis. "Langston Hughes Describes the Genesis of his TAMBOURINES TO GLORY." NEW YORK TIMES, 27 Oct. 1963, Sec. 2, p. 3.

Spencer, J.T., and Clarence Rivers. "Langston Hughes: His Style and Optimism." DRAMA CRITIQUE, 7 (Spring 1964), 99-102.

Turner, Darwin T. "Langston Hughes as Playwright." CLA JOURNAL, 11 (1968), 297-309. Also in LANGSTON HUGHES, BLACK GENIUS. Ed. Therman O'Daniel. New York: William Morrow, 1972, pp. 81-95.

HURSTON, ZORA NEALE (1903-60)

Published Plays

"The First One." In EBONY AND TOPAZ. Ed. Charles S. Johnson. New York: National Urban League, 1927. Freeport, N.Y.: Books for Libraries, 1971, pp. 53-57.

> One-act drama about Noah's curse on Ham and his sons. Winner of 1927 OPPORTUNITY prize.

"Mule Bone." See Published Plays under Langston Hughes, above.

Unpublished Plays

"Fast and Furious." 1931.

> A musical in two acts, September 1931. Written in collaboration with Clinton Fletcher and Jim Moore.

"From Sun to Sun."

"Great Day." 1927.

"Polk County, a Comedy of Negro Life on a Sawmill." 1944.

> Written with Dorothy Waring.

Biography and Criticism

Hurston, Zora Neale. DUST TRACKS ON A ROAD. Philadelphia: Lippincott, 1942. 294 p.

> Autobiography.

JOHNSON, GEORGIA DOUGLAS (1886-1966)

Published Plays

"Blue Blood." In CONTEMPORARY ONE-ACT PLAYS, 4th Series, 1927. Also in FIFTY MORE CONTEMPORARY ONE-ACT PLAYS. Ed. Frank Shay. New York: Appleton-Century, 1928.

> A drama of miscegenation that ends well. Performed by Krigwa Players, 1927(?).

"Frederick Douglass." In Richardson NHTP, pp. 143-62.

> One-act drama on the famous black leader's escape from slavery.

PLUMES. New York: Samuel French, 1927. 15 p. Also in OPPORTUNITY, 5 (July 1927), 200-201, 217-18; Locke PNL, pp. 287-99, and ANTHOLOGY OF AMERICAN NEGRO LITERATURE. Ed. V.F. Calverton. New York: Modern Library, 1929, pp. 147-56.

> A one-act folk tragedy of the South: a mother must choose between spending money on her daughter's operation or funeral. Winner of the first prize for drama in the 1927 OPPORTUNITY contest.

"A Sunday Morning in the South." In Hatch BTU, pp. 213-17.

> One-act tragedy on the lynching of an innocent black by a white mob. Written around 1925.

"William and Ellen Craft." In Richardson NHTP, pp. 163-86.

> One-act drama about a black family's escape from slaveholders.

Unpublished Plays

"The Starting Point."

Biography and Criticism

"Georgia Douglas Johnson." CRISIS, 32 (1926), 193.

LAMB, ARTHUR CLIFTON (1909-)

Published Plays

"Portrait of a Pioneer." NEGRO HISTORY BULLETIN, 12 (Apr. 1949).

> Radio play about black actor and playwright Ira Aldridge.

"The Two Gifts." In GRINNELL PLAYS. Chicago: Dramatic Publishing Co., 1934.

> One-act Christmas miracle play. Written 1932. Produced Dec. 1932, A.M.E. Church, Muscatine, Iowa.

Unpublished Plays

"Roughshod Up the Mountain." 1956.

LIPSCOMB, C.D.

Published Plays

"Frances." OPPORTUNITY, 3 (1925), 148-53.

> One-act play about a black farmer who gives his daughter to a white landowner in order to obtain land from him.

Unpublished Plays

"Compromise." 1925.

LIVINGSTON, MYRTLE (1901-)

Published Plays

"For Unborn Children." CRISIS, 32 (1926), 122-25. In Hatch BTU, pp. 185-87.

> Drama on the theme of miscegenation, which is opposed by the author.

McCOO, EDWARD J.

Published Plays

ETHIOPIA AT THE BAR OF JUSTICE. Newport, Ky.: Published by the author, 1924. Also in Richardson PP, pp. 345-73.

> First performed at A.M.E. Church Quadrennial Conference, 1924.

MATHEUS, JOHN F. (1887-)

Published Plays

"Black Damp." CAROLINA MAGAZINE, 59 (Apr. 1929), 26-34.

> One-act play on the tragedy of black and white coal miners trapped by a cave-in.

"'Cruiter." In Locke PNL, pp. 189-204. Also in ANTHOLOGY OF AMERICAN NEGRO LITERATURE. Ed. V.F. Calverton. New York: Modern Library, 1929, pp. 157-71; and in Hatch BTU, pp. 226-32.

> Drama on the practice of recruiting southern black labor for the ammunition factories of the North in 1918. Written 1926; winner of second prize in 1926 OPPORTUNITY contest.

"Ti Yette." In Richardson PP, pp. 77-105.

> One-act drama about a black who comes to hate his Creole sister because she responds to the advances of a white man during Mardi Gras in New Orleans. Written 1928.

Unpublished Plays

"Ouanga." 1929.

> Opera with music by Clarence Cameron White.

"Tambour." 1929.

> One-act folk play with music by Clarence Cameron White.

Biography and Criticism

Matheus, John F. "Ouanga: My Venture in Libretto Creation." CLA JOURNAL, 15 (1972), 428-40.

MILLER, ALLEN C.

Published Plays

"The Opener of Doors." In ONE ACT PLAYS, Vol. 40 (1923) [excerpt].

> Produced by the Federal Theatre Project.

MILLER, MAY

Published Plays

"Christophe's Daughter." In Richardson NHTP, pp. 241-64.

> The tragedy of the daughter of the King of Haiti confronted with her father's suicide.

"Graven Images." In Richardson PP, pp. 109-37. Also in Hatch BTU, pp. 354-59.

> One-act ritualistic play for children about the introduction of prejudice in the Bible, yet showing the black man as essential to God's creation.

"Harriet Tubman." In Richardson NHTP, pp. 265-88.

> Drama on the "Moses of her people" and the Underground Railroad.

"Riding the Goat." In Richardson PP, pp. 141-76.

> A one-act comedy about a black doctor among the bourgeoisie and how the girl he loves solves his problems.

"Samory." In Richardson NHTP, pp. 289-311.

> Historical epic on the African chief and his resistance to colonization by the French.

"Scratches." CAROLINA MAGAZINE, 59 (Apr. 1929), 36-44.

> One-act play on black youth life in a ghetto pool hall, where a scratch stands as a symbol for "the aim at one thing that hits two."

"Sojourner Truth." In Richardson NHTP, pp. 313-33.

> One-act play in celebration of the militant black woman, showing how her preaching changed the minds of hostile black boys.

Unpublished Plays

"The Bog Guide." 1925.

> Winner, first OPPORTUNITY contest.

"The Cussed Thing."

"Stragglers in the Dusk."

MITCHELL, JOSEPH S.

Published Plays

"Help Wanted." SATURDAY EVENING QUILL, No. 2 (1929), 62-71.

"Son-Boy." SATURDAY EVENING QUILL, No. 1 (1928), 38-45.

PAWLEY, THOMAS D., JR. (1917-)

Published Plays

"Jedgement Day." In THE NEGRO CARAVAN. Ed. Sterling Brown et al. New York: Dryden Press, 1941, pp. 534-43.

> One-act comedy on the guilt feelings of a lazy parishioner.

"The Tumult and the Shouting." In Hatch BTU, pp. 473-513.

First performed 1969 at the Lincoln University Institute of Dramatic Arts. Two-act domestic drama on the disillusionment of a southern black schoolteacher who believes in the American Dream.

Unpublished Plays

"Crispus Attucks." 1947.

"F.F.V." 1963.
> Full-length drama on prejudice in colored aristocracy.

"Freedom in My Soul." 1938.
> One-act play.

"Messiah: A Play in Eight Scenes." 1948.

"Smokey." 1939.
> One-act play, written 1929.

"Son of Liberty." 1938.
> Three-act play.

"Zebedee." 1949.

Biography and Criticism

Reardon BTDA, pp. 13-64.
> Section 1 deals with Pawley's theatre activities in the 1960s.

PAYTON, LEW (1873- ?)

Published Plays

"A Bitter Pill." In DID ADAM SIN? (see under Collected Plays, below), pp. 59-78.

"Did Adam Sin?" In DID ADAM SIN? (see under Collected Plays, below), pp. 13-58.

"A Flyin' Fool." In DID ADAM SIN? (see under Collected Plays, below), pp. 115-20.

"Some Sweet Day." In DID ADAM SIN? (see under Collected Plays, below), pp. 79-96.

"Two Sons of Ham." In DID ADAM SIN? (see under Collected Plays, below), pp. 97-114.

"Who Is de Boss?" In DID ADAM SIN? (see Collected Plays, below), pp. 121-24.

Collected Plays

DID ADAM SIN? ALSO STORIES OF NEGRO LIFE IN COMEDY-DRAMA AND SKETCHES. Los Angeles: Published by the author, 1937. 132 p.

PRICE, DORIS D.

Published Plays

"The Bright Medallion." In UNIVERSITY OF MICHIGAN PLAYS. Ed. Kenneth T. Rowe. Ann Arbor: Univ. of Michigan Press, 1932, pp. 275-315.

> One-act drama about a black man who rescues a baby from a burning house and dies, thus proving better than his reputation as a shiftless vagrant.

"The Eyes of Old." In UNIVERSITY OF MICHIGAN PLAYS. Ed. Kenneth T. Rowe. Ann Arbor: Univ. of Michigan Press, 1932, pp. 317-38.

> A young black girl elopes, tired of the routine life with her mother. One-act drama.

"Two Gods: A Minaret." OPPORTUNITY, 10 (1932), 380-83, 389.

> One-act play.

RICHARDSON, WILLIS (1889-)

Published Plays

"Antonio Maceo." In Richardson NHTP, pp. 3-28.

> One-act historical tragedy on the black Cuban patriot whose wife avenges his death after his physician helps murder him.

"Attucks the Martyr." In Richardson NHTP, pp. 29-61.

> One-act dramatization of the heroism of the first man to be killed in the American Revolution.

"The Black Horseman." In Richardson PP, pp. 179-218.

> One-act historical drama glorifying the black race through the
> epic character of Massinissa, King of Numidia. Written 1929.
> First performed October 12, 1931, by Playground Athletic League,
> Baltimore, Maryland.

"The Broken Banjo." CRISIS, 31 (1926), 167, 225. Also in Locke PNL,
pp. 303-20; and in BLACK AMERICAN WRITERS. Ed. Richard Barksdale and
Keneth Kinnamon. New York: Macmillan, 1972, pp. 639-45.

> The folk tragedy of a "bad nigger" accidentally guilty of murder.
> First prize, 1925 CRISIS contest. First performed August 1925 by
> Krigwa Players. The typescript revised in the 1930s is at the
> Schomburg Collection, New York Public Library.

"The Chip Woman's Fortune." In Patterson AANT, pp. 87-98. Also in Turner
BDA, pp. 25-47.

> Domestic drama: an old black woman's savings are given, by her
> son, to save a poor family who cared for her. First performed
> January 29, 1923, by Chicago Ethiopian Art Players. Three-act
> version completed in 1927.

"Compromise: A Folk Play." In THE NEW NEGRO. Ed. Alain Locke. New
York: Boni, 1925, pp. 168-95.

"The Deacon's Awakening." CRISIS, 21 (Nov. 1920), 10-15.

> One-act militant drama on women seeking the right to vote. First
> performed 1921 by the St. Paul, Minnesota, Players.

"The Dragon's Tooth." In THE KING'S DILEMMA AND OTHER PLAYS FOR
CHILDREN (see under Collected Plays, below).

> Children contending for leadership steal a dragon's tooth bearing
> the inscription "Love and Brotherhood." Written in the 1930s.

"The Elder Dumas." In Richardson NHTP, pp. 63-94.

> One-act play on Alexandre Dumas Pere, the famous writer, de-
> picted in unsympathetic terms because of his commercialism.

"The Flight of the Natives." In Locke PNL, pp. 97-116. Also in Hatch BTU,
pp. 383-89.

> One-act drama on fugitive slaves from South Carolina in the early
> 1860s. First performed May 7, 1927, by the Krigwa Players,
> Washington, D.C.

"The Gipsy's Finger Ring." In THE KING'S DILEMMA AND OTHER PLAYS FOR CHILDREN (see under Collected Plays, below).

> Children meet a gypsy and are shown the three ages of man: slavery, wage slavery, and freedom.

"The House of Sham." In Richardson PP, pp. 241-91. Also in AMERICAN LITERATURE BY NEGRO AUTHORS. Ed. Herman Dreer. New York: Macmillan, 1950, pp. 284-305.

> Domestic drama of a black middle-class family who live beyond their means. First performed 1928.

"The Idle Head." CAROLINA MAGAZINE, 59 (Apr. 1929), 16-25. Also in Hatch BTU, pp. 234-40.

> One-act drama on the difficulties of a black man who cannot find a job for lack of subservience.

"In Menelik's Court." In Richardson NHTP, pp. 109-39.

> One-act drama of love and intrigue at the court of the King of Abyssinia in 1898.

"The King's Dilemma." In Richardson PP, pp. 219-39.

> A king prefers to resign his power to the people rather than let a black man, his son's friend, rule it in part. First performed in Washington, D.C., and awarded the Public School Prize in May 1926.

"Man of Magic." In THE KING'S DILEMMA AND OTHER PLAYS FOR CHILDREN (see under Collected Plays, below).

> One-act play on a magician who belongs to a new race, neither white nor black.

"Mortgaged." In READINGS FROM NEGRO AUTHORS. Ed. Otelia Cromwell, Eva B. Dykes, and Lorenzo D. Turner. New York: Harcourt, 1931.

> Drama about two middle-class black brothers with conflicting aims: exploitative moneymaking vs. uplifting the race through scientific discoveries. Written 1923; first performed March 29, 1924, by Howard University Players.

"Near Calvary." In Richardson NHTP, pp. 95-107. Also in THE KING'S DILEMMA AND OTHER PLAYS FOR CHILDREN (see under Collected Plays, below).

> One-act Easter play, dramatizing the bravery of Simon, who carried the cross for Jesus, and Simon's brother Laban, who refused to deny Jesus.

"The New Santa Claus." In THE KING'S DILEMMA AND OTHER PLAYS FOR CHILDREN (see under Collected Plays, below).

> A Christmas play in one act, in which a vagabond Santa Claus replaces the traditional figure.

Unpublished Plays

"The Amateur Prostitute."

"Bold Lover."

"The Bootblack Lover." 1926.

> First prize, 1926 CRISIS contest.

"The Brown Boy."

"The Curse of the Shell-Road Witch."

"The Dark Haven."

"Ghost of the Past."

"Hope of the Lonely."

"Imp of the Devil."

"The Jail Bird."

"Joy Rider."

"The Man Who Married a Young Wife."

"Miss or Mrs." 1941.

> One-act play.

"Nude Siren."

"The Peacock's Feather." 1928.

> One-act play.

"A Pillar of the Church."

"Protest."

"Rooms for Rent." 1926.

"Sacrifice." 1930.

"The Victim."

"The Visiting Lady."

Collected Plays

THE KING'S DILEMMA AND OTHER PLAYS FOR CHILDREN. New York: Exposition, 1956. 71 p.

> Five plays: "The Dragon's Tooth," "The Gipsy's Finger Ring,"
> "The King's Dilemma," "Man of Magic," "The New Santa Claus."
> Also see Drama, part 1, section 4, for play collections edited by
> Richardson.

Biography and Criticism

Peterson, Bernard L., Jr. "Willis Richardson, Pioneer Playwright." BLACK
WORLD, 26 (Apr. 1975), 40-48, 86-88.

Richardson, Willis. "The Hope of a Negro Drama." CRISIS, 19 (1919), 338-
39.

ROSS, JOHN M.

Published Plays

ONE CLEAR CALL. Nashville, Tenn.: Fisk University, 1936.

> A tragicomedy on black life.

RHO KAPPA EPSILON. Nashville, Tenn.: Fisk University, 1935.

> A three-act tragicomedy.

WANGA DOLL. New Orleans: Dillard University, 1954.

> A three-act tragedy of 1820.

Unpublished Plays

"Aztec Qzin." 1928.

"Dog's Place." 1935.

"House or No House." 1967.

"I Will Repay." 1963.

"Strivin." 1937.

"The Sword." 1948.

SEBREE, CHARLES

Published Plays

"The Dry August." In Hatch BTU, pp. 659-70.

> A dream comedy about the problems and agonies of black youth. Shortened version of a full-length 1949 script from which Sebree and Greer Johnson adapted the Broadway musical, "Mrs. Patterson," in 1954.

SPENCE, EULALIE (1894-)

Published Plays

FOOL'S ERRAND. New York: Samuel French, 1927. 26 p.

> One-act black domestic comedy on how the neighborhood forces a boy to marry his supposedly pregnant girlfriend. First performed 1927 by Krigwa Players at Frolic Theatre, New York City.

FOREIGN MAIL. New York: Samuel French, 1927.

> Second prize in 1926 CRISIS contest. First performed 1927, New York City.

"Help Wanted." BOSTON SATURDAY EVENING QUILL, Apr. 1929.

"The Starter." In Locke PNL, pp. 205-14.

> One-act domestic comedy about a young black woman who tries to have her boyfriend marry her. Written in 1926; 3rd prize, 1926 OPPORTUNITY contest.

"Undertow." CAROLINA MAGAZINE, 59 (Apr. 1929), 5-15. Also in Hatch BTU, pp. 193-200.

One-act melodrama set in a Harlem rooming house--on the wife, husband, and mistress theme.

Unpublished Plays

"Brothers and Sisters of the Church Council." 1920s.

"Her." 1927.
One-act play.

"The Hunch." 1927.
One-act comedy of Harlem life; 2nd prize, 1927 OPPORTUNITY contest.

"The Whipping."

STREATOR, GEORGE W.

Published Plays

"Two Plays: New Courage; A Sign." CRISIS, 41 (Jan. 1934), 9 ff.
The first is a one-act play about a black woman who takes a racist bus driver's name and number; the second is a one-act play about reactions to the lynching of kidnappers in California.

TILLMAN, KATHERINE DAVIS

Published Plays

AUNT BETSY'S THANKSGIVING. Philadelphia: A.M.E. Book Concern, 191?. 8 p.

FIFTY YEARS OF FREEDOM; OR, FROM CABIN TO CONGRESS: A DRAMA IN FIVE ACTS. Philadelphia: A.M.E. Book Concern, 1910. 52 p.

TOOMER, JEAN (1894-1967)

Published Plays

"Balo." In Locke PNL, pp. 271-86. Also in Hatch BTU, pp. 219-24.
A one-act sketch on the domestic life of Georgia black folks. Written in 1922 for the Howard Players' 1923-24 season.

"Kabnis." In CANE. New York: Boni, 1923. Rpt. New York: Harper Torchbooks, 1969, pp. 157-239.

> Dramatic dialogue on black life in the South and a black intellectual's acceptance of his racial roots.

Unpublished Plays

"Natalie Mann." 1923.

> On the plight of the middle-class black woman.

"The Sacred Factory." 1920s.

> On the same subject.

Biography and Criticism

See also the entries on Toomer under Poetry, part 2: Individual Authors, 1901-45.

Goede, William J. "Jean Toomer's Ralph Kabnis." PHYLON, 30 (1969), 73-85.

Krasny, Michael. "Design in Jean Toomer's BALO." NEGRO AMERICAN LITERATURE FORUM, 7 (Fall 1973), 103-4.

Turner, Darwin T. "The Failure of a Playwright." CLA JOURNAL, 10 (1966), 308-18.

WARD, THEODORE (1902-)

Published Plays

"Big White Fog." In THE NEGRO CARAVAN. Ed. Sterling Brown et al. New York: Dryden, 1941, pp. 562-73 [Act III only]. Full text in Hatch BTU pp. 281-319.

> A three-act political drama: When black capitalism and the Garvey movement fail to help the plight of black Americans, socialism is proposed as a solution. First performed 1938 by Chicago Federal Theatre Project.

"The Daubers." In Childress BIS, pp. 79-89 [extract].

"John Brown." MASSES AND MAINSTREAM, 2 (Oct. 1949), [Act 1, sc. 2 only].

Historical and political drama. First performed April 28, 1950, by People's Drama, New York City. Revised in 1964 as "Of Human Grandeur." Ms. of February 1950 version at Library of Congress.

"Our Lan'." In A THEATER IN YOUR HEAD. Ed. Kenneth Thorpe Rowe. New York: Funk & Wagnalls, 1960, pp. 261-425. Also in Turner BDA, pp. 115-203.

Full-length drama on the difficulties and struggles of black freedmen who try to acquire and retain land of their own after the Civil War. Written 1941; new version 1946; first performed 1946 at Henry Street Playhouse; modified version performed Fall 1946 at Royale Theatre, Broadway.

Unpublished Plays

"The Bell and the Light." 1962.

"Big Money." 1962.

"Candle in the Wind." 1966.

"Charity." 1960.

"Deliver the Goods." 1941.

"Even the Dead Arise." 1935.

"Falcon of Adowa." 1935.

"John the Conqueror." 1953.

"Madison." 1956.

"Shout Hallelujah." 1941.

"Sick and Tired" (Also "Sick and Tiah'd"). 1937.

"Throwback." 1952.

"Whole Hog or Nothing." 1952.

Biography and Criticism

Abramson NP, pp. 109-36.

"Interview with Playwright Ted Ward." AFRIKA MUST UNITE, 2, No. 15, 17 (1973), 9-11.

Mitchell BD, pp. 113-14, 133-44.

WILSON, FRANK (1886-)

Published Plays

"Sugar Cane." OPPORTUNITY, 4 (1926), 181-84, 201-3. Also in Locke PNL, pp. 167-86.

> One-act drama on the life of black sharecroppers in contemporary Georgia. First prize, 1925 OPPORTUNITY contest.

Unpublished Plays

"Back Home Again."

"The Good Sister Jones."

"Meek Mose." 1928.

> See BEST PLAYS OF 1929-1930, edited by Burns Mantle. First performed February 6, 1928, at the Princess Theatre, New York City; revised version for the Federal Theatre Project written in 1937 and titled "Brother Mose: A Comedy of Negro Life with Music and Spirituals" (U.S. National Archives, National Service Bureau Publication, No. 7, mimeographed).

"The Prison Life."

"Walk Together Children" (also "Walk Together Chillun"). 1936.

> First performed February 5, 1936, at Lafayette Theatre, New York City.

Biography and Criticism

Abramson NP, pp. 54-59.

Housman, John. RUN-THROUGH. New York: Curtis, 1972, pp. 187-89.

WRIGHT, RICHARD (1908-60)

Published Plays

NATIVE SON (THE BIOGRAPHY OF A YOUNG AMERICAN): A PLAY IN TEN SCENES, FROM THE NOVEL BY RICHARD WRIGHT. New York: Harper, 1941. 148 p. Also in Hatch BTU, pp. 394-431.

> The tragedy of Bigger Thomas, a black child of the slums, who achieves a sense of himself through murder and is ruthlessly destroyed by society. Adaptation written in collaboration by Wright and Paul Green; production scripts at the New York Public Library. First performed March 25, 1941, at St. James Theatre, New York City.

Unpublished Plays

"The Burkes." 1937.

> Incomplete.

"Daddy Goodness." 1959.

> Adapted from PAPA BON DIEU (1958), by French dramatist Louis Sapin. Performed February 19, 1959, by American Theatre Association in Paris, France; first U.S. performance June 1968 by Negro Ensemble Company, New York City.

"The Farmer in the Dell." Late 1940s.

> On the problems of dramatizing NATIVE SON.

"3314."

> Incomplete drama based on LAWD TODAY.

Biography and Criticism

Abramson NP, pp. 136-63.

Bailey, Peter. "Daddy Goodness." BLACK THEATRE, No. 1 (1968), p. 31.

Fabre, Michel. THE UNFINISHED QUEST OF RICHARD WRIGHT. New York: William Morrow, 1973. 652 p.

> Bibliography. See pp. 207-14, 322-24, 444-46, 520.

Housman, John. RUN-THROUGH. New York: Curtis, 1972, pp. 461-75.

> On NATIVE SON.

Mitchell BD, pp. 114-15.

Riley, Clayton. "Daddy Goodness." LIBERATOR, 8 (July 1968), 21.

3. 1951-75

The dramatists are listed below alphabetically for the period 1951 to 1975.
Under each author, sequences of listings, wherever applicable, are as follows:
published plays, unpublished plays, collected plays, and biography and criticism. Pagination for monographs is given if discovered in the course of work
with primary or secondary sources. Anonymous and/or collected plays are
listed under Anonymous.

ABRAMSON, DOLORES

Published Plays

"The Light." In THREE HUNDRED AND SIXTY DEGREES OF BLACKNESS
COMIN AT YOU. Ed. Sonia Sanchez. New York: 5 X Publishing Co.,
1971, pp. 137-38.

> This one-act ritual consists of a dialogue between God and the
> Devil about what each of them thinks should be the proper behavior
> for a black woman of the Nation of Islam.

AHMAD, DOROTHY

Published Plays

"Papa's Daughter." DRAMA REVIEW, 12 (1968), 139-45.

> One-act play on the domestic problems of a girl compelled to
> grow up prematurely; it especially explores her relationship with
> her father. First performed by Dillard University Players Guild,
> 1969.

ALLEN, RICHARD

Published Plays

"Take Me to Your Leader." In WE ARE BLACK. Chicago: Science Research
Associates, 1969.

> A one-act comedy for children about the arrival of visitors from
> the planet Mars and their reactions to the automobile in America.

AMIS, LOLA JONES (1930-)

Published Plays

"Helen." In THREE PLAYS (see under Collected Plays, below).

> Two-act drama about a mother who loses her daughter's respect by treating her as a peer.

"The Other Side of the Wall." In THREE PLAYS (see under Collected Plays, below).

> Three-act domestic play on the conflict-ridden relationship between a sensitive wife and a crude husband. First performed April 1971 at Norfolk Public Library Black Culture Center by Morgan State College students.

"Places of Wrath." In THREE PLAYS (see under Collected Plays, below).

> Domestic drama in three acts about a husband's infidelity, which causes his wife's furious reactions and his daughter's suicide.

Collected Plays

THREE PLAYS: THE OTHER SIDE OF THE WALL, PLACES OF WRATH AND HELEN. New York: Exposition, 1965. 88 p.

ANDERSON, ODIE (1943-)

Published Plays

TRIAL OF GOD. New York: Exposition, 1970. 49 p.

> A play in verse.

Anonymous and/or Collective Plays

"At a Black Community Village Night." NKOMBO, No. 8 (Aug. 1972), pp. 17-25.

> Black consciousness ritual in the form of a short fragment of a message session; created by the Sudan/Arts Theatre Group.

TO RAISE THE DEAD AND FORETELL THE FUTURE. New York: New Lafayette Theatre, 1970. 16 p.

> A collective creation of the New Lafayette Theatre described as a "ritual spirit/epic." Performed in 1970 by the New Lafayette Theatre, directed by Robert Macbeth.

"The Turn of the Century. A Set for Our Rising." NKOMBO, No. 8 (Aug. 1972), pp. 43-58.

> A ritual created by Kalamu, Kwesi, Nyumba, and the Blackart-south Group.

ARANHA, RAY

Published Plays

MY SISTER, MY SISTER. New York: Samuel French, 1973. 80 p.

ATKINS, RUSSELL (1926-)

Published Plays

"The Abortionist." FREE LANCE, Vol. 2, no. 1 (Spring 1954).

> "Poem in Play Form, To be Set in Music." One-act poetic drama about a doctor who avenges himself on a colleague by giving the colleague's daughter a violent abortion. Slightly revised 1963 version published in TWO BY ATKINS. Cleveland: Free Lance Press, 1963, pp. 1-12.

"The Corpse." WESTERN REVIEW, Jan. 1954. Also in TWO BY ATKINS. Cleveland: Free Lance Press, 1963, pp. 14-31.

> "Poem in Play Form." One-act poetic drama about a widow who revisits her husband's tomb to watch his corpse rot.

"The Drop of Blood." In PHENOMENA. Wilberforce, Ohio: Wilberforce Univ. Press, 1961.

> One-act poem in play form, about domestic life between an older woman and her younger husband. Written in 1959.

"The Exoneration." In PHENOMENA. Wilberforce, Ohio: Wilberforce Univ. Press, 1961.

> One-act poetic drama. Protest about the false arrest of a black suspect. Written in 1959.

THE NAIL. Cleveland: Free Lance Press, 1971.

> A love drama about a Spanish woman fugitive. Written in 1957. Poetry libretto in three acts for an opera, adapted from the story by the same title by Pedro Antonio de Alarcon.

"The Seventh Circle." In HERETOFORE. London: Breman, 1968, pp. 17-27.

"Poem in radio format" on the theme of political and social involvement. Written in 1957 for EXPERIMENT MAGAZINE's drama issue.

BALDWIN, JAMES (1924-)

Published Plays

THE AMEN CORNER. New York: Dial, 1967. 81 p. Also in Hatch BTU, pp. 516-46.

Three acts on the domestic and spiritual problems of a woman pastor confronted by her Harlem storefront church congregation when her musician husband returns home. Written 1954; performed 1955 at Howard University; first performance on Broadway April 15, 1965, at the Ethel Barrymore Theatre.

BLUES FOR MISTER CHARLIE. New York: Dial, 1964. 212 p. New York: Dell Paperback, 1964. Also in Oliver CBD, pp. 233-314.

Full-length drama of race conflict in the South, centering around the acquittal of the white murderer of a proud black. Intended to show the inadequacy of nonviolent civil rights militancy and the ambiguous role of white liberals. First performed April 23, 1964, at the ANTA Theatre, New York City.

ONE DAY WHEN I WAS LOST: A SCENARIO BASED ON "THE AUTOBIOGRAPHY OF MALCOLM X." London: Michael Joseph, 1972. 166 p.

Biography and Criticism

Bigsby, C.W.E. "The Committed Writer: James Baldwin as a Dramatist." TWENTIETH CENTURY LITERATURE, 12 (1967), 39-48.

Driver, Tom F. "Blues for Mister Charlie." NEGRO DIGEST, 13 (Sept. 1964), 34-49.

Review.

Eckman, Fern Marja. THE FURIOUS PASSAGE OF JAMES BALDWIN. New York: M. Evans, 1966. 254 p.

Biography.

Featherstone, Joseph. "Blues for Mr. Baldwin." NEW REPUBLIC, 163 (2 Nov. 1965), 34-36.

Hernton, Calvin. "The Masculinization of James Baldwin." In UMBRA ANTHOLOGY 1967-68, pp. 19-22.

Kinnamon, Keneth A., ed. JAMES BALDWIN: A COLLECTION OF CRITI-
CAL ESSAYS. Englewood Cliffs, N.J.: Prentice-Hall, 1974. 169 p.

Macebuh, Stanley. JAMES BALDWIN: A CRITICAL STUDY. New York:
Third Press, 1973. 194 p.

Markholt, Ottilie. "White Critic, Black Playwright: Water and Fire." NE-
GRO DIGEST, 16 (Apr. 1967), 54-60.

Meserve, Walter. "James Baldwin's 'Agony Way.'" In Bigsby BAW2, pp. 171-
86.

Phillips, Louis. "The Novelist as Playwright: Baldwin, McCullers, Bellow."
In MODERN AMERICAN DRAMA. Ed. William E. Taylor. Deland, Fla.:
Edwards, 1968, pp. 145-62.

Roth, Philip. "Blues for Mister Charlie." NEW YORK REVIEW OF BOOKS,
2 (28 May 1964), 10-13.

> Review article.

Silvera, Frank. "Towards a Theatre of Understanding." NEGRO DIGEST, 18
(Apr. 1969), 33-35.

> Comments mostly on THE AMEN CORNER.

Simmons, Bill. "A Playwright at Work: James Baldwin." PLAYBILL, 1 (July
1964), 15.

BARAKA, AMIRI. See JONES, LeROI, below.

BARBOUR, FLOYD

Published Plays

"The Bird Cage." In Childress BLS, pp. 19-27 [extract].

> A contemporary scene set in a small southern town.

BASCOMBE, RONALD D.

Published Plays

"The Unifier." In THREE HUNDRED AND SIXTY DEGREES OF BLACKNESS
COMIN AT YOU. Ed. Sonia Sanchez. New York: 5 X Publishing Co., 1971,
pp. 122-31.

One-act satire on an Uncle Tom who pretends to lead blacks to progress but tries only to keep them contented and quiet.

BASS, GEORGE HOUSTON (1938-)

Published Plays

"Games." In INTRODUCTION TO BLACK LITERATURE IN AMERICA. Ed. Lindsay Patterson. New York: Publishers Co., 1968, pp. 268-71.

> Original title: "Loop the Loop"; movie adaptation: THE GAME. First performed May 1966 by Mobilization for Youth Drama Group, New York City.

Unpublished Plays

"African Vibrations." 1973.

"Black Blues." 1968.

"Black Masque." 1971.

"Dreamdust." 1974.

"The How Long Sweet." 1968.

"Once I Heard Buddy Bolden Play." 1965.

"The Third Party." 1968.

"A Trio for the Living." 1968.

BASS, KINGSLEY B., JR. See under BULLINS, ED, "We Righteous Bombers."

BATSON, SUSAN

Published Plays

"Hoodoo Talkin'." In THREE HUNDRED AND SIXTY DEGREES OF BLACKNESS COMIN AT YOU. Ed. Sonia Sanchez. New York: 5 X Publishing Co., 1971, pp. 145-78.

> One-act play. Dialogue between four black women on different aspects of their racial commitment.

BRANCH, WILLIAM (1927-)

Published Plays

"In Splendid Error." In Hatch BTU, pp. 588-617.

> Three-act historical drama on the relationship between Frederick Douglass and John Brown at the time of Harper's Ferry. Written 1952-53; original title: "Frederick Douglass"; first performed as such in 1953. First performed as "In Splendid Error" October 26, 1954, at Greenwich Mews Theatre, New York City.

"A Medal for Willie." In King BDA, pp. 439-73.

> Seven scenes on white hypocrisy and black fortitude when the mother of a dead black hero refuses his posthumous medal and honors. First performed October 1951 at the Club Baron, New York City.

"To Follow the Phoenix." In Childress BLS, pp. 57-66 [excerpt].

> Commissioned by the Delta Sigma Theta sorority in commemoration of the life, work, and inspiration of March Church Terrell (1863-1954). Written and performed in Chicago, 1960.

Unpublished Plays

"Baccalaureate." 1954.

"Experiment in Black."

"Light in the Southern Sky." 1958.

> NBC-TV drama on the life of Mary McLeod Bethune.

"A Wreath for Udomo." 1959.

> Adapted from Peter Abraham's novel of the same title. Performed in Cleveland, Karamu Theatre, 1959.

Biography and Criticism

Abramson NP, pp. 171-88.

Evans, Donald T. "Bring It All Back Home: Playwrights of the Fifties." BLACK WORLD, 20 (Feb. 1971), 41-45.

Mitchell BD, pp. 151-52, 167-68, 215-18.

BROWN, WESLEY

Published Plays

"And Now, Will the Real Bud Jones Stand Up." In THREE HUNDRED AND SIXTY DEGREES OF BLACKNESS COMIN AT YOU. Ed. Sonia Sanchez. New York: 5 X Publishing Co., 1971, pp. 129-44.

> A one-act ritual on a black man's progress and discovery of what the truth is for him.

BULLINS, ED (1935-)

Published Plays

"The American Flag Ritual (A Short Play or Film Scenario)." In THE THEME IS BLACKNESS (see under Collected Plays, below), p. 15.

> A short script on the American flag. Dated May 21, 1969, Harlem.

"The Black Revolutionary Commercial." DRAMA REVIEW, 13 (Summer 1969), 144-45. Also published as "Black Commercial No. 2," in THE THEME IS BLACKNESS (see under Collected Plays, below), pp. 131-34.

> On how to stop a fight between two black brothers. First performed April 12, 1967, at the Black House, San Francisco.

"The Box Office." BLACK THEATRE, No. 3 (1969), pp. 18-19.

> "Scenario for a short film . . . as related by Robert Macbeth." See Macbeth, Robert, below.

"Clara's Ole Man--A Play of Lost Innocence." DRAMA REVIEW, 12 (1968), 159-71. Also in FIVE PLAYS (see under Collected Plays, below), pp. 249-82; and in CAVALCADE. Ed. Arthur P. Davis and Saunders Redding. Boston: Houghton, Mifflin, 1971, pp. 658-75.

> One-act comedy of black life: a college boyfriend of Clara calls on her, but her dominant father knows how to handle his pretentious eloquence as well as the vulgarity of gang members. Written 1965; first performed August 5, 1965, by Firehouse Repertory Theater, San Francisco.

"The Corner." In THE THEME IS BLACKNESS (see under Collected Plays, below), pp. 98-126. Also in King BDA, pp. 77-88.

> How a pimp gives up the street corner and his slick friends to become a respectable family man.

"Death List." BLACK THEATRE, No. 5 (1971), pp. 38-43. Also in FOUR
DYNAMITE PLAYS (see under Collected Plays, below), pp. 17-38.

> A black man eliminates other blacks who oppose revolution while
> his woman argues about the righteousness of such a radical solu-
> tion. First performed October 16, 1970, by Theatre Black, Uni-
> versity of the Streets Auditorium, New York City.

"Dialect Determinism (or 'The Rally')." ANTE MAGAZINE (Los Angeles), 1966.
Also in THE THEME IS BLACKNESS (see under Collected Plays, below), pp. 17-
37.

> A parody of the "theatre of the lip" and a black ritual of retribu-
> tion and unification through martyrdom. First performed August 3,
> 1965, Firehouse Repertory Theatre, San Francisco.

THE DUPLEX: A BLACK LOVE FABLE IN FOUR MOVEMENTS. New York:
William Morrow, 1971. 166 p.

> On the search for love and self-completeness in dream fantasies
> away from the hell of "cool dark little lives." First performed
> June 1, 1970, New Dramatists' Workshop, New York City.

"The Electronic Nigger, A Tragicomedy." In NEW AMERICAN PLAYS.
Vol. 3. Ed. William M. Hoffman. New York: Hill & Wang, 1969. Also in
FIVE PLAYS (see under Collected Plays, below), pp. 215-47.

> A play showing the triumph of affectation, pompous oratory, and
> intellectual automatism in a class in creativity. First performed
> March 24, 1968, at the American Place Theatre, New York City.

"The Fabulous Miss Marie." SCRIPTS, 1 (Feb. 1972), 57-80. Also in Bullins
NLTP, pp. 7-71.

> A comedy of manners, scored to music and dance, about black
> people who fall in and out of love, are indifferent to civil rights
> strife, and try to make the most of their "miserable mean exis-
> tence." First performed March 5, 1971, New Lafayette Theatre,
> New York City.

THE GENTLEMAN CALLER. Santa Fe, N. Mex.: Illuminations Press, 1971.
15 p. Mimeographed. Also in BQ, pp. 117-36; in THE BEST SHORT PLAYS
OF 1970. Ed. Richard Stanley. Philadelphia: Chilton Books, 1970, pp. 127-
47; and in Oliver CBD, pp. 365-80.

> During the silent visit of a black gentleman, the "dutiful" black
> maid of a white household expediently gets rid of her masters.
> Copyrighted 1966. First performed April 27, 1969.

"Goin' a Buffalo. A Tragifantasy." In Couch NBP, pp. 181-245. Also in

FIVE PLAYS (see under Collected Plays, below), pp. 1-98; and in Hatch BTU, pp. 828-53.

> A black hustler is betrayed by the man he had befriended and trusted. The play shifts from realism to fantasy, from present to past, and explores moods and aspirations amid the sordidness of existence. Copyrighted 1966. First performed June 6, 1968, American Place Theatre, New York City.

"The Helper." In THE THEME IS BLACKNESS (see under Collected Plays, below), pp. 56-77.

> One-act play on a black family moving out of one apartment and into another. Written 1966. First performed June 1, 1970, New Dramatists' Workshop, New York City.

"How Do You Do? A Nonsense Drama." BLACK DIALOGUE, 1 (July 1965), 55-61. Published separately as HOW DO YOU DO. Mill Valley, Calif.: Illuminations Press, 1967. 31 p. Also in Jones BF, pp. 595-604.

> Sophisticated Negroes who try to be refined and yet know they are stereotypical "niggers" are confronted with a genuine black poet-musician determined to destroy institutionalized logic and language. Copyrighted 1965; first performed August 1965 by the Firehouse Repertory Theatre, San Francisco.

"In New England Winter." In Bullins NPBT, pp. 129-73.

> Long one-act drama relating a story of love and betrayal, of commitment and antagonism, between male and female, between brothers and friends. Copyrighted 1967. First performed Spring 1968, New Lafayette Theatre, New York City.

"In the Wine Time." In FIVE PLAYS (see under Collected Plays, below), pp. 101-82.

> A drama about the life, problems, and good times of lower-class blacks; a man hopes to see his nephew break the circle of oppression which relegates him to failure, lies, and dreams. First performed December 10, 1968. New Lafayette Theatre, New York City.

"It Bees That Way." In FOUR DYNAMITE PLAYS (see under Collected Plays, below), pp. 1-16. Also in THE AMERICAN THEATRE 1968-1969. New York: International Theatre Institute, 1970, pp. 120-32.

> Black actors who have been playing the "nigger game" suddenly confront their white audience with the true game of the revolution; a ritual on the changes that must be brought about in black theatre, and racial relations on the scene of life. First performed September 21, 1970, at the Ambiance Lunch Hour Theatre Club, London.

"It Has No Choice." In THE THEME IS BLACKNESS (see under Collected Plays, below), pp. 38-55.

> Short play on the relationship between a black man and a white woman with its moods of violence, humiliation, endurance, and ecstasy. First performed by Black Arts/West Repertory Theatre School, San Francisco, Spring 1966.

"Malcolm: '71, or Publishing Blackness." BLACK SCHOLAR, 6 (June 1975), 84-86.

> A one-act telephone exchange between a black publisher and a pseudo-liberal white girl doing a radical anthology.

"The Man Who Dug Fish." In THE THEME IS BLACKNESS (see under Collected Plays, below, pp. 85-87.

> A fable about a man, a fish, a shovel, and a safe. Written 1967. New Dramatists' reading, June 1970, New York City.

"A Minor Scene." In THE THEME IS BLACKNESS (see under Collected Plays, below), pp. 78-83.

> Dialogue between a black man and a young white woman at a bus stop. First performed Spring 1966 by Black Arts/West Repertory Theatre, San Francisco.

"Night of the Beast. A Screenplay." In FOUR DYNAMITE PLAYS (see under Collected Plays, below), pp. 119-79.

> Harlem Corner Day, at the time of the revolutionary fight against the oppressive system.

"One Minute Commercial (For Black Community Broadcasting)." In THE THEME IS BLACKNESS (see under Collected Plays, below), pp. 138-40.

> Sketch on the New Lafayette Theatre. Dated Harlem, December 26, 1969.

"The Pig Pen." In FOUR DYNAMITE PLAYS (see under Collected Plays, below), pp. 40-118.

> The death of Malcolm X is announced during a party; rhythm and blues clash with didacticism. First performed Spring 1970, American Place Theatre, New York City.

"The Play of the Play." In THE THEME IS BLACKNESS (see under Collected Plays, below), p. 183.

> A script on involving the audience through use of light, images, sound, music, poetry, and dance in order to achieve a sort of ritual-happening. Dated December 1970.

"A Short Play for a Small Theatre." BLACK WORLD, 20 (Apr. 1971), 39.
Also in THE THEME IS BLACKNESS (see under Collected Plays, below), p. 182.

> Directions for a ritual of death with a black man shooting white
> people in the audience.

"A Son, Come Home." NEGRO DIGEST, 17 (Apr. 1968), 54-73. Also in
FIVE PLAYS (see under Collected Plays, below), pp. 185-213.

> Four characters, switching roles, enact various scenes with a vari-
> ety of moods. First performed March 26, 1968, American Place
> Theatre, New York City.

"State Office Building Curse (A Scenario to Ultimate Action)." NEGRO DI-
GEST, 19 (Apr. 1970), 54-55. Also in DRAMA REVIEW, 14 (Sept. 1970), 93;
and in THE THEME IS BLACKNESS (see under Collected Plays, below), pp. 136-
37.

> A ritual of the destruction of the white man's presence in Harlem
> celebrating the building of a new black nation. Dated Harlem,
> November 12, 1969. Performed early 1970, New Lafayette The-
> atre, New York City.

"A Street Play." In THE THEME IS BLACKNESS (see under Collected Plays,
below), pp. 141-43.

> A black man of the street tries to understand the political scene.
> Dated May 1970.

"Street Sounds." In THE THEME IS BLACKNESS (see under Collected Plays,
below), pp. 144-81.

> A pageant of street characters, experimenting with the ways of
> speech of the "blues people" and exploring the various moods and
> life-styles of the black experience. Dated Harlem, August 3,
> 1970. First performed October 1970 by La Mama Experimental
> Theatre's G.P.A. Nucleus, New York City.

"The Theme is Blackness (A One-Act Play to be Given before Predominantly
White Audiences)." In THE THEME IS BLACKNESS (see under Collected Plays,
below), p. 84.

> The play leaves the audience literally in the dark. Performed
> 1973 at City College, New York City.

"We Righteous Bombers." In Bullins NPBT, pp. 21-96. Also in Turner BDA,
pp. 557-625.

> A close adaptation from LES JUSTES (The Just), by Albert Camus,
> reflecting the black terrorists' conflicting attitudes towards the
> necessity of killing innocents while blowing up their enemies.

Written under the pseudonym of Kingsley B. Bass, Jr. First performed April 18, 1969, New Lafayette Theatre, New York City.

"You Gonna Let Me Take You Out Tonight, Baby?" In BLACK ARTS. Ed. Ahmed Alhamisi and Harun Wangara. Detroit: Black Arts Publications, 1969, pp. 45-51.

A man raps on the phone, trying to persuade a woman to go out with him; a brief play exploring moods and black use of language.

Unpublished Plays

"The Game of Adam and Eve."

One-act play written in collaboration with Shirley Tarbel.

"Home Boy." 1973.

Collected Plays

FIVE PLAYS BY ED BULLINS. Indianapolis: Bobbs-Merrill, 1969. 282 p.

Includes "Goin' a Buffalo," "In the Wine Time," "A Son Come Home," "The Electronic Nigger," and "Clara's Ole Man."

FOUR DYNAMITE PLAYS. New York: William Morrow, 1972. 179 p.

Includes "It Bees That Way," "Death List," "The Pig Pen," and "Night of the Beast."

THE THEME IS BLACKNESS: "THE CORNER" AND OTHER PLAYS. New York: William Morrow, 1972. 183 p.

Includes an introduction on black theatre in the sixties, "Dialect Determinism," "The Helper," "It Has No Choice," "A Minor Scene," "The Theme is Blackness," "The Man Who Dug Fish," "The Corner," "The Black Revolutionary Commercial" (introduction), "Black Commercial no. 2," "The American Flag Ritual," "State Office Building Curse," "One Minute Commercial," "A Street Play," "Street Sounds," "A Short Play for a Small Theater," and "The Play of the Play."

For collections of plays edited by Ed Bullins, see Drama: part 1, section 4.

Biography and Criticism

Bullins, Ed. THE HUNGERED ONE: EARLY WRITINGS. New York: William Morrow, 1971. 149 p.

Autobiographical and short fiction pieces, often later turned into plays, like "The Rally," "The Helper," and "In the Wine Time."

Giles, James R. "Tenderness and Brutality in the Plays of Ed Bullins." PLAYERS, 48 (Oct. 1972), 32-33.

Hord, Fred. "Power in the Blood." BLACK BOOKS BULLETIN, 2 (1974), 11-14.

Jeffers, Lance. "Bullins, Baraka and Elder, The Dawn of Grandeur in Black Drama." CLA JOURNAL, 16 (Dec. 1972), 32-48.

"Lafayette Reactions to Bombers." BLACK THEATRE, No. 4 (1969), pp. 16-26.

Robert Macbeth, Askia M. Toure, Marvin X, Larry Neal, E. Mkalimoto, and Amiri Baraka discuss "We Righteous Bombers."

Macbeth, Robert. "The Electronic Nigger Meets the Gold Dust Twins." BLACK THEATRE, No. 1 (Summer 1968), pp. 24-29.

On the origins and aims of the New Lafayette Theatre.

Marvin X. "Interview with Ed Bullins." NEGRO DIGEST, 18 (Apr. 1969), 9-16.

O'Brien, John. "Interview with Ed Bullins." NEGRO AMERICAN LITERATURE FORUM, 7 (1973), 108-12.

Riley, Clayton. "On Black Theater." In Gayle BA, pp. 313-32.

Mostly on Bullins and Jones.

Wesley, Richard. "Interview with Ed Bullins." BLACK CREATION, 4 (Winter 1973), 8-10.

CALDWELL, BEN

Published Plays

"All White Caste: After the Separation. A Slow Paced One Act Play." In King BDA, pp. 389-99.

A disenchanted picture of the possible future of black upheaval; repression and manipulation in black-abandoned Harlem, which has become a prison-tenement for white sympathizers to the black cause.

"Family Portrait (or My Son, the Black Nationalist)." In Bullins NPBT, pp. 189-94.

> One-act diatribe against black accommodationism, using the plot of a son's failure to change his parents' outlook and convictions.

"Hypnotism." In AFRO-ARTS ANTHOLOGY. Newark, N.J.: Jihad, 1969.

> One-act revolutionary play about a magician who enslaves the minds of blacks to prevent them from resisting. Written 1966.

"The Job." DRAMA REVIEW, 12 (Summer 1968), 41-42.

> A variation on the "now is the time" theme and call to revolt in racial vengeance. First performed 1966.

"The King of Soul, or The Devil and Otis Redding. A One-Act Musical Tragedy." BLACK THEATRE, No. 3 (1969), pp. 28-33. Also in Bullins NPBT, pp. 175-88.

> On the theme of the devil's visitations to a great black musician. First performed 1968.

"Mission Accomplished." DRAMA REVIEW, 12 (Summer 1968), 50-52.

> A vignette, satirizing the spread of Christianity to the Dark Continent. First performed 1967.

"An Obscene Play (for Adults Only)." ALAFIA, 1 (Winter 1971), 14-15.

PRAYER MEETING (OR THE FIRST MILITANT MINISTER). Newark, N.J.: Jihad, 1967. 11 p. Also in Jones BF, pp. 589-94; and in BQ, pp. 27-36.

> A burglar plays the part of God in answering a black preacher's prayer and advises him to lead his militant congregation along the path of racial protest. First performed April 1967 by Spirit House Movers and Players as "Militant Preacher."

"Riot Sale, or Dollar Psyche Fake-Out." DRAMA REVIEW, 12 (Summer 1968), 41-42.

> An autopsy and exposure of the antipoverty program, inspired by the urban riots and violent black and white confrontations of the 1960s. First performed 1966.

"Top Secret, or a Few Millions after B.C." DRAMA REVIEW, 12 (Summer 1968), 47-50.

> The president of the United States calls up his cabinet for a solution to the black demographic rise--another play exposing the work-

ings of white domination. First performed early 1969 by Performing Arts Society, Los Angeles.

"The Wall." SCRIPTS, 1 (May 1972), 91-93.

Youngsters write racial slogans on a New York City wall. Copyrighted 1967.

Unpublished Plays

"The Fanatic." 1968.

One-act play.

"Recognition." 1968.

One-act play.

"Run Around." June 1970.

Performed at Third World House, New York City. One-act play.

"Unpresidented." 1968.

One-act play.

CARTER, STEVE

Published Plays

"One Last Look." In Childress BLS, pp. 91-97 [excerpt].

One scene from a domestic drama centering around the funeral of Eustace Baylor. Copyrighted 1970. First performed St. Marks Playhouse, New York City.

Unpublished Plays

"As You Can See." 1968.

One-act play.

"The Terraced Apartment." 1968.

CHARLES, MARTIE EVANS

Published Plays

"Black Cycle. An Invocation and Two Acts." In King BDA, pp. 525-51.

Social and psychological drama of a black girl's rebellion against
the established order and the older generation; an invocation to
the spirits of black womanhood. First performed 1971, Black Theatre Workshop, New Lafayette Theatre, New York City.

"Job Security." In Hatch BTU, pp. 766-71.

A social drama showing how black teachers play the game of the
educational establishment in order to retain their jobs. First performed June 25, 1970, by the Black Magicians at Third World
House, New York City.

Unpublished Plays

"Jammima." 1971.

Black Playwrights Workshop, New York City. On the difficulties
of a black woman in love.

"Where We At?" 1971.

Black Playwrights Workshop, New York City. On the degradation
of a selfish black woman.

CHILDRESS, ALICE (1920-)

Published Plays

"The African Garden." In Childress BLS, pp. 137-46 [excerpt].

Black pride in Harlem after the 1960s riots.

"Florence, A One-Act Drama." MASSES AND MAINSTREAM, 3 (Oct. 1950),
34-47.

A subtle confrontation between a black woman and a rich white
woman. Written 1949; first performed by People's Drama, New
York City.

"Mojo, A Black Love Story." BLACK WORLD, 20 (Apr. 1971), 54-82. Also
in MOJO AND STRING. New York: Dramatists Play Service, 1971, pp. 3-
23.

Black men and women can work out their differences if they love
and respect themselves and others as equals. First performed October 1970, New Heritage Theatre, New York City.

"String." In MOJO AND STRING. New York: Dramatists Play Service, 1971.

"A very free adaptation of a Guy de Maupassant story . . . 'A

Piece of String' . . . the story of a gentle man--abused by vulgar-
ians." One-act play, set during a picnic given in 1968 by the
Neighborhood Association. The play parodies neighborhoods'
promoting of togetherness.

WEDDING BAND: A LOVE/HATE STORY IN BLACK AND WHITE. New York:
Samuel French, 1973. 73 p.

First performed at the University of Michigan, 1966; performed
Off-Broadway at the Public Theatre, 1972.

WHEN THE RATTLESNAKE SOUNDS. New York: Coward, 1975.

WINE IN THE WILDERNESS: A COMEDY-DRAMA. New York: Dramatists
Play Service, 1969. 43 p. Also in Hatch BTU, pp. 738-55.

A TV play on the radicalization of the children of the black
bourgeoisie and in praise of the survival of authentic black womanhood. First performed 1969.

"The World on a Hill." In PLAYS TO REMEMBER. Literary Heritage Series.
New York: Macmillan, 1968.

One-act drama about a meeting between a young West Indian and
an unhappy white woman and her son who emerge with a better
grasp of their own lives.

Unpublished Plays

"Gold Thru the Trees." 1952.

First performed April 1952, Club Baron, New York City.

"Just a Little Simple." 1950.

First performed September 1940 at Club Baron, New York City.
Adapted from Langston Hughes's SIMPLE SPEAKS HIS MIND.

"A Man Bearing a Pitcher." 1955(?).

"Martin Luther King at Montgomery, Alabama" or "Young Martin Luther King,
Jr." 1969.

"Trouble in Mind." 1955.

First performed November 1955 at Greenwich Mews Theatre, New
York City; winner Obie Award 1955-56.

For a collection of plays edited by Alice Childress, see Drama: part 1, section 4.

Biography and Criticism

Abramson NP, pp. 188-204.

Evans, Donald T. "Bring It All Back Home: Playwrights of the Fifties."
BLACK WORLD, 20 (Feb. 1971), 41-45.

Mitchell BD, pp. 145-47, 168-69.

CLARK, CHINA DEBRA (1950-)

Published Plays

"Perfection in Black." SCRIPTS, 1 (May 1972), 81-85.

> A black man who accuses a woman of not deserving her name, whereas another brings her the perfection she is looking for. First performed January 1971, Negro Ensemble Company, New York City.

Unpublished Plays

"In Sorrow's Room." 1974.

> First performed January, 1974, Henry Street Playhouse, New York City.

CLARKE, SEBASTIAN (Born in Trinidad, West Indies)

Published Plays

"Helliocentric World." SCRIPTS, 1 (May 1972), 86-90.

> A succession of scenes of violence climaxes in total explosion, and a new nation is born.

COFFMAN, STEVEN

Published Plays

"Black Sabbath." NEGRO AMERICAN LITERATURE FORUM, 7 (Fall 1973), 91-102.

> A black poet, who is writing the musical play as it progresses, articulates the problems and rising race-consciousness of a group

of ghetto dwellers whose thinking is spurred by a young militant.

DANIEL, EDDIE-MARY

Published Plays

"For a Friend." PHAT MAMA, 1 (1970), 29-48.

DAVIDSON, NORBERT R., JR. (1940-)

Published Plays

"The Black Studies Lecture." NKOMBO, No. 8 (Aug. 1972), pp. 16-17.
> Three young blacks cut short the pseudo "black" studies course of a white liberal teacher.

"El Hajj Malik." In Bullins NPBT, pp. 201-46.
> "A Play about Malcolm X," which moves with great fluidity from one episode of his life to another. First performed Fall 1968, Dillard University Players, New Orleans.

Unpublished Plays

"Falling Scarlet." 1971.
> Musical play, first performed 1971 by Dashiki Theatre, Blkarts/ South.

"The Further Emasculation of. . . ." 1970.
> July 1970, Dillard University, New Orleans. One-act play.

"Jammer." 1970.
> August 1970, Dashiki Theatre Project, New Orleans.

"Short Fun." 1970.
> One-act play first performed July 1970, Dillard University, New Orleans.

"Window." 1971.
> One-act play first performed August 1971, Dashiki Theatre Project, New Orleans.

DAVIS, OSSIE (1917-)

Published Plays

"Curtain Call, Mr. Aldridge, Sir. A Dramatic Reading." In Reardon BTDA, pp. 233-53.

> A tribute to the outstanding career of Ira Aldridge, the major Afro-American actor and dramatist of the nineteenth century. First performed 1963.

PURLIE VICTORIOUS. New York: Samuel French, 1961. 90 p. Also in Brasmer BD, pp. 273-365; in Turner BDA, pp. 465-533; and in Oliver CBD, pp. 121-86.

> A full-length comedy presenting a group of blacks who fight southern oligarchy under the leadership of a man who talks big but knows how to turn his wishes into reality. First performed September 28, 1961, at the Court Theatre, New York City.

Unpublished Plays

"Alexis is Fallen." 1947.

"Alice in Wonder." 1952.

> One-act play, first performed September 1952 at Elks Community Theatre, New York City; expanded as "The Big Deal," first performed 1953, New Playwrights Theatre, New York City.

"Clay's Rebellion." 1951.

"Goldbricken." 1945.

"A Last Dance for Sybil." 1950s.

"The Major of Harlem." 1949.

"Montgomery Footprints." 1956.

> One-act play.

"Point Blank." 1049.

"School Teacher." 1963.

"They Seek a City." 1947.

"What Can You Say for Mississippi?" 1955.

> One-act play.

Biography and Criticism

Bigsby, C.W.E. "Three Black Playwrights: Loften Mitchell, Ossie Davis, Douglas T. Ward." In Bigsby BAW2, pp. 137-56.

Davis, Ossie. "Purlie Told Me." In HARLEM USA. Ed. John H. Clarke. Berlin, N.H.: Seven Seas, 1964, pp. 152-57.

_____. "The Wonderful World of Law and Order." In ANGER AND BEYOND. Ed. Herbert Hill. New York: Harper, 1965, pp. 154-80.

> On black humor, from Stepin Fetchit to Purlie.

Leaks, Sylvester. "Purlie Victorious." FREEDOMWAYS, 1 (1961), 347.

Mitchell BD, pp. 155-56.

DEAN, PHILLIP HAYES

Published Plays

FREEMAN. New York: Dramatists Play Service, 1973. 76 p.

> Two-act political play: a black militant fails to be elected because of fraud at the polls and resorts to violence against a "Liberal" Community Center. Domestic problems merge with political conflict. First produced February 5, 1973, American Place Theatre, New York City.

"The Minstrel Boy." In AMERICAN NIGHT CRY (see under Collected Plays, below), pp. 33-46. Also in THE STY OF THE BLIND PIG AND OTHER PLAYS (see under Collected Plays, below), pp. 144-57.

> Rainbow Rivers, a black "Minstrel Boy," hangs himself when his wife pretends that his white show business colleague and friend is dead. Is he the victim of his own complexes and fantasies or of the conjuring tricks of his wife, who has been his "friend's" lover? Copyrighted 1970.

"The Owl Killer." In King BDA, pp. 301-24.

> A family drama in which a dead owl is the only message left by the runaway son pursued by the police; an exploration of the struggle each family member consequently has to wage with the

outside world. First performed 1957(?) by Harlem Workshop.

THE STY OF THE BLIND PIG. New York: Dramatists Play Service, 1972. 70 p. Also in THE STY OF THE BLIND PIG AND OTHER PLAYS. (see under Collected Plays, below), pp. 1-80.

> A three-act variation on the theme "the heart is a lonely hunter," involving a black mother, her daughter, a blind man, and the church.

THIS BIRD OF DAWNING SINGETH ALL NIGHT LONG: A SHORT PLAY. New York: Dramatists Play Service, 1971. 30 p. Also in THE STY OF THE BLIND PIG AND OTHER PLAYS (see under Collected Plays, below), pp. 117-43.

> Surrealistic events happen when black Nancy intrudes upon white Anne's cozy life. Fear forces the latter to acknowledge her "sisterhood" after entreaties have failed; she dies after having stabbed her black double. First performed at Chelsea Theatre Center, Brooklyn, 1967-68 season.

"Thunder in the Index." In AMERICAN NIGHT CRY (see under Collected Plays, below), pp. 5-31. Also in THE STY OF THE BLIND PIG AND OTHER PLAYS (see under Collected Plays, below), pp. 83-116.

> A black man who refused to play the social game dialogues in a psychiatric ward with a Jewish doctor who turns out to be another inmate. First performed 1968 at Chelsea Theater Center, Brooklyn.

Unpublished Plays

"Every Night When the Sun Goes Down." 1969.

> Produced at the American Place Theatre.

"The Flight of the Koo-Koo Bird." 1970(?).

> Tucom Public Theatre.

"Johnny Ghost." 1969.

> TV script.

"Noah." 1969(?).

> Harlem Workshop Theatre.

Collected Plays

AMERICAN NIGHT CRY: TWO ONE-ACT PLAYS. New York: Dramatists Play Service, 1972. 46 p.

Includes "Thunder in the Index" and "The Minstrel Boy."

THE STY OF THE BLIND PIG AND OTHER PLAYS. Indianapolis: Bobbs-Merrill, 1973. 157 p.

Includes the title play and "American Night Cry: A Trilogy," consisting of "Thunder in the Index," "This Bird of Dawning Singeth All Night Long," and "Minstrel Boy."

DeANDA, PETER

Published Plays

"Ladies in Waiting." In King BDA, pp. 475-524.

Two-act drama on life in prison among black and Jewish female inmates and their matron. First performed Summer 1968, Negro Ensemble Company, New York City.

Unpublished Plays

"Sweetbread."

DENT, TOM [KUSH]

Published Plays

"Inner Black Blues, A Poem/Play." NKOMBO, No. 8 (Aug. 1972), pp. 26-42.

A drama in four parts for the raising of black consciousness, centering on youngsters rapping and fighting on a Saturday night, but ending on the black narrator's victory over the brainwashing voice of the white world.

"Snapshot." BLKARTSOUTH, 2 (Dec. 1969), 85-90.

One-act play. First performed Fall 1969 by the Free Southern Theater.

"Song of Survival." BLKARTSOUTH, 2 (Dec. 1969), pp. 91-100.

One-act ritual about black consciousness. Written with Val Ferdinand. First performed 1969 by Free Southern Theater.

Unpublished Plays

"Feathers and Stuff." 1970.

Free Southern Theater Workshop, early 1970.

"Negro Study No. 34 A." 1969.

> One-act play, Free Southern Theater, 1969.

"Riot Duty." 1969.

> Free Southern Theater, 1969.

"Ritual Murder." 1967.

> One-act play, Free Southern Theater, 1967.

Biography and Criticism

Dent FST, passim.

DOLAN, HARRY (1927-)

Published Plays

"Losers Weepers." In FROM THE ASHES: VOICES OF WATTS. Ed. Budd Schulberg. New York: New American Library, 1967. New York: World Publishers, Meridian Books, 1969, pp. 45-57.

> Two-act tragedy of a father who is accused of being responsible for his wife's death and whose children have been persistently taught to hate him. Written 1966 and first performed February 19, 1967, as an NBC-TV production under title "Love Song for a Delinquent."

Unpublished Plays

"The Iron Hand of Nat Turner." 1970.

> Watts Writers Workshop, 1970.

DOUGLAS, RODNEY

Published Plays

VOICE OF THE GHETTO. New York: Samuel French, 1968. 26 p.

> A ghetto politician, after denouncing racial and economic injustices in front of a street crowd, protests the suspension of his goddaughter from school. Welcomed with polite sarcasm at the suspension hearing, he denounces the educational system and warns those in authority to produce solutions quickly.

DRAYTON, RONALD

Published Plays

"Nocturne on the Rhine." In Jones BF, pp. 570-73.

> A priest comes to give the last rites to a thief before he is exe-
> cuted, but the priest's message cannot compare to the thief's aware-
> ness of world injustice and sense of religion and solidarity.

"Notes from a Savage God." In Jones BF, pp. 566-69.

> The monologue of a young black sitting in despair and destitution
> in his room ends with his realization that only through crime can
> he find himself and be liberated.

Unpublished Plays

"Black Chaos." 1968(?).

"The Conquest of Africa." 1968.

DuPREE, HERBERT H.

Published Plays

"How White is the Moon (A Light Comedy in a Serious Vein)." BLACK EXPRES-
SION, 2 (Fall 1968), 52-54.

> One-act conversation between the passengers of a spaceship, mostly
> whites, who flee to the moon to escape blackness and find, to
> their dismay, that its inhabitants are colored.

ELDER, LONNE III

Published Plays

CEREMONIES IN DARK OLD MEN. New York: Farrar, Straus and Giroux,
1969. 179 p.

> A realistic drama of oppression based on the story of a former
> vaudevillian who operates a corn whiskey still in the back room of
> his barber shop. Study of the relationships of black male dreamers
> and their practical sister who serves as breadwinner. Copyrighted
> 1965. First performed February 4, 1969, by the Negro Ensemble
> Company at St. Mark's Playhouse, New York City.

"Charades on East Fourth Street." In King BDA, pp. 147-66.

A ritual of vengeance, including verbal assault and physical torture, enacted by teenage youths upon a blindfolded police officer. Commissioned by Mobilization for Youth in 1967.

Unpublished Plays

"A Hysterical Turtle in a Rabbit Race." 1961.

"Kissin' Rattlesnakes Can Be Fun." 1966.
>One-act play.

"Seven Comes Up, Seven Comes Down." 1966.
>One-act play.

Biography and Criticism

Elder, Lonne III. "An Interview." In Bigsby BAW2, pp. 219-26.

Gant, Liz. "An Interview with Lonne Elder." BLACK WORLD, 22 (Apr. 1973), 38-48.

Jeffers, Lance. "Bullins, Baraka and Elder: The Dawn of Grandeur in Black Drama." CLA JOURNAL, 16 (1972), 32-48.

Williams, Jim. "Pieces on Black Theater and the Black Theater Worker." FREEDOMWAYS, 9 (1969), 146-55.

EVANS, DON (1938-)

Published Plays

"Sugar Mouth Sam Don't Dance No More." BLACK WORLD, 22 (Apr. 1973), 54-77.

>A one-act play about a wandering "jive time nigger" visiting a woman who has long been awaiting his return. First performed Fall 1972, H.B. Playhouse, New York City.

Unpublished Plays

"Orrin." 1973.

>First performed 1973 at ANTA matinee series, New York City.

FERDINAND, VAL [KALAMU YA SALAAM] (1947-)

Published Plays

"Blk Love Song #1." In Hatch BTU, pp. 865-74.

> A ritual designed to raise black consciousness in America through a return to African roots in view of the building of a black nation. Written and first performed 1969.

"The Destruction of the American Stage (A Set for Non-Believers)." BLACK WORLD, 21 (Apr. 1972), 54-69.

> A ritual that teaches blacks self-pride and togetherness, shows the evil white man in his lack of humanity, and advises white liberals to leave blacks alone and deal with the beast in themselves.

"Homecoming." NKOMBO, No. 8 (Aug. 1972), pp. 3-15.

> One-act drama revealing different possible attitudes towards the black struggle in the United States. First performed 1968, Free Southern Theater.

"Sudan/Arts. At a Black Community Village Night." NKOMBO, No. 8 (Aug. 1972), pp. 18-27.

> Short segment of a message session, a "Black confession session"; script to be performed with dance and music, with incantatory denunciations of the white American consumer society and evocations of the African power of Muntu. Written with other members of BLKARTSOUTH around 1970.

"The Turn of the Century. A set/for our rising. . . ." NKOMBO, No. 8 (Aug. 1972), pp. 43-58.

> Montage of music and poetry pieces by contemporary black poets on the theme "Black is Beautiful." Written in collaboration with Kwesi and Nyumba of BLKARTSOUTH.

Unpublished Plays

"Black Liberation Army." 1969.

> One-act play on black revolutionary struggle. Free Southern Theater.

"Cop Killer." 1968.

> One-act play.

"Happy Birthday, Jesus." 1969.

> Free Southern Theater.

"Mama." 1969.

> One-act play. Free Southern Theater, March 1969.

"New Love."

"Picket." 1970.

> One-act play. Free Southern Theater.

"Song of Survival." 1969.

> Written with Tom Dent. Free Southern Theater.

Biography and Criticism

Dent FST, passim.

FLAGG, ANN

Published Plays

GREAT GETTIN' UP MORNIN'. New York: Samuel French, 1964. 20 p.

> The first morning of school integration for a small girl. First performed at American Place Theatre, New York City.

FRANKLIN, J[ENNIE] E[LIZABETH] (1937-)

Published Plays

BLACK GIRL: A PLAY IN TWO ACTS. New York: Dramatists Play Service, 1971. 50 p.

> Domestic drama in a small Texas town, centering around the relations and conflicts of Billie Jean, a college girl who wants to become a dancer, with her practical-minded family. Copyrighted 1969. First performed June 16, 1971, by the New Federal Theatre at the Theatre de Lys, New York City.

THE PRODIGAL SISTER: A NEW BLACK MUSICAL. New York: Samuel French, 1975. 59 p.

> Lyrics in collaboration with Micki Grant, who wrote the music. Two-act play at Theatre de Lys, New York City, 1976.

Unpublished Plays

"Cut In the Lights and Call the Law." 1972.
April 1972, New Federal Theatre.

"First Step to Freedom." 1964.
Performed 1964, Sharom Waite Community Center, Harmony, Mississippi.

"The In Crowd." 1967.
Mobilization for Youth at Montreal Exposition.

"Mau Mau Room." 1969.
Negro Ensemble Company Workshop, 1969.

"Prodigal Daughter."
Street Theatre project.

"Two Flowers." 1970s(?).
New Feminist Theatre.

Biography and Criticism

Beauford, Fred. "Black Girl's J.E. Franklin." BLACK CREATION, 2 (Fall 1971), 38-40.

FREEMAN, CAROL (1941-)

Published Plays

"The Suicide." In Jones BF, pp. 631-36.
One-act domestic play: A woman's wake for her dead husband is shared by the preacher but interrupted by the neighbors' noise and subsequent fighting. Performed 1971, Black Folks Theater, Northwestern University, Evanston, Illinois.

FULLER, CHARLES H., JR. (1939-)

Published Plays

"The Rise. A Play in Four Acts." In Bullins NPBT, pp. 247-304.
A four-act drama on Marcus Garvey and the fate of a political

leader mistrusted and intimidated by blacks; establishes a parallel
between the 1920s and the 1960s. Copyrighted 1968. First title:
"Brother Marcus."

Unpublished Plays

"Candidate."

"The Conductor." 1969.

"In My Many Names and Days." 1972.
New Federal Theatre.

"In the Deepest Part of Sleep."

"Love Song for Robert Lee." 1968.
One-act play.

"The Perfect Part, or The Village: A Party (a play about friends)." 1969.

"The Sunflowers." 1969.
A 1969 series of plays: "Ain't Nobody Sarah But Me," "Cain,"
"Indian Givers," "JJ's Game," "The Layout," and "The Sunflower
Majorette."

"An Untitled Play." 1970.
Afro-American Arts Theatre, Philadelphia.

FURMAN, ROGER

Published Plays

"To Kill a Devil." In Childress BLS, pp. 11-18 [excerpt].
Scene from a domestic drama of black life. First performed April
1970, Columbia University School of the Arts, New York City.

Unpublished Plays

"Fool's Paradise." 1952.
One-act play.

"The Gimmick." April 1970.
  Columbia University School of the Arts.

"The Long Black Block." 1972.
  New York, Heritage Theater.

"The Quiet Laughter." 1952.
  One-act play.

"Three Shades of Harlem." 1964.
  With Doris Brunson.

GAINES, J.E. [SONNY JIM]

Published Plays

"What If It Had Turned Up Heads." In Bullins NLTP, pp. 71-116.
  Two-act drama on fate playing heads and tails with worn and beaten human beings who ultimately manage to survive. First performed American Place Theatre, New York City, March 1972.

GARRETT, JIMMY

Published Plays

"And We Own the Night; A Play of Blackness." DRAMA REVIEW, 12 (Summer 1968), 62-69. Also in Jones BF, pp. 527-40.
  A dying black revolutionary ends by killing his mother, who persisted in viewing life through the eyes of the whites. First performed 1967 by Spirit House Movers and Players, Newark, N.J.

GEARY, BRUCE C.

Published Plays

"Cadillac Alley." In WHO TOOK THE WEIGHT? BLACK VOICES FROM NORFOLK PRISON. Boston: Little, Brown, 1972, pp. 158-74.
  One-act plays dealing with drug addiction, prostitution, and the various social manipulations that confront ghetto blacks.

GORDON, CHARLES F. [OYAMO] (1943-)

Published Plays

"The Breakout." In King BDA, pp. 407-26.

Social and political one-act play about the occupation of a site by black militants. Raises the issue of white participation and the place of well-meaning but brainwashed blacks in the nationalist struggle.

"His First Step." In Bullins NLTP, pp. 133-60.

Two-act satirical play dealing with the contradictions of life as felt by young blacks groping towards liberation. First performed New York Public Theatre, June 1972. Written 1969.

"Out of Site." BLACK THEATRE, No. 4 (1969), pp. 28-31.

One-act satire on the dictatorial practices of nationalists: a black is beaten "Out of site" by organizers of the black nation.

"The Thieves." BLACK DIALOGUE, 4 (Summer 1970), 22-25.

A morality play in one act showing the contradictions in black capitalism.

Unpublished Plays

"The Advantage of Dope." 1971.

Two-act play; also a film script.

"The Barbarians." 1972.

Two-act play; revolutionary ritual.

"The Breakout." 1972.

One-act play. Performed June 1972.

"Called Up Fear." 1972.

Performed July 1974.

"Chumpanzee" or "Chumpanzees." 1973.

Performed July 1973; street ritual.

"Chump Changes." 1971.

"Crazy Niggers." 1971.
Three-act play performed May 1975.

"Fuck Money." 1969.

"The Juice Problem, an Erotic Love Chartune." 1974.
Three-act play, July 1974.

"Kindest of the Finest." 1973.
One-act play.

"Last Party." 1969.
Street ritual.

"The Lovers." 1970.
Street ritual. Performed Black Magic Circus.

"The Negroes." 1969.
Street ritual.

"Nine as One." 1972.
Three-act play-film.

"The Ravishing Moose." 1972.

"The Revelation." 1970.
Ritual.

"Screamers." 1973.
Three-act play.

"A Star Is Born Again." 1975.
Children's play adapted from Gordon's own story "The Star That Could Not Play."

"The Store." 1969.

"The Surveyors." 1969.

"Unemployment." 1969.

"Upcrusted." 1969.

"When Our Spirit Awakes, When Black Theatre Opens." 1969.
Four-act play.

"Willie Bignigga." 1969.
One-act street ritual. Performed 1970.

GORDONE, CHARLES (1925-   )

Published Plays

NO PLACE TO BE SOMEBODY: A BLACK BLACK COMEDY IN THREE ACTS.
Indianapolis: Bobbs-Merrill, 1969. 115 p. New York: Samuel French, 1969.
112 p. Also in Oliver CBD, pp. 381-451.

A play which begins in humor and ends in melodrama, on the theme
of race identity as featured by some black inhabitants of New York.
First performed May 2, 1969, New York Shakespeare Festival Public Theatre.

Unpublished Plays

"Worl's Champeen/Lip Dansuh An' Wahtah Mellon Jooglah." 1969.

Biography and Criticism

Walcott, Ronald. "Ellison, Gordone and Tolson, Some Notes on the Blues,
Style and Space." BLACK WORLD, 22 (Dec. 1972), 4-29.

GOSS, CLAY (1946-   )

Published Plays

"Andrew." In HOMECOOKIN' (see under Collected Plays, below), pp. 49-64.

One-act morality drama about three former gang members and the
tragic circumstances of the death of one of them. First performed
New York Shakespeare Festival Public Theater, 1972.

"Homecookin'." In HOMECOOKIN' (see under Collected Plays, below), pp. 15-
48.

One-act play about the meeting of two childhood friends, one a
Marine back from Vietnam and the other an aspiring writer.

"Mars: Monument to the Last Black Eunuch (title from a sculpture by Ed Love)."

In Harrison KD, pp. 241-47. Also in HOMECOOKIN' (see under Collected Plays, below), pp. 81-88.

> Two-act drama about unfulfilled desires and unrealized fantasies, creativity, and the regeneration of spirit. A middle-aged black dreams of going to Mars "where the real life is." First performed Howard University, January 1972.

"On Being Hit." In HOMECOOKIN' (see under Collected Plays, below), pp. 65-80. Also in Bullins NLTP, pp. 117-32.

> A one-act drama about a former boxing champion who ends up as a janitor, his career being a metaphor for the life struggle of a soulful people.

"Our Sides." In HOMECOOKIN' (see under Collected Plays, below), pp. 1-14.

> One-act play of black life and consciousness.

Unpublished Plays

"Billy McGhee." 1974.

> One-act domestic comedy. Performed September 1974.

"Hip Rumpelstiltzkin."

> One-act soul version of fairy tale.

"Keys to the Kingdom."

> Three-act domestic drama.

"Ornette." 1972.

> Three-act drama. Performed 1972, Howard University.

Collected Plays

HOMECOOKIN'. Washington, D.C.: Howard Univ. Press, 1974. 89 p.

GRAHAM, ARTHUR J.

Published Plays

THE LAST SHINE. San Diego, Calif.: Black Book Productions, 1969. 39 p.

> One-act drama about an old shoe-shine "boy" discovering the implications of his racial status.

THE NATIONALS: A BLACK HAPPENING IN THREE ACTS. San Diego, Calif.: Black Book Productions, 1968. 87 p.

> Three-act play on the revolutionary coming of age of derelicts, winos, and prostitutes who conquer their low self-esteem through blackness.

GREAVES, DONALD (1943-)

Published Plays

"The Marriage: A Play in Two Acts." In King BDA, pp. 253-300.

> A play of black experience focussing on dramatic family relationships between sexes and generations.

Unpublished Plays

"Kitsu Mensin." 1972.

> Verse drama.

GREENWOOD, FRANK

Published Plays

"Cry in the Night." LIBERATOR, 3 (Sept. 1963), 18-19.

> Short play about black militant awareness.

Unpublished Plays

"Burn, Baby, Burn." 1966.

GUNN, BILL [WILLIAM HARRISON GUNN] (1943-)

Published Plays

BLACK PICTURE SHOW. Berkeley, Calif.: Reed, Cannon & Johnson Communications Co., 1975. 119 p.

"Johnnas." DRAMA REVIEW, 12 (Summer 1968), 126-38.

> A short drama on the fate of black entertainers in white society. First performed 1966, Brooklyn Theatre Center.

Unpublished Plays

"Marcus in the High Grass." 1960.

> Performed 1960, Greenwich Mews Theatre.

HALSEY, WILLIAM

Published Plays

"Judgement." BLACK DIALOGUE, 4 (Spring 1969), 40-43.

> One-act play about a black artist who leads the revolution in killing the court by whom he is being tried.

HANSBERRY, LORRAINE (1930-65)

Published Plays

"Les Blancs." In LES BLANCS (see under Collected Plays, below), pp. 47-173.

> Two-act psychological and social drama of a European-educated African who returns home to join the struggle against Colonialism. Written 1961-66; first performed November 15, 1970, at the Long Acre Theatre, New York City. Final text adaptation reworked by Robert Nemiroff.

"The Drinking Gourd." In LES BLANCS (see under Collected Plays, below), pp. 217-311. Also in Hatch BTU, pp. 714-36.

> A three-act ninety-minute television drama on slavery and emancipation seen through the story of a black woman. Commissioned by NBC-TV in 1961.

A RAISIN IN THE SUN. New York: Random House, 1959. 146 p. Acting version, New York: Samuel French, 1959. 113 p. New York: New American Library, 1961. 126 p. Also in A RAISIN IN THE SUN AND THE SIGN IN SIDNEY BRUSTEIN'S WINDOW. New York: Signet, 1966, pp. 11-130; and in Oliver CBD, pp. 27-120.

> Three-act domestic drama on the problems of a family struggling for a better life and racial self-assertion; centers on the relationship between the black mother and her daughter and son, who go through an identity crisis. First performed March 11, 1959, at the Ethel Barrymore Theatre, New York City; winner of the New York Drama Circle Critics award for 1958-59. Later adapted as a musical by Robert Nemiroff and Charlotte Zaltberg.

THE SIGN IN SIDNEY BRUSTEIN'S WINDOW. New York: Random House, 1965. Acting version, New York: Samuel French, 1965. Also in A RAISIN IN THE SUN AND THE SIGN IN SIDNEY BRUSTEIN'S WINDOW. New York: Signet, 1966, pp. 190-318; and in THREE NEGRO PLAYS. Hammondsworth, England: Penguin, 1969, pp. 99-207.

> A three-act drama on the intellectual climate and mood of America in the early 1960s, centering on the problems of white Greenwich Village liberals. First performed October 15, 1964, at the Long Acre Theatre, New York City. The New American Library edition

includes several dozen lines from French actress Simone Signoret's version of Act III, scene 1.

"What Use Are Flowers?" In WORKS IN PROGRESS, No. 5. New York: Literary Guild, Doubleday, 1972, pp. 11-62. Also in LES BLANCS (see under Collected Plays below), pp. 323-69.

"A Fable in One Act." In a devastated world, an old hermit tries to impart to children the knowledge of the remnants of a civilization which he had once renounced. First written 1961-62 as a television fantasy, titled "Who Knows Where?" Final version, 1967.

Collected Plays

LES BLANCS: THE COLLECTED LAST PLAYS OF LORRAINE HANSBERRY. Ed. Robert Nemiroff. New York: Random House, 1972. 369 p.

Includes "Les Blancs," "The Drinking Gourd," and "What Use Are Flowers?" Also contains critical background by Robert Nemiroff and introduction by Julius Lester.

Biography and Criticism

Abramson, NP, pp. 239-54.

Baldwin, James. "Sweet Lorraine." ESQUIRE, 72 (Nov. 1969), 139-40.

Cruse, Harold. THE CRISIS OF THE NEGRO INTELLECTUAL. New York: Morrow, 1967, pp. 267-84.

Davis, Ossie. "The Significance of Lorraine Hansberry." FREEDOMWAYS, 5 (1965), 397-402.

Farrison, W. Edward. "Lorraine Hansberry's Last Dramas." CLA JOURNAL, 16 (Dec. 1972), 188-97.

France, Arthur. "A Raisin Revisited." FREEDOMWAYS, 5 (1965), 403-10.

Isaacs, Harold. THE NEW WORLD OF NEGRO AMERICANS. New York: Viking, 1964, pp. 277-87.

Killens, John O. "Broadway in Black and White." AFRICAN FORUM, 1 (Winter 1966), 66-76.

Lewis, Theophilus. "Social Protest in A RAISIN IN THE SUN." CATHOLIC WORLD, 190 (Oct. 1959), 31-35.

Miller, Jordan Y. "Lorraine Hansberry." In Bigsby BAW2, pp. 157-70;

Mitchell BD, pp. 180-82.

Nemiroff, Robert. "The 101 'Final' Performances of SIDNEY BRUSTEIN." In A RAISIN IN THE SUN AND THE SIGN IN SIDNEY BRUSTEIN'S WINDOW, by Lorraine Hansberry. New York: Signet, 1966, pp. 138-85.

_____. TO BE YOUNG, GIFTED AND BLACK: LORRAINE HANSBERRY IN HER OWN WORDS. Englewood Cliffs, N.J.: Prentice-Hall, 1969. 266 p. New York: New American Library, 1970. 271 p.

> The playscript of this stage adaptation, first performed January 2, 1969, at the Cherry Lane Theatre, New York City, was published by Samuel French, 1971.

Ness, Dabid B. "Black Playwright Looks at White America." FREEDOMWAYS, 11 (1971), 359-66.

_____. "Lorraine Hansberry's LES BLANCS: The Victory of the Man Who Must." FREEDOMWAYS, 13 (1974), 294-306.

Weales, Gerald. "Thoughts on 'A Raisin in the Sun.'" COMMENTARY, 28 (1959), 527-30.

HARRIS, CLARENCE

Published Plays

"The Trip." In BLACK VOICES FROM PRISON. Ed. Etheridge Knight. New York: Pathfinder Press, 1970, pp. 77-83.

> A natural black man overcomes an Uncle Tomming landlady and the policeman she called.

HARRIS, NEIL (1936-)

Published Plays

"Cop and Blows." SCRIPTS, 1 (May 1972), 72-80.

> White and black detectives try to blackmail hustlers who speak of starting an investment company. A play on "how to stay alert in these mean streets." First performed Public Theatre Annex, New York City, February 1972.

Unpublished Plays

"Players Inn." 1972.

> New York Public Theatre Annex.

"The Portrait." 1971(?).

New Lafayette Workshop, New York City.

HARRIS, TOM

Published Plays

"Always with Love." In NEW AMERICAN PLAYS, vol. 3. Ed. William M. Hoffman. New York: Hill & Wang, 1969.

Two-act drama about a maid who murders her white employer's family.

Unpublished Plays

"Beverly Hills Olympics." 1964.

"City beneath the Skin." 1961.

"Cleaning Day." 1969.
One-act play.

"Daddy Hugs and Kisses." 1963.
One-act play.

"The Dark Years." 1958.
One-act play.

"Death of Daddy Hugs and Kisses." 1963.

"Divorce Negro Style." 1968.

"Fall of an Iron Horse." 1959.

"The Golden Spear." 1969.
One-act play.

"Moving Day." 1969.
One-act play.

"The Number One Family." 1958.
One-act play.

"Pray for Daniel Adams."   1958.

   One-act play.

"The Relic."   1967.

"Shopping Day."   1969.

   One-act play.

"Who Killed Sweetie."   1967.

"Woman in the House."   1958.

   One-act play.

HARRISON, PAUL CARTER (1936-)

Published Plays

AIN'T SUPPOSED TO DIE A NATURAL DEATH.   New York: Bantam Books, 1973.   156 p.

   First performed 1971, Sacramento State College.   Musical adaptation from Melvin Van Peebles' poetry.

"The Experimental Leader."   PODIUM MAGAZINE (Amsterdam), 1965.

   One-act expressionistic drama on racial relations in which a powerless black leader confronts an integrationist couple.

"Folly 4 Two."   PODIUM MAGAZINE (Amsterdam), 1967.

   One-act drama on the encounter between an African and a colonial Englishman, resulting in the former's liberation through a game of folly.

"The Great Mac Daddy."   In Harrison KD, pp. 259-352.

   "A ritualized African/American event inspired by the African storytelling technique," in primal and terminal rhythms and seven beats; the odyssey of a lazy and rich young black and his gradual achievement of meaningful aims.   First performed May 12, 1972.

"Pavane for a Deadpan Minstrel."   In PODIUM MAGAZINE (Amsterdam), 1965.

   One-act play; a black in white face and a white in black face set out to seduce a white girl, in an expressionistic confrontation.

378

"Tabernacle." In Couch NBP, pp. 93-180.

> A ritual dealing with the forces that kill two Harlem youngsters; "a Black Experience in Total Theatre." First performed March 1969, by Howard University Players at Wesleyan University Black Arts Festival.

Unpublished Plays

"Brer Soul." 1970.

"Pawns." 1966.

> One-act play.

"The Pestclerks." 1961.

> One-act play.

"Top Hat." 1965.

> A dramatic tone-poem, first performed 1965 at Buffalo University Summer Theater; revised for production by Negro Ensemble Company, 1972.

> For work edited by Harrison, see Drama, part 1, section 5a, above.

Biography and Criticism

Harrison, Paul C. THE DRAMA OF NOMMO. See Drama, part 1, section 5a, above.

HIMES, CHESTER (1909-)

Published Plays

"Baby Sister." In BLACK ON BLACK. New York: Doubleday, 1973, pp. 11-121.

> Screenplay set in Harlem.

HUNTLEY, ELIZABETH MADDOX

Published Plays

"Legion, the Demoniac." In AMERICAN LITERATURE BY NEGRO AUTHORS. Ed. Herman Dreer. New York: Macmillan, 1950, pp. 306-9.

WHAT YE SOW. New York: Comet Press, 1955. 97 p.

IMAN, YUSEF

Published Plays

PRAISE THE LORD, BUT PASS THE AMMUNITION. Newark, N.J.: Jihad
Productions, 1967. 12 p.

> One-act confrontation between self-defense and nonviolent strate-
> gies. First performed Spirit House, Newark, 1967.

JACKMON, MARVIN E. (1944-) [Marvin X, or Nazzam Al Fitnah, or Nazzam Al Sudan, or Bismillah-r-rahim, or El Muhajir]

Published Plays

"The Black Bird (Al Tair Aswad); A One-Act Play." In Bullins NP, pp. 109-
18.

> A play for children based on "The Black Bird, a Parable," by the
> same author.

"Flowers for the Trashman." In BLACK DIALOGUE, 1 (Winter 1966), 20-31.
Also in Jones BF, pp. 541-58.

> A black college student, his hoodlum friend, and a young black
> parolee talk in jail about the Man, and about their relationship
> to their fathers. One-act drama. Other titles: "Flowers for the
> Whiteman" and "Take Care of Business." First performed Spring
> 1966, by Blackarts/West, San Francisco.

"The Resurrection of the Dead." BLACK THEATRE, No. 3 (1969), pp. 26-27.

> Directions for a black ritual in four movements, designed to raise
> black consciousness. Performed New Lafayette Theatre, 1969.

Unpublished Plays

"A Black Ritual." 1970.

"Come Next Summer."

> First performed in 1969 by Blackarts/West, San Francisco.

> For Jackmon's poetry, see MARVIN X under Poetry, part 2: Indi-
> vidual Authors, 1946-75.

JACKSON, C. BERNARD

Published Plays

"Fly Blackbird." In Reardon BTDA, pp. 135-232. Also in Hatch BTU, pp. 671-94.

A musical play on the sit-in movement of the late 1960s. First performed as a one-act play at Shoebox Theatre, Los Angeles, Fall 1960; full-length script performed February 10, 1961, at Metro Theatre, Los Angeles; a greatly revised version performed in New York City won an Obie award for 1962. Written in collaboration with James V. Hatch.

Unpublished Plays

"Blood of the Lamb." 1964.

Oratorio on the dilemma of faith.

"The Departure." 1965.

Full-length musical about man's struggle for survival.

JACKSON, ELAINE

Published Plays

"Toe Jam." In King BDA, pp. 641-71.

Two acts; a young girl who wants to write for the theatre learns that she must begin to deal, "barefoot," with everyday reality.

JACKSON, JOSEPHINE. See "The Believers" under WALKER, JOSEPH, below.

JOHNSON, CHRISTINE C.

Published Plays

ZWADI YA AFRIKA KWA DUNWA (AFRICA'S GIFT TO THE WORLD). A HISTORICAL PLAY IN TWO PARTS FOR YOUNG PEOPLE AND CHILDREN. Chicago: Free Black Press, [196-?]. 21 p.

The outgrowth of a classroom study unit emphasizing Africa's contributions to civilization.

JONES, [EVERETT] LEROI [IMAMU AMIRI BARAKA] (1934-)

Published Plays

"Arm Yrself or Harm Yrself." Newark, N.J.: Jihad Productions, 1967. 11 p. Mimeographed.

A black nationalist revolutionary fable; the new dramatist must achieve new images in order not to be self-destructive. First performed 1967 at Spirit House, Newark.

"The Baptism." In THE BAPTISM AND THE TOILET. New York: Grove Press, 1967, pp. 8-32.

> One-act play dramatizing the dichotomy of attitudes towards the black church, indicting Christianity as a debaser of the black man's psyche and hinting of a baptism that would end all humiliations. Copyrighted 1966. First performed March 23, 1964, at the Writer's Stage Theatre, New York City.

"Ba-Ra-Ka." In SPONTANEOUS COMBUSTION. Ed. Rochelle Owens. New York: Winter House, 1972, p. 175.

> One-act ritual-poem-play celebrating the black race.

"A Black Mass." LIBERATOR, 6 (June 1966), 14-17. Also in FOUR BLACK REVOLUTIONARY PLAYS (see under Collected Plays, below), pp. 17-39.

> A mythology according to the Yacub myth on the accidental creation of the White Beast by a black magician. Written 1965. First performed May 1966 at Proctor's Theatre, Newark.

"Black Power Chant." BLACK THEATRE, No. 4 (1970), p. 35.

> A rhapsodic song urging mumbling and shuffling Negroes to scream and strike out against their oppressors. Written and first performed 1968 at Spirit House, Newark.

"Bloodrites. A Ritual." In King BDA, pp. 25-32.

> Chants, dances, and pantomime on the death struggle against the white devils, and on the coming together of a new race.

"Chant." BLACK THEATRE, No. 5 (1971), pp. 16-17.

> Directions and words for a chant and ritual on blackness. Written 1968.

"The Coronation of the Black Queen." BLACK SCHOLAR, 1 (June 1970), 46-48.

> A ritual modeled after African ceremonies.

"The Death of Malcolm X." In Bullins NPBT, pp. 21-39.

> A montage exposing the white conspiracy against black militancy in a strongly organized, highly technological, yet thoroughly grotesque society. Written 1965(?). First performed 1965.

"Dutchman." In DUTCHMAN AND THE SLAVE. New York: William Morrow, 1964. Paper ed. New York: Apollo, 1968, pp. 1-38. Also in Oliver CBD, pp. 207-32.

The ritual of seduction and destruction between White America (a sexy bitch) and the Black Man (a young middle-class intellectual) in a symbolical underground train. First performed March 24, 1964, at Cherry Lane Theatre, New York City.

"The Eighth Ditch (Is Drama)." In THE SYSTEM OF DANTE'S HELL. New York: Grove, 1965, pp. 79-91.

A modern parallel to the False Comforters theme in Dante's IN-FERNO. First performed 1961 at the Off-Bowery Theatre, New York City.

"Experimental Death Unit No. 1." In FOUR BLACK REVOLUTIONARY PLAYS (see under Collected Plays, below), pp. 1-15.

Two white men seek sexual contact with a black woman; young black revolutionaries bring their contest to an abrupt end: murder alone can purify the race from its corrupted members who prostitute themselves to the white world. Written 1964. First performed March 1, 1965, at St. Mark's Playhouse, New York City.

"Great Goodness of Life: A Coon Show." In BEST SHORT PLAYS OF THE WORLD THEATRE. Ed. Stanley Richards. New York: Grove Press, 1968. Also in FOUR BLACK REVOLUTIONARY PLAYS (see under Collected Plays, below), pp. 41-63; in BQ, pp. 139-58; and in Harrison KD, pp. 155-69.

A middle-aged black postal employee held captive to an unseen (white) voice accepts the blood rite that will set him free by killing his own son, sentenced for murder. Written 1966; first performed November 1967 at Spirit House, Newark.

"Home on the Range. (A Play to be Performed with the Music of Albert Ayler Improvised in the Background)." DRAMA REVIEW, 12 (Summer 1968), 10-11.

Expressionistic one-act play about a black criminal trespassing in the home of an American family who speak an unintelligible language. Read 1967 at Black Community Projects, New York City; first performed early 1968 at Spirit House, Newark.

JELLO. Chicago: Third World Press, 1970. 38 p.

A farce and parody of a famous radio and television show making broad use of theatrical conventions, folklore, and mythology in order to suggest new racial implications. Written 1965; first performed 1965 by Black Arts Repertory Theatre, New York City.

"Junkies Are Full of (SHHH . . .) ." In King BDA, pp. 11-24.

One-act didactic play showing what drugs are really for, political-ly, through the conflict among a dope-pusher, junkies, and a black militant. First performed as "Junkie" at Spirit House, Newark, 1968(?).

"Madheart: A Morality Play." In Jones BF, pp. 574-88. Also in FOUR BLACK REVOLUTIONARY PLAYS (see under Collected Plays, below), pp. 65-87.

> A black couple save a soul sister and a mother from perversion and symbolical death, demonstrating the perverted attraction of whiteness. Written 1966; first performed May 1967 at San Francisco State College.

"Police." DRAMA REVIEW, 12 (Summer 1968), 11-16.

> One-act play on the predicament of a black policeman equally hated by his race brothers and his white colleagues who will eat his body when he commits suicide.

"The Slave. A Fable in a Prologue and Two Acts." In DUTCHMAN AND THE SLAVE. New York: William Morrow, 1964, pp. 30-88. Also in Hatch BTU, pp. 813-25.

> During a racial war, a radical black leader crosses the battle line to visit his white ex-wife and her liberal husband; verbal and physical violence echo the violence of the revolution raging outside. First performed December 16, 1964, at St. Mark's Playhouse, New York City.

"Slave Ship: A Historical Pageant." NEGRO DIGEST, 16 (Apr. 1967), 62-74. Published separately as "Slave Ship: An Historical Pageant." Newark, N.J.: Jihad, 1967. 13 p. Mimeographed.

"The Toilet." KULCHUR, No. 9 (1964). Also in THE BAPTISM AND THE TOILET. New York: Grove Press, 1967, pp. 33-62; and in Turner BDA, pp. 541-55.

> One-act play dealing with race conflict, frustrations, and homosexual love among teenagers: a black boy is forced by his gang to beat up his white friend as an expiation for his betrayal of their image of integrity and virility. Copyrighted 1963. First performed December 16, 1964, at St. Mark's Playhouse City.

Unpublished Plays

"Board of Education." 1968.

> One-act play; performed at Spirit House, Newark.

"A Good Girl is Hard to Find." 1958.

"Insurrection."   1968.

> One-act play; performed at Spirit House, Newark.

"The Kid Poeta Tragical."   1969.

"A Recent Killing."   1964.

"Revolt of the Moonflowers."

"The Sidney Poet Heroical, of If in Danger of Suit."   1975.

> Performed May 1975 by New Federal Theatre.

Collected Plays

FOUR BLACK REVOLUTIONARY PLAYS.   Indianapolis: Bobbs-Merrill, 1969.
89 p.

> Includes: "Why No J-E-L-L-O?" (an afterword), "Experimental
> Death Unit No. 1," "A Black Mass," "Great Goodness of Life,"
> and "Madheart."

Biography and Criticism

See also the entries on Jones under Poetry, part 2:   Individual Authors, 1946-75.

Adams, George R.   "'My Christ' in DUTCHMAN."   CLA JOURNAL, 15 (1971), 54-58.

Brady, Owen E.   "Baraka's Experimental Death Unit No. 1."   NEGRO AMERICAN LITERATURE FORUM, 9 (1975), 59-61.

Brecht, Stephen.   "Slaveship."   DRAMA REVIEW, 14 (1970), 212-19.

Brown, Cecil M.   "Apotheosis of a Prodigal Son."   KENYON REVIEW, 30 (1968), 654-61, 668.

> On DUTCHMAN.

_____.   "Black Literature and LeRoi Jones."   BLACK WORLD, 19 (June 1970), 24-31.

> On the form and style of DUTCHMAN and THE SLAVE.

Burford, W.S. "From Existentialism to Apostle of Black Nationalism." PLAY-ERS, 47 (Dec. 1972), 60-64.

Clurman, Harold. "LeRoi Jones; Naughton's Alfie." NATION, 200 (1965), 16-17.

_____. "Three at Cherry Lane." NATION, 198 (1964), 383-84.
On DUTCHMAN.

Costello, Donald B. "LeRoi Jones: Black Man as a Victim." COMMON-WEAL, 3 (1968), 436-40.

Dace, Leticia. LeROI JONES (IMAMU AMIRI BARAKA): A CHECKLIST OF WORKS BY AND ABOUT HIM. London: Nether Press, 1971. 196 p.

Dennison, G. "The Demagogy of LeRoi Jones." COMMENTARY, 34 (Feb. 1965), 67-76.
On THE TOILET and THE SLAVE.

Ferguson, John. "Dutchman and THE SLAVE." MODERN DRAMA, 13 (1971), 398-406.

Hudson, Theodore H. FROM LeROI JONES TO AMIRI BARAKA: THE LITER-ARY WORKS. Durham, N.C.: Duke Univ. Press, 1973. 222 p.
A study dealing at some length with Jones as a dramatist.

Hughes, Langston. "That Boy LeRoi." CHICAGO DEFENDER, 11 Jan. 1965. Also in Patterson AANT, pp. 1205-6.

Jackson, Kathryn. "LeRoi Jones and the New Black Writers of the Sixties." FREEDOMWAYS, 9 (1969), 222-47.

Jeffers, Lance. "Bullins, Baraka and Elder: The Dawn of Grandeur in Black Drama." CLA JOURNAL, 16 (1972), 32-48.

Jones, LeRoi. "Black Art (Drama) Is the Same as Black Life." EBONY, 26 (Feb. 1971), 74-76, 78, 80, 82.
Of special interest for Baraka's development as a playwright.

_____. "LeRoi Jones Talks with Marvin X and Faruk." BLACK THEATRE, No. 2 (1969), pp. 14-18.

_____. RAISE RACE RAYS RAZE: ESSAYS SINCE 1965. New York: Random House, 1971. New York: Vintage Books, 1972. 169 p.

Of special interest for Baraka's development as a playwright.

Kempton, Murray. "Newark: Keeping Up with LeRoi Jones." NEW YORK REVIEW OF BOOKS, 2 July 1970, pp. 21-23.

Lederer, Richard. "The Language of LeRoi Jones' THE SLAVE." STUDIES IN BLACK LITERATURE, 4 (Spring 1973), 14-16.

Lee, Eugene. "SLAVESHIP: Notes and Design." YALE/THEATRE, 3 (Fall, 1970), 32-36.

Lewis, Ida. "Conversation with LeRoi Jones." ESSENCE, 1 (Sept. 1970), 20-25.

Lindenberg, Daniel. "Un theatre militant." TEMPS MODERNES, 21 (1966), 1918-20.

Llorens, David. "Ameer (LeRoi Jones) Baraka." EBONY, 24 (Aug. 1969), 75-78, 80-83.

Valuable account of Baraka's political and dramatic activities in Newark.

Marvin X. "An Interview with LeRoi Jones." BLACK THEATRE, No. 1 (1968), pp. 16-23.

Miller, Jeanne-Marie A. "The Plays of LeRoi Jones." CLA JOURNAL, 14 (1971), 331-39.

Mitchell BD, pp. 199-205, 207.

Mootry, Maria K. "Themes and Symbols in Two of LeRoi Jones' Plays." NEGRO DIGEST, 18 (Apr. 1969), 42-47.

On THE TOILET and THE BAPTISM.

Moser, Norman. "A Revolutionary Art: LeRoi Jones, Ed Bullins and the Black Revolution." DECEMBER, 12 (1970), 180-90.

Neal, Lawrence. "The Black Arts Movement." DRAMA REVIEW, 8 (Summer 1968), 32-37.

On DUTCHMAN, THE SLAVE, and SLAVE SHIP.

_____. "Development of LeRoi Jones." LIBERATOR, 6 (Jan. 1966), 4-5; (Feb. 1966), 18-19.

_____. "THE SLAVE and THE TOILET." LIBERATOR, 5 (Feb. 1965), 22.

Nelson, Hugh. "LeRoi Jones's DUTCHMAN: A Brief Ride on a Doomed Ship." EDUCATIONAL THEATRE JOURNAL, 20 (Feb. 1968), 53-59.

Peary, Charles D. "Myth, Manhood and Magic in LeRoi Jones' MADHEART." STUDIES IN BLACK LITERATURE, 1 (Summer 1970), 12-20.

Phillips, Louis. "LeRoi Jones and Contemporary Black Drama." In Bigsby BAW2, pp. 203-17.

Reck, Tom S. "Archetypes in LeRoi Jones' DUTCHMAN." STUDIES IN BLACK LITERATURE, 1 (Spring 1970), 66-68.

Reed, Daphne S. "Jones High Priest of BART Movement." EDUCATIONAL THEATRE JOURNAL, 22 (Mar. 1970), 53-59.

Ricard, Alain. THEATRE ET NATIONALISME: WOLE SOYINKA ET LEROI JONES. Paris: Presence Africaine, 1972. 234 p.

Rice, Julian. "LeRoi Jones' DUTCHMAN: A Reading." CONTEMPORARY LITERATURE, 12 (1971), 42-59.

Schneck, Stephen. "LeRoi Jones, or Poetics and Policemen, or Trying Heart, Bleeding Heart." RAMPARTS, 6 (28 June 1968), 14-19. Also in FIVE BLACK WRITERS. Ed. Donald Gibson. New York: New York Univ. Press, 1970, 193-205.

Toure, Askia Muhammad, Marvin X, and Faruk. "An Interview with Amiri Baraka." JOURNAL OF BLACK POETRY, 1 (Fall 1968), 2-14. Also in BLACK THEATRE, No. 2 (1968), pp. 14-18.

Weales, Gerald. "The Day LeRoi Jones Spoke. . . ." NEW YORK TIMES MAGAZINE, 4 May 1968, p. 38.

_____. "Islam and Black Art: An Interview with LeRoi Jones." NEGRO DIGEST, 18 (Sept. 1969), 4-10, 77-80.

KENNEDY, ADRIENNE (1931-)

Published Plays

"A Beast Story." In Harrison KD, pp. 192-201.

> This one-act surrealist tragedy takes place in a black family in which the daughter kills her lover. Written 1966. Performed 1969 by Public Theatre, New York City, with "The Owl Answers."

FUNNYHOUSE OF A NEGRO. New York: Samuel French, 1969. 24 p. Also in Patterson AANT, pp. 281-90; in Brasmer BD, pp. 247-72; in THE BEST SHORT PLAYS OF 1970. Ed. Richard Stanley. Philadelphia: Chilton Books, 1970; and in Oliver CBD, pp. 187-206.

> Expressionistic drama on the hallucinatory world of a girl of mixed ancestry who plays out in a fantasy of racial dreams her anguish of discovering her selfhood. First performed January 18, 1964, by the Circle in the Square Workshop at the Cricket Theatre, New York City; winner of an Obie award.

"A Lesson in Dead Language." In COLLISION COURSE. Ed. Edward Parone. New York: Random House, 1968; New York: Vintage Books, 1969, pp. 35-40.

> A teacher and her seven girl students repeat a religious masochistic lesson in a surrealistic setting. Written 1964. Performed 1967.

"The Owl Answers." In NEW AMERICAN PLAYS. Ed. William M. Hoffman. New York: Hill & Wang, 1968. Also in Harrison KD, pp. 170-87; and in Hatch BTU, pp. 757-64.

> A young girl is torn between white and black, past and present, body and soul. Her identity quest among both real and imaginary places and characters is answered only by the hooting of the owl. Written 1963. Performed 1969 by Public Theatre, New York City, with "A Beast Story." Under general title "Cities in Bezique."

"A Rat's Mass." In Couch NBP, pp. 83-92.

> Short fable: a rat family keep their holy rituals in spite of Nazi oppression, but they are doomed to extinction. Copyrighted 1967.

"Sun: A Poem for Malcolm X Inspired by His Murder." SCRIPTS, 1 (Nov. 1971), 51-56.

> A symbolic scene in which moon and sun, red and black, fight for domination among images of fragmentation, disembodiment, and martyrdom.

Unpublished Plays

"Evening with Dead Essex." 1973.

"In His Own Write." 1968.

> An adaptation of the writings of John Lennon; London, National Theatre, 1968.

KILLENS, JOHN O. See "Ballad of the Winter Soldiers," under MITCHELL, LOFTEN, below.

KIMBALL, KATHLEEN

Published Plays

"Meat Rack." SCRIPTS, 1 (May 1972), 5-28.

> In this humorous fantasy, an ex-prostitute travels in time and space, becoming a revolutionary leader, a plantation slave, and her former pimp's angel.

LANG, JAMES A.

Published Plays

"The Plague (Please Don't Let the Joneses Get You Down)." In WHO TOOK THE WEIGHT? BLACK VOICES FROM NORFOLK PRISON. Boston: Little, Brown, 1972, pp. 175-204.

> The inner conflict of a black man split between his desire to get together with his family and his hanging on to his life with the cats on the block.

LINCOLN, ABBEY

Published Plays

"A Streak o' Lean." In Childress BIIS, pp. 49-56 [excerpt].

> A scene about the power of money, which a poor black man keeps when he finds it, in spite of conventional morality. Copyrighted 1967.

MACBETH, ROBERT

Published Plays

"A Black Ritual." BLACK THEATRE, No. 2 (1969), pp. 8-9. Also in DRAMA REVIEW, 13 (Summer 1969), 129-30.

> Ritual for the raising of black consciousness and the conquest of

the white monster. Performed 1968, New Lafayette Theatre Work-shop, New York City.

"The Box Office." BLACK THEATRE, No. 3 (1969), pp. 18-19.

A street scene about the people's curiosity and reactions when a theatre opens in their neighborhood. Probably written in collabo-ration with Ed Bullins.

Biography and Criticism

Marvin X. "The Black Ritual Theatre, an Interview with Robert Macbeth." BLACK THEATRE, No. 3 (1969), pp. 20-24.

McBROWN, GERTRUDE PARTHENIA

Published Plays

"Birthday Surprise." NEGRO HISTORY BULLETIN, 16 (Feb. 1953), 16.

Sketch on the career of Paul Laurence Dunbar.

"Bought with Cookies." NEGRO HISTORY BULLETIN, 12 (Apr. 1949).

A children's play about Frederick Douglass.

McCRAY, NETTIE [SALIMU]

Published Plays

"Growin' into Blackness." BLACK THEATRE, No. 2 (1969), pp. 20-22. Also in Bullins NPBT, pp. 195-200.

A black girl prefers to leave home rather than get rid of her Afro and obey her mother.

MACKEY, WILLIAM WELLINGTON

Published Plays

BEHOLD: COMETH THE VANDERKELLANS! Denver: Azazel Books, 1966. 83 p.

The changes suffered by a black middle-class family which has pro-vided college presidents for generations, when black students in the 1960s envision new racial perspectives. First performed 1965, Denver, Colorado.

"Family Meeting. A Play in One Act." In Couch NBP, pp. 247-85.

One-act surreal psychodrama on the self-destructive tendencies of blacks unable to cope with their racial identity.

"Requiem for Brother X." In King BDA, pp. 325-47.

The members of a black family vent their frustrations while a white girl gives birth to the child conceived by one of their sons. Words are the only weapons left to those who live in the ghetto gutter. Written in 1966. First performed 1968 at the Hull House Theatre, Chicago; titled "A Requiem for Malcolm X" in 1969.

Unpublished Plays

"Billy Noname." 1969.

Two-act musical first performed March 1970, New York City.

"Love Me, Love Me, Daddy--or I Swear I'm Gonna Kill You."

Three-act play.

MADDEN, WILL ANTHONY

Published Plays

"The Killer and the Girl." In TWO AND ONE. Ed. Will Madden. Exposition Press, 1961. 50 p.

A drama based on the poem "Killer" by Paris Flammonde.

MARVIN X. See MARVIN E. JACKMON.

MASON, CLIFFORD (1932-)

Published Plays

"Gabriel: The Story of a Slave Rebellion." In King BDA, pp. 167-227.

A dramatization of Prosser's slave rebellion based upon the antithetic portraits of two different slaveholders, two rebels and two brothers.

Unpublished Plays

"Half-Way Tree Brown." 1972.

"Jimmy X."

"Sister Sadie." 1970.

> Performed by the O'Neill Memorial Foundation, Waterford, Connecticut.

MAUTI

Published Plays

"Cop 'n Blow." In WHO TOOK THE WEIGHT: BLACK VOICES FROM NORFOLK PRISON. Boston: Little, Brown, 1972, pp. 151-57.

> An ironical play about black experience, centering on a slum dweller with employment problems.

MAYFIELD, JULIAN (1928-)

Published Plays

"417." In Childress BIS, pp. 67-76 [excerpt].

> One-act domestic and social drama of Harlem life in the early 1950s.

Unpublished Plays

"The Other Foot." 1952.

> One-act play.

"A World Full of Men." 1962.

> One-act play.

Biography and Criticism

Mitchell BD, pp. 156-57.

MILLER, CLIFFORD L.

Published Plays

WINGS OVER DARK WATERS. New York: Great-Concord Publishers, 1954. 270 p.

> A verse drama on the Afro-American historical experience.

MILNER, RON (1938-)

Published Plays

"(M)ego and the Great Ball of Freedom." BLACK WORLD, 20 (Apr. 1971), 40-45.

> One-act symbolical representation of a two-sided world (death and life, destruction and freedom, insanity and hope) through voices and figures.

"The Monster: a One Act Play." DRAMA REVIEW, 12 (Summer 1968), 94-105. Also in BLACK ARTS. Ed. Ahmed Alhamisi and Harun K. Wangara. Detroit: Black Arts Publications, 1969, pp. 52-70.

> A parody presenting the black dean of a college as a Frankenstein creature manipulated alternately by the white establishment and militant black students. First performed late October 1969 at the Louis Theatre, Chicago.

"The Warning--A Theme for Linda: A One-Act Play in Four Scenes." NEGRO DIGEST, 18 (Apr. 1969), 53-68 [excerpt]. Full text in BQ, pp. 37-114.

> Linda refuses to step into the pattern set by the other women in the family and moves towards self-liberation. First performed April 24, 1969, at the Chelsea Theatre Center, Brooklyn, New York.

WHAT THE WINE-SELLERS BUY: A THREE ACT PLAY. New York: Samuel French, 1974. 96 p.

> Performed May 1972, New Federal Theatre, New York City.

"Who's Got His Own." In King BDA, pp. 89-145.

> A domestic drama about the hostility sparked between the members of a black household in the Detroit ghetto by the return of a wayward son; the true nature of a dead father and his relationships to his family gradually emerge as they reveal their innermost feelings and hidden secrets. First performed October 12, 1966, at the American Place Theatre, New York City.

Unpublished Plays

"Color Struck." 1970(?).

"Life Agony." 1971(?).

> One-act play. Detroit Concept East Theatre.

"These Three."

Biography and Criticism

Jeanpierre, Wendell. "Who's Got His Own." CRISIS, 74 (1967), 423.

Mitchell BD, pp. 223-24.

"New Playwright: Ron Milner." NEGRO DIGEST, 15 (Oct. 1966), 49-50.

"Who's Got His Own." CRISIS, 74 (1967), 31-34.

"WHO'S GOT HIS OWN at Cheyney." NEGRO DIGEST, 19 (Apr. 1970), 43-48.

MITCHELL, LOFTEN (1919-)

Published Plays

A LAND BEYOND THE RIVER. Cody, Wyo.: Pioneer Drama Service, 1963. 86 p. Also in Reardon BTDA, pp. 301-96.

> A three-act drama on the commitment of a southern black preacher and his fight against segregation in the school system. First performed March 28, 1957, at the Greenwich Mews Theatre, New York City.

"Star of the Morning: Scenes in the Life of Bert Williams." In King BDA, pp. 575-639. Also in Hatch BDU, pp. 620-52.

> A two-act musical play on the career of the famous black actor and entertainer Bert Williams. First performed 1965; music and lyrics by Louis Mitchell and Romare Bearden.

"Tell Pharaoh." In Reardon BTDA, pp. 255-99.

> A stage presentation of the story of black theatre in the United States, consisting of a series of sketches and scenes on its major representatives.

Unpublished Plays

"The Afro-Philadelphian." 1970.

"Ballad for Bimshire." 1963.

> Performed October 15, 1963, Mayfair Theatre, New York City; music by Irving Burgie.

"Ballad of a Blackbird." 1968.

> On the theatre career of Florence Mills.

"Ballad of the Winter Soldiers." 1965.

> In collaboration with John O. Killens.

"The Bancroft Dynasty." 1948.

> Harlem Showcase Theatre.

"The Phonograph." 1961.

"The World of a Harlem Playwright." 1968.

"Young Man of Williamsburg." 1950s.

Biography and Criticism

Abramson, NP, pp. 204-20.

Bigsby, C.E.W. "The Black Playwrights." In BAW2, pp. 137-56.

Mitchell, Loften. BLACK DRAMA. New York: Hawthorn, 1967. 248 p.

> This history of Afro-American theatre deals in part with the author's own experience.

MOLETTE, CARLTON W[OODWARD] II (1939-)

Published Plays

"Doctor B.S. Black." ENCORE, 13 (1970).

> Adaptation from Moliere's play, later revised into a musical with the collaboration of Charles Mann. First produced by Morehouse-Spelman Players November 10, 1969, Atlanta.

ROSALEE PRITCHETT. New York: Dramatists Play Service, 1972. 27 p. Also in BLACK WRITERS OF AMERICA. Ed. Richard Barksdale and Keneth Kinnamon. New York: Macmillan, 1972, pp. 825-35.

> Three scenes; satire of the black middle class and their loss of all sense of identification with their race. Centers on the drama of Rosalee who was raped by members of the National Guard sent to protect her neighborhood. First performed March 20, 1970, by the Morehouse-Spelman Players. Written in collaboration with Barbara J. Molette.

Unpublished Plays

"Booji Wooji." 1972.

> Performed July 8, 1971, Atlanta University Summer Theatre. A black lawyer's problems of identity and allegiances.

"Rosche." 1970(?).

MOSES, GILBERT (1942-)

Published Plays

"Roots." In Dent FST, pp. 185-206.

> An old black couple in the Deep South go through their daily ritual and exchange a few words before one of them finds his end in a rat trap. First performed September 1966, Free Southern Theatre, New Orleans.

Biography and Criticism

Dent FST, pp. 181-84.

Jones, Martha M. "Interview with Gilbert Moses." BLACK CREATION, 3 (Winter 1972), 19-20.

NSABE, NIA

Published Plays

"Moma Don't Know What Love Is." In THREE HUNDRED AND SIXTY DEGREES OF BLACKNESS COMIN AT YOU. Ed. Sonia Sanchez. New York: 5 X Publishing Co., 1971, pp. 179-90.

> A pregnant black girl's confrontation with her mother who does not want her to live the life that the mother herself led.

O'NEAL, REGINA

Published Plays

"And Then the Harvest." In AND THEN THE HARVEST (see Collected Plays, below), pp. 69-103.

> A thirty-minute teleplay set in the late summer of 1967 in a large city of the North. To explain the recent riots, the play focuses

on the frustrations suffered by a black family at the hands of whites.

"Night Watch." In AND THEN THE HARVEST (see under Collected Plays, below), pp. 105-42.

Set in 1971 in a suburban area of a large city, this drama exposes the shallowness of white liberalism.

"Walk a Tight Rope." In AND THEN THE HARVEST (see under Collected Plays, below), pp. 16-67.

Set in a midwestern city in the early 1960s, the play explores the problems and conflicts of a young teacher, the first black to be assigned to an all-white school.

Collected Plays

AND THEN THE HARVEST: THREE TELEVISION PLAYS. Detroit: Broadside Press, 1974. 142 p.

Includes "Walk a Tight Rope," "And Then the Harvest," and "Night Watch."

OYAMO. See GORDON, CHARLES F., above, this section.

OYEDELE, OBOMOLA

Published Plays

"The Struggle Must Advance to a Higher Level." BLACK THEATRE, No. 6 (1972), pp. 12-13.

A short agitprop piece in which a narrator skeptically watches black nationalist revolutionaries joining hands with white radicals.

PATTERSON, CHARLES (1941-)

Published Plays

"Black-Ice." In Jones BF, pp. 559-65.

The wife of a black revolutionist executes a congressman kept as a hostage when the police shoot her husband and his friends.

"Legacy." In 19 NECROMANCERS FROM NOW. Ed. Ishmael Reed. New York: Doubleday, 1970, pp. 191-234.

Two-act play; a black girl leaves home to join the liberation struggle.

Unpublished Plays

"Circle in the Square."

"The Clowns."

"The Liberal."

"Longhair."

"The Super." 1965.

PETERSON, LOUIS (1922-)

Published Plays

TAKE A GIANT STEP. New York: Samuel French, 1954. 111 p. In Turner BDA, pp. 297-375; and in Hatch BTU, pp. 549-84.

> Two-act psychological and social drama on the problems of an educated northern young black who becomes isolated from his former white school friends as he grows up, and who cannot adjust to the blacks in the streets. Copyrighted 1952 as "Merry Let Us Part." First performed September 21, 1953, at Lyceum Theatre, New York City.

Unpublished Plays

"Entertain a Ghost." 1962.

Biography and Criticism

Abramson NP, pp. 221-39.

Evans, Donald T. "Bring It All Back Home: Playwrights of the Fifties." BLACK WORLD, 20 (Feb. 1971), 41-45.

"Louis Takes a 'Giant Step.'" OUR WORLD, 9 (Jan. 1954), 45-48.

PITCHER, OLIVER

Published Plays

"The Bite." In ATLANTA UNIVERSITY CENTER SAMPLER. Ed. Oliver Pitcher. Atlanta: Atlanta Univ., [1972?], pp. 105-22.

Black college girls affirm their racial identity through intellectual debunking of white myths and resistance to oppression.

"The One." In King BDA, pp. 243-51.

The monologue of a black ex-soldier who has accepted his color, not the role he has been assigned to play. First performed 1970(?), Negro Ensemble Company.

"Shampoo." In ATLANTA UNIVERSITY CENTER SAMPLER #3. Ed. Oliver Pitcher. Atlanta: Atlanta Univ., [1973?], 50-86.

"So How're You Wearing Your Straitjacket (An Excerpt from a One-Act Play)." UMBRA, 1 (Winter 1963), 13-16.

PRINGLE, RONALD J. (1942-)

Published Plays

"The Finger Meal." In 19 NECROMANCERS FROM NOW. Ed. Ishmael Reed. New York: Doubleday, 1970, pp. 237-55.

A play on the traditional southern master-slave relationship.

Unpublished Plays

"Dead Flowers on a Great Man's Grave."

"Deep Root of Rotted Wood."

"The Fall of the Chandelier."

"Feed the Lion."

"A Lesser Sleep."

"The Price."

PROVIDENCE, WAYNE

Published Plays

"Where Are You Black Dream." In THREE HUNDRED AND SIXTY DEGREES OF BLACKNESS COMIN AT YOU. Ed. Sonia Sanchez. New York: 5 X Publishing Co., 1971, pp. 132-36.

One-act ritual on the revitalizing prospects of black drama and
the deleterious effects of black ignorance and inaction.

RANDOLPH, JEREMY

Published Plays

BLOW UP IN A MAJOR: A SATIRICAL COMEDY IN ONE ACT. New York:
Rannick Playwrights Co., 1971. 63 p.

On the political wrongdoings of senators who try to plant a scheme
against blacks.

RAYNER, STEPHEN [ETIENNE]

Published Plays

THE JAZZMAN AND HIS LADY FARE. N.p.: n.p., 1965. 24 p. Mimeographed.

REED, EDWINA

Published Plays

"A Man Always Keeps His Word." NEGRO HISTORY BULLETIN, 26 (1963),
138-40.

One-act play on Abraham Lincoln's decision to issue the Emancipation Proclamation.

REILLY, J. TERRENCE (1945-)

Published Plays

"Bogey." In BLACK! (see under Collected Plays, below), pp. 9-27.

The problems of Bogey Price, a black cab driver, who nearly wins
at the race tracks.

"Enter at Your Own Risk." In BLACK! (see under Collected Plays, below),
pp. 3-8.

Three black actors "in an age-old script" gradually assault and
shoot the white audience in a small studio theatre in the round.

"Jejune Ju Ju." In BLACK! (see under Collected Plays, below), pp. 29-36.

Poem-like monologue on the "black is beautiful" theme.

"Montage: An All Black Play." In BLACK! (see under Collected Plays, below), pp. 39-45.

> E.Z. Rapper gets shot by the Shades at the end of his flamboyant pro- Puerto-Rican speech.

"Waiting on the Man." In BLACK! (see under Collected Plays, below), pp. 49-64.

> Three blacks in the anteroom of a New York office talk about the death of Kuumba, who has been written out of a play called "Niggers Ain't Performing No More."

Collected Plays

BLACK! Poughkeepsie, N.Y.: Myra House, 1972. 64 p.

> Includes "Enter at your Own Risk," "Bogey," "Jejune Ju Ju," "Montage," and "Waiting on the Man."

RUSSELL, CHARLIE (1932-)

Published Plays

FIVE ON THE BLACK HAND SIDE. New York: Samuel French, 1970. 83 p.

> A funny satire about a black family trying to become "truly" black, with the quiet, long-suffering mother turning into a late-model militant in order to hold her domineering husband at bay. Public reading, June 10, 1969, at the American Place Theatre Writers' program as "Gladys"; first performed December 10, 1969, American Place Theatre, New York City.

SALIMU. See McCRAY, NETTIE, above, this section.

SANCHEZ, SONIA (1934-)

Published Plays

"The Bronx Is Next." DRAMA REVIEW, 12 (Summer 1968), 78-83.

> The portrait of black people who must face certain truths about themselves and their relationship to each other at a time of revolutionary struggle. First performed October 3, 1970, by Theatre Black, University of the Streets, New York.

"Dirty Hearts." SCRIPTS, 1 (Nov. 1971), 46-50.

> Psychological drama on the acceptance of blackness: a black man

who plays a game of dreams and cards with various marginal characters; he is given the queen of spades.

"Malcolm/Man Don't Live Here No Mo." BLACK THEATRE, No. 6 (1972), pp. 24-27.

A call and response song in which a chorus asks questions that are answered by a man representing Malcolm X at different stages of his career, and by a woman embodying historical or archetypal concepts.

"Sister Son/ji." In Bullins NPBT, pp. 97-108.

A dramatic monologue by a black woman re-creating moments in her life that parallel the growth of the black struggle. First performed at New York Festival Public Theatre, 1972.

"Uh, Uh; But How Do It Free Us?" In Bullins NLTP, pp. 165-219.

A series of antithetic and complementary dramatic vignettes illustrating several stages and moments of black consciousness.

Biography and Criticism

Walker, Barbara. "Sonia Sanchez Creates Poetry for the Stage." BLACK CREATION, 5 (Fall 1973), 12-15.

SHEARS, CARL L. [SAGGITTARUS (sic)]

Published Plays

I AM ISHMAEL, SON OF BLACKAMOOR. Washington, D.C.: NuClassics and Science Publishing Co., 1975. 76 p.

Four-act play on the difficulties and problems encountered by the first black president of the United States and his white wife.

SHEPP, ARCHIE (1937-)

Published Plays

"Junebug Graduates Tonight: A Jazz Allegory." In King BDA, pp. 33-76.

A prologue and two acts; builds an allegory of young black's relation to America and Uncle Sam: Junebug graduates into a world other than the white one and the play ends melodramatically with bombs and guns. Written 1967. First performed February 20, 1971, Church of the Holy Apostles, New York City; first full-length performance at Chelsea Theatre Center.

Unpublished Plays

"Revolution." 1969.

> A one-act play in three scenes; performed Brooklyn College, 1969.

"Skulls." 1969.

> A farce in one act with incidental music.

Biography and Criticism

Abramson NP, pp. 281-84.

SHINE, TED (1931-)

Published Plays

"Contribution." In CONTRIBUTIONS (see under Collected Plays, below), pp. 49-66. Also in Brasmer BD, pp. 371-89.

> One-act comedy about a black woman servant who poisons the enemies of her race and wins respect from the younger generation. Written 1968; first performed Spring 1969 by Negro Ensemble Company, New York City.

"Herbert III." In Hatch BTU, pp. 855-63.

> Exploration of the relationship between a black husband and wife, their contrasting approaches to their children's education, and their difficulties in communicating at a later stage of their marriage.

"Morning, Noon and Night." In Reardon BTDA, pp. 397-487.

> Domestic and psychological drama of a boy's struggle to escape from his powerful and authoritative grandmother and to achieve his identity. Written 1964. First performed 1964, Howard University.

"Plantation." In CONTRIBUTIONS (see under Collected Plays, below), pp. 5-20.

> One-act comedy; black servants take over their master's plantation by cunning, after a black child is born in his family. First performed March 9, 1970, at Tambellini's Gate Theatre, New York City.

"Shoes." ENCORE MAGAZINE (Florida A & M University), 12 (1969). Also in CONTRIBUTIONS (see under Collected Plays, below), pp. 27-48.

Social comedy and drama in which shoes become a mark of status
for a poor black youth suffering from parental neglect and lack of
love. First performed Howard University, October, 1969.

"Sho' Is Hot in the Cotton Patch." ENCORE MAGAZINE (Florida A & M University), 11 (1967).

One-act play written 1951. First performed Howard University,
1961; performed 1968 by the Negro Ensemble Company, New York
City, as "Miss Weaver."

Unpublished Plays

"The Bats Out of Hell." 1955.

"The Coca Cola Boys." 1969.
One-act play.

"Cold Day in August." 1950.
One-act play.

"Comeback after the Fire." 1969.

"Dry August." 1952.
Comic drama.

"Entourage Royale." 1958.
Musical.

"Epitaph for a Bluebird." 1958.
Comedy fantasy.

"Flora's Kisses." 1969.
One-act comedy.

"Hamburgers at Hamburger Heaven Are Impersonal." 1969.
One-act comedy.

"Idabel's Fortune." 1969.
One-act play.

"Jeanne West." 1968.
Musical.

"Miss Victoria." 1965.
One-act play.

"The Night of Baker's End." 1974.
Tragedy.

"Packard." 1971.
Comedy.

"Pontiac." 1967.

"A Rat's Revolt." 1959.

"Waiting Room." 1969.

Collected Plays

CONTRIBUTIONS: THREE ONE ACT PLAYS. New York: Dramatists Play Service, 1970. 66 p.
Includes "Plantation," "Shoes," and "Contribution."

SMITH, JEAN

Published Plays

"O.C.'s Heart. Excerpts from a Three Act Play." NEGRO DIGEST, 19 (Apr. 1970), 57-76.
Racial revenge and psychological drama: the brother of a dead black boy gets back his heart, which had been transplanted to the body of a white man.

STEVENSON, WILLIAM ADELL III (1948-)

Published Plays

"One the Two of Us." SCRIPTS, 1 (May 1972), 93-98.
A one-act play about a black revolutionary couple who are also dream weavers and whose hopes for a better life are destroyed by

murder which entails retribution. Copyrighted 1971. First performed Langston Hughes House of Kuumba, Harlem, 1971.

STEWART, JAMES T.

Published Plays

"Abganli and the Hunter." BLACK LINES, 2 (Fall 1971), 43-45.

"The Gourd Cup." BLACK LINES, 2 (Fall 1971), 51-52.

"How Men Came into the World." BLACK LINES, 2 (Fall 1971), 48-51.

"JoJo, the Story Teller." BLACK LINES, 2 (Fall 1971), 52-54.

"The Messenger of God." BLACK LINES, 2 (Fall 1971), 45-48.

STOKES, BOB

Published Plays

"Cool Jerk: A Morality Play." SISEHTNYS, 1 (1974), 30-44.

STOKES, HERBERT [DAMU]

Published Plays

"The Man Who Trusted the Devil Twice." In Bullins NPBT, pp. 119-28.
>A black principal betrays a group of revolutionary black students
>to the establishment and they are saved only by the intervention
>of black militants.

"The Uncle Toms." DRAMA REVIEW, 12 (Summer 1968), 58-60.
>Political play emphasizing black racial solidarity. One-act play
>first performed at Spirit House, Newark, 1968.

VAN PEEBLES, MELVIN (1932-)

Published Plays

AIN'T SUPPOSED TO DIE A NATURAL DEATH. New York: Bantam Books,
1973. 156 p.
>An orchestration of blues and moods of people struggling to survive

in the black ghetto. Written in collaboration with Paul C. Harrison. Performed October 1971 at Ambassador Theatre, New York City.

DON'T PLAY US CHEAP: A HARLEM PARTY. New York: Bantam Books, 1973. 124 p.

Saturday night partying time in Harlem: two imps sent by the devil to break up a party find out, from surprise to surprise, that nothing can destroy black laughter and lust for life. Written 1967; published in story form as LA FETE A HARLEM (Paris: Jerome Martineau, 1967; 102 p.) together with LA PERMISSION (script for film). First performed May 1972 as a musical comedy at the Ethel Barrymore Theatre.

SWEET SWEETBACK'S BAADASSSSS SONG. New York: Lancer Books, 1971. 192 p.

The humorous story of a ghetto brothel-boy who fights the white system in order to survive. (The story of the film precedes the shooting script and final dialogue, with photo illustrations.) Script written 1970; movie completed early 1972.

Biography and Criticism

Coleman, Horace W. "Melvin Van Peebles." JOURNAL OF POPULAR CULTURE, 5 (1972), 368-84.

Murray, James P. "Running with Sweetback." BLACK CREATION, 3 (Fall 1971), 10-12.

WALKER, JOSEPH

Published Plays

"Ododo (Truth). A Musical Epic in Three Acts." In King BDA, pp. 349-88.

A musical epic retracing the history of Africans in the United States from the times of the slave trade. Written 1968 in collaboration with Dorothy Dinroe. First performed Fall 1970 by Negro Ensemble Company, New York City.

THE RIVER NIGER. New York: Hill & Wang, 1973. 177 p.

Three-act drama about a black family, presenting generational relationships and diverse reactions concerning the black liberation struggle. First performed December 5, 1972, by Negro Ensemble Company, New York City.

Unpublished Plays

"The Believers." 1968.

> Three-act drama written in collaboration with Josephine Jackson.
> First performed May 1968 at the Garrick Theatre, New York City.
> Cast and production details in BEST PLAYS OF 1967-1968. Ed.
> O. Guerney. New York: Dodd, Mead, 1968, p. 407.

"The Harangues." 1970.

> Negro Ensemble Company. Three one-act plays. See BEST PLAYS
> OF 1971 (New York: Avon, 1971) for "Tribal Harangue, Two."

"Themes of the Black Struggle." 1970.

> Performed Fall 1970, Negro Ensemble Company.

"Yin Yang." 1972.

> Performed June 1972, Afro-American Studio, New York City.

Biography and Criticism

Johnson, H.H. "Ododo." BLACK WORLD, 20 (Apr. 1971), 47-48.

WALKER, MARK

Published Plays

"A Near Fatality." BLACK EXPRESSION, 2 (Fall 1968), 48-51.

> "A two-scene statement . . . for niggers only." A "black national-
> ist" professor proves to be a servant of the system designed to de-
> flect militancy from its proper aims.

WALLACE, G.L.

Published Plays

THEM NEXT DOOR: A PLAY IN ONE ACT. New York: Samuel French,
1974. 35 p.

> Social drama on the theme of racial relations in a neighborhood
> where blacks and whites try uneasily to live together.

WARD, DOUGLAS TURNER (1931-)

Published Plays

BROTHERHOOD. New York: Dramatists Play Service, 1970. 17 p.

> One-act comedy; the conversation of a white middle-class couple reveals their prejudices after they have extended an invitation to black "friends" with whom they manage to keep a carefully planned ritual of brotherhood. First performed March 20, 1970, by Negro Ensemble Company, New York City.

"Day of Absence." In HAPPY ENDING AND DAY OF ABSENCE. New York: Dramatists Play Service, 1966. Also in Couch NBP, pp. 47-81; in Brasmer BD, pp. 221-46; in Oliver CBD, pp. 324-64; and in Hatch BTU, pp. 696-710.

> Satirical fantasy about the dismay of white southerners when they discover that "their" Negroes have left town. First performed November 15, 1965, by Negro Ensemble Company, New York City. Winner of the Drama Desk award and Obie award with "Happy Ending."

"Happy Ending." LIBERATOR, 4 (1964), 18 [excerpt]. Full text in HAPPY ENDING AND DAY OF ABSENCE. New York: Dramatists Play Service, 1966. Also in Couch NBP, pp. 27-46; in Brasmer BD, pp. 179-220; and in Oliver CBD, pp. 315-23.

> One-act satirical comedy on the way black maids manage to deceive their white employers. First performed November 15, 1965, at St. Mark's Playhouse, New York City; winner of the Obie award and Drama Desk award with "Day of Absence."

THE RECKONING: A SURREAL SOUTHERN FABLE. New York: Dramatists Play Service, 1970. 43 p.

> One-act comedy; a black pimp deceives a corrupt and tricky southern governor. First performed September 4, 1969, at St. Mark's Playhouse, New York City.

Biography and Criticism

Bigsby, C.W.E. "The Black Playwrights." In Bigsby BAW2, pp. 135-56.

Kupa, Kushawi. "The Reckoning." BLACK THEATRE, No. 4 (1970), p. 42.

Mitchell BD, pp. 209-11, 215-16.

WATT, BILLIE LOU

Published Plays

PHILLIS: A PLAY WITH MUSIC. New York: Friendship Press, 1969.

> Historical drama on the life of poetess Phillis Wheatley.

WESLEY, RICHARD (1945-)

Published Plays

"Black Terror: A Revolutionary Adventure Story." SCRIPTS, 1 (Dec. 1971), 72-101. Also in Bullins NLTP, pp. 219-301.

> One-act drama dealing with revolution: a black terrorist comes into conflict with his group and is expelled; his lover, the daughter of the next victim, is given the mission he refused to accomplish. First performed February 1971 by WASTSA at Ira Aldridge Theatre, Washington, D.C.

Unpublished Plays

"Ace Boon Coon." 1972.

> One-act play. Performed February 1972, Blackarts/West, San Francisco.

"Getting It Together." 1970

> One-act drama. Theatre Black, New York City.

"Goin' Thru Changes." 1974.

> One-act play.

"Knock-Knock, Who Dat?" 1970.

> Black Theatre, University of the Streets, New York City.

"The Mighty Gents." 1973.

> One-act play.

"The Past Is the Past." 1973.

> Performed Spring 1973, New Lafayette Theatre, New York City.

"Put My Dignity on 307." 1965.

> Performed WRC-TV, Washington, D.C., 1965.

"The Sirens." 1973.

  Full-length drama.

"Springtime High." 1968(?).

"Strike Heaven in the Face." 1972.

  Full-length drama on the black experience.

Biography and Criticism

Bailey, Peter. "Black Terror." JET, 13 Jan. 1972, pp. 60-61.

Jone, Martha. "Richard Wesley's BLACK TERROR." BLACK CREATION, 3 (Spring 1972), 12-14.

WHITE, EDGAR (Born in Montserrat, West Indies)

Published Plays

"The Burghers of Calais, A Play in Three Acts." In UNDERGROUND (see under Collected Plays, below), pp. 5-55.

  The lunatic inmates of a drug prison put on a play about the Scottsboro Boys and pursue a dramatic exchange among themselves, the audience, the characters they represent, and the author of the play.

"The Cathedral of Chartres." LIBERATOR, 8 (July 1968), 16-19.

  First performed 1969.

"The Crucificado." In THE CRUCIFICADO (see under Collected Plays, below), pp. 67-146.

  A son is offered a trip to Europe to complete his education before inheriting his father's business. Upon his return he refuses the fortune and eliminates the father, who had nothing to give him but corrupt money. First performed June 1972, Urban Arts Group, New York City.

"Dija." SCRIPTS, 1 (Oct. 1972), 15-17.

  A play for children: a little girl sets out on a long journey in order to find Father Time and persuade him to give her a birthday.

"Fun in Lethe, or the Feast of Misrule (Three Acts--A British Tragicomedy)." In UNDERGROUND (see under Collected Plays, below), pp. 63-119.

A West Indian poet, traveling through Great Britain, finds himself in various situations and indulges in reverie.

"The Life and Times of J. Walter Smintheus." SCRIPTS, 1 (Apr. 1972), 4-28. Also in THE CRUCIFICADO (see under Collected Plays, below), pp. 5-65.

A statement on the impotence and castration of black intellectuals; one of them, in a psychiatric hospital, relives stages in his career and his correspondence with a friend who writes him from prison and whose thoughts often parallel and ironically comment upon his own success and failure. First performed February 1971, A.N.T.A. Series, Theatre de Lys, New York City.

"The Mummer's Play." In UNDERGROUND (see under Collected Plays, below), 123-69.

One-act play. A character's trip through Harlem's night life, his encounters with friends and a humorous reality to which he reacts wittily. First performed 1971, New York Public Theatre.

"The Rastafarian." SCRIPTS, 1 (Oct. 1972), 13-14.

A tale for children; an old man dies, visits a child in a dream, predicts that his house will be plundered by "niggers," and teaches the child some African pieces of wisdom. The boy accepts the juxtaposition of life and death.

"Seigismundo's Tricycle." In BLACK REVIEW, No. 1. Ed. Mel Watkins. New York: William Morrow, 1972, pp. 130-54.

An old white man on a tricycle and his black servant on crutches debate life and death, the white man ultimately preferring solitude to a companion who proves too wise.

"The Wonderfull Yeare." In UNDERGROUND (see under Collected Plays, below), pp. 173-245.

A swift-moving fantasy in the tradition of the comedia dell'arte with romantic, obscene, quixotic, and Machiavellian characters performing quickly in a picaresque atmosphere. First performed New Public Theatre, 1971.

Collected Plays

THE CRUCIFICADO: TWO PLAYS. New York: William Morrow, 1973. 146 p.

Includes "The Life and Times of J. Walter Smintheus" and "The Crucificado."

UNDERGROUND: FOUR PLAYS. New York: William Morrow, 1970. 243 p.

Includes "The Burghers of Calais," "Fun in Lethe," "The Mummer's Play," and "The Wonderfull Yeare."

WHITE, JOSEPH (1933-)

Published Plays

"The Leader." In Jones BF, pp. 605-30.

> One-act satire about a black leader who cares more about his prestige and a white woman than about his organization. First performed 1968, Newark Community Workshop.

"Old Judge Mose Is Dead." DRAMA REVIEW, 12 (Summer 1968), 151-56.

> First performed October 18, 1968, Freedom Center College, Newark. Also titled "Old Judge Mose."

Unpublished Plays

"The Blue Boy in Black." 1962.

> See BEST PLAYS OF 1962-63.

"The Hustle." 1970.

> Performed at Kumba House Theatre, Newark.

WHITEHEAD, JAMES X.

Published Plays

"Justice of Just Us (Part II)." In WHO TOOK THE WEIGHT? BLACK VOICES FROM NORFOLK PRISON. Boston: Little, Brown, 1972, pp. 148-51.

> One-act play on a prisoner's reasons why the parole board is not fit to determine whether a prisoner is ready to enter society again.

WHITTAKER, FRANCIS SCOTT KEY

Published Plays

THIRTY PIECES OF SILVER: THE BETRAYAL OF THE CHRIST. New York: Exposition, 1951. 47 p.

WILLIAMS, MANCE

Published Plays

"What's the Use of Hanging On?" ROOTS, 1 (1970), 137-41.

"A Brief Play for For-Real Black Brothers and Sisters." Two soul brothers discuss the possibilities and aims of rebellion and conclude they have to "hang on."

WILSON, ALICE T. (1908-)

Published Plays

HOW AN AMERICAN POET MADE MONEY AND FORGET-ME-NOT. New York: Pageant, 1968. 63 p.

Screenplay and poems.

WRIGHT, JAY (1935-)

Published Plays

BALLOONS: A COMEDY IN ONE ACT. Boston: Baker's Plays, 1968. 17 p.

YOUNG, WHITNEY

Published Plays

"The Coming of the Pink Cheeks." In WE ARE BLACK. Chicago: Science Research Associates, 1969.

A three-act historical play for children on the coming of the white man to Africa.

Unpublished Plays

"The Crossing."

"The Death of Mr. Parker."

Radio play.

"The Final Celebration."

"Leon Nadeau's Fortunate Fall."

"The Turner's Land."
    Radio play.

"The Unfinished Saint."

"The Wedding at Temazcalli."
    Radio play.

"The Woman with the Charm."
    Radio play.

ZUBER, RON [ERON ZUBA]

Published Plays

"Three X Love." In King BDA, pp. 426-38.
    A song with several voices in praise of black womanhood, mother-
    hood, and sisterhood. First performed 1969 by Spirit of Shango,
    Detroit.

INDEXES

AUTHOR INDEX

In addition to authors, this index includes all editors, compilers, and transla-
tors cited in the text. It is alphabetized letter by letter. Numbers refer to
page numbers. See subject index (p. 465) for page references to authors
whose works are listed in this bibliography.

A

Author Index

Author Index

Author Index

Author Index

42, 46, 48, 77, 92, 100, 166, 200, 203, 227, 232
Randall, James 42
Randall, Jon 42
Ransom, Reverdy C. 63
Ransom, Stanley Austin, Jr. 66, 67
Rap, B. See Hardeman, Beauregard Andrew, Jr.
Raphael, Lennox 50
Rapp, William 254, 256
Rawlins, Eric 50
Rawls, Isetta Crawford 46
Reardon, William R. 266, 271, 275, 291
Reck, Tom S. 388
Record, C. Wilson 26
Reddick, La Bertha 26
Reddick, Lawrence D. 242
Redding, Jay Saunders 5, 13, 26, 36, 344
Redmond, Eugene 27, 46, 143, 168, 189
Reed, Daphne S. 388
Reed, Ishmael 25, 38, 50, 398, 400
Reese, Carolyn 27, 67
Reilly, John M. 137
Reimherr, Beulah 99
Reisner, Robert George 190
Renfro, G. Herbert 83
Rexroth, Kenneth 27
Rhode, Gerald 46
Rhodes, Gene 205
Ricah, W.A.D. 291
Ricard, Alain 388
Rice, C.Y. 97
Rice, Elmer 316
Rice, Julian 388
Richards, I.A. 123
Richards, Stanley 273, 383
Richardson, Willis 49, 254, 266, 273, 274, 330
Richmond, Merle A. 70, 84
Ridge, Delores F. 211
Riggins, Linda N. 68
Riley, Clayton 265, 274, 293, 337, 350
Riley, James Whitcomb 77
Rive, Richard 114

Rivers, Clarehce 319
Rivers, Conrad Kent 15, 33, 38, 46, 157
Robeson, Eslanda Goode 282
Robinson, Billy Hand(s) 45
Robinson, James H. 34
Robinson, William H. 46, 77, 78, 84
Rochon, Noel J. 47
Rodgers, Bertha 61
Rodgers, Carolyn 15, 27, 33, 239
Rogers, John William 273
Rogers, Ray 294
Rollins, Charlemae H. 5, 27, 47, 114, 277
Romero, Patricia W. 23
Rose, Arnold 11
Rosenfeld, Paul 137
Roth, Philip 341
Rowe, Kenneth Thorpe 326, 334
Rowell, Charles H. 92, 149, 240
Rowland, Mabel 282
Roy, J.M. 75
Rubin, Louis D., Jr. 21–22
Rudwick, Elliott M. 102
Rush, Theressa Gunnels 12
Rushing, Andrea Benton 27
Russell, Charles 196, 260
Ryan, Pat M. 12
Ryder, A.H. 90

S

Sackheim, Eric 53
Salaam, Kalamu Ya 270
Salimu. See McCray, Netti (Salimu)
Salk, Erwin A. 12
Salkey, Andrew 179
Sanchez, Sonia 26, 31, 47, 274, 337, 341, 342, 344, 397, 400
Sandle, Floyd L. 277
Saunders, Doris 282
Saunders, Redding 36
Sayles, Dorothy 224
Scarborough, Dorothy 54
Scarborough, W.S. 63
Schatt, Stanley 112
Schatz, Walter 12, 267

Author Index

TITLE INDEX

This index includes all titles of books which are cited in the text. In some cases the titles have been shortened. This index is alphabetized letter by letter. Numbers refer to page numbers.

Title Index

436

Title Index

Title Index

Title Index

Title Index

Title Index

W

SUBJECT INDEX

This index is alphabetized letter by letter. Underlined page numbers refer to main areas within the subject.

Subject Index

Subject Index

Boyd, Raven Freemont 89
Boyd, Sue Abbott 153
Boyd, Tom 153
Boyer, Jill Witherspoon 42, 154
Boze, Arthur 154
Bradley, Henry T. 89
Bragg, Linda Brown 154
Braithwaite, William Stanley
    Beaumont 90
Branch, William 258, 273, 274,
    275, 286, 343
Brawley, Benjamin 90-91
Brewer, John Mason 91
Briggs, Christina Moody. See
    Moody, Christina
Brisby, Stewart 154
Britt, Nellie 154
Broadside Press 7, 46
Broadway, Afro-American plays and
    actors on 254, 270, 277,
    281, 282, 289, 334, 375
Brooklyn College, theater and
    theaters of 404
Brooklyn Theatre Center 373
Brooks, Gwendolyn 18, 26, 33, 44,
    154-57
Brooks, Helen Morgan 157
Brooks, Jonathan Henderson 157
Brooks, Robert 258
Brooks, Walter Henderson 91
Brown, Charles E. 157
Brown, Herbert G. 157
Brown, Herman. See Mumba (Herman
    Brown)
Brown, Joe C. 157
Brown, John
    drama about 333, 343
    poetry about 56, 86
Brown, Lennox 263, 273
Brown, Mattye Jeanette 91
Brown, Robert Harvey 157
Brown, Samuel E. 91
Brown, Sterling 18, 30, 92
Brown, Wesley 344
Brown, William Wells 253, 257,
    273, 298
Browne, Elaine 48
Browne, Theodore 257, 273, 274,
    300-301
Browning, Alice C. 158

Brownlee, Julius Pinkney 92
Bruce, Richard 273, 301
Brunson, Doris 368
Bryant, Franklin Henry 92
Bryant, Frederick James, Jr. 158
Bryant, Joseph G. 93
Buffalo University. Summer Theatre
    379
Buford, Elmer. See Felton, B.
Buford, Lorenzo Neil 158
Bullins, Ed. 260, 268, 270, 273,
    274, 275, 285, 294, 344-50,
    363, 386, 387, 391
Burgie, Irving 395
Burke, Inez M. 257, 274, 301
Burleigh, Benny 158
Burnett, Denise. See Damali
    (Denise Burnett)
Burns, Robert 114
Burrell, Louis V. 93
Burrill, Mary 255, 273, 301
Burroughs, Margaret Taylor Gross
    49, 158
Burroughs, Nannie Helen 301
Bush, Oliva Ward
    drama of 302
    poetry of 93
Butcher, J.W. 256
Butcher, James W., Jr. 302
Butler, Anna Land 158
Butler, James Alpheus 159
Byer, D.P. 93
Byron, Asaman B.W. 159

C

Cain, Johnnie Mae 159
Caldwell, Ben 259, 274, 275,
    350-52
Calhoun Colored School 52
California, poetry about 235
California, University of at Los
    Angeles. Library. George
    P. Johnson Negro Film Col-
    lection 267
California, University of at Santa
    Barbara. Institute of Dra-
    matic Art (1968) 293
Campbell, Alfred Gibbs 57
Campbell, James Edwin 57

Subject Index

Subject Index

Subject Index

Ridout, Daniel Lyman 130
Riley, James W. 130
Rios, Carlos Robert 224
Riots
  drama about 351, 397-98
  poetry about 127, 155, 221
Rivers, Conrad Kent 33, 38, 224-25
Robbin, William Allston 225
Roberson, Ed. 225
Roberts, D.L. 225
Robeson, Paul 253, 282
Robinson, Eugene E. 225
Robinson, Jerrilyn 225
Rodgers, Carolyn M. 33, 226
Roe, Helene 226
Rogers, Elymas Payson 75
Rogers, J. Overton 226
Rogers, John Williams 273
Rollins, Bryant 226
Romantic poetry, anthologies 46.
        See also Love, poetry about
Roosevelt, Franklin Delano, poetry
        about 160, 200
Rose McClendon Players. See Mc-
        Clendon (Rose) Players
Ross, John M. 330-31
Rowe, George Clinton 75-76
Rowland, Ida 130
Royale Theatre (N.Y. City) 334
Royster, Philip M. 226
Royster, Sandra 226
Ruff, Robert L. 227
Russell, Beth Duvall 227
Russell, Charles 260, 402
Rutledge, Doris 227

S

Sacramento State College, theater
        and theaters of 378
Saggittarus. See Shears, Carl L.
        (Saggittarus)
St. James Theatre (N.Y. City) 336
St. John, Primus 227
St. Louis. See East St. Louis
St. Marks Playhouse (N.Y. City)
        352, 362, 383, 384, 410
St. Paul (Minn.) Players 327
St. Peter, poetry about 118
St. Thomas, poetry about 88

St. Thomas, V.I., poetry about 97,
        135
Salaam, Kalamu Ya. See Ferdinand,
        Val, III
Salgado, Lionel 227
Salimu. See McCray, Nettie
        (Salimu)
Samuels, Calvin Henry McNeal 227
Sanchez, Sonia
  drama of 274, 402-3
  poetry of 26, 31, 177, 201,
        227-28
Sanchez (Sonia) Writers Workshop
        (Harlem) 47
San Francisco
  poetry about 233
  theater and theaters of 344, 345,
        346, 347, 380
San Francisco State College, theater
        and theaters of 384
Sapin, Louis, dramatic adaptations
        of 336
Sarten, Lavon 228
Satire
  in drama 251, 259, 260, 293,
        318, 342, 369, 396, 410,
        414
    comedic 311, 315, 401, 402,
        410
  in poetry 237
Savage, Eudora W. 131
Schultz, M. 294
Scott, Emory Elrage 131
Scott, Johnie 47
Scott, Lewis E. 228
Scott, Raleigh Alonzo 131
Scott-Heron, Gil 228
Seattle, theater and theaters of 284,
        300
Sebree, Charles 273, 331
Segregation. See Integration and
        segregation
Sejour, Victor 263, 273
Selma, Ala., poetry about 225
Seminole Indians, poetry about 85
Sentimental poetry 133
Sermons, Afro-American 65, 118
Seuell, Malchus M. 228
Seward, Walter Eddie 131

Subject Index

Seymour, Alexander 131
Shabazz, Jomo Don 228
Shabazz, Turhan Abdul 229
Shabazz, Zakariah H. 229
Shackelford, Otis M. 131
Shackelford, Theodore Henry 131
Shackelford, William Henry 132
Shakespeare, William
  dramatic adaptations of 297
  poetry about 111
Shands, Annette Oliver 229
Shange, Ntosake 229
Sharp, Saundra 229
Shaw, Esther Popel. See Popel,
  Esther A.W.
Shears, Carl L. (Saggittarus)
  drama of 403
  poetry of 229
Shelley, William 229
Sheperd, John H. 229
Shepp, Archie 259, 275, 403–4
Sherman, Joe 318
Shields, Anna E. 132
Shields, Ruth E. 230
Shine, Ted 272, 273, 274, 404–6
Shipps, Charles Kadia 230
Shoebox Theatre (Los Angeles) 381
Shoeman, Charles Henry 76
Shokunbi, Mae Gleaton 132
Sidney, Robert Y. 76
Signoret, Simone 375
Silcott, W. Llewellyn 132
Silvera, John 314
Simmons, Gerald L., Jr. 230
Simmons, Herbert A. 48
Simmons, James W. 230
Simmons, Judy Dothard 230
Simmons, Rhoza W. 230
Simmons, Virginia Lee 132
Simpkins, Thomas V. 230
Simpson, Joshua McCarter 76
Sims, Lillian 231
Singleton, Yatunde. See Yatunde
  (Yatunde Singleton)
Skyloft Players (Chicago) 318
Slaves
  drama about 256, 257, 305, 307,
    318, 320, 321, 327, 328
    374, 384, 385, 387, 388,
    392, 400

dramatic entertainment by 251
poetry about 56, 57, 62, 69,
  76, 211
songs of 41, 46, 51, 52
See also Abolitionism; Freedmen;
  Fugitive Slave Law; Missouri
  Compromise; Underground
  railroad
Smith, Arthur Lee 231
Smith, David 231
Smith, Demon 231
Smith, Frances Laurence 231
Smith, Ivory H. 231
Smith, J. Pauline 132
Smith, Jean 270, 406
Smith, Lucy 231
Smith, Margaret L. 231
Smith, Milton. See Mbembe (Milton
  Smith)
Smith, S.P. 132
Smith, Sidney R. 232
Smith, Welton 232
Smith, Willie Wesley, Sr. 232
Snelling, Rolland. See Toure, Askia
  Muhammad
Social drama 255–56, 260, 308,
  311, 313, 317, 340, 353,
  368, 369, 374, 393, 399,
  405, 409. See also Domes-
  tic drama; Protest in litera-
  ture
Socialism, drama about 333
Soldiers. See War
Soledad Prison, writings from 34
Songs, Afro-American 50, 72, 76,
  89, 91, 123, 174, 202,
  210
  gospel 316, 318
  See also Ballads; Folk songs; Hymns,
    Afro-American; Opera,
    librettos for; Spirituals
Sonnets 74, 88, 159, 216, 242
  critical studies of 19, 184
South (The)
  drama about 256, 333, 340, 357,
    410
  poetry about 55, 68, 85, 88,
    107, 131, 184
South Carolina, poetry about 129
Southerland, Ellease 232

Subject Index

WITHDRAWAL